An American Woman in Kuwait

An American Woman in Kuwait

Stephanie C. Fox, J.D.

QueenBeeBooks

Bloomfield, Connecticut, U.S.A.

Copyright September 9, 2010 © by Stephanie Carole Fox

All rights reserved. Published in the United States by QueenBeeBooks, Connecticut.

Library of Congress Cataloging-in-Publication Data
Name: Fox, Stephanie C., author.
Title: An American Woman in Kuwait / Stephanie C. Fox.
Description: Connecticut: QueenBeeBooks, [2010].
Identifiers: ISBN: 978-0-9996395-0-4 (paperback)
Subjects: HISTORY / Middle East / General. TRAVEL / General. HUMOR / Topic / Men, Women & Relationships.

www.queenbeeedit.com

Cover design by Stephanie C. Fox
Cover photograph by David D. Haines
Printed in the United States of America

This is a true story.

Any similarity to persons living or dead is purely intentional.

The names of the individuals described here
have all been changed to protect the identities
of the guilty as well as the innocent.

The names of real places have not been changed.

Also by Stephanie C. Fox

The Book of Thieves

The Bear Guarding the Beehive

*Scheherazade Cat:
The Story of a War Hero*

*Nae-Née
Birth Control: Infallible, with
Nanites and Convenience for All*

*Vaccine: The Cull
Nae-Née Wasn't Enough*

*New World Order Underwater
The Nae-Née Inventors Strike Back*

What the Small Gray Visitor Said

Intrigue On a Longship Cruise

*Elephant's Kitchen
– An Aspergirl's Study in Difference*

Almost a Meal – A True Tale of Horror

*Hawai'i – Stolen Paradise:
A Travelogue*

*Hawai'i – Stolen Paradise:
A Brief History*

This book is dedicated to my husband, David,
for taking me to Kuwait,
and to our cat, Scheherazade,
for enduring a trip back to her homeland.

An American Woman in Kuwait
By Stephanie C. Fox, J.D.

An American Woman in Kuwait is a travelogue written by an American lawyer who accompanied her husband, a Ph.D. immunologist, to Kuwait. It is more academic than armchair reading, a memoir of details and impressions. The trip spanned almost six months, during the cooler parts of the year, from November 2004 to May 2005.

Kuwait is a tiny nation covered almost entirely by barren desert. Its huge petroleum reserves and strategic location have made it a playing field on which great military conflicts have been settled during the past two decades. The country, located at the northern end of the Persian Gulf, became one of the wealthiest nations in history following discovery of oil in 1938 and development of the oil fields brought its citizens an unparalleled level of personal comfort.

During the time span of a single generation, Kuwaitis made the transition from a society based on animal herding, fishing and local trade, to an ultra-modern welfare state, offering its citizens lifetime security and comfort at a level unimaginable to most of the world.

This remarkable rags-to-riches transformation has had adverse consequences. One particularly ugly effect of wealth on Kuwaitis and their culture is a sense of entitlement, which has evolved into arrogance and contempt for people who are less fortunate. Unskilled laborers, primarily from Bangladesh and Pakistan, hired on contract to perform menial jobs, are paid subsistence level wages and often treated brutally. Brutality towards those who are perceived as inferiors, including women, is an aspect of Kuwait masked by the veneer of modernity.

Stephanie C. Fox strips away this veneer to explore features of the nation not widely known or appreciated by the public worldwide. A major focus of her work is the degree to which the traditions and prejudices of the tribes from which Kuwaitis claim ancestry act to maintain an inferior status for women. Outwardly, Kuwait appears enlightened with respect to issues of women's rights. The rigid dress codes and other restrictive laws regulating the behavior of women in Saudi Arabia are absent. Many Kuwaiti women hold prestigious and high-profile positions, particularly in academia. Inwardly, many of these same Kuwaiti women live their private lives much as they have for centuries, entirely available to their husbands while at home.

While in Kuwait, the author lived among Kuwaitis, ate traditional foods, mingled with Kuwaitis, studied Kuwaiti history, visited most of its museums, and spent a weekend with her husband at the Wafra Farms Oasis as Kuwaitis celebrated their Independence and Liberation Day holidays. She was even lucky enough to meet Kuwait's most famous woman suffragist, Rola A. Al-Dashti, Ph.D., who later became a member of the country's National Assembly.

Stephanie made friends with Kuwaitis. She and her husband met people from Kuwait's large community of expatriates – Egyptians, Turks, Syrians, even one man from Saudi Arabia, which led to a hilarious encounter.

The author, armed with a digital camera and a laptop, recorded everything she saw, heard, tasted, smelled, and touched. Keeping a detailed journal of her experiences led to a book full of photographs that catalogues various aspects of Kuwaiti life and history.

Kuwaiti business customs are described as the author had a rare opportunity to attend a diwaniya, something that is usually closed off to women. Kuwaiti hospitality is also detailed, as she was able to visit many homes, some of them on several occasions.

The restaurants of Kuwait range from casual to formal, fast food to gourmet, and open to closed – in small rooms along the perimeter of a given establishment. The food varies widely in cuisine, quality and presentation, the most memorable item being one called "Genius Meal" – in homage to American liberators.

Their cat, a Kuwaiti war veteran herself, accompanied Stephanie to Kuwait. She was named Scheherazade. Stephanie's husband, David D. Haines, Ph.D., encountered their pet as a U.S. Army officer during the aftermath of the war in Kuwait, on Failaka Island. The cat was just a kitten playing with a cluster munition, and this warning saved the lives of the men in his unit, so he adopted her. *An American Woman in Kuwait* is the perfect guide for travel with a pet in the Middle East.

The book is a gloves-off, unvarnished description of life in this desert nation that many Westerners will find similar to that in their home countries. However, the book reveals that the trappings of a modern state are woven into deeply conservative social values that remain aggressively intolerant of concepts such as gender equality and individual freedom, things that are taken for granted in the West.

Table of Contents

Chapter 1: Finding Out We Were Going.. 1

Chapter 2: Kuwait's Brief History – In Brief 8

Chapter 3: Getting There Was Half the Hassle...and Fun 34

Chapter 4: Apartments and Houses in Kuwait............................ 50

Chapter 5: Shopping for Household Goods and Groceries 76

Chapter 6: Tea, Coffee, and Customs in Kuwait 102

Chapter 7: Genius Meals – Dining Out in Kuwait..................... 152

Chapter 8: Laundry – A Comedy of Inconvenience 210

Chapter 9: Let's All Go to the Mall – Souq Tours.................... 230

Chapter 10: Ghosts, Jinni, and Superstitions............................ 260

Chapter 11: Invisibility Cloaks and Abbeyas............................ 269

Chapter 12: A Day Off From Men 313

Chapter 13: Additional Wives – The OTHER Women 329

Chapter 14: Crime, Victims, and the Kuwaiti Media................ 347

Chapter 15: Invasion Stories.. 354

Chapter 16: The Retched Blessings of ZamZam 363

Chapter 17: Holiday Weekend at the Wafra Oasis 395

Chapter 18: The Museums and Crafts of Kuwait 437

Chapter 19: Kuwait's Woman Suffrage Movement 475

Chapter 20: Home – Culture Shock All Over Again................ 509

Glossary of Arabic Words 514

Bibliography 518

Chapter 1
Finding Out We Were Going

In September of 2004, my husband startled me with the announcement that we were going to Kuwait for 6 months. Really...and why were we going to do that?

David, a Ph.D. immunologist, was going to do an asthma study and research nutraceuticals there. He would work with his old Kuwaiti colleague, an M.D.-Ph.D. immunologist on the asthma study, and learn about the nutraceuticals – plant-based cosmetics and dental products made of herbs and whatever other natural items from the area, plus regional foods...whatever proved to be indigenous to the area.

What was I going to do there, just be dragged along because my husband had a reason to go there? A woman in an Islamic country? How could it be at all acceptable? I would be treated as an afterthought, with nothing to do, and expected and required to focus on little kids and housework. No way would I go along with that – I like cats, not kids, and so does my husband. We had married each other because we liked and disliked the same things.

I thought it over some more. What else could go wrong? Would religious Muslims try to convert me? It wouldn't work, but it would leave me in a terminal bad mood. What a great way to spend half a year.

A Middle Eastern nation...how could this go well? I thought they didn't like us much. I thought of 9/11, and the images of the reactions of people from the region on that day. Some had partied, dancing and acting like they were happy about it...

I thought about it some more.

Kuwait...that was the country that Saddam Hussein had invaded in 1990.

I knew the outcome: his armies were forcibly ousted, and the Kuwaiti people moved back into their own country. The United States had been responsible for a large part of that action.

So, Kuwait was a Middle Eastern country full of people who actually liked Americans. David had lived there after serving in the U.S. Army during the Gulf War as a chemical weapons officer. He spent 3 years there, during which time he made friends with this Kuwaiti colleague, a flighty guy who resembled an Arab Santa Claus, a genius who didn't fit into his own society very well but who had worked in the Kuwaiti resistance against the Iraqi invaders.

That was where our lovely cat, Scheherazade, was from.

We had just spent almost 9 months at a cat sanctuary in rural Connecticut, my home state, with our cat. The woman who ran the place was a published author and a retired homicide reporter for the Associated Press. She had called a local reporter to do a story on our cat when David got the invitation to return to Kuwait.

My mission, should I choose to accept it, was to follow David sometime shortly after he went to Kuwait, with our cat.

The message did not self-destruct after I heard it – there was nothing tangible in front of me that might go up in smoke. Too bad; it would have been satisfying.

Thus far, I had traveled up and down the east coast of the United States and into Canada – to Québèc, Prince Edward Island, New Brunswick, etc. – and Western Europe. I could speak French (Parisian) fairly well, and had been there 3 times.

The previous November, this same California company that wanted David to go to Kuwait and do an asthma study had sent him to Salzburg, Austria – Mozart's town – for a scientific conference. We had wanted to go there someday, but I had not been with him on that trip due to a lack of funds.

The Middle East was not a place that I longed to visit. My background in women's history and women's studies had persuaded me of this. Women's rights there were not what they are in the West.

I told David that I would not agree to go unless and until my research into the laws of Kuwait assured me that I would not have to wear a veil and that I could control my own life – carry my passport, etc. He was not happy.

He wanted to get things underway immediately. We were not doing well with the business of making a living, not getting grant money any too quickly, not self-sufficient.

I didn't care – I would rather starve at home that let a patriarchal culture control my life. I needed to sort out a few unknowns.

Not that I was about to summarily refuse to consider Kuwait and just stay with my parents…I just wanted to know as much about what I was agreeing to before I formally, officially, agreed.

I am not obedient, and I always question authority.

David was not happy about my hesitation, but what I just said about my character are some of the primary reasons why he married me.

Shortly I acquired a Lonely Planet guide to the Middle East and scoured its section on Kuwait. I have a law degree, so I went straight to the legal section, and the part about women.

Soon I was feeling a lot better. I told David what I had learned: I could dress as I usually did, with my hair showing, and control my own passport, so I would go.

As long as we came back to the United States to stay when this adventure was over…because knowing that I could go home at the end of it all was how I would be able to cope with the whole idea. The travel section of my curriculum vitae needed some geographic variety anyway – someplace out of my usual comfort zone.

Deal.

Once I had settled into the idea of actually going to Kuwait, I decided to keep a journal of the experience every day while I was there. After all, few Americans travel to the Middle East, and even fewer of them do so as civilian women who are not there as corporate wives. I would be a scientist's wife, a lawyer, and one with an interest in learning about the history and culture of the people whose country I was visiting. It would be pointless to go there without learning whatever I could. The mere idea of not doing so was simply incomprehensible to me.

Granted, I did not really want to spend months in some Islamic desert nation, but this one at least didn't require that I wear a shroud of cloth over any part of my body, so I guessed it wouldn't be too great an imposition on me to be there for 6 months. As long as I could come home to my own culture and climate and everything else that mattered to me when that time was up, I would go there.

Some Muslims Who Actually Like Us

When I realized that we would be visiting Kuwait for approximately six months, I thought it would be an excellent opportunity to find out what the citizens of that country – plus anyone else living there – were like as people.

One thing that made me think so is the fact that unlike almost every other Islamic nation that came to mind, Kuwait was not one that was likely to have citizens who hate either the United States government or American citizens. After all, Americans had thrown out some terrifying and destructive invaders within the recent memories of most of the current Kuwaiti population.

I was starting to talk myself into being okay with the idea of going there.

With that in mind, I didn't foresee much difficulty or discomfort in conversations that I anticipated having with Kuwaitis.

The only obstacle – yet also the only advantage – that I foresaw in my immediate future there was my gender. Being a woman could both help and hinder my efforts to interact with Muslims.

It could help me because I could go into the women's areas of any place that my husband and I were to visit, while he often would not be allowed to do so.

It could hinder me because sooner or later I would find myself "apartheided" out of other situations – more interesting adventures – by that same attribute, my gender.

Doubtlessly, there would be times when I would rather not be stuck in one place while something intriguing was taking place elsewhere, yet polite behavior would dictate that I stick around and acquiesce to the ennui of convention.

Would I be an "honorary man" or an American woman? If I had anything to say about it, I would opt for being an American woman every time, yet still able to see more of the inner thoughts of a Kuwaiti than a foreign male could. This would depend as much upon my own willingness and determination to understand the Kuwaitis' point of view and culture as it would my opportunities to visit them in various situations.

Because I am no anthropologist or sociologist, I would not try to become invisible. I didn't want to do that anyway – not at all.

An added dividend to all this was the fact that Kuwait was now completely rebuilt, complete with working indoor plumbing and electricity – things I am loathe to spend a day away from for any reason. Plus, the place isn't known for suicide bombings or other conflicts. I didn't want to deal with suicide bombers…sharp objects flying at you at any time in any place, maiming and killing, turning me into an ugly, disabled widow…but I could relax. We weren't going to a place like that.

In short, it was exactly what I kept reassuring my trepid female American friends before departing: a wealthy, mall-saturated country that is not at war and that happens to be populated by Muslims.

I figured it would be a chance to see what people who are Arab Muslims were like. It would be a change from politically correct, culturally and religiously diverse America – or so I imagined.

I also wondered about something that I came to think of as the invisibility factor: women who lead traditional Islamic lives to whatever degree that they do that. As an American woman, I refuse to be invisible, and I was eager to examine the contrast between Kuwaiti women's behavior and that of American women. That is a subject for later, after I had observed this.

As it turned out, I would be observing Muslim women who were not all Kuwaitis. One of them was an Egyptian professor who lived in Kuwait and was our friend. But that was fine with me. It would all be new and different to me; I would learn plenty.

Why Travel Anywhere – Including Kuwait

"How can you go to that terrible place?" came the response to news that I would soon be joining my husband for 6 months in Kuwait.

This is the question I found myself being asked every time I informed someone that I would be traveling to Kuwait. It didn't matter who I was talking to – a friend of my mother's or grandmother's (the above is a direct quote from a friend of my grandmother's, in fact), or my own friends – all seemed to think that Kuwait was a dangerous and inhospitable place to visit, and that I would be taking my safety and probably my life in my hands merely by setting foot on its deserts.

Why do you ask me that question, was my reply? Do you think that the 1990-1991 Gulf War isn't over? This is 2004, I reminded people. The war is over. Yes, Kuwait is in the Middle East, yes, it is next door to Iraq, yes, it is in a desert environment, and yes, it is populated by Arabs and Muslims. They do live there, you know. I do realize – at least in theory – what it will be like.

That being said, I reassured my listeners over and over again that Kuwait is just a benign, wealthy, quiet country that is no longer a war zone. It is now a developed, modernized country filled with people who are a lot like Americans – just imagine people who are mostly Muslim, mostly Arabs, who have homes, jobs, routines, holidays, Sabbaths that fall on Fridays, and who go to the mall and the coffee shop and the movies just as we do.

The war was far enough in the past that almost all physical evidence of it had been cleaned up and eradicated, one way or another.

Suppressing the urge to laugh when I realized that my grandmother's friend apparently believed that the Iraqi invaders were still wreaking havoc and mayhem there, I calmly informed her that Kuwait is a wealthy, mall-saturated country, one that happens to be populated by Muslims, and that it is at peace. This became my standard line, almost like a mantra, oft-repeated until I left the U.S.

Still, all the fuss over the idea made me think: why travel anywhere, let alone to a country such as Kuwait?

To answer this, I considered my own reasons for making the trip – beyond merely keeping my husband company and avoiding loneliness. Why would I go there? What would interest me about that country and culture? This brought me back to an even more basic question: why travel?

The reason for traveling is to see and hear and otherwise learn about that which is unfamiliar. For those who don't care to know about or even experience such things, by all means, stay home and live usual and often dull routines. As for those of us who wish to live a varied and memorable existence, we travel.

But that isn't enough. People are human everywhere, yet they are different. This means that they behave differently depending upon their life experiences, language, culture, and religion.

My husband and I spend a significant amount of our time communicating with people from the Middle East, thus the necessity of learning to understand them on their own terms. He has colleagues from Iran and Kuwait, Egypt, Syria, Hungary, France, and the U.S. Scientists who study immunology and chemical weapons-induced illnesses are from many places and cultures; they are not conveniently and locally situated near or in Connecticut. We must know how and why they think as they do.

Our world keeps shrinking. People keep traveling all over this planet, going outside of their own cultures. Without learning to understand one another, we can expect nothing but problems – unnecessary and preventable problems – from these future interactions.

Chapter 2
Kuwait's Brief History – In Brief

The first people known to have settled in what is known today as Kuwaiti territory were not the ancestors of the people who live there today. They were Greeks. They were a group of people sent by Alexander the Great as he spread his empire through the Middle East to India, swallowing up all of Mesopotamia as he went. Alexander did not go to Kuwait personally; he ordered a group of his followers to set up a community on an island, which they named Ikaros. It is now known as Failaka Island, and it has the ruins of a temple to Artemis on it. The Greeks lived there for over 2 centuries, starting in the 4th century B.C. Next came the Parthians, followed by the Sassanids. It was a fishing community until the late 20th century. Now it is in ruins, uninhabited.

Kuwait was settled in 1715 by the Al-Sabah tribe. Their name means "morning" and they were a family of goat herders. That became their claim to being the ruling family of Kuwait: first come, first served. They are now Kuwait's royal family, and they live in Seif Palace overlooking Kuwait Bay, in Kuwait City. Perhaps that is where their ancestors first set up their tents when they arrived. The family now comprises a huge extended group of sheikhs (princes) and sheikhas (princesses). They use these titles interchangeably with king and queen, shah and shahbanoo, emperor and empress, sultan and sultana, rajah and rani. These are all the titles used by the rulers of nation, varying with each culture. The Kuwaitis seem satisfied with translating the terms to mean "ruling princes" and leave it at that.

The official ruler of Kuwait is called the Emir, and the first one was elected in 1756, from the Sabah family. His name was Sabah I bin Jaber (bin means "son of"). Since that time, all of the Emirs have been from the Sabah family, the most famous being Mubarak the Great, who ruled from 1897 to 1915.

Religion

The Kuwaitis are Arabs, and their religion is Islam. The majority are Sunni Muslim, which is the branch practiced by the Saudis next door, who are the keepers of Mecca and Medina, the holy cities of the Prophet Mohammad. The Al-Sabah royal family is Sunni. There is also a significant minority of the Kuwaiti population which practices Shia Islam, a religion that resulted from a schism in the believers over politics, causing a bloody war and leaving lots of martyrs for the believers to remember and devote shrines to and worship at. If one travels in the Middle East, there is never any dearth of shrines, mosques, or reminders of religion.

5 times each day, whether one wants to hear it or not, a call to prayer issues loudly from the minarets – tall, thin towers that jut upwards from mosques – amplified by loudspeakers. The reason why hearing the call of the muzzein (the one who sings the call) is unavoidable is that the Quran, Islam's holy book, dictates that mosques be placed at regular intervals throughout neighborhoods so as to leave no chance of anyone missing a prayer. Add to this the modern convenience of loudspeakers and the effect is like a religious boom-box of sound in-your-conscious-thoughts.

The Bedouin People of Kuwait

Some Kuwaitis lived in tents well into the 20th century. They are the Bedouins, and they made their tents themselves. It was the women who did this, using a variety of wools from animals their families raised and cared for themselves: goats, sheep, and camels. The outsides of the tents were plain, mostly dark brown with some cream and black stripes, while the insides were divided into rooms – half for the women and half for the men – by intricately woven, long hangings.

Some examples of interior hangings woven by Kuwaiti Bedouin women. Note the different weave patterns.

These hangings were crafted by a variety of weaves to form specific patterns, usually in red, white and black. The greater the skill of the woman, the greater the pride of the husband when entertaining guests…because that was all of the woman that the guests would see. Kuwait's government – made up of people who were not Bedouins – moved the tent-dwellers into cement-bloc housing in the mid-20th century, and many of the Bedouins ceased to weave. Some Bedouin women still keep their native craft alive, however.

Traditional Kuwaiti Homes

Kuwaitis did not live only in tents in the past. They built lovely houses of gypsum and crushed coral (pale mud bricks), and used thin wooden slats from India and palm leaves for the roofs. The doors were also made of wood with beautiful hammered metal hinges and handles. Some of these homes still exist today, though most new buildings are made of marble, cement blocks, tile, and metal. Only the wealthiest of Kuwaitis still build their homes in the traditional architectural style using the old materials.

A view of the interior of a house in Kuwait built with traditional materials, showing walls, a door, and the ceiling.

A typical, traditional Kuwaiti home – the gypsum-and-coral kind – followed a standard architectural plan: 2 squares connected in the center with 2 front doors that each had a different door-knocker. The knockers made different sounds, one that men would answer and one that women would answer. This was a signal to the residents as to whom the visitor sought to see. Each square enclosed a separate courtyard, where chickens and plants could grow. Half of the house was for the women, and half for the men. The men's half was called the diwan; the women's half was called the harim. Children could run between both sections freely, but mostly they kept to the women's side of the house.

Kuwaiti Towns

A town had many such homes plus at least one mosque, a coffee house, a souq for buying groceries and other goods, and a madrassah school where boys were sent to memorize the Quran by rote. There would also be a building called, just like the men's sections of homes, a diwan – a meeting house for the men, where they could socialize together, play games and eat snacks. These meetings still go on today, and are called diwaniyas. Women are excluded from them, which makes conducting business either an exclusively male pursuit or an obstacle that entrepreneurial women struggle against, thus expending much of their energy on non-business related activities while the men don't have to. Business is not discussed at diwans; men only meet each other, and then discuss business in other venues after that. The purpose of the diwaniya is to establish and maintain influence – called wasta – for each family.

Currency

The Kuwait monetary unit is called the dinar, and each dinar consists of 1,000 fils. The dinars are issued in paper form, and the fils as coins. The currency reflects the history of the nation's economy, attractively depicting what powered it in the past as well as in the present.

Professions

Kuwaitis had just a few professions before they struck oil in the 1930s: goat-herding, sheep-herding and camel-raising, were possibilities; fishing for shrimp and fin-fish on boats called dhows in the Gulf were another; pearl-diving was yet another; ship-building was another; and finally merchant vessels offered another option.

The merchant ships were called booms, and they traveled down the Arabian Gulf (Arabs flatly refuse to call it the Persian Gulf out of cultural pride – can't blame them) to India and Africa, sometimes as far as Madagascar and Calicut, India. They would then bring back the goods – spices, wood, dates, and horses – that had been bought in those faraway places to sell in the local souqs – yet another line of work available to Kuwaitis, along with the coffee houses where ship-owners (who doubled as sea captains and rich merchants) would relax and chat while waiting for sailors to come to the coffee houses and apply to work on their ships.

Politics and Autonomy

Before oil, Kuwait was left largely on its own, despite being claimed as part of the territory of Mesopotamia (now mostly Iraq), the Ottoman Empire, the British Empire, the French, the Germans, and even Saudi territory. Kuwait is roughly the size of the state of Rhode Island, but that didn't stop foreign powers from wanting it. It has a 310-mile-long shoreline, which makes any nation more valuable. This was one of several reasons why Saddam Hussein coveted it – Iraq's shoreline is a mere 35 miles long. As if that weren't enough, Iraq had long considered its boundaries to encompass Kuwait City. But more on that later.

Mubarak the Great (who ruled Kuwait from 1897 to 1915) is credited with maintaining Kuwait's sovereignty in practice, since it could not be maintained in name. With all of those foreign claims on his country, Mubarak had to be clever and cordial with each foreign representative who came to visit him. By then, Seif Palace existed (not open to the public – the royal family lives in it; Muslims do not allow strangers to tour their homes). He had a place in which to receive visitors. He also gave asylum to his Saudi neighbors during his reign, until Ibn Saud was able to return home and rule. (Ibn Saud had been deposed from the rule of his own territory in the Najd Desert of central Saudi Arabia. He later became the founding king of that country, after the British restored him to power.)

The Ottomans had attempted to assert control over Kuwait while competing with the British Empire. Mubarak felt stronger ties to the surrounding Arab tribes – cultural, financial, and political – so he cultivated a political friendship with the British. His intent was to end the necessity of paying into the coffers of the Ottomans. It worked out well; Mubarak assumed office, let the Ottomans demand that the British stop interfering in Kuwait, and then invited the British to bring their gunboats to Kuwait's coastline. That caused the Ottomans to back off, as they could not afford the expense of a war.

Sheikh Mubarak the Great (ruled 1897-1915).

Kuwait then became a British protectorate. 2 years later, Mubarak signed an agreement with the British: Kuwait would never cede any of its territory to any other foreign power nor receive any agents from said powers without British consent. Britain now controlled Kuwait's foreign policy, and Mubarak controlled its internal affairs. It wasn't perfect, but it was better than what Kuwait had before. Mubarak the Great had 2 sons who succeeded him, and the agreement continued until 1961, when the British granted Kuwait independence.

The Red Fort at Jahrah and The Wall of Kuwait City

In the town of Jahrah, inland and west of Kuwait City, there is a famous museum. It is a fort – called the Red Fort at Al-Jahrah – where a battle took place in 1920, fought by 2,000 Kuwaiti men. The siege was led by a deputy of Ibn Saud, who wanted Kuwait for himself. With his ally Mubarak the Great dead, this was the thanks he was giving the Kuwaitis for sheltering him when he could not live in and rule his own country. The British helped the Kuwaitis just as all seemed lost, after the Saudi commander, an Ekhwan tribesman named Faisal Al-Dawish, had captured the fort. The British forced Al-Dawish to withdraw, and life went on for the survivors. It had been a very unpleasant battle as the water in the well became rancid, and the men were trapped inside the fort, running short on supplies.

David D. Haines, Ph.D. at the Red Fort at Jahrah.

1920 was an eventful year for Kuwait: the Saudi attack on Jahrah wasn't their only problem. They also wanted Kuwait City. To defend the place, Sheikh Yousef Bin Isa Al-Qana'i orchestrated the construction of a wall around it, complete with 4 gates: Al Maqsab Gate, Jahrah Gate, Shamiya Gate, and Sha'ab Gate. Each is 4 meters tall, and they are still standing today in Kuwait City. The Sheikh tried to save the wall from being torn down during an urban renewal project in 1957, but he was unsuccessful. He had helped to build it in a hurry back in 1920, but now all that remains of it are the 4 original gates plus a fifth that was added later in 1927, called Dasman Gate.

The original wall had 126 watch towers, was 2 meters tall, and was 5 miles long, spreading into a semicircle around Kuwait City. The first 4 gates are somewhat close together, and are grouped on the southern side of Kuwait City, while the 5th is to the northeast, well apart from them, in the northeast part of the city. The wall had the effect of making the city live up to its name, which means fort, and was built between June 14, 1920 and early September of that year.

The reason for the urgency was an imminent attack by the Ekhwan tribe, which lived out in the nearby desert. Oddly enough, all this work merely bought some peace of mind for the Kuwaitis, because the siege was out at Jahrah, at the Red Fort. The Emir, Sheikh Salem had moved out there, so that was where the Ekhwan attacked, using their favorite scare tactic of firing 4,000 rifles at once – one huge bang – to intimidate the Kuwaitis. Things didn't look good when everyone in the fort ran out of food and had to subsist on some vile water from the one well in the center of the fort, but then the British showed up and bailed them out. The Ekhwan had to retreat and surrender.

As for the new wall, it was not the first one that the Kuwaitis had ever built around their city, but it was the last. The most interesting thing about it was the work schedule for its construction: entirely at night, so as not to interfere with prayer schedules. Each district of the city was responsible for its own section of the wall, and men turned out after evening prayers with lanterns and flags to do the work. As they worked, other people beat drums and sang war songs, just to keep up a cheerful mood and motivate the builders. Sheikh Yousef wrote some of his best poetry during this time, in between supervising construction.

A convenient coincidence helped to promote this schedule: the Kuwaitis were lucky in that their enemy was also Muslim, because that gave them the luxury of counting on the prayer schedule as times when the attack would not come. It also helped that the Emir wasn't even in Kuwait City, which meant that the fighting was elsewhere. It does make one wonder how well they would have done without the British and inside the new wall. As it was, the Red Fort was never meant to withstand a prolonged attack, and all would have been lost without the British. After the siege at Jahrah, however, things were quiet in Kuwait for a long time.

The Dicksons – British Foreign Political Agent and Oil

The British installed a foreign political agent in the country, and in December of 1922, after the Oxford-educated explorer and author Gertrude Bell had completed decades of visits with the sheikhs of the region, her work was adopted in the form of a map of the Middle East. The map outlined the boundaries of each nation, including Kuwait, which the British treated as a neutral zone because they suspected – rightly – that it contained oil.

The most famous of the British Foreign Political Agents was Harold R.P. Dickson who, along with his wife Violet Dickson, lived in Kuwait for most of his adult life (with one brief stint as political agent in Persia).

He was the political agent until 1936, with a 2-year interlude, after which he resumed the post in Kuwait until 1941. He and his wife retired in Kuwait, living in the house where he had been a political agent. She outlived him by 30 years, returning home to England only in the summer to escape the oppressive heat in the country.

Harold R.P. Dickson, British Foreign Political Agent.

Dickson House on Arabian Gulf Street in Kuwait City.

Their home is now a museum on Arabian Gulf Street, not far from Seif Palace. Violet used to ride her horse around the neighborhood (it is no longer a neighborhood; it is now a busy thoroughfare with commercial property all around), pausing to chat with the Emir as he sat in his car with the back window rolled down. She went out with expatriate British residents to view the local archaeological sites, visited with the Sheikhs, and sat in her rattan chair looking out at the dhows on Kuwait Bay. She and Harold had a son and a daughter, both with Arab names: Saud and Zahra, who live in England today.

Harold Dickson was the reason why the first of Kuwait's oil was found. There is a photograph of Harold Dickson standing under a sidr tree with a Kuwaiti man in the house where he lived. This tree, which stands in the Burqan desert, appeared in a dream that Harold Dickson had…5 times. After he had had this dream a few times, he woke up and prodded his wife awake, and asked her to write it all down in detail, which she did. It had to be significant, Harold thought, because the dream kept recurring, and because it featured a spring of water, so he got some Kuwaiti friends to help him find it. Harold had the dream interpreted by a local Bedouin wise woman, and it led not to water but to oil – the first successful location of an oil well in Kuwait, in the Burqan fields. (Kuwait has a Burqan Bank – named for these fields.) Thus, Harold helped to make Kuwait Oil Company a successful enterprise. For this, he and Violet were handsomely rewarded with certain retirement benefits: the right to own their house, which was unheard of for foreigners, a new, chauffeured Mercedes each year, and free health care at Kuwait Oil Company Hospital (in Ahmadi City – there are more oil fields in Ahmadi).

Violet was unable to handle staying in Kuwait during its hot summers, so she would visit relatives in England, where she would comment, in an incredulous tone, that they did not serve dates with the coffee. She had become assimilated as an expatriate resident of Kuwait, where she felt most at home. It was her husband's wish that she continue to live in Kuwait after his death, and she was happy to oblige.

Climate

Kuwaitis endured horrendous heat before air-conditioning became a standard part of their lives. Temperatures reach above 110°F during the summers. Water would be brought by water carriers in leather bags made of goat and sheepskin, already scalding hot just from the trek to each home. The heat was exhausting, and many people would cope by doing as little as possible during the day, staying inside in shaded areas, sleeping on their roofs at night. In the winter, the weather in Kuwait is rather mild, and feels like fall or spring in the areas of the planet that have 4 seasons. It rains sometimes, and at other times there are dust storms. During the dust storms, visibility is reduced to near zero.

Driving a car is dangerous; camels wander onto highways and roads, causing lots of crashes. Going outside is inadvisable; at the very least, sand blows into one's eyes. Most people just stay inside and wait out the storm, as they have done in the past.

Oil, Industrialization, and Modern Conveniences

A craze of industrialization and modernization took off after 1961. Electricity, plumbing, air-conditioning, and the construction of housing for all rapidly got underway, and schools were set up for all children, including girls, where students learned more than just the rote memorization of their holy book. This construction continues today, mostly carried out by foreigners. A group of German engineers designed Kuwait's first plumbing infrastructure, and an Italian firm built it, supplying the pipes and other parts. (Unfortunately, they used cheap pipes that contained some lead – proved by the tests of an endocrinologist living in Kuwait – we spoke with him about it while we were there.)

Today, most Kuwaitis live with all the comforts and conveniences of any first-world, developed nation. They have electricity, running water, they can either buy drinking water or filter their own, they have washing machines and dryers, dishwashers, air-conditioning both in their homes and cars, and a huge labor pool of foreigners to operate a lot of this for them. Of 2.2 million people living in Kuwait, under a million of them are Kuwaiti citizens. The rest are foreign professionals from the United States, Britain, Europe, Australia and Japan, and laborers from South Egypt, Pakistan, Indonesia, Malaysia, India, and the Philippines, to name a few countries.

The Majlis – Kuwait's National Assembly

Many of the nations in the Islamic world have Parliaments, and the word for this in Arabic is Majlis. Another commonly used term for a legislative assembly is National Assembly; Kuwaitis use both, and call theirs the Majlis Al-Umma, or House of the Nation. Kuwait has a beautiful, modern building on Arabian Gulf Street in its capital city, facing Kuwait Bay that evokes its past with sailing and fishing and trading ships. It was designed by the Danish architect Jörn Utzon.

Elections for its 50 seats are held once every 4 years. There is a Speaker of the House in the Majlis, and the Prime Minister has 15 Cabinet Members, named to head the various government ministries.

These 15 Cabinet Members can vote on issues along with the 50 Members of the Majlis – unless the 50 MPs are holding a "no confidence" vote against one of the Cabinet Members – and they may not sit on any governmental committee. The Emir has the constitutional right to dissolve the Majlis, as long as he allows elections to be held within 2 months. However, Emir Jaber Al-Sabah broke this law in 1986, and it wasn't until 1992 that he ordered new elections. There are 5 electoral districts, geographically distributed, and every eligible citizen may cast 4 votes – or choose to cast just one. The 10 candidates of each district with the most votes win seats in the Majlis.

For most of Kuwait's history, only male citizens over the age of 21 could vote in any elections or hold political office. Kuwaiti women had no voice in their own government, and no way to influence the selection of their political representatives. Much has changed: Kuwait women now attend universities both in Kuwait and elsewhere, so they are educated and informed about women in other cultures and nations. Emir Jaber Al-Sabah thought that women ought to have the right to vote, and he pushed for this change along with Kuwait's woman suffragists until they won it on May 16th, 2005. Precisely 4 years later, 4 women were elected to sit in the Majlis.

Emir Jaber died on January 15th, 2006, happy to have seen this come to pass.

Sheikh Jaber Al-Sabah, the Emir.

Kuwait University

Just 5 years after Kuwait officially got its independence from the British, Kuwait University was established. This was done by a decree from the Emir. It began with a Faculty (Department) of Science, Art and Administration, and a Women's College, but women now attend the many other Faculties which have since been set up: Allied Health Sciences; Business Administration; Medicine; Dentistry; Pharmacy; Education; Engineering and Petroleum; and Law. The university started off with just 31 professors and 418 students, but has since expanded to over 1,000 professors and over 19,000 students. Many of the professors are not Kuwaitis; again, Kuwait functions in part by acting as a brain drain to other nations, with a large expatriate population of educated professionals. The university has 4 campuses in various towns of Kuwait, with Faculties in Shuwaikh, Khaldiya, Adailiah, and Keyfan.

Kuwait University: Panoramic view of faculty and graduate housing, and the Business School.

Kuwait University is not the only source of a college diploma for Kuwaitis. There is a branch of the American University in Salmiya, and the Kuwaiti government pays the tuition of any student, male or female, who applies to and is accepted by a foreign university. While David and I were in Kuwait, we met many Kuwaitis who had attended places such as Johns Hopkins University, the University of Pittsburgh, Case Western University, Cairo University, Harvard University, and MIT. Many Kuwaitis hold bachelor's, master's and doctoral diplomas from these and other foreign educational institutions. Almost all Kuwaitis speak fluent English – many with an American accent.

Kuwait International Airport

Kuwait has a beautiful airport with state-of-the-art equipment and shopping areas. It suffered heavy damage during the invasion and occupation by the Iraqis in 1990-1991, but after they left the country, the entire complex was rebuilt and made over into a luxurious complex. Many U.S. military people pass through this airport on their way to a base in northern Kuwait; I saw them when I was arriving and leaving; I smiled and waved to some American woman soldiers. They grinned and waved back to me.

The airport can be reached by driving south on Airport Road to a parking garage and the front entrance of the complex. Inside are the shops, which must be visited before going to the terminal gates. Once you have passed through security, that's it. The shops I saw included Birkenstock Shoes, which came as a surprise to me, plus there were some duty-free shops. Down the escalators and into the lower level are various restaurants which ranged from familiar American fast-food joints to somewhat upscale cafés.

Many different airlines from nations all over the planet operate through Kuwait International Airport, such as Air France and KLM. During my visit to Kuwait I became aware of the names of the airlines of the Gulf States, which operate top-of-the-line, all-frills services: Kuwait Airways (of course); Air Arabia, Bahrain Air, Egypt Air, Emirates, Etihad Airways, Falcon Express Cargo Airways, Gulf Air, Iran Air, Iran Asseman Airlines, Jazeera Airways, Mahan Air (out of Mashaad, Iran), Middle East Airlines, Nas Air (out of Jeddah, Saudi Arabia), Oman Air, Qatar Airways, Royal Jordanian, Saudi Arabian Airlines, Syria Air, Wataniya Airways, and Yemenia. All of these names were new to me; I was fascinated.

There is also the Kuwait Air Force Museum, housed at the airport, but I didn't see it.

The Al-Sabah royal family – with the exception of one member who deliberately stayed behind to organize a resistance to the invaders – all managed to board planes out of Kuwait before the invaders arrived in Kuwait City and the surrounding towns, most of which are clustered directly south of the capital city. Once the invaders arrived, they destroyed as much of the infrastructure as they could – especially the airport and any planes that remained. One would never have known this looking at the place over a decade after the invasion. All traces of destruction had been obliterated, presenting only the glittering images of prosperity and luxury.

The Invasion and War of 1990 to 1991

The invasion of Kuwait came as something of a surprise to the Kuwaiti people and their government. They had long feared both the

Iranians and the Iraqis, and sought to protect themselves by cultivating as allies the U.S. and, oddly enough, the Iraqis.

It was the Islamic Revolution of Iran that that first made them nervous. The reason for this was that Iran had just deposed its monarch, Shah Reza Pahlavi, and Kuwait had a royal family. Iran wasn't far away – it was just across the Gulf, and separated from Kuwait by a small amount of shoreline in Iraq. So the Kuwaiti government responded by sending roughly $5 billion (U.S.) to the Iraqis to help with the ensuing 1980-1988 war between Iraq and Iran. Iran responded by attacking Kuwaiti oil tankers, and as Kuwait's navy consisted of a mere 3 ships, Kuwait asked the United States for help. The U.S. sent warships to the Arabian/Persian Gulf.

As a thank-you for their financial assistance, Saddam Hussein ordered his troops to invade Kuwait on August 2nd of 1990. He claimed that Kuwait was actually an Iraqi province and that he was therefore annexing it to Iraq, adding that Kuwait had provoked this by drilling Iraqi oil. The accusation was that Kuwaiti oil drills had been sent underground on a slant, diagonally into Iraq, where they were sucking up Iraqi oil and thus enriching Kuwait rather than Iraq. The claim was not substantiated, but all that an invader usually needs is an outrageous claim to get an atrocity underway, so Saddam had his excuse. He also accused Kuwait of overproducing oil; what angered him was the exponential increase in wealth that this generated for the Kuwaiti government.

As the Iraqi troops rolled into Kuwait City, the people who couldn't get away in time hid inside their homes, hoping not to meet the invaders. Many of their prayers were not to be answered; groceries were still needed, and when the electricity and water were cut off, life became quite uncomfortable. A lucky few managed to drive overland, off of the roads, over the desert, and into Saudi Arabia where they could go on to any other country by plane. Others were stopped and turned back at the borders by Iraqi soldiers, who confiscated their passports and identity cards, thus making proof of nationality a severe problem should they be lucky enough to escape later on and then need to seek help at Kuwaiti consulates in other countries.

The Kuwaiti military was outgunned as the invaders moved in, and too passive to put up much of a fight. The soldiers had been ordered to wait for instructions to fire on the invaders, so all but one unit, which did receive those orders, went down without a fight.

It was dangerous for anyone – citizens, visitors, or servants – to go outside. Kuwaiti homes are surrounded by walls, or else they are apartment buildings. People were afraid to go outside to buy groceries, and if they dared venture out to do so, their vehicles could be confiscated by the invaders. If that didn't happen, the soldiers would sometimes order one woman out and send the vehicle away, with the occupants horrified as they realized that rape was in her near future. Sometimes the invaders treated female captives like animals, brutally mutilating as well raping servant women, then leaving them alive on the ground where they had fallen. In other crimes, they would break into a home to attack women.

Meanwhile, in Ahmadi City at Kuwait Oil Company Hospital, Violet Dickson was a patient. She had been losing her memory for some time, and had been checked in after having a stroke. The staff decided to evacuate her without letting on who she was; she was famous in the region as an informal ambassador of goodwill between Kuwait and Britain, she had been knighted by Queen Elizabeth II, and the Iraqis would undoubtedly have considered her to be a valuable hostage. 2 Indian nurses carefully walked her onto a small airplane, which they were lucky to secure, without disclosing her identity. Dame Violet was a large, tall woman, and the 2 short-statured, small-boned nurses had a difficult time walking with the confused, elderly woman, but they got her onto the plane and then the pressure eased. When the plane landed in England, they handed her off to her children and other caregivers, and made it home to India and safety until the war ended.

Meanwhile, the rest of the world was watching, while a massive buildup of military forces took place in Saudi Arabia as help arrived and got organized. Help came from the United States, whose President, George H.W. Bush, saw Kuwait as one of its foreign gas stations (one might as well be honest about the selfish motives behind helping Kuwait), plus Britain and a total of 34 nations. My husband was among the U.S. Army officers who went to help – he was a chemical weapons expert who had passed through a special military training program. He thought that this mission would be the end of his life, and that the Iraqis would deploy lethal poisons to maintain control of Kuwait, but they didn't.

Instead, the invaders left vats of their poisons behind in warehouses in Kuwait City, which the Americans found after the fighting was over. Unfortunately, they were ordered to blow these up, and an unknown recipe of chemicals was sent into the upper atmosphere, where it then precipitated back down on the region, causing unexplained illnesses among the local population and anyone else who was visiting the area. My husband returned as a civilian scientist to study this problem and assist with developing treatments for patients who were suffering from the ill effects. I am happy to say that some progress has been made.

Thanks to air-to-ground superiority and plenty of machinery, several weeks after the fighting began, it was over. A final push of 4 days, ending on February 26th of 1991, and the Iraqis were out of Kuwait. They set fire to the oil wells, and looted Kuwait City before departing, where they kidnapped many Kuwaiti citizens, seizing vehicles and goods. They stayed until the absolute last moment that the U.S.-issued ultimatum had allowed them to be in Kuwait, which meant that they were still driving up the highway, on Abdaly Road towards Iraq, when U.S. planes released napalm on the caravan of purloined people and property. The result was a blackened highway of horror.

But the invaders were gone, and that was what mattered most to everyone. Because of this, Kuwait now has a secular national holiday: Liberation Day. It is celebrated each year on February 26th, the day after Independence Day, which is about gaining political independence from the British Empire. Kuwaitis like to make a holiday vacation out of it. The reasons for the celebration are still in the living memories of most of the people of this country, so it's understandable.

Oil Fires and Environmental Damage

When I first saw Kuwait from the air as the plane descended towards Kuwait International Airport, I was looking at a beige landscape – the desert. I live in the northeastern part of the United States, where I see 4 seasons each year and expanses of brilliantly-hued green grass all around. I love the green, and the pink, blue, purple and other flowers that sprout up each spring. The desert seemed like a dead, ugly, barren landscape to me as I contemplated it from the air, but logic told me that no part of the planet could truly be devoid of life. I would just have to get to know the plants and animals native to Kuwait, either by meeting them up close or by reading about them.

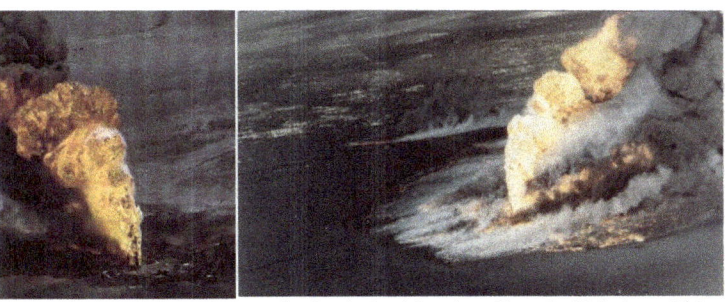

Flaming Kuwaiti oil wells, set on fire by the Iraqi invaders. Photo by U.S. Army 1st Lt. David D. Haines, Ph.D., taken during the liberation of Kuwait.

It turned out that I had chances to learn, and I was right about the methods: one chance was at the Wafra Farms Oasis, and the other was from a book by a Kuwaiti environmental scientist by the name of Jassim Mohammed Al-Hassan, Ph.D., who taught at Kuwait University. It was titled *The Iraqi Invasion of Kuwait, An Environmental Catastrophe* and printed in Kuwait in 1992. The book detailed the various flora and fauna of Kuwait, both before and after the catastrophe, so it provided a great basis for comparison. Kuwait has a species of tree called sidr, which grows lovely, small, pitted fruits called knar.

A box of knar fruit.

The weekend at the Oasis, in the southern part of Kuwait, provided an opportunity to walk through desert brush, watch the unearthing of native truffle mushrooms, and see homes that were out in the countryside.

A party hunting for Kuwait's desert truffle mushrooms; note the brush, shrubs and flowers – and trees.

Professor Al-Hassan's book was full of photos of desert foxes, one of whom had lost a leg in the oil spills, birds that had been washed clean of thick, black coatings of oil, and so on. The Iraqis had taken the attitude that if they couldn't have Kuwait, then no one could, and they had set about ruining everything and anything that they could before leaving once they knew that they could not hope to remain in control there. They set off plumes of oil spewing, uncontrolled, from well after well after well, flooding the land around them, destroying, among other things, many graveyards – including Harold Dickson's grave. The waters of the Gulf were fouled with oil, killing off lots of marine life – coral, seaweed, fish and shellfish – and deoxygenating the waters. Then they set fire to the plumes, making Kuwait's skies black with smoke, choking anyone in the vicinity and reducing visibility to near zero, just as in sandstorms only worse, because when the fires were put out, everything had been laid waste.

Desert plants and animals could not simply go on with their lives, hunting, fishing, drinking and converting carbon dioxide to oxygen. The birds were covered with black crud, and some died and became fossilized reminders of the desecration. The plants that were not washed clean quickly died. Sand could no longer support indigenous species of plants. Some Japanese people assisted with the remediation of the land where they could, turning (just one example) a large swath of land in Ahmadi City near Kuwait Oil Company Hospital into a garden. The soil they managed to develop did not resemble anything that Kuwaitis had previously known, however; it supports plants that normally thrive in cooler environments.

Further reading about Kuwait society, plus conversations with adult Kuwaitis who have worked in this society in their chosen professions for a number of years, led to the conclusion that Kuwait suffers from an overload of a combination of wasta (influence) and nepotism. This combination cripples its administrators' ability to effectively and efficiently manage Kuwait's resources. Public administrators need to consider work ethics and the merit of job applicants before granting employment merely on the basis of political and family connections. Kuwaiti administrators often don't know how to manage resources, let alone care to expend the necessary effort to do so properly. Too many Kuwaitis simply expect to be given prestigious, high-paying jobs that require a minimum of effort. They would rather let the system carry them from the cradle to the grave with free health care, education, social security, and even easy jobs.

This deficiency showed itself in the Kuwaiti effort to clean up the nation's environment after Saddam's troops vacated the country. If –

and this is a huge "if" – Kuwaiti public administrators had been better prepared to manage what resources remained to them after the invasion and destruction, the Kuwaiti environment might have fared much better much sooner.

The chief resource that remained to Kuwaitis after the disaster was human. People were still here. This is their country, and those whose home needs remediation tend to be those who care most about remediating it. Had Kuwait University had an M.P.A. program in place in the 1980s, some graduates of it might have been well-equipped to handle this situation and to properly assist and organize the environmental scientists who freely gave of their time and skills to repair Kuwait. But they were not.

Dr. Al-Hassan talks about a lack of organization among Kuwaiti environmental administrators, which meant that the freely given efforts of the Kuwait Environmental Action Team (KEAT) were not fully utilized by all who needed them.

There is no excuse for this; there are only explanations. Foreign environmental scientists also came to Kuwait, but none of them communicated at all with their Kuwaiti counterparts, who were all working on the same problem. That Kuwait was not paying the way of these foreign teams is merely an explanation. The failure of both Kuwaitis and international visitors to share their findings and resources with one another resulted in a terrible and needless waste of their skills and efforts. A wonderful opportunity of international cooperation and communication presented itself, and all sides dropped the ball. If they had assembled their findings neatly into one user-friendly report in all languages, these environmental scientists would have had the most effective remediation tool possible in terms of world and Kuwaiti efforts to protect everyone from the poisons dumped into the desert, the Gulf, the marshes, and the air.

These prayer-bound people needed a lot of help in order to restore and maintain their rather closed and rigid lifestyle. Kuwait is a small country that was attacked by a larger one. With equal levels of technology but grossly unequal numbers of fighting forces, there was no way that they were going to regain control of their territory without outside help. The Saudis couldn't do much more than host that help in 1990-1991 when the British, Europeans, Americans, Japanese and others came to their rescue. They offered geographic proximity and a launching point while the visiting militias did the rescuing. It was a time when women – in those militias – drove cars and went about uncovered and fully visible in Saudi Arabic, to save Kuwait and its environment and get oil production back underway. Kuwait is still the gas station of many other nations, and for that it can count on rescuers to come as long as oil supplies last.

The bill for the damage inflicted by the Iraqis: $5 billion U.S. dollars.

Land Mines – The End of Life on Failaka Island

There was another lasting form of damage inflicted upon Kuwait because of the Iraqi invasion: Failaka Island is currently abandoned and unsafe. This is because the place is randomly littered with a kind of land mine called cluster munitions. They are also called cluster bomblets, and are roughly the size of golf balls, which were dropped onto Failaka to get rid of the Iraqis. This was done from planes by the Americans and the French in cylindrical canisters (called cluster bombs), which broke open above the ground, dropping their contents on the ground, where they spread widely. Many detonated on impact, but many others just sat on the ground, inert until nudged, awaiting their chance to make ground meat out of anyone who touched them. Still others are duds. There is no way to know without touching them, so walking on the island is inadvisable.

Failaka Island now shows the ruins of a late 20th century Kuwait fishing community. There is a diwan and a mosque, there are many residences, and there are the archaeological remains of the old diwan and the ancient Greek temple to the goddess Artemis, plus the outlines of the ancient Greek community that surrounded the temple. All of this is uninhabited and uninhabitable. There used to be small boats for fishing and fishing nets set up on the beach, but the people who maintained them are gone.

What happened there was this: the Iraqis arrived and ordered the residents to leave – all of them. Most of them did, but some few stubborn ones refused to leave their homes. The Iraqis shot them and piles their corpses in the town square to rot. The island had lots of cats – small, shorthaired cats, with black-and-orange-and-white female calicos and grey-and-white males – who had existed in a symbiotic relationship with the Kuwaiti residents. There was suddenly no one left to feed them. The cats ate the human corpses first, and then attempted to subsist on whatever rodents they could catch, but that wasn't enough. Meanwhile, the Iraqis used them as target practice. Soon they did not trust humans.

Then the liberators arrived – American and French soldiers. They set up camp on the island, and began searching for whatever equipment was salvageable. They also cleared away some but not all of the remaining cluster munitions that still litter the island. It was too enormous of a job to complete without investing more time in the effort, and their commanders had not authorized it.

My husband, David, was one of the Americans on this island. One day, while leading his unit across the island from his camp, he saw a kitten – a cute little calico – batting something small around with her paws. It was a cluster bomblet. He called a halt, and for a moment, he and the kitten stared into each other's eyes. Then he ordered the soldiers to step backwards into their own footprints until they had left that burst pattern of bombs. They were all terrified of dying; 2 of them had been killed by the frightening contents of cluster bomblets on the day that they had arrived. David found another way to get where they were going.

The next day, they decided to reward that kitten – she deserved it for saving their lives, inadvertent or not. They laid out some scraps of their MRE rations (Meals Ready to Eat) and waited. Soon lots of starving cats were rushing forward, heedless of their prior fears of humans. They recognized their heroine quickly, and one of the soldiers rushed up to her and grabbed her by the shoulders. "Got it, sir!" he said happily. David took her and their eyes met again. He named her Scheherazade, for the philosopher woman in *The Arabian Nights* who had saved many lives with her stories. This cat had one great story. David left her with some Kuwaiti friends when his tour of duty ended in the spring. He returned at the end of the summer as a civilian scientist and took her back, and she was his wonderful pet cat for the rest of her life.

Scheherazade Cat – sleeping happily between David's feet.

Failaka Island is still unsafe, still uninhabitable, and still fascinating, so the Kuwaiti government decided to move some of the ancient temple ruins to its National Museum in Kuwait City. The public can now view them without the threat of being blown up. It is not the same as wandering among the ancient ruins of the temple to Artemis in the desert while smelling the salty air from the Arabian Gulf, however.

Water Towers and Kuwait Towers

All over Kuwait, one can see huge water towers and some small ones, all of which are fascinating to look at: they are works of art, some whimsical, some representational and depicting such things as the doors of old souqs (markets), or oil jugs, or water bottles.

3 different examples of small water towers in Kuwait: souq doors, an oil jug, and a water bottle.

The most famous water towers, which are the most remarkable, are called by the equally unremarkable name of Kuwait Towers. They consist of a trio of spikes, 2 of which actually hold water, which is kept in the balls on these spikes. One spike has just one ball, and is not open to visitors. The other has 2 balls, both of which allow visitors, with the top ball being smaller than the bottom one. The top ball has a café, gift shop, and revolving viewing deck, and the other one has a restaurant – also revolving – with a private dining room one floor below. These areas are reached by elevator, and there is an entrance fee. The third spike serves to light up the other two at night. The towers were designed by the Swedish architects Sune Lindström and Malene Björn, and opened to the public in 1979. Collectively, they hold 4,500 cubic meters of water.

These towers were one of many pieces of Kuwaiti property that was damaged during the Iraqi invasion of 1990. Bullets and shell casings damaged the outside, and the inside suffered electrical damage.

Foreign workers were murdered inside the towers, and their bodies were left behind among the wreckage to putrefy and decay. 10 days after the Iraqis were expelled from Kuwait, my husband, David D. Haines, Ph.D., a 1st Lieutenant in the U.S. Army, entered the tower that has only one ball with his rifle and found 10 corpses – 9 men and one woman. They had all been shot and left to rot. Today, all is cleaned up and disinfected, the equipment is up and running and the Towers are open to the public.

Kuwait Towers – lit up and night, and seen from a distance in Salmiya.

From the viewing deck on the top ball of the other Tower, as well as from inside the restaurant below, one can enjoy a view of the Gulf and Kuwait Bay; the Towers are situated on the cusp of Kuwait City, allowing for a panoramic look at the waters that comprise Kuwait's shoreline. Below the Towers is a children's theme park with swimming pools and water slides, and some picnic areas.

A buffet spread in the restaurant of Kuwait Towers, complete with a miniature depiction of the Towers.

Chapter 3
Getting There Was Half the Hassle...and Fun

"Americans have no history – no culture," Arpad boomed as he sat in my parents' kitchen. The scientist and dean of the Faculty of Pharmacy at Debrecen University was having dinner with us, and picking up some documents that David had left behind for him before leaving for the Middle East. This was one of Arpad's standard short visits from Hungary on one of his many trips to the United States. He always acted as though he had one foot out the door, like we were keeping him from something.

[It didn't take me long after my arrival in Kuwait to realize just how colossally incorrect Arpad's remark was. Granted, it was merely the typical grand generalization that Europeans often make when they compare the time span and originality of source that makes up each of their individual nation's cultures with that of the United States.]

With Arpad's scathing commentary on my mind, I prepared myself as best I could to defend American culture. American culture exists: we have original music of our own, including rock and classical genres, famous artists, authors, poets and historic figures; we have a laid back, egalitarian, open mindset, comic book superheroes, and humor as social and political commentary.

I was set to join David in Kuwait in a few weeks. We would meet up after he had detoured to Teheran, Iran to lecture at a scientific conference and after I had secured all necessary travel and health documents for our pet cat, Scheherazade, a former Kuwaiti citizen herself.

This had proven to be more difficult than securing permission for a human being to travel there. All I had to do, according to our Kuwaiti friend Dr. Saleh Al-Hamdullilah, was approach a desk at Kuwait International Airport, show my passport, and ask for a visa.

But never did I feel our own American culture so strongly as I did once I was physically removed so far from it, both geographically and socially. I was suddenly in a culture that was so opposite to my own that I rapidly and continually felt a profound and abiding gratitude for my own culture.

Planning, Preparations, and the Cat

It was October of 2004, and I had just returned to my parents' house at the end of September, with my husband, who was to leave the following week for the Middle East, at least 6 weeks ahead of me. We would be traveling on different airlines, and at different times. The reason was our cat, Scheherazade, a beautiful black-and-orange-and-white calico with green eyes. David's ticket was bought first, by the California company that had contracted him to do an asthma study and nutraceutical survey in Kuwait.

My ticket would be bought later, after I found out what I had to do to get the cat ready to go with me, and how long I would need to do all of that. I could not take her out of the United States or into another country unless and until all medical and legal requirements of the starting point, the stopover, and the destination were all met.

By the time all those questions had even begun to be asked, it was clear to both me and the nice secretary in California who was helping arrange this that I would go on a French airline, because the French are the most pet-friendly. No way would I put a cat in the hold of any airplane, to be terrified and made sick – possibly killed – by wildly fluctuating temperatures and pressure changes.

My husband, David D. Haines, Ph.D. in immunology, had been in Kuwait 14 years earlier, first as a soldier and then as a civilian scientist, and had stayed for over 3 years. He had made friends with various scientists, and kept in touch with them, working on patents and publishing over 50 articles in scientific journals while studying for his Ph.D. in Connecticut. His name can be found on Medline, a computer database for scientific articles.

I am a graduate of the University of Connecticut's School of Law, and before that I studied history and women's studies as an undergraduate. I traveled with my husband and wrote about our time in Kuwait, from mid-November of 2004 to May of 2005. I am a writer with an editing business, and I edit my husband's publications.

David had gone on ahead of me to the Middle East, to a 10-day scientific conference in Iran (this was his third trip there), and then on to Kuwait. Our friend, Dr. Saleh A. Al-Hamdullilah, M.D., Ph.D., an immunologist, would meet him and help him get settled. They were to conduct the asthma study and submit the results of their research to a California-based company. I would follow with our cat soon, and then help with the asthma study, coordinating details with Saleh and David.

One amusing aside about David's trip to Iran: he took 48 small cans of cat food and 3 or 4 bags of dry cat food with him. When I follow with our cat, I would bring more. We didn't believe that we could buy this particular food in the Middle East (and as it turned out, we were right). David stayed in a 5-star hotel in Tehran, Iran, courtesy of the company in California. One day, he returned to find 2 empty cans of cat food plus some pita bread fragments in the garbage can –

the hotel cleaning staff had had pita-pocket cat food sandwiches! Apparently, they are transient workers who have little money for a decent meal. David stowed the cat food with a colleague at Tehran University after that.

I prepared for the trip by spending a couple of afternoons each week at Borders Books and Music. I liked to browse the store and sit in the café for a few hours. It's very relaxing. That was where I found my Lonely Planet guide to the Middle East, which went with me to Kuwait.

I had been finishing the Christmas and birthday shopping for my relatives while going to Borders, because I would not be around for the holidays. My grandmother, who was 90 years old at the time, was particularly worried about this trip. I never let her remarks deter me, however; she has never done any serious travel, so of course she would worry that it was just all too dangerous to be attempted at all.

My mother offered to help me assemble gifts to bring to people in Kuwait. In all seriousness, she informed me that I must be ready with the standard hostess gifts that Americans and Europeans bring when traveling: chocolates and wine. I told her that no, I absolutely must not bring wine, because Kuwait is a dry country – Muslims don't drink wine, they tend to make its mere possession illegal, and carrying it would only get me arrested at the airport, and of course the hostess gifts would be confiscated (and possibly consumed by the area's rule-breakers). No, I would just bring chocolate to our friends. She was horrified, and also grateful that I had researched the culture so well. [Actually, I had learned this from Muslim scientist friends years earlier, when they visited me.]

I love geography, so I knew exactly where I was going. People and other cultures fascinate me, but I needed something to say to my grandmother and her friends. Everywhere I went in those final weeks before departing, I used the same hopefully helpful line: "It's fine – it's a wealthy, fully developed, mall-saturated country with lots of Americans, Brits, and Dutch people living there. Those people are there because Kuwait is a gas station to many other countries, such as Exxon, British Petroleum, and Shell, which are U.S., British, and Dutch companies, respectively."

This seemed to satisfy just about anyone who asked about my trip. To prepare, I bought myself a blank-paged book at Borders. I planned to write a journal while travelling. I hoped to be able to switch to a computer, but I would have to buy another blank-paged book if I couldn't, or a notebook, or just use loose paper if I that didn't work out. The blank-paged book was pretty – blue, with Vincent Van Gogh's 1889 *Irises* painting on its cover.

David left on October 2nd for Iran. I took him to the bus station, and bought him a ticket for the Connecticut Limo, which runs directly to JFK Airport. The ticket agent was very nice to me when I heard that you need a 2-day reservation just to buy the ticket; I nearly cried when I told him that the web site with the schedule for the airport limo didn't mention this. He made a call, and then sold me the ticket without any problem. I watched until the limo pulled out of sight with David in it, grinning and waving.

It turned out that it would be over a month before I could go to Kuwait to join him. The reason was, just as I had suspected, our cat, Scheherazade. U.S. law required that she have a rabies vaccination before we left the country. That wasn't all – the shot had to be a month old, and she had to have a United States Department of Agriculture Veterinary Health Certificate to travel with. The certificate must be issued within a couple weeks after the rabies shot, and used within 10 days of receipt.

As if that weren't complicated enough, I would need to carry a file with me including: 1. the story of the cat's life, 2. the original rabies vaccination certificate signed by the veterinarian, 3. the U.S.D.A. Veterinary certificate, 4. a paper stating that she can handle temperature fluctuations during air travel, 5. a Home Again Microchip record (she had a microchip installed under the scruff of her neck with a reference number for her address and I.D.), 6. a faxed copy of an animal import permit from the Kuwait Ministry of Animal Health. To enter Kuwait, she needed the rabies shot and a feline distemper shot. After all that, I was sure that this cat would not need any more medical care for a while, and she was in perfect health. She was 14 years old when we left.

Another consideration had been how to travel with her. That nice secretary at that California company, Pat, helped me arrange everything. She was worried about the cat (she had 3 cats herself). I was quite lucky to have a sympathetic person doing the planning with me on that end. Thus far, we had decided that I would be going on Air France, because everything I found out about this airline told me that they would treat my cat very well and let her ride with me in the cabin. David flew on British Airways. That airline would make the cat ride in the cargo hold, so we would have to come back to the States separately as well.

I know enough French to travel effectively – also a plus. I thought that the cat might have to enter Kuwait on a cargo jet, but later found out that that was not true – what a relief. That would have made everything much harder. After discovering that all I needed to comply with were individual airline rules, I called Air France.

For $70 I could take the cat as carry-on luggage in a cat kennel that fit under the seat in front of me. I put address labels on 3 sides of her carrier, including the microchip number, and e-mailed the label to David in Kuwait. With Saleh's help, he arranged for the Kuwaiti permit for bringing the cat.

The 6-week delay had gotten me out of having to go to Iran with him – organizing trips from the U.S. to Iran to Kuwait in such a short time was too much, and I didn't really want to go around with no makeup and a scarf and long black coat on anyway. I was very happy and thankful toward our pet for getting me off the hook about that!

Air France had a rule: 8 pets may ride in the cabin with their owners, provided that each one weighs 5 kilos or less. Scheherazade weighed 7.2 pounds = 3.5 kilos, so we were in. I made her reservation, and was to pay for her ride when we checked in at the airport, which would be Newark Airport in New Jersey. The airport limo wouldn't take us – a problem, because that would have been a mere $68 dollars. Taxis would charge $200+ to take us, which I can't afford. Luckily, my parents wanted to see me off, so they drove us there – me and the cat.

I am lucky that way; they teach me to learn and investigate how to solve my own life problems, but rescue me if after my best efforts it doesn't work. I never want to be alone. People who are utterly alone and who have no money must have a terrible time in life. I have almost no money, but I am not alone. Thinking about this makes me feel appreciative of what I do have. They even had an early Thanksgiving dinner, just for me.

It was a nice 6 weeks, and I got to see my other cat, Cookie, a black-and-white male again. He silently watched me assemble the contents of my luggage – gifts, etc.

Adventure, Anxiety, and Determination

I knew that I would feel no sense of culture shock – no difference – until I stepped off the plane in the land of my destination. There was a stopover in France – another land of the familiar – at the Charles de Gaulle Airport. France is the land of everything beautiful: language, music, sights, sounds, smells, tastes, aesthetics, everything. I knew it from studying French all through high school and traveling there a few times, once for 2 weeks with my high school teachers, again to see the exchange family whose son had stayed at my house the year before, and again for a weekend when I spent a fall college term in London, England.

Kuwait was the unknown.

It made little difference that I had studied and researched what I could before going, just to get a sense of how of its laws and culture would affect my life as a woman. I would miss the occasional glass of wine, but life as a teetotaler would be okay for the duration of this adventure. I could handle this because I knew what to expect. I would hear, see, smell and feel all of it with great intensity. If only I knew more…

What was unknown was how it would feel to be there, and that terrified me.

I have a terrible problem with anxiety whenever my environment changes. It's part of Asperger's, which is high-functioning autism.

This makes going anywhere – moving or traveling – difficult, to say the very least. When it comes to moving, I am usually dead set against it. What's the point of moving? Better to keep all of one's familiar possessions in their familiar places, and myself as well. But travel – that is a different story. Travel, by its very definition, is supposed to be temporary. When the adventure is over, one can go back to the familiar place. That makes it possible for me to face the adventure.

I can't say that I embrace adventure. Only that I want some of it in my life, so that I can learn new things, experience new things, meet people who think differently from the way I think, and bring back evidence in the form of books, photos and souvenirs as proof of my adventure.

Connecting with people who differ from us and understanding them is what is important. Writing about it and being remembered for doing it matters to me.

And so I travel when I can, anxiety be damned.

I was going anyway.

The climate, the air, the smells, the way people would look at me – or not look at me sometimes – would all be a huge change from what I was used to.

Toting my things around scared me – I didn't want the bother of lost luggage.

I had to bring our cat as it was, even though I am great at planning in advance for such things. I had the option of leaving her in Connecticut where she would be well cared for, but I had to bring her, or I would forever feel defeated by the idea that it was all just too much for me to handle.

So when my mother suggested, after my parents had driven me and the cat all the way to Newark Airport, our luggage had been checked and I was wheeling my carry-on bags and the cat in her carrier around the shops, that I didn't have to go to Kuwait, that I could come home with her and perhaps just get a job, even as I was seeing haze around me and hearing static in the throes of an anxiety attack, I said no.

I was going to travel all those miles away to Kuwait.

Going

I left on a Thursday, November 17th, 2004. My father, as usual, packed the car with precision, leaving plenty of room so that he could see to drive from all angles, but fitting everything in just so with the cat's carrier next to me and facing front, so as to allow her to see where we were going.

The night before that, anxiety had bothered me. I had spent the day laying out everything that I was bringing: clothes, toiletries, odds and ends that I managed to fit neatly into my new Vera Bradley handbag (my first one), books, boxes of chocolates, and gift-wrapped books of American art – which I was bringing instead of wine. I also had 2 suitcases in which to put it all. With that, the enormity of the change I was about to undergo loomed menacingly before me, and although I have never had asthma and am quite healthy, I began to have trouble breathing. Next, I began to cry. How would I arrange it all in the suitcases properly? It was hard enough to actually go; packing felt like torture. I was suddenly terrified.

This is not a new thing for me.

Every time I went back to college – an 8-hour drive from Connecticut to William Smith College in Geneva, New York – I had felt a wild sense of panic. It usually went away once I was in my dorm room, alone (after that first year with a partying roommate, I made certain to get my own room – no cost difference). It had only been for the first term that the panic lasted for 4 days. No…it happened again for just as long in London junior year.

Law school was a 12-minute drive from home. I was able to just focus on my studies and enjoy learning.

Anxiety is a nuisance, but I was very determined…to have a college and graduate degree with the term "doctorate" in it, to get married to my best friend and stay that way, to travel, to bring our cat…to write and publish books that will be sold in big bookstores…

Damn the panic that blocks me.

I had to get going.

My mother helped me.

I hate to admit how bad it gets, but she helped me and I will always appreciate it.

The next day was a bit easier, because I could just eat breakfast, get dressed, grab the stuff, and depart. No more fussing about with the details.

Anxiety is the reason why I plan ahead in such detail.

The more prepared I am, the less I will have to do when the anxiety hits, because it will hit, and then I will not be able to do much. I just see a haze around me, and I don't hear people too well, either.

Better to just be very, very organized.

We drove for hours – 5 of them, I think – until we got to Newark Airport.

My father didn't need directions or a map; as usual, he had memorized the route. I had chosen to go on a Wednesday because my mother, an office triage nurse, had Wednesdays off.

We all went in together, and I checked in. The anxiety came back, this time with a touch of dizziness. It was bad enough that I didn't care who noticed. I have no sense of embarrassment about it – that would just add one more problem to the mix.

We approached the check-in desk to get rid of the luggage. It was labeled both *Delta* and *Air France* – the corporations must be associated for ease of...who cared.

There were 2 people there, a man and a woman, who looked kindly at me, saw that I was quietly freaking out (very obviously having trouble focusing), and took over the transactions. The man helped, but let her lead. She was perhaps a few years older than I was, perhaps not. She had sandy hair, thick and straight, with bangs and chin-length. She wore glasses – they might have been of a dark red plastic for the frames. And she offered me her *J.Jill* pen – it was her favorite because the ink flowed so perfectly from it, she added. She managed to distract me from the anxiety for a little while.

I smiled, thanked her, and used the pen to fill out 2 luggage tags for what was going in the hold. She had me fill out other things also, and ran my credit card for the cat after weighing her in the cage. Then I set up the little wheelie with the cat, the carry-on bag, and my reading material.

We said good-bye and moved off into the various airport shops and eatery places. It would be a few hours before I was to go through the gate, and my parents intended to hang out with me. I was actually quite glad; I didn't want to roam the airport alone. I could do that in Paris, after all, when the anxiety had cleared up a bit.

We wandered around, and my mother saw a massage place. Would I like that, she offered? No thanks – I didn't want anyone touching me while I felt like this.

We paced around a bookstore, and I found a magazine called *Archaeology*. I picked it up and found that there was something in there about Pompeii. I had a fiction novel about the day that Mount Vesuvius erupted with *Pompeii* for its title. What a coincidence – I planned to read it on the plane…planes. My mother, still trying to induce a sense of calm in me, bought it for me. I put it in the carry-on bag with the cat care supplies and the historical novel. [I read almost all of that book on the plane rides.]

After what felt like forever, it was time to go through the gate with the cat.

Once I was through the gate and waiting to board the plane, with my parents having walked away after watching me go through security with the cat (I had to extract the unwilling little creature from her cage with the assistance of a security woman and then put her back in…that was the easy part), once that was over, I began to sit quietly and space out, and to calm down.

I noticed that another lady – a French woman with a huge portfolio, and a husband – she too had a pet in a carrier. Hers was a not plastic, however, but a black canvas bag with a zipper and a side made of black netting, and her pet was a dog who laid quietly, looking up around him, not barking. Perhaps he was drugged; he just looked up at her with big, brown, calm eyes. I showed her my cat, and she smiled, and said, in English, "We love them." That was all.

I noticed the nice lady who had seen that I was starting to feel that near-crippling anxiety as I checked my bags and weighed the cat in her carrier. She was here to see us off, onto the plane, when we were allowed to board.

The journey was okay, and I loved the Paris airport, trying out my rusty French skills, eating wonderful pastries, and touring the entire terminal. The cat didn't mind all that walking around, either. She was a world traveler anyway by this time. David had taken her from Kuwait to Rome to New York to Connecticut, so this was not new. I checked on her now and then as I roamed the shops and sat down to eat and people-watch; she was fine. She would just coo and meow at me, then lie down on her bed again.

2 days after I had arrived and slept off jet lag, I wrote about the journey. Before that, I slept while not letting David out of my sight; he watched television in the living room of the apartment he had rented, fretting about not doing work. I told him he could just stay put and not leave me in this strange place until I was rested enough to assimilate, and so he did. He only left once, to get our dinner. He came back quickly.

An E-Mail to My Parents and Aunt

Bringing the cat had proved to be the most complicated part of traveling. I had brought my clothes, lots of cat food, gifts, a FedEx package for David's work that weighed a lot and arrived 2 days before I was to leave, more of David's clothing, and some *X-Men* comics (I wanted to see the paintings from time to time). I had also packed more books, some favorites and a couple that I and David hadn't read yet – who knew what reading materials I would be able to find in this place? I understood that reading choices are limited in the Islamic world, so I was bringing the books and comics to prevent homesickness. I had to pay extra to take all this stuff on the plane, because it meant one more bag plus extra weight, but I did it, and then I was off with my cat and my parents in the airport, less concerned about the effects of censorship where I was going.

The cat seemed fine. She had 2 towels, a cloth bag-bed, and 2 cloth catnip toys in her kennel. I had pet tranquilizer pills for her – she seemed not to need any, so I stopped trying to give them to her. I fed her and gave her water during each flight, and carried a bag full of litter box supplies, plus her file and some books for me to read. We got to Kuwait okay, and David met us.

Kuwait is 6 hours ahead of the eastern United States during Daylight Savings Time, which is when I went there. I had gone on an 8-hour trans-Atlantic flight after waiting for about 4 hours to go. After 6 hours in the Charles de Gaulle Airport terminal near Paris, France, I boarded a 5-hour flight to Kuwait City. Another hour later and I was meeting David, having passed all checkpoints.

I sent my parents a long e-mail detailing our journey a couple of days after we arrived, greeting them and our cat, with a copy to my aunt. Here it is…

Date:	Fri, 19 Nov 2004 22:30:44 -0800 (PST)
From:	"Stephanie C. Fox"
Subject:	Re: HI MOMMY! WE'RE IN KUWAIT!
To:	"Carole Fox"
CC:	"Joan A. Fox LaCaisson"

Hi Mommy!

I love you - and Daddy and Cookie Cat.

Hi Aunt Joan! Hi Amber!

I love you too.

I slept all day on Friday - and David went out and got a haircut to look nice for me. 😊 He looked okay - his hair wasn't anywhere near as scruffy as before his previous haircut - but he was ready for another haircut.

The apartment sucks - the toilet doesn't work very well. He forgot to get towels, so we dry off with his T-shirts. We will move to another place, perhaps today. I sure hope so. It sounds pretty good - newer, fully functional, etc. I'll let you know when we get there. We will have to borrow stuff, but that is all arranged. What is especially good about the next place is that it will be in the same building as the clinics that David and Saleh are setting up - just 2 floors up, on the 9th floor. The commute will consist of an elevator ride.

Right now I am at Kuwait Gulf Oil Company Hospital. Saleh Al-Hamdullilah is seeing a few patients in his office. We saw him. A Philippina nurse (Head Nurse) named Eudora gave us a ride here. She gives David lots of rides here. I guess Saleh takes him home.

When I arrived, Saleh's son Ali and David met me and Scheherazade Cat at Kuwait International Airport. The officials didn't even look at the paperwork on the cat - incredible! But what if I didn't have it and there had been problems?! All the officials wanted to know was: Did I have any wine with me? No, of course not, I said; I knew they didn't want me to bring any of that, so I didn't bring it. The customs official seemed pleased with that, and I went through. I had to go to a desk for an entry Visa first - that was simple.

David has agreed that we will not waste our nonrefundable plane tickets home. We will use them. We might come back here, we might stay home and set up a home - I want to stay home, of course. I even managed to extract a promise from David that he wouldn't go to Iraq until I am convinced that it is okay. He'll never pull that off, so wish me luck keeping him out of there. I won't go; I have to take care of our cat.

The plane rides: Air France is definitely the way to go, but we knew that from all my research about which airline would let me take the cat. So many American ones simply refuse to take pets internationally or, if at all, only as cargo. Scheherazade would not have done well in cargo. She did very well in the cabin. The first plane had 2 aisles with 2 seats by the windows and 4 seats in the middle. I was on the right by the window. No one sat next to me.

For the Newark to Paris flight, she lost her tranquilizer pill somewhere inside her cage just as a French stewardess told me to keep the cage door shut - she was worried that the cat would get out. I shut the door and told her what I was trying to do, and that I wasn't going to bother trying again. The cat seemed okay. A little while later I put the cat carrier up on the empty seat next to me so Scheherazade could look around at the inside of the plane and see the other passengers in the vicinity. A nice French couple was 2 seats away with a 14-year-old Welsh Corgi dog - very quiet. I met them before we boarded. The wife had a huge black portfolio - maybe she was an artist. She looked at my cat, I complimented her dog, and she smiled and said, "We love them," meaning our pets. Ms. Ahearn - the lady who took my bags and helped us when we first got to the airport - watched us all board the plane. I told her I felt much calmer now that we were about to board the plane. She was very nice.

Those stewardesses were all very pretty and chic, and smelled wonderful - those French perfumes... A very nice steward waited on me, and smiled when I wrote something in French and English on my menu. "You wrote all this?" he asked me. I said yes, and that I could speak French, but too slowly, so that French people always switch to English when they talk to me. He smiled, and promised to bring me a dinner that I could eat - they had either beef or salmon, and yoghurt, and lemon poppy seed cake, and prosciutto with cantaloupe melon, and Brie cheese.

I got a window seat for each flight. During the first flight, after I ate, I got out the cat carrier, and used that white plastic dish that hooks onto the inside of the cage door. I put some dry cat food in it, and the cat ate most of it, then turned away, but couldn't sit comfortably. I took this to mean that she was finished eating, so I took it out, put the leftovers back in the zip-lock bag, and then put water in the dish and put it in the cage door. She turned around and happily drank a lot of it. She refused to accept any more water out of the syringe. Good idea, though. Thanks for getting me those. When she turned around again, I knew she was through, so I dried the dish with my napkin and put it away.

Next, I brought the cat in her carrier, my handbag (just because I wouldn't leave it), and the black bag of cat care supplies into the toilet. I set up her litter box and let her out. She just meowed and walked around. No sale. I wasn't surprised. I went to the bathroom myself and packed everything back up. The cat was okay.

There was a Global Positioning System display on screens on the walls and on the backs of all the seats showing where we were with readouts on temperature around the plane, altitude, ground speed - roughly 500 mph (it gave it in kilometers as well) - and we could switch to movies and news and music. I tuned in to classical music - earphones were part of the free packages that we all got. Right across from me were an aunt and niece from Manchester, England. They were both young, blond, and I thought they were just 2 friends traveling together. The aunt was overweight and uncomfortable, and the stewardesses tried hard to help her. She was okay, though. They went back to England on a plane that left from the same gate that mine left from later on.

The breakfast was pretty good, too: yogurt with granola, coffee or tea, more Brie, etc.

The food on the flight to Kuwait, however...I don't know what happened there. The French stewardesses were just as beautiful and friendly, but even the soldier next to me rejected some of the food. Soldiers will usually eat any old crap, so this had to be pretty bad. It was a cross between quiche and fruitcake. I told the stewardess that it was so bad that even the military guy rejected it, and she said that she would tell the woman who buys the food, and that they would most likely never have that again.

I was seated next to the window again, with a guy who drives tanks in Iraq. He had just gone home to visit his wife and kids in Colorado. A French-speaking Arab (in Western clothing) with prayer beads sat in the other seat. This plane had one aisle with 2 rows of 3 seats. The soldier was wearing jeans, and so were the other soldiers he was traveling with. His commanding officer was behind him and on the other side, and asked how he was doing. "Fine, sir, I've got a cat to sit with, sir." Laughter.

The cat meowed a lot during takeoff and landing on each flight. I couldn't feed her until our food was removed, then I did the same thing as before - no problem. But a couple of minutes before dinner...something stank. I hoped that it was just the guy in front of me farting, but I suspected that it was only wishful thinking. [Pretty sad when your fantasies are about guys farting.] It was the cat. I checked her cage. She shat in the old blue towel, but not as much as she needed to. As soon as I could get up, I took the cat, the handbag and the other bag into the toilet. This time, she decided that the better part of valor was to use the litter box, and she did. I turned the bag - saved in a zip-lock bag from the first attempted use - inside out and threw it down the garbage chute. I washed the towels and stored them, wet, in the zip-lock bag. The pink bag bed and the 4 catnip toys survived the ordeal unscathed, so I put them back in the cage with the cat. She was fine after that - didn't need another bathroom visit.

I often put my fingers into the cage and she would purr and rub against me. No biting - she just wanted attention. When I went through security in Paris, I had to do the same thing you saw me do at Newark Airport - take off shoes, put coat and keys in a box, and take the cat out and carry her through the metal detector. She didn't want to come out, so the French security lady had to hold the carrier and pull while I pulled the cat out. I had to ask her, "S'il vous plaît, tirez la boîte and je vais tirez la chatte." The security lady laughed and helped me. I ran through and put everything back together, like I knew the drill well, which I did, from doing it in Newark.

The Paris airport was neat - lots of shops. I wandered around looking at everything, wheeling my cat and other stuff around on that thing you bought for me - it's great! No one minded the cat. I had saved some of David's Euro coins from last winter - his Austria trip - in the pitcher from Ibiza in my room. You know - the little one in which I keep international coins. I took those with me and used 3.30 Euros to buy a container of orange juice at the airport. David was pleased with my resourcefulness when I told him about it.

The apartment we will stay in when we move is available now, and we are allowed to move into it now. We're thrilled - we hate this one. Saleh will help us move. We can pay for it when the California people send the money to us - the owners are okay with that. We're so glad about that. Now that the cat and I are here, she doesn't scream and yell - what a relief. She let me sleep all day yesterday, only joining me to purr and sleep next to me. I'm sure it's because there are no other cats here. And she likes me better than ever for taking good care of her on the 2 flights.

Print this e-mail and let Nana look at it.

I've got my blank-paged book. I will write about this trip in it, though having these e-mails is good for that purpose, too. I save copies of these letters in my Sent Items [e-mail] folder.

I love you!

Love,

Stephanie.

That was what I told my family in writing, from the library computers at Kuwait Oil Company Hospital in Ahmadi City that Saturday.

But there was plenty more to it – about arriving in the airport and smelling, hearing, seeing and feeling all those new, intense things.

Just Off the Plane

I had looked down at the ground in the fading light as the plane descended toward Kuwait International Airport's runways, and seen the beige sand all around. It was as I had expected: too much beige everywhere. I told myself that this would be better than another white, icy-cold winter. Just as well to have left that part of the planet for once before the next snowstorm (the first one had been the previous week).

The soldier next to me on the plane had warned me that it would be a whole different life, or something like that. I believed him. I had looked out the windows a lot, and seen the northeast-pointing peninsula of Cyprus with the mid-day sunlight shining on the water of the Mediterranean Sea halfway through that ride, and now I was looking out at a desert in twilight. I looked for signs of plant life, and thought I could see some brush here and there. It looked scratchy. I planned to find out what plants and animals were indigenous to Kuwait one way or another. At least it would give me something to do.

We disembarked, and I reassembled the wheelie with the cat in her carrier, the carry-on bag with the file on the cat in easy reach, and my handbag yet again. Out of the plane we all went, and into the terminal. Now I would feel culture shock, I told myself.

Everyone headed through a quiet building with sand-colored granite tile to a desk with one quiet Middle Eastern guy in a standard guard's uniform: dark blue pants, light blue buttoned shirt. He had black hair and a mustache.

I remembered what I was to do: get an entrance visa from him. How was I to do that, I wondered?

I hung back and watched other people get theirs. Nothing dramatic appeared to be necessary: just had over one's passport, wait for him to do something on his computer, watch while a sheet of partly Arabic and partly English spools out of his printer, accept it and one's passport from him, and follow the others downstairs. I did that.

Before I went on, however, I looked upwards at a distant balcony.

Several women were walking around up there.

All of them were completely shrouded in black, with long robes, veils, and another piece of cloth over their faces from the bridges of their noses down. Only their eyes and hands showed. I had read about Saudi princesses before; this was how they dressed when they went out anywhere.

I looked up at them, and they looked down at me.

Conversation was not possible. They were all the way up there, and I was supposed to descend even further down. I did.

Downstairs, I saw few other Americans and no other women – just a 12-year-old girl arriving with her father. I knew that Kuwait employed many foreign men from India and Egypt, and I line of Indian men had formed off to one side.

I chose another line, with only a couple of people in it, and waited.

Soon I was called over to a booth with one man in it, seated a bit high up.

I gave him my paperwork, and the cat's.

He leafed through it quickly, gave it back to me, and waved me on. I don't think he spoke English, and my Arabic had a long way to go (the glossary at the end of this book was the result of my stay in Kuwait, after all).

What about the cat, I thought? All those papers I had been required to prepare, and he had barely noticed them!

I waved to get his attention. He looked up.

"Don't you want to check my cat and her papers?" I asked.

He looked confused; he had obviously hoped to avoid the necessity of actually talking with me.

Unable to make sense of what I was asking, he stepped out of his booth and down, as I kept pointing into the cage door at the cat.

He peered in.

I showed him her paperwork, and asked again if he needed to do anything with it.

"Ah!" Now he had caught on. "No – all fine – just go." He smiled.

Okay, I thought. I made every effort to follow the law. If the officials here didn't care, I wouldn't worry about it. I said thank you, smiled, and pulled the wheelie over to the next stop.

It was an X-ray machine.

I put all my stuff through; somewhere between the entrance with those lines and the guy who didn't feel the need to look at the cat's papers I had reacquired my luggage. At least, as the nice lady from

Delta had assured me, the airlines had not lost my luggage. The worst was probably over. That's when I got the questions that I had expected:

The guy running the station had seen the shapes of the huge shampoo bottles I had brought, and asked about them. Were they bottles of wine? No – they were shampoo, because I had wanted to use a familiar kind when I first arrived in Kuwait. He seemed to believe me, but asked about wine again – had I brought any with me?

"No," I said. "I knew you didn't want any of that in Kuwait, so I didn't bring it."

With that, he was satisfied.

Only now, thinking back, does it dawn on me that his tone betrayed a touch of disappointment. Perhaps the airport guys hope to nab some booze from Westerners who don't check Islamic law before arriving, and then enjoy it themselves!

I didn't want to experience legal problems in my own culture, let alone the Islamic world. I have a law degree – and a perfect record. I like it that way. I wasn't going to bring wine to Kuwait!

It seemed that there was nothing left to do but head out to a spot where I hoped I would see David. I reassembled the wheelie for the last time, and started walking.

A foreign worker appeared and grabbed the suitcases, smiling and wanting to help. I was so tired that I let him, watching this stranger carefully. He stayed in my sight, not too far off.

"Stephanie!" David rushed up to me and hugged me, no doubt violating the host culture's rules of decorum. I hugged back, asking if it were allowed. David hugged me again and said he didn't care.

He tipped the smiling porter, took the suitcases, and led me out.

Chapter 4
Apartments and Houses in Kuwait

As David led me away, I suddenly felt quite calm. The anxiety was still there, though just barely. I would not let him leave me alone until I was rested and somewhat settled.

We had only walked a couple of paces before I heard a voice call out: "Mrs. Haines!"

I looked to the left; it was Asim Al-Hamdullilah, Saleh's 3rd son.

He was probably 19 years old now; I had last seen him when he was 12. He had accompanied his father on a visit to the United States, back in 1998. Asim had been under the mistaken impression that the wasp nest he had found behind the apartment was a bee's nest. He told David, "I found a beehive – I'm going to get some honey!" and then he took off. David had looked puzzled for a moment, and then realized what was up. "Saleh!" he yelled, and took off, trying to round them up before Asim could touch anything...

Asim had come with David to drive us.

I went over to him and said Hi, thanked him, and told him that it was Ms. Fox, but that he should just call me Stephanie. He smiled and said okay.

Off we went, out the front of the building which led directly to a covered parking area.

David and Asim loaded the trunk with the stuff; I got into the back seat with my carry-on bag and handbag, Asim got into the driver's seat, and David got into the front seat with the cat carrier. Asim stepped on the gas, and David immediately opened the cage door.

"Cat!" he shouted happily into her face.

"Mrrow!" she greeted him back, just as loudly. She leapt out at him to be petted.

"Cat!" he shouted again. After a brief greeting, he shut her back inside.

Asim pulled up outside a large building, which I later understood to be the Souq Sharq Mall. People were coming out, walking together, some dressed in traditional Kuwaiti outfits, and other in Western clothing. All seemed, to my as yet untrained eyes, to be Kuwaitis.

David went inside to buy a few things – he does all of his shopping at the last minute. I had e-mailed him to say that he must buy certain things before the cat and I entered whatever apartment he had found for us: cat litter, cereal, milk, and orange juice. That was what he was doing. He appeared after Asim and I had chatted for about 20 minutes.

Asim was preparing to apply to medical school, hoping to follow in his father's footsteps. I wished him luck; I hoped it would all work out.

David came back and we were off.

The apartment was well south of Kuwait City, it turned out. I later realized that Asim had gone straight north from the airport to that grocery store. David is not a planner...

Our destination was a town called Manqaf, directly east of Ahmadi City, where Saleh worked as an internist at Kuwait Oil Company Hospital, which is next to the Ahmadi oil fields. Manqaf is on the shoreline, facing the Gulf.

Our Apartment in Manqaf

David had another apartment, one in Manqaf, but we left it after just 2 days. Its toilet could not be fixed. No need to say more. What it had was a proximity to mosques, from whence we could hear muezzins calling worshippers to prayer on loudspeakers at 4 a.m. plus 4 other times each day. [In the old days, these guys would climb up the mosques' minarets and call out their songs from there, but not now. The advent of technology has made minarets mere architectural decorations.] Also in common are the many small and soon-to-be-fingerless children who play with fireworks outside. The possession of fireworks is legal in Kuwait.

This was the living room in the Manqaf apartment, and the bedroom. The place was furnished, complete with curtains and linens. Next to David, on the coffee table, is the bag from the Indian take-out joint where he got the first Kuwait dinner that we ate together.

The entire apartment was furnished with used furniture, used linens and curtains. It was dimly lit day and night, thanks to the closeness all around of other buildings of equal height to ours. The elevator was unreliable, David told me as he helped me drag the luggage into the apartment that first night. The stove looked old and grungy, and there was a dreadful smell emanating from the bathroom. It reminded me the descriptions of mountain trolls in British novels about magic in ancient times: like a dirty toilet.

David told me that something was wrong with the toilet, that he had been waiting for the landlord to have it fixed. Wonderful...

I let our cat out of her carrier at last and set up all of her things – food, water, litter box, bed (I put that in the bedroom, because I wanted her to sleep near us). I unpacked just enough stuff to be able to brush my teeth and change clothes. I was getting tired, and was not happy to think that I could not rely on the bathroom.

David turned on the television and announced that he was going out to get our dinner. What would I like? I didn't know what to say. What sorts of choices were there? There was Indian food, Chinese food, Thai food – all cheap take-out joints. Oh. Indian food, I said, not wanting any major food adventures until I felt more settled. Okay – off he went to get it.

I looked around, and so did the cat. Neither us loved the place.

I couldn't see much, and I was feeling anxious again. I decided not to let David go anywhere the next day while I slept off the jet lag. I had just been up for nearly 48 hours, I guesstimated, and I was getting shaky. I didn't want to be left alone in this awful apartment where I couldn't see out while Saleh took off with David.

When David returned, I told him so. Friday is like Sunday in Kuwait, so I thought he ought to be able to just take it off, especially since I had just arrived. He wasn't thrilled with this idea, but he agreed. Saleh called the next day, and I told him the same thing. Saleh probably would have just driven him to meet more scientists and business people, but they had months and months to do that, so he agreed to forget it for that day, and we all went out the next day, to K.O.C. Hospital, where David worked on the computers all days and Saleh saw patients.

We ate the Indian food, and I went to bed.

It was a long sleep, punctuated here and there by the sounds of a muezzin calling Muslims to prayer 5 times. I was too out of it to be really bothered by this. The cat went between rooms all day, to alternate sleeping spots, and David stayed home and watched television. The sheets smelled odd – like nothing familiar – not David, not cleanliness, not anything good.

I got up at the end of the day and looked out, just to make sure about the views. Just as I had thought in the darkness, I couldn't see past the other buildings out the living room and bedroom windows. I could see a bit more from the kitchen, but nothing much.

I decided to take a shower, and with no curtain and a tub that I was unwilling to sit down in, it was awkward. Just as in France, I noticed that the bathtub had a faucet and a shower nozzle on a hose. One could activate the nozzle, lift the hose, and control the water. That, at least, made it possible not to flood the bathroom. The awful smell continued to emanate from both the toilet and the drain the middle of the tiled floor.

There were no towels, so I dried myself on one of David's tee shirts, which he brought for me. We had to move – and buy our own towels.

The fact that David would object to spending money on this concerned me not at all.

This was the view out of our bedroom – looking at the front door, the table, and the fridge. Above, our cat inspects the bathroom. The whole place reeked of…bathroom. The toilet didn't work.

Our cat was usually very vocal. She said nothing in the apartment. She just walked around and around it, inspecting and smelling things. It was her first taste of freedom after a 6-hour car ride, followed by a 4-hour wait in Newark Airport, followed by an 8-hour flight to Paris, followed by 6 more hours in the Charles de Gaulle terminal (interesting hours for us as we wandered around eating and looking at all the shops), followed by another flight that lasted for 6 hours, followed by another 2 hours before being let out in this awful-smelling dump.

I don't think she approved of the place. I made note of this to David.

Looking out all of the windows in the Manqaf apartment, through the old, off-smelling curtains, was a rather claustrophobic view, and I realized that if we stayed there, I would be hemmed in with nothing to see for hours, and that horrible smell all around me. Perhaps I would be unable to go to the bathroom in this place, even after an attempt at repairs was made. Perhaps it would be a recurring problem, while I stayed home and David was out for who knew how long…so I refused to accept it.

This was the view from the windows of the Manqaf apartment. To the left, I saw a rooftop on which someone had hung their laundry out to dry, with a mosque in the distance, across the highway. To the right, I saw the rooftops of the buildings immediately across the street from our building, with water tanks on them.

If I was going to in Kuwait for months on end, I was going to smell nothing amiss in our home, and I would be able to see out. David was a bit disappointed that I wanted out, because it would mean getting our own furniture and linens – paying for them – but he saw my point of view. He didn't have much of an argument to make for keeping the used ones and the awful smell with no view but me spending lots of time in such an environment, so we told Saleh that we needed to move.

Sure enough, Saleh knew of an alternative, and showed it to us the very day that he brought us with him to the Kuwait Oil Company Hospital. That was Saturday, November 20, 2004, when he had to work all day. When he was free for the day, we all got into his dark green BMW sedan and headed north.

This was the building that we moved into, in Abraq Khaitan. Our apartment was on the top floor, the 9th, around to the right, in the back. We could look out of our bedroom and living room windows to the right, and out our kitchen window to the back.

It turned out that he lived in an area called South Surra, which was brand new and mostly still under construction. Just west of that area, on the east side of Airport Road, directly south of Kuwait City, was an area called Abraq Khaitan. Looking out over Airport Road was a newly constructed building – full of apartments. Some were rented out, others were not, and the first 2 floors were a huge, wide open space meant for businesses. There was no little attachment, as so many of these buildings had, for a convenience store or tiny take-out joint.

We went to this building, and rode the elevator up to the top floor – the 9th. Each floor that did have apartments had 4 of them. There was a stairwell at the back of the building, and a pair of elevators across from each other at the center of the structure. We got off the elevator and Saleh led us down a hall to the right. A set of keys was hanging out of the lock on the left door. He turned it, and we went in.

It was a new apartment, empty, with dust from construction on the floors. Everything worked, and nothing smelled bad. I looked out all of the windows. I could see every which way, unimpeded, and whatever new buildings that were going up were only to be seen out the kitchen window, at the back of the building. Out the living room window was a great view of Airport Road, looking south, showing Kuwait International Airport off in the distance, and the town of Farwaniya across the highway. We could see a lot out the kitchen window even though some buildings were out there, including views of a cluster of striped, peg-like water towers in the distance along the northern perimeter of South Surra.

Above to the left is the view from our kitchen, showing an apartment building that was nearly completed. It stayed nearly completed for most of the time that we lived there, with a wooden skeleton for a top and tenants living below. Above to the right was the view out our bedroom window, which I shot when I opened the window and reached out slightly. Seeing what was happening in the neighborhood was easy from here, and interesting.

Here are the same views months later, when it was almost time to go home to the States. The top of the building out the kitchen window and the tall green one across the lot from the bedroom window were almost complete.

I liked this place, and could easily imagine living in it, so I told my husband and Saleh this. Great! Saleh handed us the keys, and said he would arrange for us to be driven with our stuff to this place tomorrow, and lend us some pillows and blankets until we got furniture. He would also take us furniture shopping the next evening, because otherwise we would have to keep sleeping on the floors, which would have been unpleasant…and was for a few days.

Didn't we have to contact the landlord and ask about this first? I wondered, but Saleh just took the keys, locked the door, and said that taking the keys would amount to taking possession of the apartment. Okay.

This was the view out of our living room window, looking at Farwaniya across Airport Road, which ran north-south – north to Kuwait City and south to Kuwait International Airport, Ahmadi City, and the Wafra Oasis.

We rode the elevator down to the mezzanine level and got out. It was a huge open space meant for a business. It turned out that Saleh and David had plans of setting up a clinical laboratory in this very building. Saleh was showing it to David now, and with that, David was sold on the idea of this particular apartment. If all went according to plan (it didn't!), he could just ride the elevator down to work. It all hinged upon the success of one Dr. Nazila in getting a license to set it all up. That way, Saleh could work both at K.O.C. Hospital and here...

Nazila was utterly unreliable and it never happened, but we had found our apartment.

We were close to most of the people we would need to see on a regular basis, and I would be in a decent location for hours on end when David was out. I had no delusions about how my life would be in an Islamic country: I would be home alone for hours, left to my own devices. Being alone is something that I am fairly good at, and practiced at. I read lots of books, watch television – but not daytime television – movies, mostly, and write on the computer. And I watch what goes on outside. I would be able to see while being so high up and remotely visible as to be able to see without being seen at home.

It was the perfect home for an observer in a strange new land.

Our Apartment in Abraq Khaitan

We settled into the flat located in a suburb of Kuwait City called Abraq Khaitan. It could also be spelled Kheitan, but I liked the other way better. David liked Kheitan. Our address was:

> Building 23
> Apartment/Flat 32, 9th Floor
> Blocks 54 + 69, or Block 8
> Airport Road
> Abraq Khaitan
> KUWAIT

There should have been a code # of 5 digits as part of this address, but I didn't have it, so it wouldn't work as a mailing address. As it turned out, we had our one package from my mother sent to Fatin, our Egyptian friend and a scientific colleague of David's, at her office. She taught biochemistry at the Kuwait University School of Nursing.

Upon entering the apartment, one found oneself in a room with no windows, which stretched to the right. A single overhead light on the ceiling illuminated the room, and there was an intercom/doorbell contraption on the left wall. Continuing on through the break in the wall, one entered the living room, which also stretched to one's right.

This room had a large window with a little curved, painted metal railing. Either side of this could be opened, and there was a half-circle panel of glass on top of those 2 sections of glass for yet more light.

Our empty apartment: the living room; the bedroom, looking across at the kitchen; the living room again with our cat perched on the suitcases.

    Turning left, one looked directly into the bathroom, which contained a toilet on the right, complete with one of those little hoses that Arabs like to use rather than toilet paper, a sink to the left with a round mirror above it, and a tub and shower arrangement. There was a little plastic fan with a motor set into the small window near the ceiling. Stepping forward from the living room, one walked into a little rectangular hallway that led to 3 rooms: the bathroom in the middle, the bedroom to the right, and the kitchen to the left.

    The bedroom was a large room with a window just like the one in the living room, but no ledge and no railing. The kitchen had a good-sized window as well, though no half-circle section at the top. It had tiles halfway up the walls, and a set of metal-and-plastic cabinets along the wall to the right, where the sink was. That was all; no stove, no oven, no refrigerator, no nothing. Apparently, it was the norm in Kuwaiti apartment housing for the tenants to furnish these appliances themselves. I was later to realize that most tenants live permanently in their apartments, and go so far as to have wall-to-wall carpeting installed, chandeliers if desired, and even wallpaper, along with the expected custom-made curtains.

    We would not be doing any of this. This was a temporary adventure, so we would have just enough to be comfortable and to be a good host and hostess when company came to visit. That was why I bought several mugs and a sugar bowl and creamer set: tea and coffee had to be available for friends and business invitees. I found a set with matching soup plates and was happy with those, and let the mugs be random, just as I do in the States. It's fun that way.

A very nice Indian guy named Ramatallah drove us in his boss's jeep to this apartment on Sunday, the very next day. He helped us smuggle our cat in, as we were not entirely sure about the building's rules concerning resident pets. It turned out that we were worried over nothing, but we didn't know this until weeks later, when the landlord came to visit, looked right at our cat, and just smiled at her in a friendly way.

Our landlord was a young twentysomething Kuwaiti guy who drove a dark green Jaguar. He told us that he was an electrical engineering graduate of Louisiana State University. I saw him twice: once in a dishdashah with a guthra and ekal – the standard garb of Kuwaiti men – and another time in jeans and a tight-fitting, dark green shirt. He was a thin beanpole of a guy with short hair and a polite smile.

An old Egyptian man in a turban was our bouab – superintendent. His name was Abdul Mohti, and he spoke only Arabic. David told me that his name meant "Slave of God." For a while, before I got David to tell me his name as I added it to my journal, I could only remember the English translation. I didn't let this go on for long, because I didn't want to be caught saying it to any of our Muslim friends, and since we were in Kuwait, they were all Muslim friends. I didn't want to offend them over a guy's name. It sounded like a joke in English, and David enjoyed it at home.

Abu Salah was the name of our landlord. His name had a funny translation too, but I did try not to remember it (Saleh told us what it was.). Abu Salah – it's rude not to say the 2 names together, and they meant that he was the father of a boy named Salah – was a pleasant rich kid with an American accent.

We hoped to persuade Abu Salah to have the common areas of the building cleaned. Because it was newly constructed, and there was dust everywhere – floors, fixtures, stairwell, halls, etc. The elevators smelled like garbage, and had mirrored sections that needed scrubbing. Also, the elevators still had plastic gray covers over their control panels, which were peeling off as people pulled at them during rides up and down. It turned out that it was the bouab's job to mop the floors of the common areas, and this smell vanished a day or so later, when he Abdul Mohti did his job.

The health clinic – dermatologic – was planned for 2 of the floors in this building, so this cleaning job was crucial. Patients would be disgusted by the mess; we certainly were. David and I spent the following afternoon scrubbing and polishing the ceramic tile floors of our apartment, but we didn't bother with the common areas of the building – that was the superintendent's responsibility. When our furniture arrived, it would go onto a clean floor. Saleh insisted on buying furniture for us (we would pay him back when our pay was wired to Kuwait). We were able to pay him back about 10 days later.

The furniture came from a store in Safat called Al-Ghanim (described in another chapter). We shopped for it the night that we moved into the Abraq Khaitan place, and the refrigerator was brought the very next day. We had to wait until Wednesday for the rest, but just having a fridge was a huge plus – we could get breakfast foods and thus take care of basic needs right away.

At first, the apartment was terribly uncomfortable, because we had to sleep for 3 nights on the porcelain tiled floors with borrowed pillows that were flat as pancakes, but then it got a lot better when our bed was set up. The building was made of cement blocks with electricity and plumbing, and water was sent to each apartment from a huge tank on the roof. A hot water heater over the kitchen sink, on top of the upper cabinets, supplied both the kitchen and bathroom. The water in the kitchen spurted scalding streams at me every time I turned it on, but otherwise there was nothing amiss.

This was our bedroom before the furniture arrived: a quilt on the floor, and a sheet on the window. The sheet ended up staying; I refused to buy curtains, and there was no way to attach them other than tucking them into the window.

Once we got things somewhat set up, it was quite nice, and I was content to stay in it alone for hours on end. I felt safe, and it was mostly quiet…unless the family next door blasted their television or stereo or whatever it was that they had. (The landlord eventually evicted them for this, much to my satisfaction.) Soon we had every amenity necessary to approximate an American home away from home: a shower curtain on a rod with rings to hold it up – it took a while to find this – a toilet seat, which David resisted buying while I completely ignored his protests, toilet paper, soap, kitchen towels, a sugar bowl and creamer set, 6 soup plates which doubled nicely as bowls, forks, knives and spoons, a coffee maker, a microwave oven, and finally, a hair dryer, which I had to use in the kitchen for lack of an outlet.

This is how our bathroom looked once I had found everything we needed. David was glad once the deed was done, despite trying to stop me from spending so much as a Kuwaiti fil on this. Note the little metal hose to the left of the toilet; Middle Eastern people prefer this to toilet paper. We used it anyway – there's a roll on the back of the toilet.

It occurred to me that this was where Kuwaiti people would be coming to visit, with no division of the home between men and women – no separate sections. It was very American that way, and I liked it. People bring their own cultural perceptions and training with them, and that is all that they have unless and until they learn what other people's cultural background causes them to think about. I looked forward to observing our visitors, and to asking them questions.

Our kitchen essentials: refrigerator, microwave oven, and coffee maker. Note the cords that stretch off to the left, to the one outlet in the room. Our mop was propped against the wall next to all this. Across from this was the sink.

This was our bedroom, after the furniture arrived, and again, after I bought the new sheets and quilt set. We had to give the linens back to Saleh's wife. I was happier with our own.

David and Scheherazade were very happy that first evening after the furniture was brought and set up. This photo was taken before the television arrived. Indian and Egyptian guys spent half the day in our apartment with screwdrivers and other tools, assembling everything. At right, David and Saleh were hard at work writing up scientific results for journal articles, and business proposals.

This description would not be complete without telling about Abdul Mohti, the bouab. He was a nice old man from southern Egypt – a Saeedi, which means south Egyptian. Fatin taught me this word. She is from Cairo, so I asked her, because I was worried about sounding rude, whether or not it was polite. She assured me that it just literally meant a person from the southern part of Egypt, so I stopped worrying about it. Abdul Mohti lived away from his family, who were all back home in Egypt, and he sent part of his pay home to them. I felt sorry for him when I heard about this.

We did know it at first, but Abdul Mohti could not read or write when he first moved in. Our good friend who lived downstairs, a nice Kuwaiti man whose mother was from Egypt, was teaching him. Soon Abdul Mohti was attending the madrassah school across the street in the evenings, memorizing the Quran and making friends. That is what madrassahs teach: rote memorization of the Islamic holy book.

Abdul Mohti, our friendly, slightly sloppy, baksheesh-seeking bouab in the doorway of his living quarters.

He lived downstairs in a tiny, 2-room apartment with a makeshift bathroom. We saw the place once, when he had visitors and his door was wide open. We were paying our rent, which was 170 KD per month plus 5 KD more for the bouab. This 5 KD was bribe money, called baksheesh, and it was very important to him. It made him friendly towards us, and willing to help with all sorts of details necessary to living there. I supplemented this with ice cream, because that is the kind of baksheesh I am used to giving people in the States. Abdul Mohti seemed absolutely delighted, and laughed uproariously when I presented it as farawla baksheesh, which literally meant "strawberry bribe" – he loved it.

David went downstairs the day after we moved in to see if he could borrow a mop from the bouab, but came right back up to me, disgusted. He said, "I am absolutely disgusted with Slave of God. All he has are several shit-caked mops – I wasn't going to borrow any of those." So we polished the floor with damp rags, all on our hands and knees, while our cat watched. We did a pretty good job, and I bought our own blue sponge-on-a-stick mop a few days later.

Not long after we settled in, we heard some odd noises directly below our living room window, so we opened it, looked down, and saw that a large herd of goats – doubtless doomed to slaughter – had been moved into the courtyard directly below. I often looked down there, goats or no goats, because sometimes I would see a stray cat sunning itself on the rooftop.

The courtyard full of goats in the building next door. This was perfect; the building looked complete, so it would not have more stories added to block our view out. I felt sorry for the goats, but otherwise enjoyed the window.

We had no television until Fatin came over on Thursday with her spare one for us, and then David delightedly went down to her car to carry it up. It was a heavy black thing, with a 26-inch screen, and it worked perfectly. We had it connected that very night.

Mansoor

Shortly after settling in, David met a wonderful Kuwaiti guy in his late 20s named Mansoor. He became our friend while we were in Kuwait. He lived downstairs from us, on the 4th floor, with his mother and oldest sister, who was divorced and so permanently back with them. This is completely normal in Kuwaiti culture; children do not necessarily move out when they grow up. Mansoor's role was to take care of his mother, providing housing and catering to whatever wish she might have, such as enabling her to have family gatherings in the living room each week.

David met Mansoor downstairs shortly after Fatin left her spare television with us. The next thing to do was to connect it to the satellite dish on the roof, where we could pirate our entertainment like the rest of the building was doing. I was amazed by this off-the-grid, unofficial resource, but as I had no way of arranging anything different – I did not speak Arabic, after all – that was what we did. David brought Mansoor up to our living room to direct a guy in the setting up of our TV cable, and review of our channels. We later managed to acquire a printed list of them all, at which point I found the Al-Jazeera news station (operated out of Dubai in the United Arab Emirates). It's like the MSNBC of the Middle Eastern world – liberal news. I also found a channel that showed repeats of *CSI* episodes, *Without a Trace*, and the Oscars. The most watched channel turned out to be the one that showed movies – all duly censored by the Ministry of Islamic Affairs, called Awqaf (more on that later).

Mansoor: he always wore sweats or jeans, a blue jacket, sneakers and a baseball-style cap when he went out, and was bareheaded and barefoot whenever he was at home. He considered the entire building to be home – his apartment, the elevators, the area out front including the bouab's place, and any apartment that he visited. Thus, this is how he appeared whenever he came up to our place for a visit and tea. David wore gloves a lot – he had terribly dry skin on his hands – a leftover injury from being a chemical weapons officer after the Gulf War ended.

Mansoor was a wonderful friend, and a character – especially to look at: he was short, with thick, straight black hair that he wore short in the back but rather long on the top combed straight back, and he had a mustache. His complexion was tanned, and he was always smiling.

He spoke English – not perfectly, but well enough to be easily understood. Mansoor was a starry-eyed admirer of all things American, and he was as curious about us as we were about him and his culture. What started off as a brief settling-in encounter was to become a fun cultural exchange that we looked for whenever we wanted company or a chance to go out with a friend, and he was always happy to oblige us. We still miss him.

Saleh and Raidah's McMansion in South Surra

South Surra is a very nice, new place with many beautiful, upper middle class homes that are under construction. All of the homes have unique designs, with many different colors. What the occupied ones had in common was that all windows, regardless of size, had curtains covering them completely, so that one could not see in from the outside. Some windows were huge, but they were not the norm. They were usually found around stairwells, and we did see and comment on one exception with a huge glass-encased stairwell in the front of one house and the corner of another. But small windows are a hallmark of Islamic architecture, and serve to prevent outsiders from seeing into a home – even the living room must be private.

Looking at the windows of other homes from inside a moving car whenever I went out anywhere in Kuwait, I had seen that all homes had curtains close up against their windows. The reason was easy to understand – concealing the women. This feature of home décor – which, considering the cultural requirement for it was really home furnishing – stood out prominently to me because Western homes have decorative curtains. Their purpose is the make the homes look nice, but the residents don't care if you can see them walking around their living rooms and watching television. To people in Kuwait, this would have been a terrible breach of their privacy, one that was their own responsibility to prevent.

As we drove through the area, I saw desert sand stretched all around us in huge open spaces, with the exception of newly paved roads and curb cuts. Streets had been delineated, but only some of the homes planned for this upper middle class neighborhood had been completed. The construction was confined to whole blocks here and there. Off in the distance was a mosque that was clearly in the middle of its construction; it had several minarets already completed. Saleh told us that mosque construction was funded entirely by the worshippers, so it could only proceed as funds were taken in, unlike homes, which could be built with loans and then sold.

Saleh and Raidah's house was in one of the completed blocks; they hadn't lived there more than perhaps 5 years. Everything looked new and perfect. When we arrived, I saw that it was a huge building, a sort of McMansion, with at least 3 stories. The outside of the building looked like stucco, and it probably was, because stucco most closely resembles the original building material traditional used in pre-oil Kuwait: gypsum and coral. The color of the building was a pale cream-to-beige. There were medium-sized windows symmetrically placed, one on each side of the front door and on up the building to the top floor. The first floor windows had black metal, slightly curved bars, as did the front door. It resembled a decorated prison.

The front of the house had a low wall in front of it, with another gate across that. I headed in that direction, but Saleh said we would be going in through the side door, so I only got a brief look at this part of the building. The side was interesting, though. Around to the right of the building was a driveway. To its right loomed the wall of the neighboring house. To the left was Saleh and Raidah's house. Straight ahead was the servants' quarters, where the married Indian couple, a maid and a driver, lived. They were called Sarah and Abdullah, but I suspected that those were not their real names, and that Saleh and Raidah were just using familiar-sounding names on people who needed jobs.

Looking up to the left at the house, I saw more windows, but of course seeing in was not possible from where I stood – we were almost directly under them. There were no windows on the facing side of the neighboring house. We went inside, and found ourselves in a stairwell that rose into the upper stories. The floor and the stairs were made of white marble blocks, streaked with grey striations. The railings of the staircase were metal – stainless steel. Straight ahead was a door, which led into the ground floor.

Going in through it, we found that a long hallway stretched to our right into the back of the house, and to our left was a huge living room. We went down the back hallway first. There was one room to the left of the stairwell – a beautiful but unused bathroom. It had a marble floor with porcelain tiles, and the ones across the center of the walls had a pretty design of flowers and birds. I didn't see any toilet paper or towels – or soap. Continuing on down the hall to the right, there was yet another bathroom at the end, straight across from the kitchen, and a closed door across from the first bathroom.

This was Hanbal and Saidah's old room, now abandoned, and it contained most of their things. Hanbal had died a year and a half earlier in Pittsburgh, 11 hours into liver transplant surgery, and Saidah had returned to her family. Raidah had let David stay in that room for a week when he first arrived in Kuwait, and Saleh had let him know that this was a big concession for her to make. He never went upstairs, so he didn't know what the rest of the house was like.

Raidah invited me to see her in the kitchen, though all of the work for the meal was complete and she was relaxed and ready to start the visit. Her sisters were in there, but they just looked at me without speaking. I smiled politely at them; I suspected that we wouldn't be chatting. [I knew that Raidah could talk to me though; we had spoken on the phone when Saleh had visited us in Connecticut, when he son was in the States for his liver surgery. She had worried to me in perfect, coherent English about how she couldn't bear to lose another child; her second son, Mashhur, had already died of the same problem, having gone into organ rejection before the family realized what was wrong.]

I was very interested to see the kitchen, and I got a quick but thorough look at everything in it. I told Raidah that I am a gourmet cook, so she let me see it. It was about half the size of the living room, and had a huge refrigerator with glass doors. There was a stove, and all of the cabinets were made of metal. I also got a sense, as I went there with David, that he was invading a women-only territory every time he went deeper into the house. He went out to the living room to talk with Saleh while I was back in the kitchen with Raidah.

Parked along the right side of the back hallway were Hanbal's 3 high-speed motorcycles – one red, 2 black, all spotless. In the week that David stayed there, that is as far into the house as he ever went. The motorcycles were, by law, Saleh, Raidah, and Saidah's joint property until Hanbal's estate was completely settled, so they could not be sold yet. Unless and until Saidah visited and signed them over, they were frozen assets. Saidah was Iranian, and living back at home in southern Iran with her parents, which happened to be near Raidah's relatives. Saidah wouldn't communicate with Raidah when Raidah had gone home, and so Raidah felt as though she had lost a daughter. Meanwhile, Hanbal's ghost haunted her dreams with instructions about their property. What a mess!

Raidah told me that her sisters were shy and couldn't speak English, so they weren't going to eat with us. They wouldn't even come out of the kitchen, although I had been taken back there to meet them. They had greeted me politely but without smiling. Both were huge, round, tall women with finely plucked, round eyebrows. Their faces were pretty, and they wore black robes, scarves, and pants. Raidah told me that the family almost always eats upstairs.

Raidah brought me out to see the rest of the ground floor, which was grandly decorated. The walls were plain white, and there were windows that looked out a short distance. Tall, potted plants stood around here and there, and fussy, French-style sofas were all around the living, room, which stretched across the left half of the front of the house. The sofas had gold paint on the edges of the carved areas, and white paint for a base. The cushions were poufy enough, just backs, seats, and armrests, in several colors, forming a floral pattern on red. Marble and glass coffee and side and end tables completed the room, and there were framed pictures on the end and side tables.

Looking across from this, we saw the dining room: it was raised on a platform, up one step from the living room. It wasn't as large as the living room because the beautiful, unused bathroom was next to it. The dining room furniture was in the same style as the living room sofas – fussy, French chairs with ivory cloth cushions, and a long oval table. Every seat was set with pretty china and crystal and flatware, and the white tablecloth had a clear plastic cover on it.

Raidah had made a lovely, delicious feast. We ate lamb, chicken, mashed potatoes, gravy, batter-fried cauliflower, herbed Persian rice (Raidah is from the Shiraz area in Iran), and potato fries. These Asim jokingly called "patriot fries," whereupon I said that the U.S. Congress had wasted our tax money trying to rename French fries. We also had salad made of tiny pieces of lettuce, tomato and cucumber. Raidah wanted to see us eat American food, she said. We said that we love to try unfamiliar food, but she just said, "Next time," so we assured her that everything looked great. We enjoyed every bit of it.

Dessert was chocolate cake with cherries – Asim didn't like it – and those wonderful puff pastries with honey and pistachios…like a Middle Eastern version of baklava (I grew up eating the Greek version, with honey and walnuts – this was even better). The cake tasted like nothing, despite presenting the appearance of a fancy chocoholic confection. [I later found out why: different climates cause different reactions in ovens and kitchens, which affect the taste of foods that are great successes elsewhere, plus the dairy products differ from region to region, also causing different tastes.]

I really wanted to sit with Raidah a while and show her the art books that I had brought for her. Eventually, we did this, and we talked for a long time. It was nice. This enabled me to observe her personality and let her see some of mine, and we had some fun. Raidah was a huge, sad woman who smoked small, cigarette-like cigars. She wore a black robe over her clothes, and a black hijab (scarf). Under it, her grey hair was twisted up into a bun with a huge rosette tying it in place. She and Saleh both had diabetes, but neither watched what they ate.

Only 5 of us ate the cake. Hassan, the youngest boy, had stayed up half the night flying a kite in the desert, so he was too sleepy to meet us. Mohsen helped Asim bring the dishes of food out, but said he wasn't hungry and disappeared. He and Asim looked rather similar: thick, black, straight hair and dark, large eyes, and both wore dishdashahs at first. (Assim changed to jeans and a shirt later on.)

Later on in the evening, I asked Raidah whether she had any wedding photos from her wedding to Saleh, but none had been taken. Raidah enjoyed looking at mine, though – my mother had suggested that I bring them. Raidah then told me that Saidah had had a lovely wedding to Hanbal, all organized by Raidah herself. Really – I said, brightening, could I see those photographs? Raidah didn't know where they were, but said that she was disappointed in them. Why? She had hired a photographer with a reputation for doing very high quality work, but that when it came time to actually pose for the photographs, Raidah suddenly realized that in order to take the pictures of Saidah in her gown with her hair up in a bun and tiara – visible – this man would have to see Saidah's hair! This would not do, so his wife took the photographs. Of course the wife was no expert photographer, so the pictures weren't that great...although the fee certainly was.

When it got dark, I noticed something else about her house: the windows had metal shades that rolled down from the top, completely closing off any view of the inside the house. It was as if we were suddenly hermetically sealed in. Raidah went around pulling these things down, and they resembled customized covers such as the large ones that cover shops in a mall in the States. There were no curtains.

Raidah gave us more tea with sugar in it, more puff pastries with cardamom and pistachios, and coffee. We had a lovely time with the Norman Rockwell and Georgia O'Keeffe paintings, and Raidah told me all about living in Boston, Massachusetts while she attended Boston University and Saleh worked on his Ph.D. at the Harvard-Boston University laboratory. She said that that was the best time in her life, when she still had all of her kids alive. She kept photographs of Hanbal and Mashhur in her living and dining rooms. They had been toddlers then; their parents had not known that they would have health problems in the future. Raidah had completed 3 out of 4 years of her Bachelor's degree when Saleh asked her to quit so that he could focus on his Ph.D. That is why she knew English so well.

Assim and Aiesha's Family Bloc Apartment

Saleh took us out later that same evening to meet a Kuwait University professor of Business Practices, where we also met his wife, Aiesha, who taught accounting at a local community college. We ended up becoming friends, and I got into a routine of visiting Aiesha on

Friday evenings. As a result, I got to see the inside of another Kuwaiti home and learn a little bit about the lives and customs of the family who occupied it.

The house that Aiesha and Assim lived in was huge. It was in an area called Abdullah es Salem. It had no particular façade to it, only a wall around the ground floor with a metal door, and a carport off to the left. Through the metal door was a courtyard all around the house, just wide enough for a basketball hoop, which they had. After going through the gate, the door to the house was straight ahead. I was fascinated by the architecture of the house, because it was my first thorough look at the inside of an Arab home (having only seen the ground floor of Saleh and Raidah's house). This house had white marble all through it, including the stairwell, which was plain with metal railings. The moldings were made of dark red marble. This staircase was not meant to be showy – only to provide a way to go from one floor to another.

The carport outside Aiesha and Assim's house, with the metal doors to the courtyard and house.

Upstairs and to the right was a huge, high-ceilinged comfortable-looking living room with a long sofa around 2 of its walls. All of the rooms had high ceilings. A kitchen and 2 bedrooms led off from the left side of the living room, a full bathroom was straight ahead, and Assim and Aiesha's room was just behind the living room, to the right of the bathroom. The living room was cozy and full of knick-knacks on either side of the television. It had a pleasant, lived-in look to it. It also had a computer; Assim and Aiesha had just gotten a DSL Internet hook-up – and they were nice enough to let me pay our Visa bill on-line. That was a relief, because taking care of our finances at the Internet café didn't seem very safe or secure.

The kitchen was packed with food, and it had a gas stove with a lid – stoves in Kuwait all had lids (I didn't know why they were made that way; people just left the lids up all the time anyway). The 4 younger children lived in the back bedroom, which had 2 bunk beds – Hamid and Abdul Malik (ages 13 and 12, in 8th and 7th grades) have the top bunks, Aiesha told me, and Karidah and Safa'a, the little girls (ages 6 and 4), have the lower bunks. Hassan had the other bedroom all to himself, and their oldest daughter, Zahra (age 20) lived downstairs next to Assim's mother, in the apartment directly below.

There was an equally large space out in the hall to the left of the staircase, but I never saw what was there – servants, storage space, who knew – and I didn't ask right away. Later, I found out that it was an apartment just like Assim and Aiesha's – a mirror image of theirs. Assim's father had ordered this building constructed for a specific purpose: when his sons grew up and got married, they could live in these apartments with their wives and families. This house and the identical one across the street were monuments to his multiple wives and the descendants he expected to have from their resulting sons. As it turned out, most of the sons moved out into houses of their own rather than taking the apartments, despite the fact that the rent here was free.

Downstairs, on the left, were 2 sitting rooms and the formal dining room that we saw the night that we sat in the fancier of the two sitting rooms. One of the sitting rooms – the outer, fancier one – is for men, and is called a diwaniya; the other one is for women, and is called a harim. The place fascinated me, because I had never been in one like it before, except for Raidah and Saleh's, and I saw so much less of that one.

The most interesting thing that I noticed about this home was the curtains: their primary function seemed to be to completely cover the glass so that no one would see in. This had the unfortunate effect of also making it impossible to see out or enjoy the slightest bit of sunshine. The point seemed to be to make sure that the women would not be seen while being able to move about the home without worrying about their hijabs.

Fatin and Zahid's Apartment in Salwa

David has a colleague who teaches at the Kuwait University School of Nursing named Fatin. She also conducts laboratory experiments there, and they write articles for scientific journals using data that they generate from the labs that David works from in the United States. Fatin and I are friends, and we like to visit whenever we can. She has visited me in America.

Exactly 2 weeks after I arrived in Kuwait, Fatin invited me to her house in Salwa, where I met her husband and maid. I stayed all day (until 8 o'clock), saw the whole apartment, ate a delicious homemade lunch that included an Egyptian fish called shaum, which was breaded and fried, and watched a movie with Fatin. We had a great time.

Fatin and Zahid lived in a beautiful building in Salwa, on the 2nd floor of a 3 storey house (the floors are called Ground, 1st and 2nd, just like in Europe). So they actually lived on the top floor. This meant that they also had a back terrace to enjoy. The entrance they used was on the left side, and it led to a stairwell and elevator, all with white marble blocks for flooring, which was used in the hallways as well. It was very attractive, light, and open.

A typical home with upper levels for rent in Salwa, Kuwait; residents park out front and walk in through the side.

Their maid, Manisha, a Hindu lady from Hyderabad, India, lived in a room out in the hall across from the elevator. Manisha's room was accessed by going out into the hallway, across to the back door, and outside onto the terrace. She had her own full bathroom in there. I never saw it; Fatin just described it to me. Manisha was just a few years older than me, with a husband back in India and 5 children, most of whom were grown up and married (at a very young age). She spoke Hindi and Arabic only, so Fatin had to talk for her. Manisha was in Kuwait on a 3-year contract, complete with health care from her employer. She always came back to Fatin after her 2 or 3 month-long trips home, which occurred whenever the contract times ran out.

Fatin told me that during these times, she would be exhausted from having to do all of the housework herself plus the grocery shopping and her university job, and I believed her. Fatin would call Manisha often, begging and asking when she would come back. I just listened, but I really couldn't blame the maid – she must miss her family terribly!

Fatin told me that once Manisha went home and found that her husband had taken in another woman, whom she immediately and angrily tossed out of the house. Good for her – she was sacrificing the ability to live in her own home in order to pay for it, and then she found an interloper! On a later visit, it was the day of Manisha's daughter's engagement party, an elaborate ritual and celebration that Manisha had paid for but was missing. During the day, Manisha disappeared many times to call home and hear the details, thus vicariously enjoying what she could of the event. She kept coming back to check on us – we didn't need much – and sharing the happy details, which Fatin was interested to hear and translated for me.

We were both happy that she could at least experience that much of the engagement party, but it seemed to me like a pittance of enjoyment. Fatin at least was a pleasant employer who did not try to stop Manisha from calling as much as she wanted to and hearing and sharing it all. Manisha had no one other than us to share her happiness with, so we paid attention.

Fatin's apartment had 2 bedrooms with full bathrooms, a den, a kitchen, living and dining rooms. Fatin had given Manisha a television and a space heater for her room, so it sounded quite comfortable. Fatin's daughter, Nuwwar, was away at college on the Greek side of the island of Cyprus. Nuwwar's room was directly across from the den. In her bathroom was the washing machine. I wondered about a dryer, but didn't ask. I got to see Nuwwar's old school photos, and her room was still much as it had been before she had gone away to college. Fatin and Zahid's room was nice, too, and also with a bathroom inside, plus a walk-in closet. The living and dining room was one large room, with the dining set off to the side, all at the front of the house, and with beautiful, rose-toned curtains and formal furniture. The den and Nuwwar's room were at the back, by the door to the elevator and stairwell. The den had informal sofas, large and cushy, grouped around a big coffee table and facing a large television and VCR. Fatin's computer was in the corner.

    Zahid came home for lunch, and drank tea with us in the den while we finished our movie. Then he took a nap. He was quiet, but nice enough. He came from Syria, and worked as a civil engineer in Kuwait. He had 3 brothers back in Damascus, and went back for visits sometimes. Fatin's brothers had introduced them.

Chapter 5
Shopping for Household Goods and Groceries

When we moved into our apartment in Abraq Khaitan, it had no furniture at all. It also lacked a toilet seat, a refrigerator, an oven-stove setup, and curtains. Some of these things we bought, while we chose to do without others – such as curtains. We also needed eating implements, and we needed to make a decision: would we get a stove, or do without? Our decision was based upon what was involved in having one – more on that later.

The usual tasks of moving into a new area confronted us: finding a local and conveniently located grocery store. That wasn't too difficult. Grocery stores in Kuwait are called jamiyas, which literally translates as the society store, according to our friend and neighbor Mansoor. We were able to walk to one from our apartment, through a lot of rubble and cement blocks that seemed to surround every other acre of land – much of the town was under construction, where apartment tower after apartment tower was going up. Workers who lived in the area – from poor Islamic nations in Southeast Asia and northern Africa – hissed at me from the darkness. David always walked with me, or else we got rides from Mansoor.

We would also shop, whenever I got the chance to either go with Fatin on a Thursday or have a ride from Mansoor (David came along on those) to a Sultan Centre store. There were 2 of them in Kuwait: one in Souq Sharq Mall, and another one in its own building in Salmiya on Arabian Gulf Street. I really preferred those places for things like fresh produce, plus I had better luck at finding cereal and juice – juice that wasn't loaded with high-fructose syrup and other unhealthy rubbish. Once, to research nutraceuticals – foods with healthful properties that are indigenous to this region of the planet – we went to a jamiya in Kuwait City and had a tour from the manager and his staff. I took many photos. Later, Fatin and Nuwwar helped us label the collection in a PowerPoint presentation.

Our furniture and appliances all came from various branches of an outfit called Al-Ghanim. Its flagship store was in Safat, and featured fabulous showrooms of merchandise. There were many smaller branches here and there that sold little things such as hair dryers and microwave ovens.

Fatin also showed me, during one entertaining afternoon of mall visits, a famous pastry shop in Farwaniya, and once David and I wandered into a nut shop in Fahaheel.

Jamiyas

The evening that our new refrigerator arrived, we went out to the local jamiya, to buy groceries. A jamiya is a town's co-op/supermarket. Upstairs in Abraq Khaitan's jamiya were all sorts of cleaning solutions, sponges, hangers, forks, spoons, sharp knives for cutting raw fruits and vegetables, can openers, kitchen towels, oven mitts, and sets of glasses. I bought some of these things, including a pretty set of 6 glasses with flowers on them. This was necessary because of the custom of giving guests a drink of tea or fruit juice each time they visit, though we couldn't offer tea yet – no stove. (We ended up using the coffee maker that I bought a few days later to heat up bottled water.) We only had one glass and 2 plastic cups. I insisted upon being able to be a polite hostess when people came to visit us. We had also taken delivery of some furniture, with a table that seated 6 people. (Most visitors ended up sitting in the living room and using the coffee table, however.)

We went to the co-op after getting some Kuwaiti dinars – a supermarket with the usual assortment of sections, plus an upper level full of household items. I found a scrub brush to use for washing dishes, and laughed at myself for being so delighted about finding it. We also got a toilet bowl brush, but the sponges were terrible – flimsy things that held too much soap but hardly any water – so I didn't buy many. We got one of those substandard things, but I would hold out for the good kind (and I soon found them at Sultan Centre).

Moving between floors was done with an escalator that resembled a huge conveyor belt, so that shopping carts could go along for the ride. Upstairs I also found carpets, bedding, sanitary supplies, pet food, and tee shirts. Plus staring men and women shrouded in full black abbeyas, hijabs and nekhabs everywhere I looked, along with little boys who ran through the aisles to stare at the one American woman in the store. I just minded my own business and kept shopping. No one bothered me.

One product which was not as healthy as the version available everywhere in America, the search for which obsessed us, was fruit juice. We wanted pure orange juice for breakfast – though this matters to me more than to David – and not finding orange and other varieties of juice is irritating to both of us. We didn't want the kind that is from concentrate – that is water added to dehydrated, powdered fruit. Worse yet, we kept finding mixtures of 20% fruit, plus sugar, plus water, plus chemicals – fruit syrup marketed as juice! It's not a healthy thing to drink, and is sickly sweet. Imagine how insane it seemed to us, the concept of a pure food being reduced to a version of that food rather than just being that food. It was odd and disturbing.

No wonder, David said, that Kuwait's population has such a high percentage of diabetics. That poor excuse for juice, and all the rice they eat, must have something to do with it. Rice is a big part of their diet. The smaller stores on every block, called bakalas, offer nothing but this junk juice. At least the Khaitan co-op and the big grocery store at Sultan Centre stock one brand of real orange juice.

Downstairs was where the boxes of tea and frozen foods were, plus a section at the back, directly opposite the registers, with all sorts of nuts. If you wanted any, you had to ask the man behind the counter to measure some out, which David did. At the end opposite from the freezers was a staircase and a ramp. They led down to the produce area, deli, spice section, and coffees.

The spice section of the Khaitan co-op; the coffees are in the center of the photo, and close-up, above.

This was the produce section of the co-op. Many familiar and unfamiliar fruits and vegetables were for sale.

The coffees were on 3 shelves, one for each type: French Roast – a familiar, dark, bitter flavor; Arabic – a blend of tea, spice and coffee that was not ground up; and my and David's favorite, Turkish – finely ground coffee that was heavily infused with cardamom, which is the second most expensive spice in the world. The spice comes in a pod, which must either be opened and the contents ground into a powder, or added to tea and then skimmed out. It smells absolutely wonderful, and I knew this ingredient well from baking with it at home (I make all sorts of cookies from scratch). This was the coffee that we kept putting into our coffee machine, and when we couldn't find it, it seemed like a household crisis. It was that good.

As I was looking in the produce department of the co-op, I suddenly felt someone slam into me (not too hard, but it was a significant thud). I moved aside and turned around in time to see a man in a dishdashah falling down and twitching uncontrollably. David eased him to the floor and positioned his neck carefully so that he wouldn't choke (David is a former EMT). The man had epilepsy, it turned out. I thought it was a diabetic attack at first, and asked about giving him candy, but then he started drooling and I realized it was epilepsy.

The man's brother, in Western clothing, spoke to David. He said not to worry, that this happened a lot and that he takes care of him. As the seizure abated, we could see lucidity return to his eyes. I reached down and patted the sick man on the shoulder twice, out of sympathy. David said "no, don't do that," because I'm a woman. The epileptic man's eyes widened in shock and horror – but his brother stayed calm. It occurred to me that his brother must know some Western ways, dressed as he was (though he spoke only Arabic). But a sick Arab would not, so we left them alone. We walked home with the plastic grocery bags of goods – house wares, foods, everything – tramping along with it all through the sandy streets in the darkness and dim lamp lights.

When we got up to the apartment, David helped me clean the new glasses, forks, spoons and sharp knife – I washed, he dried. And then soap suds rose up out of the floor drain! The bouab (superintendent) was supposed to deal with these things, but he wanted baksheesh (bribe) money. After we paid our first month's rent, at which time we would include the bribe money, he would see a pattern being established and get into the habit of helping us. We planned to give him 5 KD. The bouab would just have to be satisfied with that (and he was).

Another evening, we went out for groceries with Mansoor. It was late, and he was too tired to take us to Salmiya, so we went to the store in Khaitan. We had hoped to visit Sultan Centre, because our printer needed new ink cartridges, but we could do that another day. We really appreciated a ride in his little red hatchback car. We came home fast with plenty of milk, strawberry juice, laban, and other good stuff, and we got to see Mansoor.

The best part of the evening was when he told us something about how soft drinks are marketed to Muslims: pointing up above the jamiya building, he indicated a huge billboard for Coca-Cola. Of course it was in Arabic, and the script of that language lent itself to the font normally used by Coca-Cola. Arabic reads from right to left, however, and translations are often inexact. In this case, the inexactitude was entirely deliberate: the soft drink had been renamed "Mecca Cola" – to attract more customers. I wondered if the ad also claimed that it would bring the consumers closer to Allah…

We thought it was hilarious, but also terrible that people in this part of the world were just having their risk for (or actual cases of) diabetes aggravated by that disgusting, fizzy drink. I'm an odd American, I had to explain to Mansoor yet again – I hate soda. I hate cold, brown, sickly sweet, fizzy drinks. Better to just drink water, coffee, tea, and pure juice with no additives. Mansoor's physique looked like it was going to seed on the American processed foods that he loved so much. He was overweight, he smoked, and he ate take-out often, either Kuwaiti take-out, which resembled American fast food, or KFC and McDonald's, which he spoke of in worshipful tones.

The next time Mansoor took us out to the grocery store, instead of calling it "society" like he usually does (short for co-operative society), he tried to say grocery store. It didn't work – it came out more like "grace something-store" – so we taught him the word he wanted. As we walked through the grocery store, chatting about things like moldy strawberries, I was suddenly impressed – very impressed – once again by how well Mansoor had learned English. He did this all by talking to people, watching American movies with Arabic subtitles, and learning a few written words in school and then building upon them in real life. He could read some words that I wrote down; it's when he wanted to do any writing in English that he got lost.

I lamented the lack of a box of all fresh and no moldy strawberries. The store packed them in medium-sized clear boxes, and at first glance, just looking at them from above, they looked like healthy red ones. Pick up the box, and one could see mold growing all over the ones on the bottom. "No problem," said Mansoor with a big grin. David came over to watch. Mansoor opened 2 boxes, transferred the good ones into one box and put the rotten ones in the other, closed both boxes, and handed me the box of beautiful red ones. Hah! We did that from then on, whenever we shopped at the jamiya. I love red berries.

We had fun wandering around the grocery store; I got stared at in every aisle as usual, with Mansoor enjoying every silly person's reaction to me. I was wearing my usual outfit: long, black pants with pockets, a tee shirt, and sandals. My feet, my lower arms, and my head and neck show in this outfit. I wore my hair up in its curved gold clip, my makeup was done, and I had my pearl earrings on. I had a dark pink jacket with a hood (waterproof, but soft fabric) that I took off when we went inside, and draped over the side of the cart. Nothing about my appearance was shocking or unusual or even risqué for my culture – not even sexy by American standards. Men in every aisle stared, though. Most of those men were accompanied by women in hijabs and even nekhabs, so it was no wonder that I was such an arresting sight to them.

Mansoor fixing the strawberry problem for me. David got a great kick out of this; he hates to be ripped off.

As Mansoor and I came up the ramp out of the produce department, I nearly walked into a fundamentalist character, who looked very put out to have come face to face with me. Mansoor looked at his reaction with pronounced disapproval; he disapproved of hateful behavior toward foreigners. Then we laughed about it – and so did David when we caught up with him. He saw the whole thing from a distance. A little boy kept appearing after I got the laban and milk, just to stare at me. He did it so much that I told him to go back to his mother. I doubt he understood me, but David started making weird, bug-eyed faces at him to make him go away. Everywhere I went, men stared at me. I met their gazes calmly enough, tedious though it was.

Sultan Centre

There were 2 and only 2 stores to visit, but they were completely worth the expense and bother of going there and buying what we needed. One was in Souq Sharq, on the western end of the mall. It had a restaurant with a buffet and outdoor seating that overlooked the marina; the other was in Salmiya where, just across the back parking lot, we could see the Gulf and a new Hard Rock Café being built (much to Nuwwar's delight). It remained under construction for the duration of our stay, not that we cared. We don't like loud, noisy rooms with flashing lights and crowds. There is also a Sultan Centre warehouse nearby, but customers don't go in there; it's just a distribution center.

The Hard Rock Café in Salmiya, Kuwait, on the beach of Arabian Gulf Street, facing the Gulf.

We were very lucky because Fatin offered to drive us to a supermarket on weekends. We had no car, so this was a big help. She ended up taking us to either of the Sultan Centre stores almost every weekend. If she couldn't do this, sometimes our friend Mansoor would happily do it, asking me numerous questions about the food and merchandise the whole time. It was fun.

The Souq Sharq of Sultan Centre

The west end of the Souq Sharq Mall had a huge grocery store on its lower level. This is Sultan Centre, a chain of grocery-and-home stores that Americans patronize. We had just gotten our new refrigerator, so we bought milk, orange juice, mango juice, berry yoghurt, cheese, pistachios, flatbreads, toilet paper, and 2 huge bath towels – one blue (for me) and one green (for David). What a thrill – seriously! After several days of drying ourselves off on tee-shirts and then on tiny borrowed towels from Saleh, this was great.

The grocery store had a fish section with a beautiful display of fish on ice, a pastry counter, a house wares section, a produce area, and many aisles of dry goods (foods), toiletries, paper and plastics, and pet supplies, all on the lower level. To enter, one can either go in through the mall, or enter from the parking lot directly (past the registers and baggers), and cut through the restaurant from the marina's promenade.

One can also walk directly away from the Sultan Centre grocery store section into the lawn furniture area, on over to the gelato and French pastry bar, and over to the seating area of the restaurant, past the buffet and on outside to the marina. By the marina was yet more restaurant seating.

The fish counter at Sultan Centre, complete with a huge Hammour; bottled water, strawberry juice, and laban. When we couldn't get decent orange juice, we had strawberry juice (produced in Saudi Arabia), because it had some real strawberry pulp in it, but it was mostly sugar syrup, so David started buying fresh-squeezed orange juice at the take-out joints nearby. Laban was a yoghurt drink that David liked. And Kuwait's water has lead in it, so we bought water that was bottled elsewhere. This meant checking the labels carefully, as Kuwait sold its own bad water, with labels saying that it was bottled in Kuwait. People just didn't know – test results hadn't been published.

Back inside, in the middle of the lower level, and with the grocery store part of the business on all sides, is a pair of long escalators. They go up to the next level, which is where toys, pillows, bed linens and books are sold. This is where I bought our pillows. They were just poufy cotton ones, not foam, so I found myself using 2 at a time, and later buying a heating pad when a nerve in my neck flared up from this arrangement. I could barely hold my head up for several days, until Saleh gave me some medicine, which solved the problem. By then I had acquired the heating pad from this store, however, and it helped too.

It was at this particular Sultan Centre that I acquired one other thing, a crucial item that I carried everywhere I went in Kuwait, and referred to constantly: a map of the entire country. I still have it; it is a bit ragged, but still easy to read, despite spending several months inside my handbag. One side is divided into 2 halves; most of the upper half is a map of the entire nation of Kuwait – complete with a legend – showing every major road and city or town, plus Failaka Island, Bubiyan Island (it's all marsh, I was told, so no one bothers with it), and the oil fields, delineated with little red lines and oil-rig symbols, Kuwait Bay, and the Gulf. To the left of that is a much smaller image showing where in the Middle East Kuwait is, plus a Business Guide for Kuwait and an Index for the State of Kuwait showing where to find particular cities. The lower half is like a small guide to the nation, full of helpful facts: Visitor Information; Topography; Climate; Flora and Fauna; Social Customs; Transport; Economy; Oil; Population, etc.

 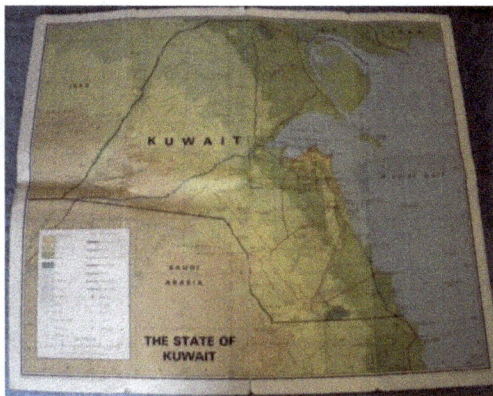

The cover of the map shows Kuwait Towers; inside was a map of the entire nation of Kuwait.

The other side of the map showed Kuwait City with almost every street name, plus famous cultural and political landmarks, including museums, souqs, banks, the stock exchange, the Grand Mosque, the city's famous 5 gates, and various government ministry building locations. This was set into the lower left side; the rest of the spreadsheet was devoted to the most heavily settled areas of Kuwait, from Jahrah to the west to Sulaibikhat to Shuwaikh Port on to Kuwait City, then moving south into Salmiya, Salwa, Manqaf and Fahaheel. I love maps; I don't go anywhere without them if I can help it. I always want to know where I am, where I've been, and where I am going.

We often ate dinner in the restaurant outside the Sultan Centre supermarket, sitting on the patio beside the marina, after buying our groceries. It was lovely – nice, mild weather and all lit up at night with a view of the Kuwait City skyline. Usually I didn't attempt any nighttime photography; I just enjoyed the outing. We would do this either on our own or with Mansoor. Once, David got an apple-flavored argeelah pipe and enjoyed puffing away until I finished shopping for groceries, chaperoned again by Mansoor. I bought Mansoor 2 boxes of Twining's tea bags: one of Earl Grey; one of English Breakfast tea, because he said he liked my tea when he visited, and because he deserved it – he was very nice to us, and lots of fun to hang out with.

The Salmiya Sultan Centre

Fatin really preferred the other branch, which stood in its own building on Arabian Gulf Street, so we were off to the Sultan Centre store in Salmiya, where lots of Americans, Brits and Europeans live. It was just as nice and as well-stocked as the one in Souq Sharq. Fatin did her weekly grocery shopping. I bought a 4-cup coffee maker, oven mitts from California (well-insulated ones, and prettier than the junk from the co-op in Khaitan), an ice cream scoop, a bottle opener, 6 table knives, a heat-resistant spoonula (I would miss those after working in Williams-Sonoma!), curtain hooks (8), 2 more bath towels, a small garbage can for the bathroom, a coffee scoop, Turkish coffee (I forgot paper coffee filters ☹), and some smoked salmon. I thoroughly enjoyed the sight of so many scarfless, bareheaded women. It was odd seeing American women all around me after being in Kuwait for just a week. I did not know any of them, I had no reason to get to know them, and yet there they were, buying groceries. They lived in Kuwait year-round, because their husbands had jobs with American corporations that were based in Kuwait.

The front of the Salmiya Sultan Centre – the entrance is down on the right. We always parked in the back – the parking lot is shown above on the right – and walked around to the front, which meant going around to the left.

One Thursday early in our stay in Kuwait, we visited both branches in one day, because Fatin wanted to do so. We went first to the Souq Sharq one, then headed straight for Sultan Centre in Salmiya, which is just north of Salwa, the area where Fatin lives. She wanted to do her grocery shopping, and I could think of a few more things to buy. Among them was more smoked salmon – David and I can have some smoked salmon sandwiches, thus giving us a break from the monotony of Egyptian take-out chickens. They're good, but eating the same thing repeatedly is starting to really bother us. I also got him some laban – low fat, because he can't get it all the time at the grocery store near us. Later, Fatin told me that Zahid doesn't like Kuwaiti laban – too sweet. In Syria, it is more sour than sweet, so he waits until he goes home for a visit to drink any rather than be disappointed in Kuwait. David was surprised; he thinks it is rather sour. It's all in what you're used to.

The layout of the store was much like the other one, except that the first floor was only about groceries, and had a huge spice section. Upstairs, which could be reached by riding up a large conveyor belt with one's shopping cart – basically an escalator with no stairs – was everything else. The quality of the goods for sale in Sultan Centre stores was much more familiar to me and seemed better than the stuff that I had found in the jamiya, and also in traditional Kuwaiti souqs. I was glad to have seen those, but I had hesitated to buy plates, towels or blankets there.

Sultan Centre had thick towels like the ones I could buy in the States, pretty dishes and, of all things, wine glasses in a country where they would never contain wine. I also found a shower curtain, a rod, and hooks – something that had eluded me elsewhere. When I saw Mansoor's apartment and realized that his mother had taken over the bathroom for laundry, and that they just used the tub with the detachable shower head on a hose, I began to suspect that Kuwaitis didn't use shower curtains. I didn't recall seeing anything like that in Raidah or Aiesha's bathrooms, either, for that matter.

In short, thanks to the Sultan Centre stores, I was able to outfit our apartment in such a way as to make it fully functional as Americans were used to enjoying their living spaces.

One evening, I walked all around inside this place chaperoned by Mansoor. He had brought us first to Haitham Restaurant, where we bought him dinner. Then he drove us to Sultan Centre in Salmiya. That was the night that I found the shower supplies, sugar for guests' tea and coffee, and real sponges – what fun. I was happy that David wouldn't flood the bathroom floor anymore. I showed Mansoor some flowers – lilies, orchids, hyacinths, irises, roses, narcissus, etc. We smelled them, too. It was a great store...they had some of everything.

Upstairs, we looked for a sugar bowl – no luck. But it was okay, because we had lots of fun looking at glasses for wine, martinis, champagne, beer, shots, etc. – all sorts of glasses for which the contents cannot be had in this country – how ironic. Mansoor had thought that they were for fruit juice! He got quite an education that night. He also insisted on accompanying me all through the store, while David disappeared into the greeting card section. Why? Because after 8 o'clock, single guys were allowed to browse in Sultan Center. Fatin had told me that they are banned before that hour, because they had made nuisances of themselves to female customers who were trying to buy groceries, and the management decided that they were bad for business. Interesting...I did notice some groups of single guys here and there, but as Mansoor was chaperoning me through every aisle, they never tried to bother me. David could just as easily have been a deterrent, but he didn't want to watch me shop, and I was never in the slightest danger.

I got a bit of an education on the way to and from Salmiya. Apparently, the Kuwaiti soccer team had just won a big game, and Kuwaiti soccer fans were out in the dark, celebrating. They were racing in their cars and jeeps, burning rubber, and getting out to dance in the streets, delaying traffic and riding on the tops of and hanging out the windows of their vehicles, all because their team won. Cops would have put a stop to such behavior in America, but there was not a cop in sight for blocks. The fans did seem to be under some semblance of self-control, however – they were just out having fun without hurting anyone.

We came back at 1:30 a.m. Mansoor went out right away to play billiards with his friends. He said he had fun with us. We had fun with him, too. ☺

The Fish Souq

Although we had no way to cook fish – no stove, and no intention of buying one – I wanted to see the Fish Souq, which was just across the lot from the Souq Sharq Sultan Centre, and next to Dhow Harbor, where the fishing boats docked. A dhow is a fishing boat. The Fish Souq looked absolutely fascinating to me; I am a gourmet at-home chef, so I wanted to at least attempt to gain an understanding of the ingredients available to anyone who had the chance to seriously cook in Kuwait. I was not disappointed.

Fatin agreed to take us there (and later on in our stay, Mansoor did also). We parked, and walked in. One long hall was for fruits, vegetables, nuts, spices, live chickens, eggs, butchers, and some fishing equipment supply shops.

Halfway down was a foyer with glass doors on either side that lead to a huge, high-ceilinged, white-tiled hall with cement floors: the fish market. Around the light fixtures, which branch out from all 4 sides of thick pillars spaced throughout the room, were beautiful sand-colored tiles. They looked like they were made out of sand, in fact, and they depicted squid, sea horses, crabs, and scallop shells. There were also huge, colorful, painted murals on the highest parts of the walls all around the perimeter of the room.

This was the hall next to the Fish Souq. At left is a butcher shop with lamb for sale. Kuwaiti customers and foreign workers wandered among fruits and vegetables on both sides of a huge hall that ran the length of the building.

These sand-like tiles surrounded every pole-mounted light fixture, depicting sea horses, shrimp, and scallop shells.

Freshly caught finfish and shellfish was displayed everywhere, mostly in the open on slanted white shelves, and in baskets. The vendors are rather aggressive in their sales tactics. They kept calling out to shoppers to look at their wares, and they gestured grandly at them if you came near their displays. I found this annoying, because I like to look in peace, without being bothered by any salespeople until I want one. It was fun strolling around, seeing tiny lobsters (some with tiny red eggs piled high on their tails!), squid, blue crabs in stacks, a few small clams, large and small shrimps, sharks (little ones), and so many species and sizes of finfish.

The selling floor of the Fish Souq, with colorful murals above, sand tiles around the lights and above them as well, and fish-mongers clad in rubber boots and aprons with scales and chalkboards next to their wares. Most of the customers were men, but some women, mostly shrouded in abbeyas and hijabs, roamed among the displays as well.

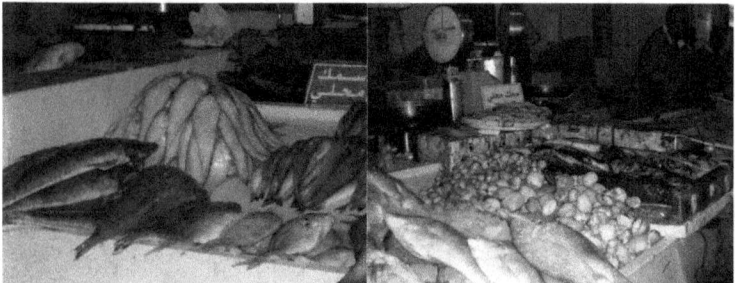

Many fish displays were set up in this way, with attractive, round piles of fillets cascading downward, and whole fish laid out in front of them. We saw piles of clams and oysters next to finfish.

More finfish laid out with their tailfins displayed prominently…the yellow-tailed fish were intriguing. They were not yellow snapper or yellow-fin tuna, so I was left, with no translator to help me identify things, wondering.

Fatin bought 2 kinds of fish to freeze and cook later. She said that the prices were good, and that the quality of the fish was excellent – no surprise there – and she was very pleased with what she found. There were some species of fish that she really wanted, including one from the River Nile called shaum. She cooked it for us later, and it was delicious.

I looked at every last display in the fish market, often staring down stupid Arab and Indian men who were not socialized at all in terms of how to politely look at women – as Western men are. American men and most Western European men take just brief moments to look at women, then look away, having seen us. They don't stare and stare, because they are taught that to do so is very rude and, in some contexts, threatening. Men in the Middle East stare. I realized that they didn't want to do any more than that. Arab men that we met and socialized with in Kuwait – and women – have assured us of this, but I nevertheless enjoyed staring them down. I can easily stare steadily back, without smiling, as if to say "Why are you staring at me?! It's rude – stop it."

This vendor at first gestured grandly at his wares, but when I brandished the camera, he grabbed a fish, held it up, and grinned happily. So did the boy at right with the Zubaidy fish – at last, one species that I knew.

But Fatin could not. She is an Egyptian Arab. She dresses elegantly in a suit with high heels – just to go to the mall – with a pretty head scarf draped over her hair (bangs showing). She stayed near me and David while looking nervously away from the oglers. This difference in our upbringing fascinates me, and gave me an odd sense of cultural pride in being able to handle such childish male nonsense with coolness and amusement.

One Friday evening Mansoor took us out to the Fish Souq, because I really wanted to take photographs of it, inside and out (I forgot to do so when Fatin took us there). So we all had a great evening there, and at a restaurant in Sultan Center.

The shellfish were amazing to see: blue-shelled crabs; shad roe with clams; lobsters, some with eggs on the bellies.

First, we got lucky in finding a parking space very shortly after arriving at the mall. We thought we would have to follow other cars around for half an hour, but no, we didn't. We immediately headed across the lot to the Fish Souq, where I photographed the beautiful sand tiles depicting several species of shellfish and all the displays of real fish, both finfish and shellfish. The vendors were funny; they got excited about having their wares photographed, and held up squid and other items for me. Then they all wanted to see their pictures on the view-screen on the back of my digital camera. Mansoor chaperoned me all over the Fish Souq while David wandered back into the grocery area.

Arabic Food Research

Late in our stay in Kuwait, David set himself the task of compiling a list of regional fruits and vegetables that could only be bought in Kuwaiti supermarkets. He had a vague idea about this before going to Kuwait, but it wasn't until I joined him armed with a digital camera – an early birthday gift from my father – that a real plan took shape. We could combine the camera and the laptop to create a PowerPoint presentation illustrating the whole topic, and Fatin could tell us the names in both English and Arabic of each item.

We gathered the data we needed late one morning after we arrived at Rola A. Al-Dashti's office only to find that she wouldn't be ready to meet with us for a couple of hours. So, we asked Rola's mother to tell us where the nearest jamiya was. She pointed us in the right direction after asking us why we didn't just go to Souq Sharq's Sultan Centre. David explained about researching foods that are locally available and preferred by Kuwaitis rather than by foreigners, and then she understood. Off we went through the Dasman area of Kuwait City to its local grocery store, and David immediately asked to meet with the store's manager. We met 2 Kuwaiti men – Ahmed, who directed floor operations downstairs, and Talal, who worked upstairs in the office.

Yemeni watermelons, Saudi watermelons, and Iranian pumpkins…and Philippines pineapples, of all things.

A huge date bar…avocadoes, garlic, onions, various potatoes…more varieties of potatoes that were new to us…

From left to right: bathinjan, which are Indian eggplants; Lebanese akudenea fruits; Jordanian quoassa.

David held out these knobbly things called karalla, from India. The herb is called helba; it is used to improve digestion, and the price: terrible bad breath.

Talal had an Indian staff member serve us glasses of cold water on a tray while David explained that we needed to photograph some produce and ask questions about each item. He had brought forms to fill out, and Talal told Ahmed to help us. Finally, we accomplished what David had wanted to do for a long time: gather information with photos on foods sold in a local Kuwaiti grocery store. We saw several unfamiliar fruits and vegetables, and Ahmed filled it all out in Arabic. We also took photos of strawberry juice jugs and laban, taking care to get the vitamin and ingredient labels. Then we saw coffee – Turkish, Arabic, French (misspelled "Frinsh" by the shippers) on an aisle marked "TEA/NESCAFE" – as well as rose and jasmine blossom water, and holy water with a cartoon of a black-shrouded woman on its label.

The Kuwaiti jamiya staff: A staff worker; the floor manager, Ahmed; and the store manager Talal.

We thanked the men and prepared to take our leave. They were very friendly and happy to help us, and they insisted upon posing for some photographs in the downstairs office before saying good-bye.

There was no way to give them the photographs, but this didn't seem to concern them at all. Apparently, they just wanted us to remember them. We certainly would – the whole experience was pleasant and interesting.

Bakalas – Convenience Stores

Bakalas (plural) are seedy little joints housed in little cement spaces at the foot of cement-block apartment buildings. A bakala is a convenience store. It is typically a tight space with a couple of small aisles of goods, plus more displayed on every bit of available wall space. A refrigerator is a the back, with milk, laban, fruits, other items, a cooler with frozen treats opposite the clerk/owner, and on and below the sales counter, just as in the West, are candy bars and energy bars. Newspapers and magazines are arrayed on a rack just outside. Long, clear plastic sheets often hang in the entryway to keep out insects and maintain a slightly more comfortable temperature than outside. This is how I kept up with the local news in Kuwait – through purchases from the local bakala.

The bakala nearest our apartment in Abraq Khaitan.

The Al-Ghanim Store in Safat

I wish I had photos of the big flagship Al-Ghanim store in Safat – but photography is forbidden inside Kuwait stores – especially in the more upscale, affluent ones. The reason is fear of competition from other businesses; if photos are shared with other businesses, the worry is that the owners will copy the style of décor and thus have increased profits. It seems like a pointless restriction given that brochures are often put out by a business, complete with photos of showrooms, and anyone can walk around inside any store, memorize the ideas, leave, and then duplicate them elsewhere if they wish to.

This was where our furniture came from. Later, we acquired a microwave oven from a smaller branch of this store in some other town, and I got a hair dryer at an Al-Ghanim that sold only appliances in yet another place. Saleh took us to the big store in Safat the night after we had moved into the apartment in Abraq Khaitan, on a Sunday evening, to choose the furniture; by then, he must have assumed, I would have had all day to contemplate what the place ought to have in it. He guessed right – I chose the bare basics, trying to spend as little as possible and form as little attachment to any of it as possible. This was meant to be temporary, and it was, despite Saleh and David's brief delusions of us having a future life in Kuwait. What a relief!

The Al-Ghanim family is a wealthy Kuwaiti tribe, and they were responsible for the mercantile dealings of this nation when it was first organized in the 1700s. Just as the Al-Sabah family took over governmental functions and became the ruling family, the Al-Ghanim family became the one that owns the largest controlling interest in home furnishings, appliances, fabrics, etc. We tried to arrange for the furniture to arrive the next day, but it didn't work...it would arrive the following Wednesday morning.

The front of the store is a huge, impressive-looking colonnade. This façade covers a 2-storey showroom. The furniture department is upstairs, with bedroom sets, living room sofa sets with coffee tables, dining room sets, and so on. Lamps are also available, all upstairs. Downstairs is the curtain department. Curtains are very important in Muslim homes, because the windows must be completely covered with cloth, thus allowing outsiders to see absolutely nothing that is inside – such as the resident women while not wearing their hijabs. The curtains were not actually made up yet; the fabrics are neatly draped all over the central part of the ground floor, allowing easy viewing without having to move any pieces out of the way. A choice of fabric and style is made, measurements are provided, and curtains are ordered. We didn't order any. It would have been too great an expense for a temporary stay.

To the right of the curtain area was a large room full of sheets, blankets, bed-in-a-bag sets that contained a quilt, 2 pillow shams and a dust ruffle in each pattern, tablecloths, bathrobes, and so on. I noticed that these items were comparable to what I was used to having at home in the States, and some were quite pretty. David and I had been married almost 2 and a half years earlier, in June of 2002, so I had recently gone through the detailed exercise of setting up a collection of house wares. Here I was doing that again on a slightly smaller scale! I had no intention of acquiring as much stuff this time – only enough to be comfortable for 6 months.

To the left of the curtain area was a small Starbucks, set into the windows of the front of the store, and between more curtain fabrics and this little area was a large doorway that led to another whole section of Al-Ghanim, which was about a quarter of the length of the home furnishings section. It was 2 levels, both connected to the 2 in the other section, and both full of electronics. The upper level contained stoves, ovens, dishwashers, washing and drying machines, and refrigerators. The lower level was full of computers – both desktops and laptops – printers, computer accessories, and a full complement of home entertainment systems.

You name it, they offered it. But we didn't need all of it, and we were trying to be judicious about what we bought, because we would be leaving in May. We were buying things at Al-Ghanim because we didn't know where to shop in Kuwait without advice, and we were buying things because we couldn't just borrow from Saleh's wife's stash indefinitely. The stuff we were using had actually belonged to her oldest son and his wife; her son had died, and his widow had returned to her relatives in southern Iran, just across the Gulf. Saleh's wife, Raidah, wanted the things that we were using back – she believed in odd things such as that her son's ghost would be unhappy if they were out of his old room for long.

Accordingly, Saleh shepherded us all over the store, encouraging us to order new things, and grinning happily as he entertained visions of us remaining permanently in Kuwait, having babies, me adopting the hijab, and David working with him for the rest of their professional lives. He had tried to talk me into staying permanently in the car on the way to K.O.C. Hospital the day before, and my anxiety level began to escalate. David told him to stop, so he merely suggested that of course I would occasionally go home to visit. No, David said, watching me.

So here we were, looking at furniture on the upper level of the store.

The first priority was to stop sleeping on the hard tile floor, so I headed straight to a plain, modern-looking set of bedroom furniture, and selected a king-sized bed (the only size they had), which came with 2 night tables and 3 wardrobes. The bed came with a mattress, and I looked forward to sleeping on it soon.

What about the living room? Saleh wouldn't let up. I chose a set of medium-to-dark blue, plain, boxy, cloth seats: one sofa, one chair. It came with a low coffee table and a small end table that matched. I noticed that none of the wooden furniture in the entire store was actually made of solid wood. All of it was made of pressed sawdust and covered with a cheap veneer.

What about the dining room? At least our apartment lacked any more rooms that could hold a set of furniture, I thought to myself, picking out a utilitarian table with a top that was made of wood that could be pulled outwards and folded back when a larger one wasn't needed. This would go in the room with no windows, and David could sit there working and holding meetings. I also chose chairs...or perhaps those metal-and-wooden things came with it.

In the appliances area, the only thing I agreed to buy was a small-to-medium sized refrigerator. No way was I getting a stove; we were only visiting Kuwait, and they were all gas stoves that operated through scary-looking tanks with hoses that connected to the burners. I didn't want to deal with the possibility of blowing up the building, let alone the hassle presented by these things.

Onward to the electronics area, Saleh announced, as David promised to pay him back as soon as our pay was wired to us (which it was the following week – the entire sum that we had been promised, rather than incremental payments). Saleh tried to induce me to buy an entire kitchen's worth of equipment, but all I would agree to was a medium-sized refrigerator with a freezer at the top part.

We went downstairs to look at laptops next. This was important, and neither David nor I had any trepidation about investing in this equipment. I only wish that I had known more about computers and which brands to avoid. I chose an Acer laptop with Microsoft and Intel software preloaded, and a Hewlett-Packard printer. We still have and use the printer, but the laptop lived precisely one year (a friend of David's in Farmington, Connecticut, where he studied for his Ph.D., managed to salvage all of our data off of it for us).

With that, we told Saleh that we would not buy anything else, and he took us home.

Precisely 2 weeks after that, Saleh drove us back to the Al-Ghanim store to pay for everything – the fridge, the laptop computer, and the furniture. He managed to save us some money on it, though not as much as we had hoped. He and David had to spend quite a while sitting at the desk in the back, so I went downstairs to take advantage of some 20%-off-if-you-pay-cash deals on bedding. Soon we had a pretty, floral bed-in-a-bag set of a comforter-quilt, bed skirt, and 2 pillow shams. The sheets were beautiful pink ones with a rose pattern interwoven into the cotton.

The Philippina women who worked there smiled and packed it all up for me, I paid them, and dragged the heavy bags upstairs. David and Saleh were almost finished with the arrangements, so I paced around a bit looking at lamps until they stood up. We could do without a lamp, I had decided – the light switches in the apartment operated perfectly good overhead bulbs; more money that would not be spent. David and Saleh took the heavy bags, and we left.

When I made up the bed later, I was quite pleased – it looked beautiful, and warm. What a relief that was. Kuwait winters seemed to be dry and chilly. Our cat was pleased, too. She was the first member of the family to actually sleep on the bed, despite having one of her own. We all took a nap in the newly outfitted bed this afternoon with Scheherazade deep down under the covers. When David got up (he needs a lot less sleep than I do), the cat moved up and rested her chin on the pillow next to me. Good cat – she was so cute.

Scheherazade Cat immediately took first possession of our newly outfitted bed, and took a nap.

We weren't warm enough, however, so on Christmas Eve, Mansoor found the place and brought us there. I got a change of sheets – identical to the others – and a blue blanket.

After a month or so of hard labor printing reports and photos, our printer needed black and color ink cartridges, so Fatin took me to an Al-Ghanim store across the highway from our apartment, in Farwaniya. That store made things complicated: you found what you wanted, a salesperson put your phone number in the computer, you waited at the counter in the front to pay, and then you paid and went back to the first guy to get your things. Meanwhile, Fatin was kept waiting with a back problem. Some stores in the States operate this way too, and no one likes it much. Al-Ghanim is such an old, big name in Kuwait that everyone accepts this complicated service from it without question.

When we had paid for our furniture, we had done so before payment was due, because this would entitle us to a coupon worth 118 KD to spend in the store. We asked Mansoor if he could take us back there months later, with little time left to spend in Kuwait. It was the principle of the thing: we had the coupon, so we would get the stuff.

Mansoor drove us during his 3-hour afternoon break from work (I didn't ask how he was allowed such a long break) to the headquarters of the Al-Ghanim home furnishings and electronics store in Safat. We were entitled to whatever we could buy in either furnishings or linens for that amount, and the Philippina women who worked there insisted that we buy exactly that much so that Al-Ghanim would have to give us the full benefit. They were very friendly and helpful. I did my best to prevent David from teasing and confusing them. David does this to every stranger he meets just for fun – bad boy!

We got pink and blue bath towels, a new shower curtain with palm trees on it, a matching guest hand towel, one pink and one white linen tablecloth, a tall black metal lamp with a dark blue shade, and a Tiffany-style stained-glass lamp that could hold 2 light bulbs. This lamp had a peacock motif. I think it's cool – I like it because it reminds me of things in museums, and have always wanted a lamp with Tiffany designs. I found a pink waffle-weave bathrobe to finish the deal off, which I still have. David said to not use any of the new house wares, but to save them for when we returned to Kuwait and got another place. (He returned alone for a few months in 2009, to help Saleh run a spa clinic, and did in fact use some of them.) I really had no interest in returning. I was making a thorough study of Kuwait, trying to finish it so that I would not actually live there in the future. Maybe a short visit to friends…

Mansoor told us the bad news that he was moving to Farwaniya on the way over, and the shocking reasons why (see the chapter called

Invisibility Cloaks for details). Then we had fun in the store. At the small Starbucks coffee shop inside, I got Fatin an insulated, metal coffee mug for the car – she had wanted one. She deserved it – she had been very nice to us, giving us her homemade food at her house and to take home, which we really appreciated. The Philippino vendor who sold it to me was gay – we could tell – and I rushed David and Mansoor away from him as David joked about having met him in Provincetown. The guy had no idea what David was talking about; I pressed the bag to David's chest, scolding him and Mansoor and ushering them back into the linens area of Al-Ghanim. Naughty boys!

A Nut and Dried Fruit Shop

On another afternoon, David and I went to meet a chemist in Fahaheel, a nice Palestinian man who lived there with his wife and children – 2 boys, a teenage daughter, and a baby. There was also an Indian maid. We were dropped off by a friend's driver, and left on a busy street far from the part of town where the chemist lived. While we waited for him to pick us up, we noticed a beautiful shop full of dried nuts, fruits, and other specialties and gourmet regional goodies. In we went – and I had my camera with me.

David had a great time inspecting everything in sight; the shopkeeper was happy to answer his questions.

The arrangement of goods would never have been allowed in the U.S.; open vats of dates, crackers, etc.

A Famous Pastry Shop

One afternoon when I was out with Fatin – without my camera, as photography tended to be discouraged in shops – I paused to stare into a sweet shop. The displays looked rather interesting, including one large, round tray with a layer of green pistachios on top – all ground up. Fatin told me that David loved that shop, and used to beg her to bring him some sweets from there whenever she came to the States. It was called the Bohsali Bakery, and was an Iranian business. There were other branches elsewhere in Kuwait, but Fatin said that this was the best one. This was also the shop that – supposedly – Osama bin Laden and Yasser Arafat liked. Of course I had to go back and buy David some treats, so I got a container of Middle Eastern baklava, made of phyllo pastry with pistachios, and half a kilo of white pistachio ice cream, a flavor that Mr. Ali's shop in Khaitan didn't offer. David was delighted. ☺

Chapter 6
Tea, Coffee, and Customs in Kuwait

Kuwaiti people have their own ways of making tea and coffee, and of serving and drinking them. I never knew how complex it would be until I was there dealing with it, but it was great fun to learn about it. They were also wise enough not to assume that I meant what a Kuwaiti person would mean as I presented the drinks. How could I? I was just learning how they did these things. In addition to these social niceties, there were many more customs to encounter and adjust to. It was endlessly fascinating.

Nescafe at K.O.C. Hospital

Kuwait Oil Company Hospital is located in Ahmadi City, well south of the most heavily settled areas of the country, which extend south and east of the capital, Kuwait City. The hospital is a small, sprawling, 2-level building with a framed, hand-drawn floor plan in the center reception area (there are at least 2 reception areas). We spent much of the day in a tiny library with 4 computers, only 2 of which were connected to the Internet. I e-mailed my family about the plane trip, and met various doctors.

A hospital administrator invited us into his office for coffee. It was there that I was told that Kuwaitis haven't a clue about making good coffee – only tea. I had yet to see a café in Kuwait, as I had only just arrived 2 days earlier. He served Nescafé as he broke the bad news to me. I decided not to just believe the first Kuwaiti person who told me I couldn't get good coffee. A little while later I was sitting in the doctors' lounge (we were invited into it), which had a tray where people could make themselves a cup of more instant Nescafé – yuck. Or they could make tea, using a hot water dispenser, which the cafeteria workers came across the hall to set up.

My First Taste of the Kuwaiti Hospitality Routine

As I mentioned earlier, we went to visit Saleh and Raidah for dinner after a week in our new apartment. Just when we were about to have dessert, we were unexpectedly interrupted. A grinning Kuwaiti named Mahmoud, whom we had met the previous day at K.O.C. Hospital, appeared at the door. Saleh hurried us out the door with him, putting a slice of Raidah's cake on a porcelain plate with a metal fork and a paper napkin, placed it on the back seat of his car with me, and sent us off in a big hurry.

This seemed very odd to me for various reasons: one, we had just been taken away from one host's home by another, with Mahmoud seeming utterly oblivious to everything and anything but the reason for taking us with him, which was to show us his shiny newly restored antique 1959 red Mercedes coupe and yellow Chevy truck; and two, this dessert had been given out on a porcelain plate, of all things. Why not just use a plastic or paper container?

Eventually, I got the answer to the last question from our friend Mansoor: it is not considered nice. Interesting…in this culture, so many homes had servants with drivers to retrieve these things that they could afford to operate this way. Not in the States; we wrap things up in foil or plastic and say good-bye to the whole gift then and there.

Why was Saleh in such a rush to hand his guests off to this guy? He was a potential investor, and Saleh hoped to start his own medical clinic. But as far as I knew, Mahmoud never invested so much as a fil toward any of that. It was all about the shiny cars…

Mahmoud himself was a comical character: tall, handsome, with thick, short dark hair, dark eyes, and a huge mole on his right cheek. He looked like a parody of Robert De Niro. When I asked Saleh about him, he told me that Mahmoud was a wealthy, retired K.O.C. employee who could afford to give us money, and he had asthma.

He whisked us off to his house in Dahar, near the Gulf coast. He lived there with his son and 2 daughters from his first wife, and Fatima, his second wife (Wife 1 had died, after which time he had married Wife 2). I had met his older daughter Haleh the day before; she was a sweet girl in her late teens who covered every bit of her hair with her hijab, and spoke to me with a quiet smile.

Fatma was young and pretty, and she wore one of those housecoats that I had seen for sale in a mall. It was long, red, with gold embroidery around its front zipper, and rather ugly. She had a staff of 3 Philippina maids, who soon brought me a piece of cake smothered in apricot sauce and a tiny glass cup of tea with sugar in it. Tea was usually served in Kuwait with no milk. These items were presented on a tiny table, which was placed directly in front of me. The tea was wonderfully fragrant, but drinking it this way disagreed with me. I decided to hold out for milk; a little while later, David told me that drinking tea with no milk puts one at risk for esophageal cancer!

I only ate 2 bites of the cake – I was still too full for more, and I had to save room for whatever Raidah wanted us to have at her house. The cake Fatima gave me was a fluffy, tasteless white sponge cake with an apricot sauce over it – probably from a freezer. I began to suspect that of all the desserts I would taste while in Kuwait, the best ones would be those made from traditional recipes native to the region, not Western imports. I was right, but I had to go on a few more visits to confirm this.

For nearly an hour, I sat in the harim with Fatima and her friends, all of whom wore their robes and scarves – abbeyas and hijabs – because Mahmoud might walk through the room. Only Fatima showed her hair. Few of the women could speak English, and so I found myself people-watching again. I noticed that many of them were overweight – plump, one might call them. After a while, Fatima and one of her friends revealed that they could converse with me by quizzing me about my husband's work – what company did he work for? It never occurred to them that he might be self-employed, which he was. When I explained this, they seemed confused and nonplussed.

More time passed. I noticed that the 12-year-old daughter from Mahmoud's first marriage had come in to sit. She had short, curly hair and jeans on, and she never smiled. I wondered how long ago her mother had died, and how soon after that he had replaced her. She seemed friendly enough with her stepmother, but unhappy.

Finally, Mahmoud came back in and told me that my husband was asking for me.

I jumped right up, thrilled to escape from the harim while keeping my expression neutral about it. I thanked Fatima and followed him out back to the garden. David was sitting there with the men. A little enclosure against the back stone fence had some rabbits and chickens in it. I noticed that the men had their own, separate bathroom to use, and that it wasn't tiled like the nice indoor one for the women. It was a backyard diwan. Haleh was summoned to sit with me; the men felt awkward having me there, but duty-bound to please David, their guest.

We chatted for quite a while longer, all the while worrying about having offended our first hosts back in South Surra. The smiling and nodding went on and on and on – like Mahmoud was trying to keep the Americans in his yard because it somehow thrilled him to have us there. After a while, I learned that many Kuwaitis are a bit starry-eyed around Americans thanks to the Gulf War and to our efficient, cool culture that seems to get things done in short order. (Well, it didn't take long to oust the invaders, but we were complete strangers to him!) Finally, I stood up, smiled sweetly, and asked Mahmoud point-blank to please drive us back to Saleh's house now.

That worked.

Saleh and Raidah weren't even upset; we ate their cake, I sat with Raidah for a while until she felt we had really visited, and then Saleh took us on some more visits. At least he was with us, and I didn't have that feeling that we ought to leave.

Assim's Diwan

Our next stop was at the home of a Kuwaiti professor who taught business courses at Kuwait University. He lived in Abdullah es Salem, north of Saleh's area, and I became friends with his wife. We had many visits, usually on Fridays, while I was in Kuwait, and kept in touch by e-mail after I left. Her name was Aiesha, and she appeared several times as we sat in Assim's diwan to bring tray after tray of food, sweets, juice and tea. Then she sat quietly next to me.

Saleh sat quietly holding his prayer beads, which are also called worry beads. They seemed to somewhat resemble the rosary beads I had been required to learn to pray with as a child, but without sections. Most beads were the same size, but there was one line hanging down, just like the section of rosary beads where it branches off toward the crucifix. I asked Saleh about the beads, and all he said was that they were "to keep my hands busy." Well, they were fulfilling that purpose.

After this visit, Assim took us to see his brother. Saleh was searching for investors again, and apparently, Assim's older brother Fahad was wealthy enough to qualify. We went to his diwan, where we proceeded not to discuss business much at all. At first I was puzzled by this, until I learned, later through constant reading about Kuwaiti culture, that business is not discussed in diwans. You meet people at the diwan, then talk business a day or so later during the day, at their offices.

Fahad's Diwan and Fly-Swatting Servant

We drove a short distance to an impressive-looking piece of property in a well-settled area, though I didn't know where. A wall surrounded the place – white, with greenery growing over it and cascading down the outside of the walls. A brass plate mounted on the wall informed us, in English and in Arabic, that this was the diwan of Fahad Al-Tikriti. Assim led us in, and we were seated promptly in a room that was similar in size to Assim's diwan, but not in décor. Whereas Assim's had had French-style chairs and sofas with fussy red cushions and gold curlicue patterns, Fahad's was decorated in the traditional Kuwaiti style: plain, with white walls and square cushions on bench-like sofas along the walls.

Fahad had an African woman maid who wore a white, eyelet-lace trimmed pants suit and a white turban. She served tea with sugar in it to his guests – us. That was the 4th time in one day and 6th cup of this overly sweetened stuff that I had had! This we could observe with all seriousness. It seemed to be a perfectly normal and dignified job to us. What we found absolutely hilarious, however, was the young Indian guy whose job it is to go around the house killing flies with a squash racket. There were probably several of these cheap, plastic things around the house for his use! I'll bet he had other duties that were not so silly, but this was all that we saw him do that night.

After another seemingly nonproductive visit – I was still learning that this was simply the norm for making business contacts in Kuwait – we said thank you and good-night to Fahad. I never saw any other part of that house, nor did I ever see Fahad again.

Arabic Coffee – a Misnomer

David and I had become addicted to a very good kind of coffee as soon as I had bought us a coffee machine at Sultan Centre. As usual, David had objected, saying that I shouldn't have bought anything, but I told him we couldn't spend 6 months without being able to so much as make our own coffee at home. He quickly settled into using it and couldn't imagine doing without it – typical behavior for him. The coffee we loved was a finely ground blend called Turkish coffee, which was heavily infused with a wonderful spice: cardamom. It was absolutely delectable.

One morning we finished our package off. David went around the corner to the bakala and bought some other stuff, and it was horrible, so we planned to go out to the co-op that very night and get more of the Turkish stuff. But I was intrigued, because I had seen it at the jamiya, so I opened it up and brewed some, just to see what it would be like.

He had bought Arabic coffee, according to the package…if you could justify calling it coffee. Instead of dark, finely ground coffee, it appeared to have tea leaves and herbs in it, is light brown, and smells almost like cocoa, but no such luck…it's just a vile, weird-tasting liquid. It brewed into a light brown, transparent concoction, which David says is often served at diwaniyas to bring the guys "closer to God." They were welcome to it – we tasted it, and it was revolting. David called it raktajino – Klingon coffee. Klingon food is always depicted as revolting to humans in *Star Trek*, so this seemed like a good name for it.

Determined to be a Good Hostess

In mid-December, we were enjoying a new microwave oven that I had insisted upon buying, not wanting to eat cold leftovers, and we had only paid 18 KD for it (it blew up a day before we left Kuwait). Wow – hot meals, leftover from eating out and buying take-out, were possible now, and tea! It was great.

In the afternoon, Mr. Hassan, our new Egyptian friend, came over for another meeting, and I offered him tea – but I still had no sugar, so he chose strawberry juice. It was delicious, made of real crushed strawberries, so at least I felt like a decent hostess, but I was determined to get a sugar bowl and creamer after having had several guests but not the proper tools for presenting tea.

That evening, we went out with our friend Mansoor.

We looked around in a mini-mall at many things, but bought very little.

Upstairs, we looked for a sugar bowl – no luck.

A week later, while I was out with Fatin's daughter Nuwwar in Salmiya, she showed me several stores that offered the sort of china that I was used to. In a Danish store, I found a sugar bowl and creamer set, and 6 matching soup plates, all with pretty pink roses on them.

I took them home and filled the sugar bowl with sugar-in-the-raw. It's delicious, and healthier than the refined white sugar that most people used.

Once I was properly set up, I began to find out much more about tea and coffee customs.

People would lift up the lid on the sugar and stop short, shocked, asking what that was. David would explain it every time, and every time, they would calmly accept it and then add 4 teaspoons full to their mugs.

I held my tongue with the people I didn't know very well. But with Mansoor and Assim, I didn't. Assim had diabetes, despite his tall, thin physique and healthy complexion (Aiesha told me it was in the early stages). Mansoor had been in the hospital with blood poisoning when he was 22 and in a coma for a while. He was okay when we knew him, but this habit of saturating the tea with sweet stuff stunned me.

Another thing that many Middle Easterners do – not just Kuwaitis – is take a cup of tea with no milk, pick up a cube of sugar, hold it between their teeth, and suck the tea through that. Tooth decay and diabetes ensue. And a risk of esophageal cancer is part of the equation with no milk. To top it all off, the tea is super-brewed – with several teabags, concentrated, and not very good ones at that.

Mansoor pointed them out to me one night at the jamiya: "That is what my mother and sister buy," he told me. There in the center of the store, stacked to the ceiling on a display near the registers, were boxes and boxes of 2 or 3 brands of Arab tea bags. I had smelled the stuff, and tasted it. With milk, it was okay, but not without.

When I went to Sultan Centre, I had bought some Twining tea – English Breakfast and Earl Grey. When Mansoor came to visit, I presented his mug with some of that – one teabag did the job nicely every time – and he was amazed. This was wonderful! What was it? I showed it to him and eventually bought one box of the stuff for him to take home.

I was fascinated by his reaction.

My Education in Tea and Coffee Continued...

There is a sound that Arabs make when they are happy about something, such as a betrothal, that to me seemed reminiscent of a Native American war cry. It sounded like both a whoop and a trill. I saw and heard it on television in Kuwait in an ad for those horrid tea bags, when a CEO in a board room meeting, wearing a dishdasha and guthra tried the tea and liked it. It made me think, what weird sounds do Americans make? Bravo...Yeah...loud whistles...Boo...Bronx cheers...the list goes on – just a reminder that we too can sound strange to people from foreign cultures.

Assim Al-Tikriti paid us another evening visit. I served him tea in the mug that mocks Saddam Hussein as a street bum ("Will Tyrannize for Food."). I used the new sugar bowl and spoons, and the new sugar bowl filled with "Sugar-in-the-Raw," and I served dates with the tea – David was in Kuwait during Ramadan (the month before I arrived...and he was glad I had missed it, when the whole country was like a closed mausoleum most of the time), and he went to many diwaniyas, where people kept giving him dates, so we had a lot of them.

When Assim sat down, I peppered him with questions about Middle Eastern tea service. He answered them all readily, happy to be able to help me understand the culture around me. I think the Kuwaiti people I knew rather enjoyed teaching me about their culture. I wanted to know all about it – about secular, everyday aspects of their lives, not just Islam. If that topic fit into the equation somewhere, of course I wanted to understand how, but it seemed to intrigue them that I was after all the other details with such interest.

Earlier that day, in late December, David had been visited by 2 scientists – a Palestinian chemist named Thamir (very nice guy), and a Jordanian biochemical engineer named Aza (who was cheating on his wife). Of course I had served hot drinks to them as well, but I had followed my own customs: I offered choices and then asked them what they would like, and when they told me, I believed them and gave it to them. This didn't seem like a mistake…

While I heated the water up, they told me more about tea and coffee customs. Apparently, there was a tradition of serving tea when guests first arrived, and Turkish coffee when the hostess or host wanted the visit to end, as a signal that the guest should leave.

It turned out that Aza preferred Turkish coffee to tea. Suddenly I wasn't sure what they would think if I served it. Then I did it anyway, and told him that I was not trying to get him to leave – I was just serving a drink that he liked. He and Thamir laughed and assured me that they didn't see any such message in the offering. It was all their fault, for telling me about the meanings behind these beverages and the timing of serving them! I am glad they told me, though. Now I will understand what is going on in future visits to other homes.

Assim confirmed these customs as he drank his tea with the sugar-in-the-raw, and thought the mug was cool.

Mansoor later added something else to the mix: if the hostess doesn't fill up the mug all the way with hot water, it means that she is trying to get the guest to leave. I was horrified; had I been offending every visitor by leaving room for milk? I did tell them what I was doing, and then add milk to my own drink…

"No, never mind," Mansoor said ("never mind" was his favorite soothing line to use). He had understood what I was doing, and never thought that I was trying to shorten a visit. How could he, when David and I kept inviting him to sit down and stay awhile and chat?

We had fun; we gave Mansoor some mango ice cream and Turkish coffee. We drank big mugs of Turkish coffee, two-thirds full of hot coffee and one-third full of cold milk. That is how Americans like it, and everywhere we went, Arabs were simultaneously fascinated and amazed. It was hilarious to watch their reactions.

On the way home from my next visit with Aiesha, as Assim drove me back, I asked him about what Mansoor had told me about filling cups all the way to the top so that visitors would not think that we wanted them to drink up quickly and go. Assim said he didn't know about the tea custom, so I would ask Aiesha, but he did say that the coffee is typically served at the end of a visit, in tiny cups, only about half full. If you don't shake the cup after finishing it, the person serving it will think you want more and come back with the pot! That explained why Mohammed Al-Hamdullilah was so determined to give us more Turkish coffee at the tent party.

The next time I saw Aiesha, she served me tea (with milk!), and honey croissants. I asked her a question – why is it so crucial to fill the cup up all the way…does it really mean hurry up, drink up and go quickly? She said no, that Mansoor is wrong, and it means simply that the hostess is not a generous person if she doesn't fill it all the way to the top. Aiesha also told me that after eight years in the States, she had started to forget Kuwaiti tea and coffee serving customs. She certainly remembered them all years later, I thought. Pour with your left hand and hold cups with your right – but she didn't know why it had to be that way.

I was getting confused, but having fun. It didn't matter; the Kuwaitis and other Arabs didn't expect me to internalize their tea and coffee customs, only to be interested in them and to attempt to be a pleasant hostess when they came to my apartment. I could certainly do that.

Traditional Turkish Coffee Served

When we visited Dr. Alim and his family, he offered us a choice of Nescafé (!) or Turkish coffee at the end of the evening. "Turkish coffee? Yes, please!" I was delighted; here was a chance to try the real thing, not just the ingredient filtered through our coffee maker. I wondered how Nadira would present it. I had to speak through Alim, but I told them both that Nescafé was just processed American junk and I really appreciated their wonderful, native, homemade food. Out it came a few minutes later, and it was wonderful.

The coffee had its wonderful cardamom scent, of course, and was very thick and frothy. It was served in a metal container with an open top and a long handle on the side, from which it was poured into small, individual cups. Milk and sugar were available, though we understood that it was traditional to drink it with only sugar. Thanks to the influence of the Ottoman Empire throughout the Middle East, people all over the region like this kind of coffee – and so do we.

Nadira's presentation of traditional Turkish coffee.

That pretty much completed my coffee and tea education.

Inside a Kuwaiti Hospital

Saleh worked as an internist at Kuwait Oil Company Hospital (K.O.C. Hospital) in Ahmadi City, south of where we lived, near the Ahmadi oil fields. It was a government-run hospital, a small, sprawling complex of older buildings that were in the process of undergoing an extensive renovation and facelift. While I was there, I saw the future look of the hospital in the small portion that had been completed – sharp, modern, clean lines.

K.O.C. Hospital's new look: outside, at the main entrance; inside, with new marble halls, plants, and tiles.

The older areas included a courtyard inhabited by many pigeons and looked liked sandstone and mud-bricks with cracking tiles. I could see why the renovation was happening. I found many interesting things: bathrooms with little hoses next to the toilets, a hole-in-the-floor for a toilet in one stall, a floor plan of the complex, and of course the older sections. There was a small gift shop that sold flowers, snacks and newspapers near the courtyard with the pigeons.

 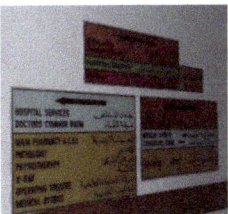

This was the floor plan of K.O.C. Hospital, mostly in Arabic, to guide visitors, and some hallway signs.

I spent my first day out and about in Kuwait wandering around this hospital, before we had even seen the apartment that we were to live in for the rest of our time there. I used the library computers to e-mail my parents that I had arrived, ate lunch with David in the greasy, unhealthy cafeteria, and saw a patient exam room because David was using a computer in it. There was a rack in a waiting area full of Islamic pamphlets, and there were separate waiting areas and pharmacies for men and women.

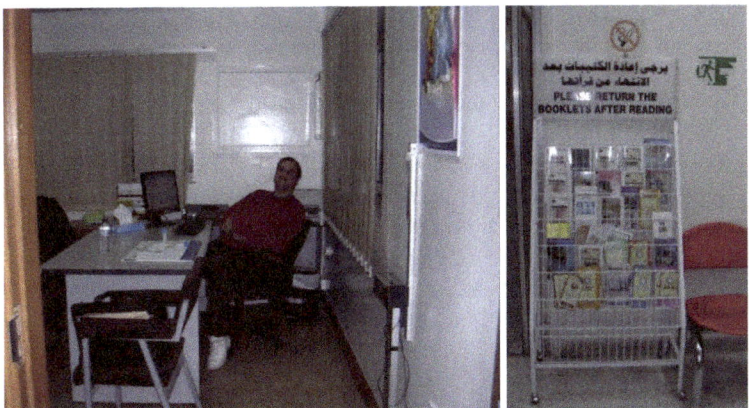

David working on a computer in an exam room, and Islamic pamphlets that were to be read and put back.

The most remarkable thing I saw was both the lack of a nurse/receptionist and a sign on an exam room door telling people to just wait and not knock on the door. The nerve of anyone to expect quiet, submissive, endless waiting without question, I couldn't help thinking to myself.

There was absolutely no sign of any nurse, or anyone else to ask about anything – all day.

Kuwait had many other hospitals, but I never saw them. A lot of them are private hospitals and so cost more to use. The private ones are more like hotels, I was told. The government run ones provided government-funded health care to Kuwaitis, while the private ones were available to Kuwaitis but also were the only option for foreign workers. So unless one's employer took care of one's health care costs, that meant that the hundreds of thousands of laborers from third-world countries would be out of luck if they got sick or injured.

It's the Arabian Gulf – NOT the Persian!

Our friend Saleh told us that on the west side of the gulf, which is inhabited by Arabs, not Persians, it is called the Arabian Gulf. When he was a schoolboy, his teacher ordered the students to cross out "Persian" and write "Arabian" wherever the term appeared in their textbooks. Obviously, this is a matter of ethnic pride, and we adjusted our terminology accordingly while in Kuwait.

New Year's Eve

We found ourselves with a very full social calendar on New Year's Eve – 3 invitations for one day. The first one was to lunch at the Salmiya apartment of an old friend of David's – a scientist that Saleh introduced him to over 10 years ago – Dr. Alim. He and his family were Syrian, so I saw how the women's dress differed from that of Kuwaiti women, and that was where we had Turkish coffee served in the traditional way, by his wife Nadira and daughter Mahibah. The second invitation was to see Aiesha, as New Year's Eve fell on a Friday, and the third took us to Salwa, to Mr. Hassan's place, the nice Egyptian engineer who had lived in Kuwait for most of his life, to celebrate New Year's Eve with his family.

Dr. Alim had called me up earlier in the week, and told me that his wife, Nadira, could talk with me in French…but it turned out that she remembered even less of it than I do, so her daughter, Mahibah, sat with us translating into English and Arabic until she had to go pray. They gave us presents: cologne for David and a transparent, red and black rose-patterned shirt for me. I thanked them, and promised myself to get Mahibah a new scarf after she showed me her colorful collection.

The main difference between Kuwaiti women's dress and Syrian was color: Syrian women wore colors, while Kuwaiti women wore all black, with a little colored embroidery decorating the edges of their abbeyas and hijabs. There appeared to be no difference in the way that they wound the hijabs into place. There were some other robes that Syrian women wore, but they preferred not to do so in Kuwait. They showed me some, very nicely bringing out 3 very different robes – different in color and decoration, not style – and holding them up while I shot a photo of each one.

I was careful when adding these photos to this chapter to crop out Nadira and Mahibah, and to just show the outfits. Everywhere I went – with the exception of the Egyptian family I was to meet later that evening – I was admonished that I could have photos of my new friends to remember them all by, but to please not show them to any men. So I keep them to look at and to show to curious women. Women can look at women, but men who do so must be their relatives or husbands. All this was about complying with the cultural code of the hijab, which is not just a scarf. It's an institution.

Syrian robes, all in different colors and with different embellishments.

Mahibah was the second oldest of their children, and the only daughter (her older brother was at college in Lebanon). She was in the 11th grade and intended to study pharmacy when she went on to a university. She and her mother both wore hijabs that hid their hair completely. They prayed on schedule, guests or no guests, but taking turns because of my visit. When Mahibah took her turn, Nadira and I sat over the tea and coffee at a literal loss for words, but we kept trying to chat. Mahibah spoke both Arabic and English fluently. I should have asked about French, just for the heck of it. Mahibah was a very nice girl; during lunch she turned to me and said, quietly, "I hope this food doesn't seem strange to you." I told her that I hoped it did, because if I wanted everything to seem familiar, then I should have stayed at home in America. That pleased the family.

They had obviously gone to some trouble to put on a delicious lunch, and we loved it. The lunch included: store-bought flatbreads; homemade Lebanese flatbreads; laban yoghurt; lamb kebabs on one round bread with one roasted tomato and one roasted red onion; a huge plate of small grape leaves filled with rice and tomato; another huge plate piled with rice and topped with slices of chicken and roasted cashews and peanuts; a smaller plate with potato fries, chicken, and tiny dumplings called kibbeh, shaped like footballs and filled with ground lamb; babaganoush, which is cold eggplant puree; hummus with olive oil on top; and a choice of orange juice, soda, or water. Everything was delicious.

Despite the determination of Mahibah and Nadira to do all the cleanup work, I helped clear the table. Then we headed back to the party. For dessert there were plates of pistachio baklava, plus 2 delicious recipes of homemade cookies: one kind was a hand-shaped oval coated with powdered sugar and full of pistachios, and the other kind was round, shaped by a mold, and full of fruit paste. All that was served in the living room with tea. (At last I tasted a local dessert, and it was delicious.) We chatted about wedding photos, school, etc. The men sat together at the cleared table discussing work, while the younger kids – 3 boys named Osama, Yaman, and Kamal (who had likely just started high school; he looked a little younger than Mahibah) disappeared. When it was over, Dr. Alim took us to see his office, which was nearby, with a view of the Gulf. Then our friend Assim Al-Tikriti picked us up.

It was a lovely party.

After a visit with Aiesha – because the next party was to be late in the evening – Assim was kind enough to take us to our next stop (and to retrieve the cell phone, which had fallen out of a hole in David's briefcase!). This was outside a Burger King in Salwa, where Mr. Hassan lived with his family. We rang in the New Year with them, and had a great time. And we met Spicy, their 7-month-old kitten. She was really cute – a fluffy calico with gray and beige spots, and huge, round golden eyes. They found her on their doorstep, which was 2 levels up – many apartment buildings in Kuwait are open from the ground level up through the stairwell – and when their 16-year-old daughter Sahar wanted her, they let her keep the kitten. Mr. Hussain met us and took us home, where Spicy, Sahar and Alima Basha, his wife, were waiting for us.

Here are: Spicy the calico kitten; the fake Christmas tree in a Muslim home; the New Year's cakes.

The apartment was beautifully decorated, with wall-to-wall carpeting in every room but the kitchen, Persian carpets, attractive furniture, pretty wall hangings of tapestry and framed artwork, tasseled cushions, and of all things, a Christmas tree! Apparently, many Egyptian people like to celebrate New Year's Eve with one, even though coniferous trees don't grow anywhere near the desert, and most Egyptians, including this family, are Muslim. The tree had all of the usual Christmas decorations: gold garlands, balls, etc. It was fake, of course.

A few minutes after we settled in, Shakir arrived, and after that the oldest child, Shakira and her husband, Tarif came over. They lived 3 blocks away, and Shakira would have their son in a few more days. They had been married for just a little more than a year, so we all had fun sharing wedding photos. Of course, being at home, Shakira could show us 2 full photo albums. We compared notes on how we had each made a few stylistic embellishments and additions to our gowns. Most women in this family of Egyptians did not cover their hair, I could see from the photos, though Alima did. One cousin, however, wore a full abbeya, hijab, and nekhab – all in white. When Shakir identified her, his sisters said, laughing, how do you know? He said it was easy – she was the only guest who wore all that stuff. More laughter.

Another thing of interest in the wedding photos was the belly dancer, who was hired as part of the entertainment. They also had a guy in funky sunglasses with a long ponytail who led what appeared to be a line dance. Everyone seemed to have had a lot of fun, and Shakira looked absolutely perfect. Now she was Sahar's high school computer teacher – poor Sahar – and would have a baby soon. Tarif was an engineer of some sort. He seemed very nice, and his in-laws liked him a lot. He was also rather quiet. The funniest thing about them was the fact that although they knew the gender of their baby, they had not chosen a name. Tarif thought something would occur to him when he saw the baby. [As it turned out, this did not help, so I joked that people would call them Umm and Abu Can'tMakeUpTheirMinds. The custom was to insert the child's name after Umm (Mother) and Abu (Father).]

Another person in the apartment was the maid. She was a cute little woman from the Philippines, and Alima told me that she had been studying at college there until a relative who was financing her studies suddenly died. Then she was forced to quit school, so she got a job as a live-in maid in Kuwait. What an upsetting story – she had had a chance at studying her way to a respectable job with opportunities for advancement, and bad luck ruined it. I went to the kitchen after midnight to give her a Happy New Year hug, as we were all making the rounds with them. I don't think anyone else did so.

Dinner was delicious. It consisted of: a turkey on a huge platter of saffron rice with lentils and golden raisins; more small stuffed grape leaves with rice and tomato inside; salad made of herbs and tomato and cucumber; and a spicy tomato-based sauce to pour onto the slices of turkey. There was plenty of bottled water, tea with milk, and 2 cakes for dessert. One was a chocolate cherry cake, and the other was a white cake with thick red fruit paste inside and on top, forming the numbers 2005.

No booze, of course. We found out what the problem is with Muslims and booze: prayers are said 5 times a day, leaving insufficient time in between for any consumed alcohol to leave one's system before the next round of prayers. Some Muslims try to beat this by having a drink immediately following a round of prayers, but who knows how effective this is.

Another family arrived just as we finished eating, and they immediately proceeded to eat. That family was Alima's friend, Asilah, a quiet, tall, thin, dignified, hijab-wearing lady, her husband, and 2 daughters, Shakira, and Manaal, who wore knee-length dresses with stockings, and wore their hair down long. They also had a son who was studying in the States. Her husband taught English at Kuwait University in Shuwaikh. Manaal was 19 or 20, and intended to study politics. She spoke perfect television English and told us that we said what everyone else who meets her says: that she would make a great newscaster. She had the demeanor of one.

Manaal and I got along quite well, and she talked with me all about something that I had wondered about since arriving in Kuwait: additional wives. This was a girl with monogamous parents, but she knew the cultural reasons for multiple wives, so I had a great discussion with her. Then she told us something about what had happened to David just before the Gulf War got underway, when he was with his army unit in Saudi Arabia: it was a common practical joke that Egyptian guys liked to play on foreign men.

We had a great evening there.

An Egyptian Practical Joke for Foreign Men

This joke is typically played by men on men. David had direct and bitter experience of it, but now that it is in his past, he considers it to be a great and funny story to tell. Manaal listened to the tale with amusement, and then explained that this is in fact an awful joke that is played over and over...

During the military buildup to the Kuwait War – also known as the Persian Gulf War of 1990-1991 – David was in Saudi Arabia with his unit, and he was lucky enough (!) to be assigned the task of liaison officer. This meant learning enough Arabic to communicate with the local population and the Saudi soldiers, in case the U.S. Army unit needed anything – which of course they soon would. Wars tend to lead to such things, after all.

Just before he went out among the Saudis to try to learn some Arabic, an Egyptian guy named Ahmed, who was working with David's unit, approached. He very helpfully offered David a list to carry around with him. David unfolded it and looked at it; it had one column of entries in English, and one in phonetic Arabic. The English column listed such useful phrases as "Hello," "Good day," "Please," "Thank you," and so on. David was very pleased, and thanked Ahmed. He stuffed the sheet of paper into his pocket and headed off down the main street of Riyadh.

He hadn't gotten far when he spotted a Saudi soldier. The guy was huge – well over 6 feet tall, with a cruel, handle-bar mustache, and of all things, an Israeli-made assault rifle slung over his shoulder. He stood silently on duty in the blithering heat, staring into space, minding his own business. He was a Bedouin tribesman, and David suspected that he had been selected solely on the basis of his imposing size.

David decided to try the words on the sheet of paper out on this guy.

He took out the list, looked for the Arabic entry across from "Good day," and saluted the Bedouin soldier smartly.

"Koos amuk!" David said with what he hoped was a friendly smile.

To his amazement, the reaction did not fit the English phrase. The Bedouin guy slowly shook his head from side to side, making a sound that Arabs make when they disapprove of something: "Tsk, tsk..." It sounds more like a clucking sound to me, though.

Puzzled, David took the list out again and scanned it.

Yep, there it was, just like he had said before.

He tried it again.

This time the reaction was a bit more pronounced; the Bedouin guy slowly and calmly took the Israeli assault rifle off of his shoulder, rode the bolt down to ready it for a shot, and pointed it at David.

David looked up at him in horror and confusion. Here he was on his first day as liaison officer, and he was about to get shot by one their own people, he thought – the Saudis were, after all, fighting on the same side as the Americans, the Europeans, and whomever else had gathered in Saudi Arabia to get the Iraqis out of Kuwait.

Before the situation had time to get any worse, a Saudi officer came tearing down the street (which sounds difficult to do, considering how hot it gets there – over 140°F). He spoke to the Bedouin guy, apparently ordering him not to shoot, and asking him why he was pointing his weapon at the American officer. They spoke briefly, and then he asked: "Lieutenant, what did you say to this man?"

"I thought I was just saying 'Good day', sir!" David said, and handed over the sheet.

The Saudi officer looked it over, turned pale, and inquired as to where David had gotten it. David told him.

"Lieutenant, do me a favor while you are in Saudi Arabia: never, ever, listen to an Egyptian."

David promised not to, and he found other means of learning Arabic.

When he got back to the base, he found Ahmed and took him aside.

Moving aside to where they would not be observed by passersby, David took out his pistol, cornered Ahmed, and held it up to his face.

"Ahmed," David said in his best menacing tone, "if you ever do that again…"

Sniveling like the wimp that he was, Ahmed swore not to mess with David ever again.

Hand-Holding Men in a Homophobic Culture

On one of my many visits with Assim and Aiesha, I was ready with a question for Aiesha, one that I had also asked Assim about in the car as he drove me over to see her.

The question was: what have they to say about Arab men holding each other's hands or wrists when walking together? Saleh sometimes tried to do it to David when leading him somewhere, and David figured that it must be a dominance thing on the part of whichever male is doing the wrist-holding. He never allowed it. I told both Assim and Aiesha about David yanking his hand or wrist free and saying, "That's Stephanie's job, Saleh!" and Saleh grunting his grudging assent to the rejection.

Both Assim and Aiesha knew about both hand-holding and kissing in greeting between Arab men, but neither is really in favor of it. Aiesha said that she doesn't see much of this, because she didn't go to the mall much, and Assim says that he just wasn't a touchy-feely person, and he didn't like to hold hands with men.

Seconds after we finished hashing out all of this, a news shot of Saudi Crown Prince Abdullah came on kissing George W. Bush and holding his hand on international television. We all roared with laughter at it, the timing was so perfect. It was almost as though the news story showed itself on cue for us. It fit perfectly into the stream of conversation. [And I was not pleased with Dubya for allowing it; an American President should never let a foreign king or prince lead him about like that.]

Joke: Is Sex Work or Fun?

Kuwait is a society in which most drudgery is done by foreign workers, so jokes such as this one are probably inevitable. The wind-up to this joke certainly should make mention of just how dependent upon foreign labor this little gas-station of a country is. This will have to do: No one has had to do any real work for 4 generations, thanks to the profits from drilling oil.

Question:
"Is Sex Work or Fun?"

American:
"It's fun, of course."

German:
Thinks about it a bit, then says, "Well, I work hard all day, then I come back home, and I still have obligations to my wife, so I think that making love to her is work."

Kuwaiti:
"Making love to my wife must be fun, because if it were work, I'd hire a Pakistani to do it."

American Celebrities

Apparently, we became celebrities among Mansoor's friends. We never knew anything about this until one evening when Mansoor told us that he had become quite popular at work, and that this was all because he was able to tell daily stories about how the Americans who lived in his building were doing, what we were doing, etc. It was as though Mansoor were his own one-man tabloid, with us as the hot item being reported on. It was surreal: people actually demanded that he tell them what David and Stephanie had been up to in the past 24 hours! What did we do for Valentine's Day? And so on... Unfortunately, they assumed that because we are Americans, we must have had wine and drugs in our apartment, and wanted to hear all about it. Their proverbial bubbles were promptly burst when Mansoor reported that we had nothing of that sort in our possession.

One afternoon over tea, oddly enough, the conversation turned to American Barbie dolls. Mansoor loves all things American, and I showed him my latest photos from Souq Sharq, which included plastic dolls dressed and painted as Kuwaitis of the past. This prompted me to write down a brief history of Mattel's Ken and Barbie dolls, which date back to the late 1950s, when the wife of the founder of Mattel Company created and named the dolls after her 2 children, Barbie and Ken. Mansoor was fascinated, and kept it.

Mansoor had thought that the dolls were husband and wife. Here is where a cultural lesson came along for him: Ken and Barbie are teenagers – probably 18 years old – and they are NOT married. They are dating! American teenagers do NOT get married – their parents expect them to just date, and put off marriage until their twenties, at least. Mansoor was fascinated, and wanted to buy a doll at Souq Sharq's Sultan Center. I promised go with him and show him the different dolls. He wanted to see if they really had dresses in colors besides pink. That is merely the most popular color, I told him, not the only one.

It is always fascinating to take a subject from one's culture at random, as we did, and see what meaning an outsider assigns to it. Without knowing the actual story, a Kuwaiti person can't help but apply their own cultural mores to it; unless and until an American explains things, they will continue to do so. Mansoor was fascinated by what I told him, and of course he accepted it. After all, I was the one who played with these toys as a child, not him. He didn't judge us or our American culture of dating as morally deficient, either. We were just different from him. It probably helped that he met us as a married couple, too.

Kuwaitis encourage their daughters to play with a different doll, also made by Mattel. Her name is Fulla, and she is made from the same mold as Barbie, but is sold only in Kuwait. She has waist-length black hair, brown eyes, and an olive complexion. She wears high-end designer clothing...under an abbeya and hijab. Both are black, with matching gold embroidery on the cuffs and collar of her abbeya and the ends of her hijab. She is a gorgeous and proper Islamic Kuwaiti woman.

I bought one of these dolls as a souvenir in the Sultan Centre store at Souq Sharq Mall. She cost 4 dinar and 600 fils as a souvenir that I had been considering for a while: a Fulla doll. The doll wears her hijab the way that my friend Aiesha does, with one side of the cloth much longer than the other, wound around her head, leaving a strip hanging loose on one side. I wanted a model of how a traditional Kuwaiti woman dresses to take home.

Fulla – the Islamic answer to Barbie. Shown next to the doll is the back of another doll's box, with various chic outfits that she might wear, all hidden under her abbeya and hijab.

Dolls weren't the only subject that we discussed with him this way: he wanted to know, hypothetically, what the cultural upbringing of American children was like, even though he knew that we planned on just having cats. He had assumed that if we had a child, she or he would automatically take only the father's culture, because that is what Kuwaitis do. "No," David said, "the kid would take both cultures, learning all about and internalizing both." Mansoor was surprised, but of course he believed us. Then we pointed something out to him that he hadn't considered: his dad was a Kuwaiti, but his mom was Egyptian, and he had already told us that he spoke Arabic with an Egyptian accent. No doubt he also knew what many Egyptian customs were, complete with the cultural backgrounds on them. Yes, that was true, he admitted. "So," we concluded, "you have absorbed both parents' cultures – you can't help it, because you inevitably spent time with both of your parents."

He agreed; it was true. Kuwaiti culture focuses on the father's culture, name and history, but children everywhere inherit their mother's culture and history too. Women are half of the world, so people can't help but absorb the cultural essence of the women in their own families.

"Excuse Me" – Sexual Harassment in Internet Cafés

Before Assim and Aiesha got a DSL Internet connection in their living room, we had no recourse but to patronize Internet cafés. Non-Kuwaitis without iqamas – work permits – could not get phone lines or Internet connections at home, so we were stuck whenever we needed to check our e-mail or do online banking.

At first we didn't know where in our area to go, so David asked around until a nice Indian guy in a phone store told us where we could find one called "Victoria," and even locked his shop to show us the way. We were the only people there, but it was still very nice of him to do that. I hated to think of snobby Kuwaiti attitudes towards Hindus, Pakistanis, Egyptians, Philippinos, Indonesians, and other foreign workers – we had just met one who was so helpful and friendly!

The Internet café was totally unmarked, so it was a very good thing that we had some help finding it. It was two floors up a small marble staircase with yellow painted railings, which led to a glass door with metal criss-crossed all inside the glass. This door led to a large billiards hall that was very dimly lit, where men sat smoking and watching television above a bar...and no doubt drinking non-alcoholic beverages. The bar was on the right. To the left, way in the back of the long, wide, room, I saw a few computers. We went over there and saw many more computers tucked away around the back walls of the pool hall. For ½ KD ($1.80), we used the Internet for 30 minutes.

During the time at the Internet café, I was annoyed by both the slowness of the computer and the failure of the disk drives, only to be further infuriated when David changed computers and sat across the room from me. In America, I would not have cared where he sat, but here, right on cue, the moment my husband moved to another seat, a 20something Kuwaiti kid in a gray dishdashah got right up and started trying to get my attention. "Excuse me, excuse me," he said. The Philippina girl who worked there – dressed in a tight red blouse with her hair down – came over to find out if his computer was working properly. It was – he paid no attention to her. He went back to his machine when I ignored him completely. Jerk – I was already frustrated at how slowly the computer was responding to my commands, and then he came over to try and distract me. Nuwwar, Fatin's daughter, had warned me about this – young men would try to harass any lone woman in public. The slightest response would just make it all worse.

Interview About Soccer – and Women

After I returned from Kuwait, I had a brief e-mail exchange with Assim about soccer. I was curious about it because I had realized that his little girl, Karidah, liked soccer as much as his boys, Hamid and Abdul Malik, did. He had mentioned once that he had taken them out to Kuwait's soccer stadium to watch a match, and that they had been thrilled when their team won. This made me wonder about Karidah – what if she wanted to go someday? Would he take her?

So I e-mailed him a list of questions, and he wrote back. His answers were in block capitals. As I expected, the outlook for Kuwaiti women seeking this sort of fun was grim – especially if they were his daughters. As it was, Aiesha never got control of her television.

Here is the Question-and-Answer list:

Do women attend soccer games in the national stadium in Kuwait?
NO – ONLY WHEN THE NATIONAL TEAM PLAYS. A SMALL NUMBER ATTEND.

Where exactly is this stadium? MANY PLACES.

Is it government controlled? YES.

And what is its name? WE ARE BUILDING NEW ONE CALLED JABER STADIUM.

Are women allowed to attend soccer games? YES.

Or do they not go to them because of custom? YES.

Rather than because of law? NO. IT IS A MEN'S GAME.

Bend It Like Beckham is a movie about women's soccer, yet from what you told me, you did not include Karidah in the trip to see that movie. She would have been 6 years old when it came out into the theaters. Why didn't you bring her to that movie, knowing that she likes soccer? Was it her age, or her gender, or both? **He didn't reply to this question.**

Do you ever keep her from attending an activity that she enjoys because of her gender – one that she could participate in if she were either male or from a family with a Western culture? **Or this one.**

Would you ever bring her to a soccer game in Kuwait? NO.

Or in the Western world – again, considering some of the above questions? YES.

Would you say that Karidah is as fascinated by soccer as Hamid and Malik are, or not? NO.

If so, do you think that she tries to dampen her own enthusiasm out of a sense that it isn't possible for her (cultural reasons) to enjoy the sport as fully as the boys can? NO.

Do you notice – and if you do, WHAT do you notice – women from other Arab/Kuwaiti families enjoying soccer? THEY WATCH ONLY AT HOME.

What I took from all this was that Assim would indulge most of his daughters' wishes if they happened to be in a culture where they blended into the general scheme of things, but not at home in Kuwait. In Kuwait, he would go with the conventional way of life and leave them at home most of the time, only sharing the thrills of the outside world with his sons. And the family was usually in Kuwait.

Awqaf, a.k.a. Big Brother

I got the distinct impression that Muslims were complacent about censorship in their culture – it was what they knew. Assim Al-Tikriti liked Awqaf versions of movies, preferring to have the swears, sex and kisses edited out for him, rather than being required to think and feel independently and decide what to ignore and what to consider. After several months away from home, I found myself looking forward to a summer in the U.S. so that I could catch up on all the movies and reruns of shows that I was missing in Kuwait, and see them in their uncut, original forms. Recently, an Awqaf version of an American movie came on. It wasn't a great movie, but Awqaf made it very confusing to follow by cutting out swear words, making messy chops in the film, and then having it repeat the words leading up to the removed profanity. It skipped and was dizzying to look at in those spots. Yet this was all fine with Assim! It was NOT fine with me, but it is typical of movie-watching experiences in Islamic societies.

The funniest instance of Awqaf's censorship was when David saw *The Blue Lagoon* on television in Kuwait. That movie is about a little boy and girl who get stranded on a tropical island, grow to be horny teenagers and best friends, then have sex on the island in great weather while spending most of their time scantily clad in rags. After whatever Islamic nation's Awqaf had finished with it, it was almost unrecognizable, and the plot no longer made any sense. All that had been chopped out. David would see a beach vista, followed by an abrupt and sharp move to yet another vista, and so on. He barely saw the cast. He started laughing, wondering what the point was to even broadcast this movie.

The Kuwaiti government pays a group of very pious (!) and very Islamic men to act as magic-marker wielding censors of all magazines, and another group of similar men to remove all sexually explicit and romantic scenes from movies and television shows before they are broadcast in the Middle East. Kuwait's government is not alone in this practice. It is standard throughout the Middle East. [In fact, most Western television programs and movies that we could find on our set in Kuwait were broadcast from Dubai, in the United Arab Emirates.]

I noticed that every bridal magazine for sale in Kuwait had at least one thick line of black magic-marker ink slashed across some unsuspecting model's cleavage. Other magazines were not exempt; it was merely easier to find evidence of Awqaf's vandalism by checking bridal magazines.

David said to look at my ruined *National Geographic* magazine as a souvenir of the Islamic world, so I will, but it amazes me that the

Awqaf clerics actually believe that someone might be turned on by the image of a naked, incompletely evolved, man. They have too much time on their hands, as my husband has said before.

Watching movies and television shows could thus be a frustrating experience, especially if one had not previously seen the movie at home in the Western world. If not, one would be forced to wonder what one was missing as a messy chop suddenly appeared in the middle of a scene, with swear words cut out or, if the scene involved sex (most disturbing to religious Muslims), or nudity (almost as bad), or romance (can't have men and women being quite so adoring towards one another – Allah must come first!), whole segments of dialogue and action missing. The viewer would have to guess what was missing each time this occurred.

And so it went.

Business Proposal: Lingerie Catalogues as Porn

Late one afternoon in April, David had a hilarious thing happen to him. A Saeedi man named Ahmed insisted that they meet, because it was "VERY important." Ahmed was a guy who David often saw in passing at one of the take-out joints in Abraq Shaitan. They would say hello and good-bye, and perhaps a few more friendly words. David agreed to meet him out of curiosity. Ahmed pulled up in his car and hurried David in, then took off down the street at a reasonable pace. David asked what the big deal was, and Ahmed started pulling some glossy, colored papers out of the back seat, showing him what he had in the car – pages from underwear and lingerie catalogues that were brought from the non-Islamic world. He sells them to other Saeedi guys!

His customers thought of these pages as pornography, and they actually bought them from him for what they saw as a cheap thrill. These catalogues are given away or mailed to people free of charge in the U.S. – and Ahmed sells them here. He said, "Dr. David, we can make money from this!" He wanted David to send him more when we return home, so that he could sell them to other guys and then share the miniscule proceeds. How absurd! Awqaf would be sure to put a stop to this, even though it is basically nothing. If this is the best that these guys can do to find and enjoy the forbidden, then it's pretty sad. I could hardly wait to go home and, among other familiar things, peruse my next Victoria's Secret catalogue, and then throw it away – yet that small thing was contraband in Kuwait.

Insh'allah Bokram'allesh

"God willing, maybe tomorrow." This is a common and infuriating Kuwaiti response to almost everything. It differs from the response of many other Middle Easterners, which leaves it at "Insh'allah" – thus giving the listener a sense of hope that whatever is being asked for might actually be done.

Kuwaitis are terrible about getting work done. They hire people to do their college term papers for them. They have free health care from cradle to grave at the expense of the government which, thanks to oil, is well able to afford it. They can get government jobs and expect job security because of preferential treatment over more competent foreigners. If they want to become rich as individuals, however, they must expend a bit more effort, taking risks through investments or working hard at whatever profession or task matters to them. Otherwise, they can just sit back, relax, take long breaks from work, take naps, and maybe, eventually, get around to doing whatever they have agreed to do…or not.

The women are a bit more motivated to work, but that is only because of gender roles; I am referring to housework and child care. Even with a maid, they still do some housework and watch their children personally.

"This is not prayer!" No kidding...

David went out running and exercising. As I was finishing up my shower, he suddenly came upstairs, laughing. He had been doing some callisthenic exercises in front of our building when he noticed 2 Yemeni kids – he recognized the accent – copying him. He thought, "good, people in this country are too fat, it's good to see them exercising." That didn't last long, though, because their dad, a short guy who only came up as far as David's chin suddenly raced up to the kids, yelled at them, and then went over to David.

He was still yelling. The Yemeni guy screamed in Arabic, "What is this?! This is not prayer!" David started laughing and couldn't stop, so he ran into the building and took the elevator upstairs to tell me all about it…definitely a hilarious cross-cultural encounter.

Forms of Islamic and Arab Dress

Early on in my visits with Aiesha upstairs, I thought to ask about all the names of Arab dress for both men and women. Assim and Aiesha both answered me, and I took notes – they didn't mind my questions and curiosity.

Women wear: 1. an abbeya – a long, black robe that goes over whatever they are wearing to hide their body shape; 2. a hijab – a scarf that covers their ears and hair; 3. a nekhab – a veil across their faces. None of these things are dictated by Kuwaiti law, and I see either the absence of a nekhab (most common), or no abbeya but a hijab over hair.

Men wear: 1. a dishdashah – a long robe-like shift, often made of the same sort of cloth that business suits are made of; 2. a khaffiah – the white hair net that goes under the outer parts of headwear to keep it all in place; 3. a guthra – the long cloth, either white or red-checked but also in other designs, that goes over the khaffiah; 4. an ekal – the [usually] black rope-like fastener that holds the guthra in place.

When all notes had been carefully taken and understood, Aiesha asked me whether I had always been interested in cultures other than my own, or had I been directed to learn these things? I replied that I have always liked to learn these things, my whole life, and I like it best when I can do it by talking directly with people from other cultures. Reading is good, but talking face to face with people is the best. She seemed very pleased about it, and glad to know me. I like her.

When Assim had picked me up, he had stopped briefly to look at some papers with me and describe what they were about. As he did so, he noticed that his pen was missing (I found it when we stood up). I said, "Do you mean that fancy one that you keep in your pocket? I've noticed that every Arab guy in a dishdashah has one really nice-looking pen – just one – in the upper pocket of his dishdashah." Assim said yes, he meant that one, and that it was part of Kuwait's bullshit culture. This, of course, was very interesting to hear. What did he mean by a bullshit culture?

He told me that Kuwaitis show off by wearing expensive wristwatches and keeping expensive pens in their pockets, and that he did what the other guys did. [He had literally bought into his own "bullshit" culture by buying an expensive pen and wristwatch, despite this view...just to blend into it.] I asked him how expensive the pens and watches typically are, because one person's idea of expensive may be another person's idea of cheap or moderate.

Assim told me that his pen, a Mont Blanc, cost $250, and the watch, Swiss by Ekel, was $1,500 – but that was nothing to what some other guys would pay. Sometimes a guy will carry a $400 pen and wear a $6,000 watch, just to show off. And then there is the matter of one's car: Kuwaitis notice each other's cars and talk about them, so they like to have a Mercedes or a Jaguar that is only a few years old at most – a Toyota or a Nissan just won't do.

This business of showing off explains why Kuwaiti bother to dress up to go out to the mall. It was amazing to see all this effort in a culture in which dating was forbidden: girls and women with beautiful makeup, high heels, and long, flowing designer clothing trolling the malls, while guys in designer sneakers, jeans and shirts or dishdashahs with gel in their hair eye them. But they are not supposed to approach each other – that is haram – bad.

Perfection of appearance is a must in this culture, even for men. The trouble with this is that when Kuwaiti men wear Western clothing, they look too perfect, right down to the gel in their hair, with not one out of place. This is fine at home in Kuwait, but if they dress like this in the West, they might be mistaken for gays, even though this is the standard look for straight guys at home. It didn't stop with the hair; their shirts were rather tightly fitted. American men wear looser tee shirts, for example. (If I needed to get David any new clothes, I wouldn't be able to find the right things in Kuwait, I realized.)

Because Kuwaiti men no longer wove bishts, no apprentices had taken up the trade. Bishts are wool jackets that are worn over dishdashahs. They come in varying colors and thicknesses, and are embroidered around the edges with gold thread. Now they are mostly just seen at weddings, worn particularly by grooms, but every day by members of the royal family. Mansoor told us that they are very expensive, running into the thousands of dinars. His brother-in-law had only one; it was bright blue and cost close to four thousand dinars. Incredible – you would expect royalty to spend that much on a piece of clothing, but not regular people. So Kuwaitis had gotten into the habit of buying foreign-made bishts, and it was a dying art.

David has a brown one and a black one – I like the black one – given to him by a Saudi man. I knew that Saudis often had money to burn, but this sounded like a pair of rather expensive gifts! David felt bad about them once he realized that the guy had spent so much for them. The last time he wore one was at Hallowe'en in Connecticut. I wore my homemade witch cape – a beautiful thing with gold-on-black zodiac patterns – and David wore a dishdashah, bisht and guthra with an ekal. We were giving the candy to trick-or-treaters at my grandmother's house. We had fun, but we also had no clue that David's costume was so expensive!

An Autographed Ostrich Egg

One day, Hamid Al-Qasim, the guy who invited us to the Wafra Oasis, sent his driver to our place with a really cool gift: an autographed ostrich egg! It was huge – 8 inches across, and heavy. It had a thick, yellowish shell, and Hamid had used a bright blue felt-tip pen to write on it. Mohsen looked at it and held it, and told us that his father once ate one, and that it was a meal on its own. Saleh saw it, too, when he came over. He looked impressed, of course. It was hard not to be. I took several photographs of it with our cat, in her bed, and a few more on the contrasting blue blanket of our bed.

Scheherazade Cat in her bed with the ostrich egg, some catnip toys, and her own newspaper story.

David intended to have holes drilled in either end to drain out the contents, and then preserve the egg shell. It would make a cool souvenir from Kuwait if we could get it home without breaking it. (We never did it, but it was a fine idea while it lasted.)

Getting Pulled Over in Kuwait

Out on the highways of Kuwait, I once noticed a police officer who had pulled over a driver on the side of the highway. The whole procedure – or lack thereof – looked very odd. The cop did have the cruiser's red-and-blue lights on, but he was parked *beyond* the car of the civilian. In America, he would pull up *behind* the civilian's car. Odder still, the civilian was out and standing next to the police cruiser. David said that this is a courtesy, a show of respect to the cop. It seemed like a huge risk for the cop to take – what if the person walked up to the cruiser window and shot the cop, I wondered? In the U.S., the highway patrol officers approach the car themselves, with one hand on their guns, and the other shining a flashlight into the car. Everything was opposite here, it seemed.

Cultural Misperceptions

Assim and I sometimes joked about perceptions about different cultures showing up in conversations when we travel. As a Kuwaiti, he had met Americans who imagined that he must be a billionaire, because he is from Kuwait, which has black gold – oil. That does not mean that he personally enjoyed that wealth. No – oil wealth is the property of the Kuwaiti government, which spends it on education and health care for its citizens.

As an American, I got other reactions from Kuwaitis. For example, the assumption I found at parties was that I must love Coca-Cola, because I am an American. Truth be told, I can't stand the stuff, and never could. Give me bottled water or fruit juice or tea or coffee, and I'm perfectly comfortable. But I hate the fizz and brown syrup of soda. It takes a lot of convincing to make people give the idea up – I just say that I am a very strange Westerner or American, and that seemed to end it more quickly.

Religiosity

One evening, I asked Assim and Aiesha what the 5 prayer times are for Muslims. I knew that there are 5 times during the day, but that was all. Aiesha and her younger boys explained it to me, and even showed me that the exact ones are published each day in an Arabic newspaper. These times are changed by a few minutes each day as the seasons change, thus affecting the times that the sun rises and sets. But to state the times simply, they are: 1. sunrise; 2. noon; 3. mid-afternoon; 4. sunset; 5. late evening.

The April 5th "Day by Day" report, which appeared, as its name implied, in each issue of *The Arab Times*, was brief and to the point, offering comments on an aspect of present-day Kuwaiti life and culture. The final news item was that an Egyptian imam had been reported as having punched a worshipper in the face...for waking him up to pray! It seemed that the guy was late for Al-Fajr prayers. This made me curious, so I turned to page 2 of the day's paper and looked at the prayer times and their names. Just for fun, I copied them into my journal:

        Fajr......................4:13 a.m.
        Sunrise..................5:34 a.m.
        Zohr.....................11:51 a.m.
        Asr.......................3:23 p.m.
        Maghrib................6:06 p.m.
        Isha.....................7:27 p.m.

It was immediately obvious why the imam was sleeping when the late worshipper disturbed him. Thinking about it just a bit more suggested 2 things: 1. of course an imam would get up, conduct services, and then go back to sleep for a while with a work schedule like this one; 2. perhaps the worshipper could have skipped the early prayers...or not. I suppose it would have worried him.

The next thought that occurred to me was – why, if Muslims are expected to pray 5 times each day, were there 6 prayer times on this list? It was like this every day. It turned out that the sunrise prayer was the extra one, though I never found out what the reason for it was. The other words needed translation: fajr = dawn; zohr = midday; asr = afternoon; maghrib = sunset; isha = night. There were other prayers for Eid – and there were different Eid celebrations in different Islamic countries. The Kuwaitis celebrated the standard one, Eid Al-Fitr, which dealt with the end of Ramadan, the holy month during which Muslims must not eat, drink anything (not even water) or have sex during daylight. No wonder they celebrated the end of that month – it must get terribly uncomfortable to the point of dehydrating, and so many of them live in arid regions.

Prayer Calluses

Everywhere we went in Kuwait, we would see a few people with an odd, permanent discoloration on their foreheads. Not everyone had this, but enough of them did to cause me to notice and comment to

David. They were prayer calluses, and the word in Arabic for that is "zebibah". Any worshipper who has repeatedly pounded their head onto either the ground or prayer stones has built up a callus of thick, dead skin in that spot, with residue from the stone permanently ground into it. Anyone could have one, from a woman with heavy makeup on her beautiful face to an older man in a polo shirt and khaki pants.

Some people seemed proud of their calluses – oddly un-Islamic.

But, I am an atheist. I observe. It's all interesting to me.

Houri – The Islamic Heaven Fantasy

The Islamic heaven fantasy is that when someone dies, if they have been a devout Muslim, they shall be waited upon by many gorgeous, voluptuous, lovely-eyed, virgin women. If the deceased is male, they will also have sex with him. If the deceased is female, she will have the maid service, but know that her husband is having his way with the houri.

The exact number of houri per person is not specified in the Quran: the numbers suggested to me were 40, 70, and 77. It certainly didn't sound as though a bevy of hot guys were waiting in heaven to spoil devout Muslim women when they died. Only men got sex in heaven.

Hajj

There is holy water flowing from a spring called ZamZam at Mecca. The spring flows in an area that is now underground, thanks to the many additions and renovations made since Mecca was established as a holy place in A.D. 632. ZamZam is one of a Muslim's first stops on Hajj. A woman who has made Hajj is called Hajjiah; a man is called Hajji.

The spring first began to flow above ground some millennia ago when Abraham's – well, Jews and Christians say slave, and Muslims say second wife, so who knows which is true – slave/second wife, Hagar, and her son, Ishmael, arrived at the place in the Arabian desert which is now called Mecca, and they needed water rather desperately. Legend has it – the story being written in the Torah, the Bible, and the Quran – that Hagar ran frantically up and down seven times and then, miraculously, water began to flow up out of the rocks in the desert. Her problem was solved.

Muslims are required to wash themselves before praying in any mosque (ablutions), and all of them have areas designated for this express purpose – usually just huge areas with sinks – one for women, and one for men. At the shrine at Mecca, they have the spring of ZamZam. I found a great book about all this in The Kuwait Bookstore – full of photos – called *Mecca The Blessed, Medina The Radiant: The Holiest Cities of Islam* book which said that worshippers are supposed to wash themselves at ZamZam before visiting the Ka'bah inside the holy shrine. It didn't mention any gender segregated spots there, and it said nothing about drinking the water from the spring – only washing at it was mentioned.

Women go to ZamZam to wash, then continue straight on to the shrine, where they worship separately from the men, except when circumambulating seven times counterclockwise around the Ka'bah. They do not change their clothing. They wear their best clothing, but it must cover all but their hands and faces. Even women who usually wear nekhabs over their faces do not wear them on Hajj. All adornments – except for wedding rings and watches, I noticed from photographs – must go.

Men have a different routine: they wash at ZamZam and change out of regular clothing and into two huge, seamless white cloths called an ihrām. One cloth goes around their waists, the other like a sash and shawl around their shoulders, usually leaving one shoulder exposed. When the Hajj is complete, the ihrām is then removed, washed at the ZamZam spring, and put away to be used as the Hajjī's death shroud. [Muslims wrap dead bodies in white cloths before burying them.]

Saleh returned from his latest Hajj – he has gone to Mecca several times, as Kuwait is next door to Saudi Arabia – with a bottle of ZamZam water for us. He had filled a water bottle with it after drinking the contents. We called Mansoor, poured some into glasses, and then drank the water, considering it carefully. It flows from some rocks, so it had a hard, mineral-like taste. I didn't love it, but it wasn't bad. David has a thoroughly undiscriminating palate, so he had to take my word for it. Mansoor simply said that he didn't like it (he hadn't been on Hajj yet).

Mohsen, Saleh's 4th son, told me that no radio equipment or other communications technology works at Mecca. Perhaps the rocks around ZamZam have something to do with this, but it seems unlikely that the Al Sa'ud family (the royal family of Saudi Arabia), the official guardians of Mecca, would ever allow any geoscientists or other scientists to analyze this. I for one am quite convinced that there is some scientific explanation for this – or maybe it's caused by the meteor on the southeast corner of the Ka'bah. That's the part that the worshippers try to touch. They also do so at other times, when they go alone or in less crowded times, at random. That's called making Umrah.

Seeing no point in debating this with a devoutly Muslim 16-year-old boy, I told Mohsen that God must have decided to keep people off the airwaves around Mecca during prayers, which are said 24 hours a day, 7 days a week, all year round there. That would mean that no one can ever use the airwaves there. He agreed – it must be true. God would not want any distractions from prayers.

A Hussainiya

Shia Muslims have places where they can hold meetings and arrange Hajj trips (by bus). They are called Hussaniyas, after the martyr Hussain, who was a grandson of the Prophet Mohammed. Hussain got killed in a battle fighting over the schism that led to separate branches of Islam: Sunni and Shia. Most of Kuwaitis, including the Al-Sabah royal family, are Sunni, but some are Shia, including our friend Saleh, the immunologist.

With my curiosity and David's willingness to answer all of my questions – plus a few trips outside to check on me and see how I was doing waiting all alone in the car – I managed to understand what the place was all about. It was a religious diwaniya, held in a social mosque called a Hussainiya. These gatherings are held in a building that is named in honor of the Hussain, who would have led some ancient caliphate if he hadn't been murdered/martyred along with his whole family in Karbala, Iraq, before he could take office. David informed me that images of male prophets were hung up inside the building, especially in the room where the Hussainiya is held (Islam does have some female prophets, but not too many).

One evening I wound up waiting for what was absolutely, no doubt about it, an extremely rude amount of time to have to wait – in the car, alone, needing a bathroom, wondering when Saleh would be ready to leave. He had stopped there with David on the way back from someplace else, to do what he usually did in the evenings: attend yet another diwaniya and network for business contacts.

He should have done this some other night, when I was already comfortably at home. The evening proved to be one Islamic-culture insult to me after another, as did the ride home in Saleh's car. Women are not welcome at diwaniyas, let alone religious diwaniyas. I found myself stuck and infuriated by this gross lack of consideration, and decided to do what I could to give Saleh some grief over this. I succeeded rather well, if I do say so myself.

The front of the Hussainiya, with a wall in front of the entrance, and a seating area off to the left. The door with the light-blue paint on its metalwork was on the side, and led to the bathroom that I might have been able to enter if only I had worn a scarf over my hair...which I didn't have, and didn't want. I had no idea we were going here.

When all was said and done, I had no regrets: not even about having been to the outside of the place, because I learned what a Hussaniya was, something that I would never have learned about or collected photos of unless this had happened.

Assim had dropped me and David off at the place and then gone off to celebrate Safa'a's 5th birthday. Later, after he heard what happened, he said he wished that he had just brought me with his family to enjoy the birthday party. I'm glad he didn't; as much as it meant to me and Safa'a that a little girl get her due share of attention and fun, I needed to learn about a Hussainiya, and I would have hated hearing him talk in a high-pitched voice to her for the rest of the evening (so many people address little kids as though they are imbeciles!).

Meanwhile, about the religious diwaniya: I did not know what it was until after I had been outside this building for perhaps 20 minutes. All I knew was that Assim drove us there because we were going to meet Saleh. We arrived maybe 25 minutes before Saleh did, so Assim waited with us until he appeared, and then drove off to meet his family.

First, an explanation of this Shi'a Muslim gathering is necessary. It's always nice to know what's going on around you, and to understand as much of it as possible. Assim told us what the place was before leaving, and said that Shia Muslims are a religious minority, so don't talk about Hussainiyas much. Odd – the whole country is Muslim, I thought. What could happen? But I didn't mention it to any Sunni friends.

Once I realized that I was being made to wait outside because I am female, I resented it with all the anger I could muster. I was being kept out in the chilly night, watching men enter and exit this building, to maintain a bastion of religious male chauvinism.

These interesting vehicles were parked outside: the one on the left was a Hajj bus, with curtains for a hot, sun-beaten ride through the Saudi deserts to and from Mecca; the one on the right was a Red Crescent ambulance. That made perfect sense: in the Western world, we have the Red Cross, so why not the Red Crescent, the Islamic religious symbol, in the Middle East?

David thought that I might be allowed in if I wore a hijab, but I was not in the habit nor did I intend to take up the habit of carrying a head scarf around in my bag. Assim Al-Tikriti actually suggested this idea to me over the phone earlier that day, but I'd be damned if I'd cater to what felt like sexist customs. It would feel like acquiescing to an insult.

David is a good husband; he concerned himself with my opinion, mood, comfort and curiosity, and kept checking on me. He also told me that it was really boring in there, but he did find a canteen where he bought a lovely bag of shelled pistachios, so it couldn't be all that bad inside.

Men kept arriving with suitcases, and I asked Assim about it. He told me that this place arranged Hajj trips, and then I noticed 2 long buses parked across the alley next to the building, with curtains in every window. [The curtains were for shielding against the extreme desert heat, not to hide women.] So those men had a place to stay overnight until it was time to go on the Hajj. Where did the women from far away stay? Did it cost them more money than the men's place? Did they even have a place? Assim didn't know. Lots of men don't bother to get answers to questions that don't concern them...yet another reason why women need to vote!

One man, dressed in Western clothing, kept going in and out. He might have been an Indian servant, or an Arab. I just couldn't tell. It was annoying enough that he kept watching me. I took several photos of the place. I was particularly determined to do so after Assim informed me that it wouldn't be appreciated. Assim, Saleh and David had left me bored for who knew how long, so I didn't care about the wishes of this little religious boys' club. In fact, I thought that that was all the more reason to take pictures for my journal – exclusionary customs make for interesting reading and viewing.

The building looked rather mundane. It was hung with some banners in Arabic. It also had bright lights illuminating the surrounding area, and beautiful tiles all around the main entrance. Teenage boys kept coming and going – perhaps they would go on a Hajj next week, though I could only guess; they seemed to be staying in that building. It had 2 upper stories, which were the hostel. There was a public water fountain with a cholera-spreading cup to share, and some swing sets.

Saleh finally showed up and gave me his car keys so I could sit inside his car after Assim drove off. He told me that if I needed a bathroom, I could go in through the side entrance to one, but "don't invade the shrine!" I told him that I didn't need a bathroom. No way was I about to go inside where a bunch of self-satisfied jerks would hassle me. I was just glad my bladder was empty.

A shrine?! Assim explained over the phone the next day that Hussainiyas are by definition shrines, and treated like mosques, even if no prophet has ever lived or died in them. I decided to make myself comfortable in the front seat of Saleh's car, the better to view everything that went on. I had a vague inkling that this would give Saleh some grief from his Shia peers – payback for leaving me there (insert evil grin here).

Sure enough, as if that wasn't obnoxious enough, when Saleh and David were finally ready to go, Saleh was upset that I was in the front seat. Some Arab guys had seen me there when they came out, so they had teased Saleh when they went back in. The cultural implication is that if a woman who is not his wife sits in the front seat, something illicit might be going on between them. Even Saleh knew that they knew that no such thing is going on! He just couldn't take the teasing. My husband was in there with them, so it was perfectly obvious that everything was as it ought to be and not otherwise. I felt no guilt over this whatsoever.

So they came outside, and David got into the back seat. Saleh got in and demanded that I switch to the back too, saying that he was going to pick up some potential financer for our clinical laboratory. Feeling extremely ill-used and rather insulted at this point, I moved to the back next to David. Saleh drove off, and never picked up anyone! He made it up to get me out of the front seat, and we felt odd sitting back there together, like Saleh was our chauffeur or something.

It got better, too – Saleh told a friend over his cell phone that "Stephanie doesn't care about our customs," as the guy teased him about me sitting in the front seat while I waited. I scolded him well – I told him that I am not indifferent to Arab customs, or Islamic customs. He only vaguely seemed to understand, so I elaborated: I care about all of their customs, and find them quite fascinating. I also care about how I am treated, and expect some sensitivity in return.

No, saying that I did not care was inaccurate. I cared very much. I cared every time I saw women not being treated as though their comfort, convenience and wishes counted equally with that of men.

We were starting to have some serious trouble getting along with Saleh. I would not have babies, wear a hijab, or put up with any of his nonsense. I have to be able to feel a sense of self-respect, and putting up with nonsense would seriously menace my ability to do so.

David was very annoyed at Saleh, and although Saleh would not have any trouble with other Kuwaitis about Americans, he was complaining a lot to us. He was like a big kid who wanted his own way. David was in Kuwait to work, but he never puts his career ahead of his wife's sense of dignity and comfort. I could not have traveled with him otherwise.

A Little Girl's 5th Birthday

About Safa'a's 5th birthday: it was duly celebrated after I was dropped off with David to wait and wait at that Hussaniya. There had been some doubt about that as the evening had progressed at Assim and Aiesha's place, but I did not just let it slide while yet another little girl in the world got ignored in favor of a brother.

She was very quiet and not at all demanding about it, even while her father seemed to be focused almost exclusively on helping her older brother. If Assim wanted us to come over and counsel his oldest son about study skills, he could not expect any of his daughters to take a back seat. I refused to participate in letting a girl be treated as less important than a boy – ever. And she was so good! She smiled all the time, and climbed up onto Hassan's lap and smiled at him. You reap what you sow in this life: Hassan went out and bought her a new Barbie doll for her birthday. She liked it. As for the other kids, Aiesha, David, and me, we all sang *Happy Birthday* to her. That helped.

Assim, however, barely thought of this 5th birthday. Aiesha told me that because it was winter break for so many families, only 3 other children had been in school that day, and all of them had happened to be boys. So she did not bother with cupcakes or cake for just 4 little kids and none of Safa'a's girl friends. She was promising Safa'a a weekend party in the women's diwan with lots of little girls.

Meanwhile, there was talk of going to Safa'a's favorite pizza place with just the family for dinner, so that her birthday would have some fanfare. The poor kid fell asleep on the sofa, waiting and hoping while her father talked loudly downstairs with his mother and brother, oblivious. He was still thinking about Hassan.

After about 45 minutes of this, I went downstairs in my socks, knocked, and smiled at him and his mother. Then I told him that Safa'a was very worried that he wasn't going to pay any attention to her 5th birthday, and that she really wanted her father to acknowledge it, and that she thought they were going out for pizza. He came upstairs right away and shouted "Happy Birthday!" and admired the doll. Then he and David started discussing an apartment or other alternative to the dorms for Hassan! Really – that could be continued after pizza, I thought.

I interrupted by scolding David, informing him that little kids usually go to bed early, it was getting later and later, and Safa'a hadn't had a pizza for her birthday yet. Assim said that this was much more important, whereupon I countered with, "What could possibly be more important than a little kid's birthday?!" After all, I have yet to meet a little kid who would understand being ignored or brushed aside like that. They gave in…sort of. But it was enough. After a few telephone calls to the States to see about the apartments, it was decided that they would stop, try a letter the next day, and go out for Safa'a's pizza.

Hassan drove his mother and younger siblings to the restaurant, while Assim drove us to a diwaniya – one with a religious twist. He met his family later on at a Lebanese restaurant (Safa'a preferred this to the pizza place, it turned out), and they all celebrated properly. Assim even ordered a big, fancy birthday cake (secretly), so that Safa'a had a thrilling surprise when it was brought.

Aunt Fill-in-Her-Name Will Take Care of You

I came across an article on the last page of *The New York Times Magazine* – that I must have brought from the United States to Kuwait and discovered sometime later – about riding the subway in Egypt. An American woman had written it after doing that. In it, she described a Middle Eastern custom aimed at discouraging naughty behavior in children, and at enlisting help with general child care from the nearest female adults in proximity: they call that woman "aunt" and try to lay a guilt-trip on a child for whatever misbehavior, or they just say "This is Aunt Fill-in-Her-Name – she'll take care of you," if her name is known and she will be around for a while.

Interesting...and I have seen something similar done here and there in my own country, but not as a general rule or custom.

When I read that article, I promised myself that I would not cooperate with any "aunt" traps, no matter who laid one for me. I even warned David. He is less tense about pressure to like and interact with kids. With that baggage not even present, he gets along with them well enough – as long as the kids leave after a while.

Travel is an adventure – a chance to see, hear, smell, taste and experience new things: museums, history lessons, and sociological intrigue, other unfamiliar places, new music or customs, musks and perfumes and aromas of a visited culture's foods, eating the foods themselves, and conversations about how people think and why they do whatever they do in their everyday lives. There is always something that differs from the way I am used to seeing things done at home.

I just wouldn't let the culture that I was observing pull me out of that role involuntarily.

Voluntarily leaving that role would be another issue entirely, however. I never pretended to be solely an academic, inflexibly invisible to the people I was writing about. I intended to let them observe me, and learn about me when the opportunity arose. And they were curious to do so on many occasions, as time went on. More on this as my story continues – later.

For Lack of an Iqama

An iqama is a work permit, issued to foreigners so that they may work in Kuwait. We never got those. We were there off the grid, and we found out halfway through our stay that the visas that the Kuwaiti airport officials issued to us upon our arrival in the terminal were only valid for 3 months. We did not have the funds to exit and return to Kuwait, either. It was suggested that we fly to Bahrain and back. Too much money!

And forget asking me to cross the border into Saudi Arabia. I was horrified by the mere thought of doing so: before entering any Islamic nation, I researched the laws concerning women in Kuwait, its abutting neighbors (Saudi Arabia and Iraq – totally unsafe there. If I were to so much as enter Saudi Arabia, I would have to be wearing an abbeya and a hijab.

That wasn't the only thing wrong with going there: Saudi Arabian law expects a husband to hold custody of his wife's passport. The officials would snatch the documents from us, process them, and then hand them back to David! If I tried to take my own passport back, the official wouldn't even glance at me (making eye contact with a forbidden woman is un-Islamic anyway). I would be David's prisoner if I went there! So forget it. I wouldn't even go. There are some adventures that I do not wish to experience.

Not to worry; the Al-Hamdullilah family sorted it out; we gave them our passports for a week or so, and a well-connected cousin with friends in the business community got them stamped with new visas allowing us to stay until our plane tickets back to the U.S. came due.

But we never got work permits, despite their best efforts. That was too complicated, because my husband's work was of the independent, by-contract sort. We were in Kuwait so that he could do an asthma study with his old immunology colleague, and so that he could learn whatever he could about the nutraceuticals of the region: food, herbal treatments, etc. That was officially what brought us to Kuwait. As his wife, my presence was easily justified and explained. As an individual, I set myself the task of keeping a detailed journal about my experiences, studying Kuwait's culture and history, and chronicling it all with my digital camera. I would have plenty of material for a book – a travelogue – when I came home. I was not just a tag-along wife with no career or interests of my own. David thought it was great, and so did I.

The only problem was David's constant hope that we would, in fact, get iqamas. What then? What sort of work might I hope to get? I knew that the Kuwaiti work-week ran from Sundays to Wednesdays, so a paying job could as easily leave me with an Islamic work-week schedule as it could a Western one (both kinds existed there). What upset me was what was always, without fail, suggested as just about the only sort of job I might be able to get in Kuwait: teaching little kids, which I have no training or interest in. It was enough to make me determined to work on adult things for free, hoping to get by on contract writing and editing jobs. Perhaps a university might have a place for me? That might work...

Well, it didn't matter. Despite the fact that I had college-level teaching experience on my curriculum vitae, no iqamas ever materialized, and we went back to our home country after 6 months. I really wasn't at all upset about that. I had my book notes, and an experience that most Americans would never have.

Bedouns a.k.a. Beepnies

Once, as we waited on a busy street for a ride, we saw several pickup trucks driven by Arabs with red-checked guthras. The trucks were all white, and were painted with orange and brown stripes on the sides. The drivers went up and down the street, slowing down and stopping for people – usually men – who were waiting at curbs, perhaps for buses or taxis. The drivers also beeped a lot as they approached. They were using their trucks as unofficial taxis.

David told me about them. These people are called Bedouns (not Bedouin – those Arabs are nomads *with* passports), and Bedoun means "without." They are without a country, without citizenship, so getting a job is impossible. They survive by driving others around in their trucks. They are usually from Iran, Iraq, and Saudi Arabia, but sometimes from Kuwait.

How did they end up without a country? David told me that it was just general selfishness on the parts of their governments to have not bothered about them. Americans call them "Beepnies" because they beep their horns so much.

Looking for Books, Not Men!

Fatin and I went out to the Virgin Megastore – a bookstore – in the Marina Crescent Mall one afternoon in mid-April. The store had been totally rearranged, with the fiction department placed in an upstairs area with a new café – just like Borders Books and Music in the U.S. To get to it, it was necessary to climb a set of stairs and peruse books while looking over a balcony at the rest of the store.

Fatin was left looking at cookbooks and other things downstairs, where a mall security guy in a white dishdashah was pacing around, staring at everyone. Poor Fatin – when I came back down with the books I wanted, she was upset. She had convinced herself that the men in the store believed that she was alone, in search of a man for an illicit rendezvous!

I refrained from telling her to relax. Instead, I reassured her that logically this could not be the case – that she could easily conclude this by recalling that the security guy informed her that I was upstairs when she started looking around for me. "She's upstairs," he had said. I must say that this was the first time that I had ever gone out anywhere with another woman and had her worry about such a thing.

This is a well-educated, professional woman who looks chaste and respectable, and still she had worried that she might be projecting an appearance of impropriety. How anyone could get that idea seemed beyond comprehension to me.

Baba Nayim...

One Thursday morning, David and Saleh attempted to do the impossible: hold a meeting with both his brother, Salman Al-Hamdullilah. The purpose of the meeting was to discuss some great idea of Salman's about funding for the clinical laboratory from someone in the United Arab Emirates – without losing a huge chunk of the profits and being thereby reduced to the level of mere employees.

(Eventually, however, we understood something: Salman had absolutely no intention of helping. In fact, he liked to make a sport of stringing people along with false hopes.) Saleh showed up early that morning to pick up David, and they went to Salman's house in Rumaithiya. So the toughest part was solved – all three guys were in the same place.

However, Saleh had just been stuck by Raidah with child-care duty: he had his out-of-control 5-year-old grandson with him. The kid shrieked his lungs out whenever either of the men attempted to speak, and he was stuffed with sweets, bouncing all over the place. (David described the scene later.)

They were shown into the house's diwan, and there they sat – for 2 hours. Salman was home, but seeing him was impossible, because he had fallen asleep, and his servants kept saying "Baba nayim," meaning "Father is asleep." Saleh wouldn't let David go and wake him up. "Don't invade!" he kept saying.

Late in my time in Kuwait, I learned that being asleep was a common ploy that men used to avoid people who were trying to reach them; it might or might not be true, but if it was, any servant who attempted to disturb a sleeping boss risked a beating. So it really worked very well as a diversion and delay tactic.

The sound of a servant on the phone drawling slowly, "Baba naaayyyimm" became one of the most annoying ones that we became accustomed to in Kuwait.

Getting Paid Back
– but he wouldn't hand the money to *me*...

In February, Saleh borrowed several hundred Kuwaiti dinars from us to get his car fixed.

We went with his son Mohsen to the BMW dealership to pay the bill, which I handled. It has always been my job in our marriage to handle our money, manage it, and know how to access it as we need it.

David trusts me; I show him what I am doing, tell him all about it, and he is satisfied. It should come as no surprise that Kuwaiti couples don't operate this way.

A few weeks later, Saleh paid us back. He had his 16-year-old son Mohsen drive over with the cash. The kid was so serious – he never cracked a smile a single time that I saw him those months. He had a wad of cash with him, and he carefully cited precisely how much money was there, and in what form of bills. It was almost funny, but still a good way to do things.

He was standing outside our building between the elevators when I found him, and David had disappeared from view because he was taking out the garbage, so Mohsen handed it to me. I put it in my pants pocket and thanked him, saying that we trusted him and would count it later. Still, the kid remained, and I wondered what for. He said he would wait for David to come back, to confirm payment.

Really – it was not just David's money, and it was not just my money – it was our money! After Mohsen left, David explained: Kuwaiti wives tend to pocket wads of cash that are paid to their husbands, say nothing, and just spend it all.

So even if a husband lets her keep it, the person who owes money and is paying it back will make absolutely sure to inform the husband personally that he has just brought the money back, so that there will be no question of repayment of the debt.

Still, I found Mohammed's behavior just a bit insulting. That wad of cash would pay for rent, groceries, taxi rides, other expenses, and gifts for relatives in the States.

Qaffer – Inhuman – Not-Monotheistic!

David taught me a new Arabic word: qaffer. It means non-human, as in anyone who does not subscribe to one of the 3 monotheistic religions of the world. This is how Bangladeshis are viewed here, he told me. Strange though; aren't Bangladeshis Muslims? Maybe this is racism, I don't know. What a raw deal; I feel sorry for them. Bangladesh is a very poor country. They have no life, they had no life, and they can expect to have no fun or future. This came back to mind during another visit with Aiesha.

I had just told her how much we loved to eat in Indian restaurants.

Aiesha told me her attitude about eating in Indian restaurants: Muslims have special rules about handling food – called halal rules – and they will only consider eating in an Indian place if they believe it is run by Muslim Indians – and Aiesha wants to be sure that both the bosses and the workers are Muslims. Hindus might handle the food differently (in what way, they weren't certain).

Thus far, I knew that Muslims won't eat pig meat, and that animals must be killed a particular way – by slitting an animal's throat and letting it bleed to death. [This sounded upsetting to me, because it sounded slow.] Interesting…and a way to limit yourself, narrow your world, and have fewer experiences. I could only assume that she knew this and didn't care.

A little while later, I got another taste of this selfishness as I helped Aiesha pack some food into her freezer. The maid had carefully bunched the spinach up in elastic bands, and then left them standing neatly in a dish of water. I asked Aiesha about her. She was Philippina, and a Muslim, probably in her twenties.

Aiesha told me that she preferred a Muslim maid, and one who could speak either English or Arabic. Sometimes she sent her pay home; sometimes she kept it for herself. What else? Aiesha didn't ask about anything else.

Why not? She wasn't interested; she had problems of her own. I said that I love to know about other people – maybe I can help, and it gives me a vacation from my own problems. Yet my friend couldn't even summon enough interest in another human being who followed the same religion as she did.

Gender Apartheid on the Trading Floor

I mentioned to Aiesha that I wanted to take a quick walk around the trading floor of the Kuwait Stock Exchange, just to see it, adding that this was because of a report that I had seen several years ago on *60 Minutes*.

It was then that I was disappointed: Aiesha informed me that the Kuwait Stock Exchange keeps a separate trading room for female stockbrokers. Great…the report took place in the men's trading room. Maybe I would go anyway. I was willing to bet that the men's trading room was grander than the women's trading room. I never got around to seeing any of it, but at least I found out about it.

All of this reminded me of a scene in the movie made from James Watson and Francis Crick's book about decoding DNA, *The Double Helix*. Watson, the American scientist, went looking for Rosalind Franklin, the scientist who took the x-ray photographs that made this possible. He tried the faculty lounge, which was full of men in wing-back chairs, smoking and reading newspapers. When he asked for Dr.

Franklin, they haughtily informed him that the room was for men only. His reply was great: "Why? What do you do in here, toilets?"

Islamic society gets excited over much less than toilets, segregating much more.

Dr. Islamic Fundamentalist Offers Me a Wrist-Shake

Late in April, we toured the Center for Islamic Medicine in Shuwaikh, a privately owned facility that produces nutraceuticals. A wealthy Kuwaiti physician owned it; he had the luxury of doing whatever he wanted for a career, and that was to run a small factory that made packets of herbal remedies for bronchial asthma and other ailments. We toured it with Dr. Aziz, the Egyptian veterinarian from the Kuwait Department of Animal Health.

David wanted Dr. Aziz to pick up where he would leave off, arranging a lecture series in Kuwait. He explained the general idea to Dr. Aziz with creative, hilarious and spontaneous examples: Dr. Majnouni (majnoun means crazy) would lecture about subcutaneous peanut butter; Dr. Harami (haram means morally bad and therefore forbidden) would lecture about chocolate in the hair. We howled with laughter as Dr. Aziz looked shocked at first, and then joined in the laughter as he realized how ludicrous these examples were...Dr. Crazy and Dr. Immoral lecturing, indeed. Dr. Aziz agreed to set up lectures about real topics – immunotherapeutics, nutraceutical remedies paired with pharmaceutical ones, etc.

We started the day at an office building that connected through a series of cloisters to a beautiful mosque. The mosque had a huge copper dome and was white with small mosaic tiles in dark blue and sepia decorating every archway. Huge double copper doors with Islamic art patterns etched into them led the way to the lobby of the Institute's office building. We went upstairs to the individual carpeted and marble-tiled offices.

The whole building appeared to be both decorated with and designed in the shape of an eight-pointed star, which is a common architectural and artistic theme in Islamic designs. The cloistered area outside was interesting to see as well: gardeners were busy with hoses, keeping the grounds well-watered and thus covered with sweet-smelling green grass and edged with impatience flowers. After spending a lot of time in a desert environment, I could not help but stare and inhale deeply.

The gold dome on the mosque of the nutraceuticals institute, and the cloisters around the lawn. The expanse of green grass smelled wonderfully sweet and made me homesick, but it didn't matter; our time in Kuwait was ending.

At last Dr. Al-Duaij appeared. He was – oddly enough – a cool-looking guy. I say "oddly" because he refused to shake my hand. After that, he smoothed the offense over by being really friendly and pleasant to all of us. David came away from the meeting feeling optimistic, because they had common interests: nutraceuticals and alternative forms of medicine.

They all posed for some photos, and I also took many photos of the grounds and building outside. I did not do this inside, however, because everywhere I went I encountered women who were shrouded in black abbeyas with nekhabs, leaving only their eyes visible.

Dr. Al-Duaij was a short man who wore wire-rimmed glasses. He kept his hair and beard, which were gray with some black, only a few centimeters long. He wore a gray suit with a beautiful blue and white-striped tie, and grinned broadly at us. His front teeth jutted out a bit but were perfectly straight; combined with his ever-present grin and his glasses perched on his forehead, he gave off an aura of sophistication.

Dr. Al-Duaij drove us to his factory, which was a small, one-level mud-brick building that overlooked Kuwait Bay. It was 20 years old, and the manager told us that they had been fighting since its inception for a newer and better building.

The manager, a Pakistani scientist, had a prayer-stained forehead, but he shook all of our hands, even mine. The guy who shared his office, however, shook hands with the men and then held his wrist out to me – so I withdrew. I was touching his wrist before I saw that; he had moved toward me as though to actually shake my hand.

This guy was interesting to look at; he had black, wavy hair and probably was overdue for a haircut, and a long scraggly beard. In short, he looked like a Muslim fundamentalist in a lab coat. He sat quietly and politely at his desk next to the manager, though, not talking but not glaring hatefully either.

Understanding this did not make me any less annoyed when the manager stopped me in the hall to treat me to an explanation of Islamic culture and behavior. I cut him off, informing him that I knew all about it – how non-hand-shakers are socialized to think and act, the religious mindset and instruction behind it, etc.

The manager gave up on the lecture and lamely ended with some words about how it is the culture, so I told him that I find it insulting even though I understand it. It felt so good to finally say this to a Muslim man, even if it wasn't to a non-hand-shaker of a Muslim man. But the other guy didn't speak English, and I don't speak Arabic.

The "Al-" in Kuwaiti Last Names

One last detail that I never forgot: the "Al-" that precedes each Kuwaiti's last name (though this is not unique to Kuwaitis) means "tribe of" whatever follows it. No Kuwaiti last name is without this prefix. David was the one who explained this to me, because I asked about it. After that, I was always careful to remember it, say it, and write it.

Chapter 7
Genius Meals – Dining Out in Kuwait

Let the litany of restaurant reviews begin…plus take-out joint reviews, and reviews of any other outside eating experiences. Kuwaiti food is very good, I am happy to report. Details follow…

The Kuwait Oil Company Hospital Cafeteria

The hospital is a small, sprawling, 2-level building with a framed, hand-drawn floor plan in the center reception area (there are at least 2 reception areas). We spent much of my first day out in Kuwait in a tiny library with 4 computers, 2 of which are Net-connected. I e-mailed my family about the plane trip, and met various doctors.

A hospital administrator invited us into his office for coffee. It was there that I learned that Kuwaitis haven't a clue about making good coffee – only tea. I had yet to see a café in Kuwait. The doctors' lounge (we were invited into it) has a tray where people can make themselves a cup of instant Nescafé – yuck. Or tea, using a hot water dispenser, which the cafeteria workers come across the hall to set up.

The cafeteria is a small room containing one refrigerator case with fruits, juices, water, soda, and a display across the bottom shelf of herbs, spices and lentils. There is a cash register next to it. Perhaps 20 tables fill the room, and at the far end is a photo, ubiquitous in Kuwait, of the Crown Prince and the Emir of Kuwait, walking together.

The Kuwait Oil Company Hospital Cafeteria – the counter and the eating area.

Their family name is Al-Sabah; all Kuwaiti last names begin with Al-, which means "tribe of" and the second part is the particular family's surname. This is how you can tell that a person is Kuwaiti, among other methods. "Sabah" means "morning."

When a member of the staff brings your food – after your second or third attempt at ordering off of a limited menu of things that aren't all available – they also bring cutlery, napkins, a tray containing salt, pepper, oil, and vinegar, and glasses of water. The food is greasy. We had tomato soup, then fries with chicken kebabs.

Medical Conference Meals...Varied

On December 17, 2004, we went out with Saleh – all day – to a cardiology conference at the Hilton Hotel Banqueting Hall in Manqaf. Just as in the U.S., doctors must attend lecture series to maintain their medical licenses – or take a test. The conference was held in a small building next to the main building. There was fresh-squeezed orange and lemon juice, tea, coffee, pastries, tarts, cakes, etc. at the back of the hall where the lectures were being given. An Arab in a dishdashah with a red-checked guthra and a 5 o'clock shadow videotaped every lecture plus the question-and-answer sessions.

The Hilton Hotel Ballroom in Manqaf, a shore-side town well south of Kuwait City.

David was very glad to meet an American cardiologist from an Episcopalian hospital, Dr. James Wilson (whose name was written as Dr. Wilson James on the programs). He talked about restenosis of stents in angioplasties, and ways of adding medicine to stent insertions.

David's nutraceuticals could be added, so Dr. Wilson wants to stay in contact with him. Cool – I'm proud of David.

The previous medical conference we had joined Saleh for had been very different: a lunchbox dinner of bitter cheese with dark green herbs in puff pastry was served, with sweets and tea and coffee. That conference had been held at Kuwait University – a no-frills affair. This conference was so over-the-top luxurious that I decided to explore the place, and the photos I took are from my tour of the hotel grounds.

For an hour, I left the conference and went out back to the beach, where a long line of rocks stretches out into the Gulf. There was a great view of the Kuwait Oil Shipping Docks, freighters, booms (merchant sailing ships), dhows (fishing boats), etc. Two American guys were standing on the rocks smoking cigars – one from Alabama, and one from everywhere and nowhere in particular (an Army brat who had spent his whole life traveling, so he had no regional accent). They saw me with my camera and insisted on photographing me on the rock outcropping. After that, we chatted for a while.

Looking back at the building where the conference was held; me on the rocks behind it.

They were in Kuwait on a construction contract until (like us) May. They had access to the U.S. PX store, and wore clothes with "Operation Iraqi Freedom" emblazoned on them – sweatshirts and tee shirts. They lived with lots of other Americans in an apartment building near the hotel, and are fed regular news reports by U.S. channels, so the latest George Dubya Bush terror alert had them spooked. These Americans are targets living all together in an apartment building, while David and I were effectively off the radar screen, blended in with the local population. What an interesting mix of risk and life choices we each had made.

I took many photos outside, and then we all walked towards the building. Those 2 American guys were sticking close to Starbucks coffee places and pizza joints – the hotel had one of each – while David and I went to other places to eat. We said good-bye, and I went towards the back door of the main hotel building. There was a Thai restaurant to the left (still outside), and decorative, mosaic, blue-tiled pools lining the buildings, plus a large swimming pool. Inside, I found several high-end shops: L'Occitane, Henckels Knives, shoe stores, clothing stores, a bookstore, etc.

The beach behind the Manqaf Hilton, and the main building facing the beach.

The book shop was great – I got a copy of *The Arab Times* for news of the terror alert and the failure of the Kuwaiti government to order the timely clearing out of the country's storm drains (resulting in flooding around Kuwait City earlier that week after a yearly bout of rain). Also, I found several beautiful post cards of sights in Kuwait – to keep as souvenirs, not to send – a detailed map of Kuwait (at last!), and a book full of photos and the history of Failaka Island. We could see where our Scheherazade Cat was born and learn all about the place! ☺

After that, I returned to the Banqueting Hall for…a banquet. The food was free to all who attended the conference. It was delicious: lentils, chick peas, tomato, eggplant, fish, chicken, cauliflower, bread, fruit salad, pistachio pastries, etc. After that, we all hung around until Saleh was able to hand in his continuing medical education credit slips, during which time I collected lots of literature on the latest high-tech medical equipment being peddled there, in case David would want it. I also shot some photos of a super-luxurious rest room.

The sign on the rest room depicted a woman with a hijab (scarf) over her hair; the facilities were beautiful.

The Local Town Square in Abraq Khaitan

The next day was fairly quiet. We stayed home until the afternoon, then went out to pay KD 3 apiece for phone cards.

We walked a couple of times in the course of the outing across a huge expanse of sand located in the center of Khaitan. Shops, banks, a McDonald's, and restaurants overlooked it. While daylight lasted, a couple of cricket games were being played in the middle of it. Cars were parked on the south and east edges, and small dumpsters could be found here and there along each side.

It was a square of undeveloped land for who knew how much longer. We saw a tent being set up on the northern side. It was dark brown and white, long, and piles of red oriental rugs, all identical, with white tassels on either end, rolled up, waited next to it. The rugs looked larger than prayer rugs, which are meant for only one person. Two mosques were also on this square – one to the west, and one to the east.

We found 2 more restaurants – side by side across from the northwest corner – that were okay for a cheap meal. One was Egyptian. The other was Indian, and it was called Maharani (Princess of Love). I looked forward to wandering around the area, and I realized that most of this exploration would take place after dark, when David was home from a day out working, or when he had stopped for the day after working at home.

An Egyptian friend of ours, an engineer in his late 20s named Shareef, visited one evening to pick up something that David was working on. He said we ought to have a tourist map of Kuwait, and I was already planning to get one. He also told us not to go out after 7 or 8 o'clock on Wednesday or Thursday nights – when the weekend is getting underway – too many bad bachelors. David wasn't worried, but I wouldn't go out without him. Shareef also advised against shortcuts across dark, desert patches, saying to stick to busy, well-lit areas.

In the end, we decided that we would go out after dark, that we would keep to well-lit areas and main routes, and that I would always walk ahead of David, so that he could see me. This suited me; I walk faster than he does. It suited him, too, both for that reason and because it was more secure to just be able to see me continuously and not have to keep checking. It worked out well – nothing bad ever happened to us.

So we went out – and I photographed Ahmed, the Egyptian owner, in front of his restaurant. He was so pleased that he stopped us on our way home to give us free glasses of hot tea with sugar, plus lots of spices and tea leaves at the bottoms of the glasses.

The Egyptian restaurant on the edge of Abraq Khaitan's desert square; the owner surrounded by his employees.

Mr. Ali's Sweet Shop

We made friends with an elderly Kuwaiti man named Mr. Ali who owned a sweet shop that sold pastries and ice cream. This nice man took care of 2 stray cats; one was a calico, and the other was black-and-white. The cats let us pet them, and I got a photograph of Mr. Ali with one of them. It turned out that the cat had kittens among the cement blocks of the building next door, which was undergoing renovation.

After meeting the store owner and the cats, we bought some ice cream – pistachio. It was soft, lighter and less creamy than ice cream in the West – perfect for hot weather. A nice Bangladeshi guy packed it in a white plastic container and covered it with tin foil for us, for 750 fils (about $2U.S.). We noticed strawberry ice cream, and planned to get some next time. We also liked the small puff pastry rolls of Middle Eastern baklava, made with honey and pistachios that he sold. We visited Mr. Ali many times over the course of our stay in Kuwait, and bought sweets from him many times.

David chatted with Mr. Ali in Arabic whenever we stopped by, and he found out that Mr. Ali had a long commute from his home in some other town each day. If I could have asked the man about all the changes that Kuwait has seen over the course of his lifetime, I certainly would have done so. He must have grown up when Kuwait was just starting to make serious money from oil drilling, before the nation was fully mechanized, modernized, and convenient.

Mr. Ali sitting at his desk inside his sweet shop; feeding and petting his cat; enjoying the cat's company; standing proudly in front of his sweet shop.

For the Winter Solstice, we went out for Indian food and groceries, and then visited Mr. Ali at his sweet shop, where we bought more of his wonderful pistachio ice cream and saw him feeding 2 calico cats. We took several pictures of him with them. Later, we brought prints of him at his shop, both outside and in, for him to keep. He was delighted, smiling more broadly than ever. His smiles were always wonderful.

Mr. Ali; ice creams for sale; wrapped trays of sweets.

Sweet Castlo

On the way home one evening, we got the usual stares from almost everyone we saw – it amused me, and I knew that I got stares because I was a bareheaded woman, and an American. We stopped in a pastry shop to get some pistachio, honey, date, coconut and puff pastry sweets. It was called Sweet Castlo – probably a mistake, we realized.

Sweet Castlo – outside and in.

They probably meant to write Sweet Castle...too late. A very nice Syrian man ran it. We spent one dinar (we didn't want a fattening amount; just enough for a little enjoyment). There was a Kuwaiti ahead of us whose wife and daughter – both in full black veils and abbeyas – had just bought some pastries. He saw us and stayed just long enough to translate for us. He asked us where we were from, and then he left. We thanked him as he walked out.

This place was a short distance away from the square, off the beaten track that we usually took to get to everything else. The pastries were similar to the ones at Mr. Ali's place, but he was so much friendlier that we stuck to his shop after trying this one a couple of times.

Take-Out Joints

We often stopped on the way home at an Egyptian chicken place. For one dinar (almost $4), we could buy a whole rotisserie-cooked chicken, smothered with cardamom on the outside. We would take it home and feast on it, then follow it up with ice cream or strawberries, usually some very red Egyptian strawberries from Sultan Center. That place also had – for a higher price – hard, red-and-white American and Australian strawberries. The Egyptian ones cost less, and were juicy and fully ripe. But then, they didn't have as far to go from the farm to the market.

The Desert Corner Egyptian Joint

There was a nice place on the corner of the desert square in Khaitan that made delicious bread in its own ovens, barbecued chicken and lamb, good herbed omelets, and fresh-squeezed orange juice. It was an Egyptian take-out place. I never found out its name (the sign was only in Arabic), but it was pretty good, as far as Egyptian take-out places went.

The men who worked there were always very friendly, smiling welcoming smiles at both of us, happy to see us, and waiting patiently while I told David what I wanted and he translated it into Arabic for them. Then they would take a chicken off of the long, metal rotisserie pole, unhooking it from its clamps.

We would watch as they went through the ritual of placing it on the center of a large, haphazardly roundish piece of flatbread, after which they would top it with wilting potato fries, and place one roasted tomato on one corner of the chicken and a roasted red onion opposite that. They would then seal it all up with tin foil, enclose a little round plastic container of thoom (garlic cream) sauce, and put it all into a brown paper bag, and then in a plastic one, tying the handles shut.

Our favorite place to buy a cardamom-coated rotisserie chicken, on the corner of the square in Abraq Khaitan.

For dinner most nights, we had that familiar cardamom chicken, sliced open in the middle and stuffed with cardamom sprinkled potato fries. It also came with a small container of white garlic sauce and some pickled carrots and cucumbers. Our cat was getting spoiled; we gave her plenty of high-quality cat food that we had toted on the plane, but now we were tearing off bits of chicken and giving it to her as we sat in the living room. She would smell it, come up alongside us, and yowl for it. She was good at loud yowls, and we were suckers.

That's wasn't all that we usually ate – we also got fried eggplant with the chicken, some falafel (chick pea) rounds with holes in the middle of each one (shaped like small doughnuts), perhaps some more potato fries, and some salad made of tomato and cucumber with chopped herbs. Some nights David would get me a cup of freshly squeezed orange juice, because the chicken places sold this, too.

Goub-Goub – But No Crab

Unfortunately, there was a horrible Egyptian place called Goub-Goub around the corner from the cardamom chicken place on the main drag of Khaitan and up the busy street a bit. It sold similar food, but somehow it always came out unappetizing, and so I told David to please never EVER shop there again. (Sometimes he would have people drop him off near the apartment building, buy dinner, and then walk home.)

Its very name sounded unappetizing – like something you would expect to cough up from the back of your throat when you have a cold. Mansoor told me that he and his sister bought food from there all the time – because they delivered. Fatin told me that Goub-Goub means crab – but that place didn't sell any. Why name a take-out restaurant after a food that it didn't sell?! Oh, well. Don't look for logic where there is none. I wished it did sell crab; the Egyptian take-out in Khaitan was so monotonous. It also offered fresh-squeezed orange juice. That was the only really good thing they had, though.

One night, I sat in the living room reading and typing into our laptop computer while David had gone out to the corner of the desert square place for barbecued chicken and juice. I wasn't sure I wanted any dinner, even though I was hungry; the food in Khaitan had become too monotonous. It was another month before we were to leave for the United States, and I had begun to miss being able to buy groceries and cook in an oven and on a stove. But…we were still glad that we had not bought a stove. It was strange to think that apartments in Kuwait did not come equipped with stoves, but that was the way it was.

I ended up eating dinner – David brought back some food from the good place on the corner of Khaitan's desert square. We ate barbecued chicken, hard-boiled eggs, grilled tomatoes, fries, and thoom. He even bought me another fresh-squeezed orange juice. I loved it when he did that, and he did it often. ☺

The Take-Out Joint on the Main Side Road

One evening, we went out – on foot – and came back again, without completing our errand. We wanted to go to the bank to wire money to the States, but it was closed, so we would try again the next day an hour earlier. Banks in Kuwait operate from 9 a.m. to 1 p.m. and then again from 5 to 7 p.m. After that, we ordered our food from the place on the corner of the desert square.

We got barbecued chicken again, and orange juice. David told me that the guys who ran that place had figured out that he usually bought orange juice for me, and omelets. They even asked him where I was sometimes when he shopped alone. They seemed nice, and David said that they had a good attitude toward their customers.

However, south of our apartment building, on a main highway that led east, was a take-out joint staffed by some very unpleasant men. They all spoke Arabic, and were from neighboring Middle Eastern countries. The food was laid out in heated metal trays, just as at other take-out joints: hard-boiled eggs, fries, roasted eggplant, tomato-and-cucumber salad, etc.

I went in with David a couple of times, peering under his arm and pointing things out that I wanted him to order. He ordered it in Arabic, and the men packed it up with the usual speed and efficiency, but I noticed a cold atmosphere in there, despite the heat from the ovens. I glanced up and saw one man hanging back, glowering venomously at me.

He was of medium height and build, dressed in a plain, Western outfit of dark chinos and a pale blue Oxford-style shirt, with very short hair and some stubble (not much) on his face. I met his gaze calmly, and stared him down for a moment. By then, I knew what was probably going through his mind, even though direct communication between us was impossible (which did not make me sorry!).

He was angry to be able to see an attractive woman whom he did not know, and blamed me for the fact that I was fully visible. I suppose I might as well have been dancing around in a bikini as far as he was concerned, tossing my long hair about. In fact, my hair was up in a clip (a chic, matte gold thing), and I was wearing my usual loose tee shirt and long, dark pants. The problem was his, I knew. At least I knew the intricacies of his problem.

The guys in the side highway take-out joint had a bad attitude, David told me. They leered at me when I went with David to that place, and he saw them do it. It made him angry – David gets angry when people are rude to me. I told him about that, but at first he didn't notice. He saw it the next time, though, and I stopped going in there. Those guys also tried to short-change David, but he watched them. This just made them dislike him more.

The chickens were good, and so was the thoom, or we wouldn't have bought anything from them. That was the place where we got Scheherazade's Christmas chicken. But they weren't the only unfriendly vendors. It caused us to go back to the desert corner place just for the smiles and friendliness, monotonous food or not.

Another night, on the way home, we passed several take-out places – as usual – all staffed by Egyptians, including that one on the east highway. David said that most of these guys were from southern, rural Egypt, like our bouab. David said that the word which refers to where they are from is "Saeedi" – which sounded like a racist and ethnocentrist word.

David assured me that it isn't a rude word; it just meant that they were from South Egypt. Unfortunately, a significant number of Saeedis often deserve their bad reputations. David said he had to watch the vendors very carefully to make sure that they didn't put anything bad in our food.

Restaurants

There were various forms of seating arrangements in Kuwaiti restaurants, which, aside from the adventure of trying new recipes, made the experience very interesting. It made it a double adventure.

One seating arrangement was familiar: everyone gets a table in a room full of tables, with each party at one of those tables in full view of the other diners. People eat, holding conversations while glancing around the room at the décor and at each other. This would not be remarkable in the Western world, but it was something that some people in the Middle East apparently saw as a deterrent to eating out.

Some of these places were beautiful, upscale, formal restaurants, clearly meant for couples on dates – married or engaged, it was meant for "respectable" couples. Of course, restaurants are good for business meetings, too.

Another one of these seating arrangements was meant only for men – single or married. What mattered was that these men were eating out without any women. These were less expensive places, and not beautifully appointed.

Foreign women from the wealthy, Western cultures of the world appeared to be exempt from such strictures, however. I ate in several such places with my husband, and no one ever made me feel unwelcome. It was as if they knew that such a thing was normal for me and my culture. The restaurant manager and/or staff always smiled and made me feel very welcome.

Still another seating arrangement was the total opposite of this one: all tables were separately enclosed inside little rooms which consisted of wooden cubicles. They came complete with doors, and the wait staff would knock before entering. The reason for this was to conceal women who wore full face veils – nekhabs – whenever they left home.

The women could take them off inside the cubicles and enjoy their meals. That way, no one other than their fiancé or husband or father or whomever a woman was dining out with could look at her face and enjoy seeing how attractive she might be.

Next seating arrangement: informal restaurants that were half public – i.e. a room full of tables – and half curtained off. The interesting aspect of the curtained off half was that people at the various tables in there could see each other, even if they did not know each other. I suppose it saved on knocking and balancing plates when delivering the food to the tables.

The curtained off halves of the restaurants were for families, and the other part was for single men. We encountered one variation of this: the place consisted of 2 large tent-like structures with glass walls – one for families and one for single men.

One more seating arrangement was another mixture of types: tables in one part of the restaurant, either half of it or the middle, and cubicles either along the perimeter or taking up the other half of the place. I'm glad I saw all this.

The Samarqand Restaurant

One morning in early December, a very nice Persian doctor came to our flat and spent 2 hours talking with David about the possibility of working as a general practitioner and liaison with the medical center in Tehran, Iran. His name was Dr. Jahanandish, and he and his family lived in Shiraz, in southern Iran, well inland. We both took a liking to him immediately – and he shook my hand. We had a lovely day with him.

When a Muslim man won't shake my hand, I hate it. I know what it means: a devout Muslim man is not supposed to touch any woman who is not a member of his own family. They believe that women are unclean – who knows, we might be menstruating, horrible creatures! Also, they might get horny if they touch one of us, menstruating or not. They worry that they might get turned on…from a mere handshake!

I learned about this in law school, from an Iranian law student who was also an ayatollah. I find this whole custom and way of thinking to be insulting to both parties, and I always offered to shake hands in Kuwait, just as in America. The reason: to find out whether the male Muslim in question was open- or parochial-minded. I wanted to know what sort of a person I was dealing with whenever I met someone new. The way a man treats a woman tells you a lot about him.

After David had talked with Dr. Jahanandish, we took a ride to Kuwait City to meet Saleh at a Persian restaurant. The taxi ride to this place was absurd. The driver didn't know where it was; he had to keep stopping to ask people for help, most of whom had no idea where it was. We finally found it, in part thanks to Saleh calling our cell phone every so often.

The cab driver apologized, but we weren't angry with him. Kuwait's cab drivers probably just pay a fee or use wasta to get their licenses, with no qualifying exams. No wonder they can't find anything! The cab drivers hang copies of their licenses over the backs of their seats. The licenses are laminated 8.5" x 14" cards with photos of the drivers and copies of their identification on them.

The restaurant was called the Samarqand, and we ate some delicious food there. The place was named for a beautiful Persian city that still exists, but it is to the northeast of Iran's borders, thanks to an inept shah who lost a lot of his country's territory in the 19th century.

We had: lentil soup; tomato-cucumber salad; Persian flatbread (it's huge and round); another soup, thicker than the first and full of lentils, potato, tomato purée and a chunk of lamb; lamb and chicken kebab in rice with tomato and red onion; and fresh-squeezed carrot or orange juice.

Inside the Samarqand restaurant. It was one level upstairs from the ground floor, and very nice.

Two other doctors met us there...and both refused to shake my hand. The heavyset one in traditional Arab clothing proceeded to treat me to a lecture on the no-handshake rule. I told him I already knew all about it – what it meant, etc. I didn't want to let them tell me the whole thing all over again. I know the old saying – if you don't like it, leave – but I was stuck there, and I refuse to just tolerate something when I trapped in an unpleasant environment. But I'm glad I went in spite of it all. An experience such as this one is certainly interesting to tell about later.

The other guy was thin and creepy, and never smiled. He wore a gray tweed suit, glasses, and had a scruffy-looking gray beard to match.

As we sat with them, though, I began to like the heavyset one a little, because he smiled. It also helped that I made David sit between me and them, as a buffer.

The restaurant had a view of the Grand Mosque of Kuwait out one window, so I took a couple of pictures, and then took a few more of the inside of the Samarqand. The décor was pretty – mostly ivory-hued tiles, with a few blue, sepia and black ones here and there. Some old framed drawings were on the walls, showing Persian men doing bong hits on elaborate hookahs, and surrounded by goats, sheep, chickens, and so on.

The bathroom presented a problematic balancing act: it had no toilet, only a flushable porcelain hole in the floor. This necessitated a squatting feat that I managed to pull off, despite my skepticism. The room was unisex, a one-room restroom with a lock on the door – but it seemed to me that such things belonged only in men's rooms, if there. At least it was as beautifully tiled as the rest of the establishment, and spotlessly clean. The sink had plenty of soap and towels, and I rejoined the lunch party of men comfortable and ready to observe the religious ones for a while longer. I spent the rest of the meal people-watching…one of my favorite activities.

The Grand Mosque of Kuwait City, seen from the window of The Samarqand.

Haitham Restaurant – Indian Food

Shortly after getting settled into our apartment in Abraq Khaitan, and after taking delivery of a refrigerator, we ate dinner at a really great Indian restaurant. We had: basmati rice with saffron, cardamom, peas, and tiny bits of fried onion on top; chapatti bread; curried boneless chicken with gravy and tomatoes; soup; salad; bottled water; and fresh-squeezed orange juice. The owner asked how it was, and I said it was the best meal out that we had yet had in Kuwait. He smiled. Haitham restaurant turned out to be our favorite local restaurant; we could walk to it on the way home from the jamiya (grocery store). The manager was always there, speaking sufficient English to translate the menu and welcome us with a smile.

Mr. Jabbar, the manager of Haitham Restaurant.

Typically, we went to the Indian place once a week to either eat there or get take-out, and often with plastic bags of groceries from the local jamiya (grocery store) on the floor next to us. It was almost always the same dinner after we had tried a few dishes and found our favorites: curry chicken and chicken tikka, both boneless recipes, with biryani rice that has saffron, cardamom, cloves and peas in it and fried onions on top. We would also order some chapatti breads, which pulled apart as we ate them. The dinner came with hot chicken noodle soup, tomato-cucumber-cabbage salad, and mustard greens with lemon wedges. We loved it.

Our friend and neighbor, Mansoor, came with us as often as not; I would quiz him endlessly about why no other women were eating inside, and what their husbands would think if in fact they did eat there, visible to men whom they did not know. It was great fun.

David has told me a story – or rather, referred many times to an incident – involving the almost exclusive patronage by U.S. troops of American fast food joints during the 1991 American occupation of Kuwait. It was recalled due to our mutual abhorrence of and refusal to eat at the McDonald's on the north side of that huge square of sand in Khaitan. We both preferred to try the local restaurants. This made David very conspicuous as an American soldier. His commanding officer wanted to know why he wasn't eating at KFC and other American fast food joints with the other troops. His reply about wanting to try new things displeased the commander. The prevailing military attitude was one of disapproval when it came to interacting with the population of the occupied country. There was also an unwritten directive to keep apart from the general population of Kuwait.

Haitham Restaurant – offering eat-in and take-out Indian food, made to order; a table inside.

The counter at Haitham restaurant with a manager taking a phone order; the menu on the wall.

We both love to meet new and different people – we don't fit the conventional mold, and we're proud of it! David disagreed with it, met many Kuwaiti people, and made friends with them. That is how he met Fatin and Saleh, and was able to come back almost immediately after demobilizing to the States and leaving the army.

One evening, we went out with Mansoor to eat at Haitham Restaurant. We hadn't gone there in a while, and we had fun visiting with him and being silly again. As usual, he insisted upon chaperoning me when I went to the sink to wash my hands at the end of the meal; Indian restaurants have sinks for washing up, but no bathrooms, and this place had a long open hallway that led to the sinks. His intent was to make sure that once I went down there, no guys would go in until I came back out. There was no door – just a hall – and you could see people at the sinks if you face it.

We had a lovely time out with Mansoor. We all had that wonderful food, the chapatti breads, curry chicken and basmati rice, and some fresh-squeezed blood orange juice (another variety of orange). I managed to ask Mansoor what I was so curious about, and get a detailed answer. Why did I never see any Kuwaiti women in this restaurant, but always and only waiting in cars while their husbands got take-out?

He told me that this Indian restaurant, with no place for families, was for single men only – but that obviously an American woman could go there with her husband. However, a Kuwaiti wife could not eat there. Why not? Because other guys would see her face, think she was pretty, and that would make her husband jealous. Also, she would be talked about for going there and being seen. This would all make her life miserable – not worth the trouble. So...if Mansoor had a wife, we could not, all 4 of us, go out to eat there together. We would have to find a family restaurant. Complicated! At least I had learned about the thinking of Kuwaiti husbands. Mansoor was divorced, so he knew how married Kuwaitis think.

The Maharani Restaurant

The Indian place had a toilet with a cover but no seat – odd. The tables were all separated into beautifully carved little wooden cubicles with sliding doors. We could hear everyone else over the tops of the walls, and the wait staff knocked before coming in – every time. The food wasn't bad, but we only ate there once, because we felt so isolated from everyone else in the place. I'm glad we tried it; now I had some idea what it must be like to be a nekhab-wearing Kuwaiti woman, having to cover her face every time a waiter came back.

The Maharani Indian Restaurant. All of the tables were enclosed in wooden cubicles.

Airport Eateries – the Jamaica Blue Café

Assim Al-Tikriti, the professor at Kuwait University, wanted to spend more time with us. He wanted some assistance with research and writing, it turned out – my specialty. So one evening in early December of 2004, he came over and took us out. We had a fun visit.

When he took us out, it was to – of all places – the airport. We went out at midnight, so it was too late to go anywhere else…nothing else was open. But all of the food places at the airport are open 24 hours a day – and so were some of the shops. We looked at shoes and sandals in a Birkenstock store before heading for the food court on the lower level. Assim told us that this whole section of the terminal was only 3 years old.

It was newly built after restoring the older section from the Iraqi invasion damage. We settled on a shop called the Jamaica Blue Café for coffee, a mocha, hot chocolate, and a chocolate cupcake, heated, with chocolate glaze and sprinkled with ground, green pistachios (I loved those; they were on many desserts in Kuwait).

Assim told us about himself. Thus far, we had known that he had a Ph.D. in business administration. Now he told us that he had done his graduate work at the University of Pittsburgh, and that that was his first academic experience that was entirely in English. He had done all previous levels of his education in Arabic in Kuwait, right through his Bachelor's degree.

He did know some English when he got to Pittsburgh, however. He had studied it during high school and college, and in Colorado for a few months before beginning graduate school in Pittsburgh. Assim also told us that he was a perfectionist when he wrote. He wrote articles for Kuwait University. He wanted me to edit them, but he needed a draft first, and he said he was very slow about generating one.

We sat with Assim for over an hour in the café. I got Assim to tell us about his life some more, and we told him about our history together – how we met at a Hallowe'en party (Assim loved Hallowe'en!), were best friends for years, and then we decided that we should be more than that. His story was quite different: he and his wife Aiesha were introduced by relatives. This was undisguised matchmaking. After a visit or two, they agreed to get married. 6 months after that, they did.

Muslim society does not allow dating – no transition time in which a couple may get to know each other. Couples must simply go from one extreme to another. They barely know each other, they marry each other, and then they set up a home together. Assim and Aiesha now had 6 kids: an older daughter, a son in college, 2 other boys, and 2 little girls.

It was such fun chatting with Assim in that café that I wanted to go out like that sometime with both Assim and Aiesha, so I asked him about it. [I thought to myself, they are well off, they have a maid, so finding a babysitter would be no obstacle.] Assim said that Aiesha couldn't come out with us because she had to watch the kids. Oh. I left it at that. It sounded like jail to me, not being able to go out, and having her husband nix the whole idea for her without even asking her.

It seemed grossly unfair that Assim could take off at all hours and do whatever he liked, while Aiesha was stuck at home with the kids. David said it was social custom that stopped her. She spoke English fluently and we could have fun, but no. As it turned out, I was able to go to her place many times and visit for hours, talking and sharing stories.

Still, I liked talking with Assim. I told him that I like mixed company: both genders, all ages, different cultures, etc. This is clearly the result of growing up in American culture, and being an American gives me the benefit of allowing and encouraging me to enjoy interacting with so many different kinds of people. If I had to give up on the idea of doing that, as Aiesha does, I would be very upset! This was an educated woman who had studied for an M.B.A. in Pennsylvania, so she must have known what she was missing.

Out for Coffee at the Mall – Complicated!

A couple of days before Christmas, I went out with Fatin's college-age daughter, Nuwwar, in Salmiya. We looked in many shops on a main city street, all upscale and full of interesting things, plus the Marina Crescent Mall, which was on that street too. I found a pretty set of 6 soup plates with little pink roses, plus a matching sugar bowl and creamer. After that, we were getting tired of walking around even though we had some more time, so we headed back to the mall.

When we went to buy coffee, we chose a place called CinneZon (it's the same as Cinnebon in the West). We had a complicated time just trying to get what we wanted. Nuwwar wanted hot foamed milk on hot coffee, while I wanted cold milk added to hot coffee. How hard could this be?

Very hard, it turned out, when the young, bespectacled Indian employee looked at me as though I had spoken ancient Sanskrit and then brought me the coffee with no milk, whereupon I asked him to add cold milk. Nuwwar's cup turned out to be full of nothing but foamed milk – I had him redo that, too. Incredible – at least he served our small Cinnebons without error.

I was careful to be nice, though – he had a hellish people-pleasing job. No wonder so many Americans buy their coffee at Starbucks; that place keeps carafes of cold milk on a side area for customers so that they can add their own. The other coffee shops here follow the British method, doing everything for the customer, but using hot milk, as Europeans supposedly want it. I'm glad I tried it and found out.

Indian Food and Hubbley-Bubbley in Hawali

For Christmas Eve, Mansoor took us out. First, he came to our flat, where we were waiting with a gift for him and his mother and sister: a platter of pistachio pastries from Mr. Ali's shop. Then he asked for tea and I was very pleased to be able to serve it to him in one of the new mugs with the new sugar bowl that I had bought with Nuwwar. At last, I was able to serve the tea properly, according to Arab custom.

When Mansoor took us out, it was to Hawali, where he lived until August of 2004, when he moved to Abraq Khaitan. David jokingly called the area hali-wali Hawali, because hali-wali means no good in Arabic, and Mansoor laughed – he loved it when David made fun of something. The first place he drove us to was his favorite Indian restaurant in Hawali, and there we learned that Kuwaitis call waiters in Indian restaurants "Ahmed" and call out to them when they want something. "Ahmed!" just as French restaurant-goers call out "Garçon!" Assuming that these guys are really called Ahmed seems a bit rude to me, though. I just say "Excuse me," when I want the server to come over to my table.

The food in the Indian place was good (but the food Haitham Restaurant was even better). Mansoor was slowly coming to understand why we don't like KFC or McDonald's, and why Americans tend to look at those places with disdain. Of course a young boy growing up in Kuwait. Mansoor was 10 years old during the Iraqi invasion; he couldn't forget that Americans played a prominent role in ousting the evildoers, so he would look at anything American with interest.

But now he was finding out more than he ever thought he would about our culture. Apparently, Kuwaitis have a penchant for saying, "You ate at McDonald's?! Wow – you are a genius, like the Americans!" They sounded so impressed, but all they would gain from the place was weight. Still, it was informative to know this about Kuwaiti popular culture and habits.

The Indian restaurant was divided into 2 sections: one for single men, and one for families. The family section was curtained off from the other one. It was nothing fancy, just as the one in Khaitan is nothing fancy – the floors were plain, the walls were even plainer, and the tables and chairs were cheap metal. Another family came in to eat before we left. The women were wearing black abbeyas and hijabs, so I asked Mansoor what happens when women with veils (called nekhabs) go out to eat. They have to carefully reach under the veils to fork their food into their mouths, he answered, pantomiming.

The Hawali Hubbley-Bubbley place: the pavilion for families, and inside with Mansoor and the staff.

Our next stop was a hubbley-bubbley (water pipe) place, also in Hawali and also equipped with separate seating arrangements. These were elaborate: there were 2 glass-walled buildings with slanted rooftops, beautifully stenciled on the ceilings inside. The one on the left was for families, so we went in there. The one on the right was for single men. A waterfall was in between them, and behind the family building was the area where the water-pipes were kept.

Waiters in Turkish-style uniforms were going around setting up the pipes and replenishing the coals as they burned out. I got strawberry juice; David and Mansoor got hubbley-bubbley pipes. Mansoor had a coffee-flavored one; David took Nuwwar's advice and tried her favorite flavor, apple. I tried it, actually managing to puff it once, and Mansoor's wasn't bad either. The place had little plastic mouthpieces, one for each person, to avoid spreading germs.

A waiter presenting a pipe with flavored coals; strawberry juice; the room out back with all the water-pipe supplies.

Le Nôtre – My Birthday Dinner

For Christmas Day, we went out on our own, touring and then eating in a great restaurant.

We toured the Souq Mubarakiya, which proved to be a fascinating self-guided tour for us, then took a cab to Kuwait's one French restaurant, Le Nôtre. We got out across the street and ran across to look for the restaurant, unsure of which way to go. We decided to ask for directions, and went up to the guardhouse of the Kuwait Armed Forces Officers Club.

We approached and saw some Kuwaitis in the comfortable room next to the little guardhouse, and an enlisted Kuwaiti with glasses inside the guardhouse. He was very nice; he came out and told us to go left, and we would find the restaurant almost immediately. We also begged him for a photograph, and he obliged. The soldier's name and rank were embroidered in gold Arabic writing on his shirt pockets, and he had Kuwaiti flags as patches on the sleeves.

David and the Kuwaiti soldier who pointed us in the right direction on Christmas evening.

We followed the soldier's directions and soon found ourselves at Le Nôtre.

The sign leading us to Le Nôtre restaurant, lit up by the driveway; inside the dining area.

This outing to Le Nôtre was my birthday treat, and it was perfect in every way – the food, the atmosphere, the service, everything! I got up and looked around; there was a chocolaterie, and the place was attractively decorated, complete with French descriptions of the desserts in gold letters on the purple walls behind them. The restaurant was in a beautiful modern building with purple-painted walls and dark wood walls, and had a view of the Arabian Gulf.

Le Nôtre had a beautiful array of French chocolate confections and patisseries laid out to entice the customers.

We had: herb-garlic dip; sun-dried tomato dip; bread and butter; smoked salmon with dill and mustard sauce; shrimp-avocado salad; curly potato fries; onion soup with Gruyère cheese melted on top; shrimp with asparagus sauce and risotto; saffron rice molded into a rounded cone shape; fish with tiny, long, thin baby carrots with the leaves left on; and a bowl of red raspberries, blackberries, red currants, blueberries, and raspberry sauce on top. Everything was delectable.

Our appetizers and meals – no need to repeat what we had; see above.

For the pièce de resistance, a Kuwaiti couple who were out celebrating their birthdays – both on December 25th, like mine – had a chocoholic Yule-log cake, called a Bûche de Noël. It was delectable: it was dark chocolate sponge cake in a thin layer, rolled with chocolate cream and covered with chocolate ganache and marzipan mushrooms dusted with cocoa. We had noticed them as we arrived, but minded our own business. This was difficult for me, because I could hear what the husband was saying:

He was talking on his cell phone in English, asking why Americans put up trees at Christmas – what does it mean, and where does that tradition come from? And what about Yule logs? Then their cake arrived, with the staff loudly singing Happy Birthday. David pointed at me and loudly said, "It's her birthday, too!" whereupon the Kuwaiti couple ordered 2 slices of their cake to be cut and served to us. We thanked them and sat with them for a few minutes, and I answered the husband's questions about Christmas. He was delighted. His company was rebuilding Iraq's hospitals, so he and David exchanged contact information.

3 people whose birthdays are all on December 25th – with cake. ☺

Kuwait Towers: The Horizon Restaurant and Café

After dinner, we went on to Kuwait Towers. To get there, we walked north, a short way up the beach. We passed an American semi-fast food restaurant (full of Americans) and a juice stand. Lots of stray cats were enjoying the beach and the restaurants' dumpsters. It was a lovely moonlit night.

We enjoyed strolling and stopping along the beach to look out at the Gulf. We also got a kick out of a misspelled sign that read "GRILLING IS PROHEPETED." It was hilarious, so we took photographs (blurred, unfortunately) of each other pointing this out.

Then we came to Kuwait Towers. There are 3 of them: a plain, tall spike that lights up the other 2; one spike has one sphere that holds water; and another spike-tower with 2 spheres which both hold water. This one was open to the public. It had a restaurant, 82 meters up, in the lower and larger sphere, and a café, 162 meters up, in the smaller sphere, with another viewing area.

The Iraqis invaders trashed both towers and murdered the workers in the one-sphere tower – 9 men and 1 woman, all foreigners. David found the bodies 10 days after the Iraqis left, when he was a U.S. Army officer. He had been ordered to go in there with his gun and check for hiding Iraqis (the smell of rotting corpses was horrendous).

We went up the fully restored 2-sphered tower and saw framed photos on display detailing the damage done by the invaders.

The ticket-selling booth at the base of Kuwait Towers; the entrance to the public tower.

Inside the top sphere, we found 2 levels: a lower level with rest rooms and the framed photos, and an upper level with a gift shop, coffee shop, and revolving viewing deck. We went up the stairs and saw the revolving viewing deck moving around the shops, and looked out. Misspelled signs talked about the views. We gazed out at the night, looking down at the water amusement park below the Towers, at the Gulf, and at Kuwait City all lit up.

It was lovely, but photography wasn't possible. I don't mean to say that it wasn't allowed – I mean that it didn't work in the dark. Instead, I looked out the windows, then bought a tee shirt and 2 mugs (unfortunately the decals began to peel off the next day!). One of them was hilarious: it showed Saddam Hussein as a homeless street person with a sign that read "Will Tyrannize for Food." David thought it was great, too.

After seeing all of this, we took the elevator down to the other sphere to look at the Horizon Restaurant, with a gourmet buffet. The place was heavy on atmosphere and light on food quality. It was fun to see the bread display: loaves baked in shapes meant to resemble Arabic letters.

We sat on the sofas in the level below the restaurant for a few minutes, which had a private party dining area – empty – and then rode the elevator down to the lobby to call a cab. A nice Lebanese concierge called it for us, and we chatted with him until it arrived.

The elevator to go up to the restaurant and café decks; the buffet at the Horizon Restaurant.

Inside the lobby on the ground floor of the Tower; David pretending to climb it, just to show the scale of it.

The cab dropped us at the place on the east highway, where we bought a chicken. We went home and put it in a dish on the floor, and then David held our cat there for a photo. It was hilarious. After that, we cut up some up and put it in the dish.

Scheherazade Cat staring in utter disbelief at her Christmas gift.

After wishing our cat a Merry Christmas, it was time to wish our relatives one. We called around, taking about an hour. Our letters hadn't arrived yet, but the family was glad to hear that some were coming, and I told them what to expect. They hadn't opened their presents from us yet – oh, well.

An Upscale Lebanese Restaurant

One evening early in January, Assim took us out to a fancy Lebanese restaurant located on Arabian Gulf Street. It was in a large, modern building with beautiful carved wooden doors and colorful hangings.

We had a lovely time eating eggplant purée with olive oil and pomegranate seeds, puffed hot breads, mango juice, kebabs, etc. Most of the women eating there wore hijabs, but at the end, 3 women arrived together – all of whom were wearing tight, revealing clothing. Assim thought that they were "upscale" prostitutes. In America, they would just seem like trashy-looking women, not prostitutes, so I found his assessment intriguing. What means one thing, and a fairly benign thing at that, can mean something very different in another culture.

The front entryway of the Lebanese restaurant that Assim took us to.

The restaurant had a seating area that was raised up on the right, and that was where we sat. There was another seating area in the center with huge, colorful, poufy cushions and resembled the inside of a tent. It had low armchairs under a round wooden pavilion with sheer curtains hanging down. It was such a focal point that sitting there clearly would have drawn continual glances from the other diners. The décor of the restaurant featured a lot of dark blue, plus other colors in the wall hangings. In addition, there was a section of the restaurant off to the left that was all dining cubicles.

The buffet area with a waiter, and the small enclosure in the center of the dining room.

As we arrived, I took out my camera and by chance caught an image of a nekhab-clad woman leaving with her husband.

A Kuwaiti woman, wearing a nekhab, leaving the restaurant with her husband. This was in the waiting area.

The Mais Al-Ghanim Restaurant

The next week, Assim took us to a wonderful place called the Mais Al-Ghanim restaurant. (He told us that he was hoping to run into his son and his friends, but he didn't want to be obvious about it. We never saw them.) The food was very good; we enjoyed it. We ate a chunky eggplant appetizer – another version of babaganoush. Next, I had quail, and David had pigeon. Assim was less adventurous – he had hummus and lamb kebab.

Here are 2 different views of the dining area. It was casual, decorated like a traditional Kuwaiti building.

The place was founded by a French employee named Emile in 1953. It used to be called the Mess Al-Ghanim, as it was meant to be a mess hall for employees of the home furnishing and appliance superstore. The big store was the one in Safat, where we had bought our furniture, refrigerator and laptop, and later our sheets and quilt.

Mais Al-Ghanim had a delivery wagon – an upscale restaurant that delivered!

The front entrance hall, above.

There are also smaller Al-Ghanim stores elsewhere, which only sell machines. Clearly, the Al-Ghanim tribe was very wealthy and influential. They had been able to convert their employee dining hall into a beautifully appointed, luxurious restaurant. The name had been made chic with "but" in French, by replacing "Mess" with "Mais" – clever.

Valentine's Day

Valentine's Day threatened to be so complicated that David hadn't even made a reservation as of the day before the holiday. I was certain the restaurant we wanted would be full by the time he figured out what to do. He wouldn't even call, because he was so sure that someone who barely spoke English would either accidentally or deliberately confuse him. The problem was that Kuwait had 2 Boom Restaurants. The old one was small, with great seafood. The new one was large with mediocre food. Of course, only the old one would do, but where was it? Kuwait had no yellow pages.

I wanted an unusual day, and a romantic one. The previous year, we had spent this day apart, with David on a Dutch airplane eating lousy food. I wanted a nice date with my husband this year. I saw shops all over Kuwait selling red roses and heart-shaped merchandise, but with dating forbidden in this culture, I wondered: who were the target customers? Were they the Americans, Brits and Europeans who live and work in Kuwait? Were they engaged and married Kuwaitis? It was hard to know. I was curious, as usual.

Well, David sorted it all out, with Mansoor's help.

We ate dinner at Al-Boom Restaurant on Valentine's Day, and had a wonderful time. It was a perfect romantic evening, the food was delectable, the ship was beautiful – inside and out – and we had a wonderful time. All this cost us only 22.500 KD ($38.70).

But it is not possible to eat in a popular tourist attraction on a particular evening without a reservation. This question had been dogging David for over 2 weeks, since he had first promised me a romantic Valentine's Day evening dinner at Al-Boom.

Our first problem was figuring out exactly where it was so as to contact the people who ran it. As I mentioned, Kuwait had no telephone book or business directory. Al-Boom wasn't even listed in the Lonely Planet's *Middle East* book. What was David planning to do? I wanted him to take care of this himself – if he did it, it would feel like a much more romantic evening, and I told him so. Now he really had a problem, because he is a workaholic who prefers to wait until the LAST minute when it comes to fun.

David decided it was time for desperate action: he would beg Mansoor to drive us to the place. When Mansoor got off work at 10 p.m., we called him. He was still in his car, driving home. I felt as though we were bothering him. We called him often to beg for rides. Now we wanted something special, and we wanted it late at night.

We piled into his car and he drove straight to…the grocery store in Abraq Khaitan, not really understanding what David was asking for. When he did understand, he said, "Can't we go tomorrow?" He must have been tired. David said no, please, tomorrow would be too late, and patiently explained that tomorrow was Valentine's Day, the very day on which he was supposed to already have this problem worked out. That did it; Mansoor drove off with us, determined.

It got strange: he headed up Airport Road, despite what we told him about where we thought the place was. He didn't get off at the Messilah or Salmiya exit and head east down the Fifth Ring Road. He went the other way, straight into Kuwait City! He wasn't sure what we were saying, and was bent on calling his friends on his cell phone to ask them whether they knew anything about this place. He always found things out this way. But he needn't have done so – we had seen the masts of the ship from the road, and David remembered where along Arabian Gulf Street to look.

But Mansoor didn't listen. He drove needlessly around almost the entire length of Arabian Gulf Street, which follows the coast of Kuwait City and on into Salmiya past Salwa. Thus, we had an impromptu and inadvertent car tour: we saw Kuwait City with the Liberation Tower lit up – again – plus the National Assembly building, Seif Palace, the Kuwait Stock Exchange, the Grand Mosque, the old American Hospital under renovation, the Red Crescent (the Red Cross of the Arab-Muslim world), Souq Sharq, Dickson House, Al-Amiri Hospital…

We drove on and on, until we came to the right place. It was on the coast, just as one would expect, surrounded on both sides by 2 hotels: the SAS Radisson Hotel on the right, and the Palm Hotel on the left. There was also a Polynesian restaurant and a Starbucks. We drove in first to the right of the main driveway, finding only private villas. Then Mansoor drove right past the main driveway and up the left side. It was easy to see why: a police checkpoint with signs saying "Mandatory Stop" and "Police" flanked either side of it, and a little farther up were 2 guys in military fatigues with assault rifles.

Mansoor pulled over and asked a private security guard at the Palm Hotel about the Boom. Up the middle driveway, came the answer. Resigned to it, Mansoor headed out onto the main drag, which meant he had to double back and make a U-turn. He did it, with both of us apologizing for the hassle and confusion, punctuated by more "never mind[s]". 26 years old, divorced, lonely, and driving an American couple with romantic intentions around – the situation was not lost on me or on David.

Around we went and back – to the police checkpoint. We showed our passports and Mansoor showed his civil I.D. to the guards, who looked them over carefully, studied our faces, and seemed satisfied. I even waved and smiled at one as he scrutinized my face – he seemed to feel that he had stared enough at that point...mortified, even, to be scrutinizing a woman he did not know.

We were in – and moving up the long driveway, past lots of parked cars and SUVs. Why all the security? Lots of V.I.P.s stay at the Radisson Hotel, David said – it was a target for terrorists. Somehow I doubted that any were lurking nearby, plotting to destroy the Al-Boom.

The place was all lit up. It was after 11 p.m. We got out and went up to a huge, open gate at the end of the driveway. The gate was impressive: it even had those rows of bolts that end in clusters of 3 bolts on the sides of its doors, which characterize old, traditional Kuwaiti doors.

We walked past a huge anchor and 2 propellers (odd, I thought – booms were wooden ships with sails for propulsion!) and through this gate. We found ourselves in a small courtyard with waterfalls and fountains and lights pointing up at the hull of the Boom. To the right was a brass sign affixed to the stone wall: Al-Boom Restaurant.

Al-Boom had this sign just before the wharf. It appeared to be mounted on coral rocks. We also saw this plaque.

All the way to the right was a beautiful wooden archway with a stone floor. It led straight ahead and slightly down, past a pair of bread ovens on the left, which were cooled off for the night. As we continued on down, I noticed some stairs leading to a lower courtyard that wound around the hull of the Boom, surrounded by water fountains. The ship was permanently docked, encased by lots of woodwork and stonework.

Looking around, I saw some beautiful double doors. Feeling glum, I paced around outside, looking and photographing. It was so late that the place had to be closed. How would we even meet anyone to ask about a reservation, let alone get one? I thought that I had better shoot as many photos as I could now, because I doubted that we would be back.

David emerged, looking miserable, and said that the place had been booked solid for 2 weeks. He had had more than 2 weeks to get a reservation, so I said in clipped tones, "Thanks, David," and took off. Let him pace and worry; I would just leave him to his own devices and take more photos. This was likely to be the most of the Boom that I would experience.

I went up some stairs outside the ship and found myself on the upper deck. There was the prow of the Boom, with its bowsprit to the right, and in the middle were masts and ropes for sails, which were no longer present – or needed. To the left was the captain's cabin, with beautiful scenes of seafaring life in stained glass all across the front of it. I went up onto the poop deck and saw the pilot's wheel, and came back down to the main deck.

When I came down the staircase, I expected to see David and Mansoor, wanting me to hurry up. Instead, they greeted me with the announcement that David and I had a reservation for tomorrow evening! I stared at them – was this a joke? No – this was for real. Before I could ask about it, a Kuwaiti in a dark dishdashah with glasses and a red-checked guthra was there, shaking my hand and raving on and on about how much Kuwaitis love Americans, and about how there would be no Kuwait without us. His name was Mr. Bassim. I just nodded and smiled.

He led us inside to look around. There were tables in the hold, with some on an upper deck at the prow of the ship, and down in the middle was a lovely salad area decorated with black metal lobsters and pots. At the entrance area was a waist-level box, full of ice and decorated with a large, gold crab on a black background. Waiters were going about their business of closing the restaurant for the night.

I glanced back and saw Mr. Bassim, the restaurant manager in the red-checked guthra, happily and grandly chatting away with David and Mansoor. No doubt, there would be some wild story. I am not at all good at lying, so I stayed back and occupied myself with the camera.

When at last I had taken all of the photos I thought reasonable or possible to take, I rejoined David, Mansoor and Mr. Bassim. He was almost finished; he gushed a bit more, and led us outside to point at the even bigger ship out back, a baghlah, called the Al-Hashemi II, which forever blocked in the small restaurant. It was also a private club. So...both ships were in the same location – we needn't have worried about being driven or directed far away from the original one. The big one was connected to a private club of the Radisson Hotel, he told us. It was decorated inside with lots of gold, and had made the Guinness Book of World Records for being the biggest wooden ship ever built. Cool.

We thanked Mr. Bassim and left with both of his business phone numbers and our reservation. As we headed back to the car, I asked Mansoor how he could live in Kuwait all of his life and never visit such a fascinating place as the Boom. "I don't need it," was all he said. Okay – I guess I've just got history and education in mind wherever I go. I'm not typical.

I waited until we were safely sealed into the car to ask how they had gotten the reservation, and their answer confirmed my impulse to stay away until the ruse was complete: they had told Mr. Bassim that David worked with the American embassy. Yes – I would have ruined it somehow, by blurting that he didn't or looking startled.

Later, David confessed that under pressure, as Mansoor suggested that they tell some such lie, he had almost said that he was the ambassador. "Too much," Mansoor had admonished him, and wisely so. No way. American security guys would spot the tall tale as such instantly.

I suggested that we now take Mansoor to a restaurant after all of his driving and maneuvering on our behalf, and we both thanked him profusely. "Welcome, welcome," he said, and drove us to Haitham Restaurant for Indian food. We bought him a nice meal, had another lovely visit, and he took us home at 1 a.m.

The Al-Boom Restaurant

On Valentine's Evening, as we got dressed to go out, I worried: could or would pretending to be an unspecified embassy employee lead to trouble? No, David assured me. Fine: we resolved to have a lovely time. I did my nails, took a long bath, and put on a semi-formal black dress with black stockings and black velvet slipper-shoes. I wore my hair down long for a change rather than twisted up into its usual gold clip. Tonight I wanted to be dressed up for David to admire. David wore a black suit and a beautiful blue shirt and tie.

David told me that Mr. Bassim had talked about bringing people over to talk to us, and David had cleverly discouraged this. He said that he just wanted to be alone with his wife for Valentine's Day. Brilliant – that is the inviolable custom of the holiday, and Kuwaitis like privacy, so Mr. Bassim bought it.

We hailed a taxi and were off, with the driver assuring us that he could get us there at approximately 7:30 p.m. He knew exactly where to go, and did such a good job that we took down his phone number for future reference. He was from Sri Lanka, spoke Tamil, and had lost some [extended] relatives to the tsunami disaster (we asked).

The cops with assault rifles inspected our passports and the trunk of the taxi, and then let us into the sacred stomping grounds of V.I.P.-dom. We got out and walked.

Red balloons adorned everything, some heart-shaped, with long red ribbons attached to them. We went through the red-ballooned double doors and into the restaurant. Our reservation was fine.

I began to relax and enjoy the date. Romantic pop music – all in English – was playing. People from non-Islamic cultures occupied most of the tables. Women all around me were bare-headed with pretty hairstyles and makeup, and attractive clothing. They must be from the U.S., Britain, Europe, Lebanon, and perhaps Egypt, I thought to myself.

We were quickly seated at Table #26 by two Indonesian waiters in traditional Kuwaiti seafaring clothing: turbans and long skirts – with aprons. Menus appeared, and our waiter showed us postcards with order cards attached, plus a pen on a string hanging from the side of our table.

Everywhere we looked, we saw beautiful wooden carvings – plus fish-shaped flower vases and red balloons.

We were to choose our dinners, mark our cards, hand them to our waiter, then raid the salad bar. I headed for the bathroom before settling in. It proved to be a beautiful one with wood-paneling, and appropriately cramped, but very comfortable with every amenity to be desired. I realized that this restaurant was a favorite for foreigners, though some Kuwaitis liked it to. It was locally famous for having wonderful fresh fish dinners.

Al-Boom's menu came with a history of the ship, which had been built to be a restaurant. Each table had a rose.

Coming back, I glanced around and realized that all of the diners seemed to be Americans – and perhaps a couple of Europeans. I saw some young and some middle-aged Americans with crew cuts and expensive polo shirts, and others wearing suits. They were all out on dates with their wives or girlfriends.

I quickly saw that everything would be just fine. It was time to enjoy the evening. The waiter came back and showed us a plate of 5 different fish – all referred to as the catch of the day. So, the catch of the day meant a choice between 5 things – not what we are used to! The choices were: Zubaidy, Sea Bream, Hammour, and 2 versions of another fish, I forget which one, but it might have been Roughy, both as a whole fish and as a fillet.

The menu offered Chicken Tikka, Dutch Steak, U.S. Sirloin Steak, Lamb Chops, and Catch of the Day for the first 5 possibilities. All for 11.250 KD apiece, with a salad bar included, a side of vegetables, plus a choice of Arabian rice, baked potato with either herbed butter or sour cream, or fries, and a sauce. The list continued: Lobster Tail, Combo Platter (choose 2 of the 1st 5 items), etc. for KD 13.750, and either possibility ended with dessert as part of the deal. The dessert was unspecified – it turned out to be the same delectable things for all.

David chose a Combo Platter of Lamb Chops and Zubaidy; I chose Sea Bream. A red rose stood in a vase on the edge of the table, and a little wooden lantern on the side facing another American couple 2 tables away and up against the hull of the boom. They had ordered steaks – on a sea-ship of a restaurant that was famous for great fish.

With our orders in, we headed for the salad bar. David whispered to me that it was also a fish bar, with smoked salmon. The bar included: 6 dressings, deviled eggs with tiny shrimp on top, large shrimp, plain and herbed smoked salmon, smoked trout, smoked spiced trout, other smoked fish which was white with yellow edges, Bibb lettuce, chick peas, hummus with olive oil, and lots of other wonderful things. David piled his plate high; I wondered how he would ever finish his dinner. I took half as much but tried everything, and managed to finish it.

Diners from many cultures, including Kuwait; me – sitting with a plate of smoked fish and fresh vegetables.

As we finished the smoked fish our entrées arrived. Then the steak-eating American couple got up. A rose had arrived for the wife during their dessert, prompting the predictable jokes about how all they would get would be the checks. The husband did not have a crew-cut (he was a civilian), and he was wearing a suit. The wife was in black, like me.

They came over to chat with us. He worked for an American company and had been in Kuwait for 2 years; she had just joined him the previous September after packing their 2 kids off to college. She taught English to kindergartners at a British school. The Kuwaiti parents didn't care that she was American and not British – only that both countries speak a version of English. She worked an Islamic week while her husband worked a Western week, so they didn't get very many days off together. The kids would join them in the summer during the blithering heat.

She talked about Sultan Centre, City Center, and seeing Bedouin people out in the desert. She said that they have married their cousins too much, that you can see it in their faces – something is oddly unattractive about them. Okay…I talked a little about the Al-Hamdullilah tent parties, but that family didn't keep up the genetically irresponsible practice of marrying cousins – they looked okay, and many of the women were pretty.

The American woman told me to watch out for becoming an American snob. What did she mean? She meant that we are foreigners in a country where Kuwaitis revere us, while they treat their foreign servants – who are from third-world countries – like dirt. Smile at these servants, she said, thank them for whatever they bring you, and they will appreciate it. I was glad to realize that I was already in the habit of doing that. We thanked them for the lovely chat and they left us to our dinners.

David had 5 or 6 Frenched lamb chops with herbs and gravy, and Zubaidy that he thought must have been previously frozen. I agreed, but the lamb chops were great (we shared our food). I tried it with my Forestière sauce, which was like more gravy and full of gourmet mushrooms. Then I gave him the rest of the sauce. My Sea Bream fish was delicious – soft and flavorful. I ate the grilled eggplant, red onion, yellow pepper and tomato, and some of the baked potato with herbed butter. The whipped butter was good on my fish. David liked my fish, too.

Heart-shaped cakes and puff pastries at Al-Boom.

Our rectangular plates were removed, and dessert was presented on some huge plates, painted and glazed with a funky fish design. Dessert consisted of several items, attractively arranged in the center of the plate: sliced cantaloupe melon, kiwi fruit, strawberry, a small, square puff pastry layered with cream, a tiny, heart-shaped pink-frosted white layer cake, a tiny, heart-shaped, chocolate layer cake with a chocolate flag shape sticking out of its top, and a flower-shaped cookie shell with a scoop of lemon sherbet in it covered with raspberry sauce. A red rose for me arrived during dessert.

We were each given a souvenir upon leaving our table: a hand-hewn nail with a folded card attached to it by a string was presented to us to take home. It had a history of this particular boom ship, plus other fun facts, which follow:

～ AL BOOM ～

This Boom, Mohammadi II, was built in 1979 in Calicut, India, using authentic drawings of Mohammadi I, which was built in 1915-16, the Largest Boom ever built in history.

Mohammadi II took 3 years to build, 17,500 cubic feet of 85-90% first class teak wood, 8,800 kgs. of hand made iron nails from 3" to 30" long, 2.5 tons of copper and 35,000 man days to build "AL BOOM" in India and Kuwait!

Facts About The Boom

Length: 39.9 Mtrs.	Breadth: 10.3 Mtrs.
Depth: 3.4 Mtrs.	Weight: 415 Tons
Iron Nails: 8800 Kgs.	Nails: 3" to 30"
Man Days: 35,000	Seating: 75 Guests
Wood: 17,500 Cu. Ft.	Built: 1979 Indian
Copper Sheeting: 2.5 Tons	
Trade: Floating Restaurant	

EVERYTHING HANDMADE TO A SPECIAL DESIGN

After dinner, we wandered all around the boom, inside and out. The heads – old ship's toilets – were just little rounded seats attached to the sides of the boom, with holes in their bottoms. The front keel of the boom had decorative crescent-shaped metal plates holding it onto the ship.

So that was how sailors went to the bathroom at sea… Imagine the death-defying feat of relieving oneself on the storm-tossed seas. Had any Kuwaiti sailors lost their lives this way? Well, this ship was just for show.

We climbed the stairs outside and saw the captain's cabin. It had beautiful stained glass windows facing the main deck, and dark, varnished wood paneling inside. It was a coffee lounge, and we found some Maxwell House cans on a shelf in the back. No one was in there.

The Captain's Cabin had 2 displays of old boom-building tools and 1 of hand-forged nails.

The Captain's Cabin, with stained glass depictions of sailing ships, a painting of the Emir's visit, and tables.

We went down to the kitchen area (just outside of it) and saw the chef working over his open kitchen, complete with the catch of the day display, which included a brass teapot engraved with "AL-BOOM" on its brass stand.

The chefs of Al-Boom hard at work in the open kitchen, and examples of their work materials.

We went down to the water fountain area to see the hull of the boom, and David gave me a nice, long, kiss. Then he hammed it up for some photos with my rose.

David with my rose – under the stern of the ship, and by the entrance with the rose in his teeth. ☺

I went back in and got a good picture of the hostess, who was wearing a traditional Kuwaiti woman's dress, in dark red over a pink blouse. She said it came in blue, too. She was from the Philippines. I thanked her for the photo – she was often asked to pose.

We noticed that there were many brass plates to the right of the doorway into the dining room, all with names of famous politicians who have eaten at Al-Boom: Madeleine Albright, Gerald Ford, Kofi Annan, etc. Bill Clinton's photo was not there, to our mild disappointment (he did visit Kuwait once while he was our President).

It was time to go home. I thought of calling the same cab driver on our cell phone, but David was sure that this would be too complicated, so we walked into the Radisson Hotel and he had someone there call us a cab. I went straight into the hotel's bookshop. There were lots of Americans sitting around the hotel lobby, and some Kuwaitis. Or were they Saudis? David told me that they dress the same, but are less friendly.

We went outside, and saw a worker baking bread in the 2 ovens, so he posed for photos – one of him by the ovens, and one of the pokers he was using to get the huge, round flatbreads out. (Later, Mansoor told us that the oven is called al tanoor.)

Whatever they were, I wanted to see the books on Kuwait, so in I went. It was worth it – I quickly found one called *Kuwait by the First Photographers*. It covered the time period of 1900-1950, and described Kuwait as it was before oil made it a wealthy nation. It showed booms being built and maintained, and most interestingly told how they were kept water-tight: each year, a boom would be dragged ashore to the shipyard, the spaces between the planks cleared, and then re-stuffed with oil soaked fiber. All this had been done by hand.

The hostess of the Al-Boom restaurant in a Kuwaiti gown; a bread baker at the tanoor in Kuwaiti sailor garb.

After a perfect evening, we went home. David fed our cat, and I put the rose in water.

The next time we had the chance, we invited Mansoor to come up and see all the photographs. He was thoroughly delighted with the whole thing, thinking it was quite a coup to have helped get us there. [Apparently, Mr. Bassim had tried to get David to take me to that Polynesian place – what would we have learned about Kuwaiti culture there?!] Mansoor laughed and enjoyed all the photos, with a cup of his favorite Twining Genius Tea (Earl Grey).

He then requested that I write down the words "Happy Valentine's Day" for him – which I did, in beautiful Chancery Italic calligraphy, thinking that he wanted to save it and give it to someone. Wrong – he wanted to spell it correctly and text-message it to someone using his cell phone. Did he have a girlfriend? I asked, hopefully. No – this was just for a regular friend. Oh well. He was lonely, so I had hoped for him. He seemed to have given up – he said that his one year of marriage was constant problems, that he didn't know how to avoid making another mistake. Did I have any advice?

Yes – make friends with a woman first, then marry her. David interrupted – "that's not possible in this culture!" "I know that," I said – "I meant to be devious…we could help!" We could keep his secrets and help with family introductions once Mansoor and some hypothetical woman decided that they wanted each other. Oh, okay…but Mansoor thought it would all be too difficult to bring off. This is much more than a mere Valentine's Day dinner.

Valentine's Day – This is not for Muslims!

A few days after this wonderful date night with David, I visited Fatin at her home again. She wanted to hear all about it, so I described everything. She had eaten there once many years ago, before the war, but it wasn't as exciting as what I had just had. She hadn't been there on a date, and not on a holiday.

The Awqaf (Ministry of Islamic Affairs) flyer demanding that Muslims ignore Valentine's Day.

Fatin and Zahid are Sunni Muslims. They attend a nearby mosque in Salwa that had handed out glossy, colored flyers dictating that they ignore Valentine's Day. She showed it to me, because I had asked whether Zahid had given her anything romantic for the holiday. It actually had photographs of a red rose, a heart-shaped box of candy, and 2 other items, and informed its parish (in Arabic) that this holiday was not for Muslims.

Only Eid and Ramadan are to be celebrated, not birthdays, not Valentine's Day, not anything else! "So nothing else for the whole year?" I asked, confirming what I was hearing. "Nothing else," she said. Besides, every day is a feast as long as you are well and happy, she added. True, but having interesting events scattered throughout the year can be very nice, I thought. Having them is not sinful!

Of course I wanted a photo of the notice. It was prepared not by the mosque but by the Ministry of Islamic Affairs, also called the Awqaf, and distributed at mosques around Kuwait. There it was, all in Arabic, with its glossy color photos of roses, candy, candles and other romantic gifts. So I now had my latest digital trophy added to the collection of photographs showing Kuwaiti, Arab, and Islamic culture.

David was intrigued and morbidly fascinated by it. His response was to say that some people definitely had entirely too much time on their hands. But David, I said, Kuwait's government pays these time-wasters to do just that! He laughed. (More on what else Awqaf spends its time on in another chapter...)

Fatin was amazed to hear that the U.S. Constitution separates religion and politics, though she realized that we have freedom of religion. I told her – and she listened, because I am an American lawyer – that that is how religion is protected. The law trumps religion, thus accommodating the free and safe expression of all religions. Islam tends to put religion ahead of law, thus allowing religious scholars to write the laws of Muslim nations.

As for Mansoor, he said that when he was married, he gave his wife roses, chocolates, and a Teddy Bear for Valentine's Day. He would have ignored Awqaf if it told him not to.

Caesar's Palace for Chinese Food in Salmiya

Late one evening in early February, at 9:45 p.m., a nice Kuwaiti named Hamid Al-Qasim arrived to take us out to dinner. He wanted to eat Chinese food. I took his photograph, and then we went out (and I forgot the camera). In the car was an Indian driver whom we had never met. Hamid told us that his other driver had left him.

Hamid seemed rather put out by this; he complained that he had gotten that other driver trained and licensed, complete with work papers, and then he went off to another employer who would pay him more. We kept our expressions sympathetic.

We would miss him, but secretly we admired him – no doubt his family really needed that money. The new driver was from Sri Lanka. He was very nice. His name was Partha, and he told us that his family members were all okay, that the tsunami of December 26 hadn't affected them. [I just had to ask.]

Hamid drove while teaching him where things are in Kuwait. (We took a liking to Partha, and I bought him a map of Kuwait, just like mine, before we left for the United States.) We went to Salmiya, where there are lots of malls, shops, a Sultan Center, and the smell of the Gulf breeze. It was nice, but Hamid had little idea of where he was taking us. He told us he didn't spend much time in Kuwait City, preferring to be at the Wafra Oasis, which is on the southern border of Kuwait. There are lots and lots of farms there, and he spends half of each week at his house there. Kuwait City provides Wafra with its recycled water for farming purposes, and Hamid found it very restful to go there, away from the crowds of the city.

He invited us to stay overnight out there during the upcoming holiday weekend, and we looked forward to it. Apparently he had access to 3 guest apartments, so he needed to plan and reserve spaces in advance. Our cat was invited, too. David had talked about Wafra many times. He was excited; he used to go there often when he lived in Kuwait in the early 1990s, when the farms were just starting to be developed. By this time, they were thoroughly built up, and lots of fruits and vegetables were grown there. It sounded really nice. Hamid wanted to barbecue duck for us. He said that animals lived at Wafra: sheep, goats, camels, Arabian horses, ostriches, etc. I could hardly wait to go there by the time he had finished describing it.

I was curious about Hamid: what had he studied? He told us that he had spent 11 years in the States, studying and working, so I wondered what he had done, about his education, and where he had studied. He told us that he had earned a B.S. in computer science, then worked. He started at Washington University in Seattle, Washington, and then switched to Pacifica University in California. When he graduated, he worked in a city located midway between San Francisco and Sacramento.

We ate at a beautiful place called Caesar's Palace, which offered some Chinese and some Indian food – no Italian food, despite the name. It was lovely there. While David was in the rest room I asked him if he had a wife – it just seemed like the polite thing to ask at that moment – and he told me that he was separated, so I dropped the subject. Later, when David asked about her – after he told us that he has 3 kids, all girls (I asked) – I told David not to ask about the wife, because I had already found out that they were separated. Hamid smiled at me appreciatively.

Hamid hinted that he wanted to sit in one of those little rooms on the perimeter of the dining room rather than at a table in the middle of the restaurant where everyone can see you eating. I caught on and voted for that, saying that David would probably be able to hear better in there, being deaf in his left ear. That settled it, and we sat down on the sofas to wait.

Waiting to be seated was fun, because across from us sat first one, then another young, engaged Kuwaiti couple. They were dating. Religious Muslims can only date once a couple is formally engaged. I could tell what their status was because the guys were each wearing silver wedding rings on their right hands; after marriage those rings go to the left hands. The first bride-to-be wore a hijab with fashionable clothing, no doubt from the popular store called Zahra, and the second wore a full abbeya, hijab and nekhab (I'm sure they got an enclosed room to eat in!). Her fiancé was bareheaded, and wore a dishdashah.

The food we ate was very, very good. We took our leftovers home. Hamid was determined to give us several appetizers, so we each got soup. He ordered 3 other things to share. David had hot and sour soup, ever in search of spicy food; I had crab soup, which was thick with real, shredded crabmeat. I had a hunch about that, after visiting the fish souq, seeing how upscale this restaurant was, knowing that Kuwait began as a fishing community, among other things. Dinner was duck with bamboo shoots and mushrooms over rice. When David also chose duck, Hamid again said he would give us duck to eat at Wafra.

Hamid wanted to argue politics a bit, so we did. He didn't seem to be very skilled at it, but he did okay. When he couldn't back up a point he wanted to make with me, he switched subjects. One thing he did say with certainty and conviction, though, was that the Americans should have taken a lesson from the British and pulled out of Iraq a long time ago. No one wanted Iraq – it has always been a hopeless mess, as the British found out in the 1920s, when they left in disgust, Hamid told us. We agreed.

I asked him more about his life in California. Hamid told us that he had lived in a gated community of apartments in an urban area, surrounded by African-American neighbors who liked to sit outside on their doorsteps. He had a funny story about a visit from his mom. She announced that she would walk to the mall. He offered to drive her, but no, she wanted to walk – she was used to walking in Kuwait.

She was quite independent after having been widowed when her kids were only half grown and raising them alone. Hamid worried that his only parent wouldn't be safe in what he thought was a rough, dangerous neighborhood. He followed her in his car, watching as she smiled and greeted everyone she saw. They just smiled back and waved to her; he stopped worrying and let her go alone after that.

He had a succession of pet dogs, including a white toy poodle, which he bathed and perfumed every day. He even remembered the name of the perfume! Hamid went on to say that whenever he invited a woman to stay overnight, he wouldn't let the dog stay in the bedroom. For revenge on each woman guest (the dog loved to sleep in his owner's bedroom), the poodle would do his best to destroy her shoes. Hamid quickly got into the habit of asking for her shoes as she arrived. She would inevitably ask why. You don't want to know – just let me put your shoes out of sight and reach, he would say.

He had worried when taking dogs on planes to London and Kuwait about whether the food he provided was ever given to the dogs, and how comfortable they were. We told him how great Air France was for our cat – that I was able to feed and water her on the way to Paris and Kuwait. He no longer kept a dog, but looked like he was taking mental notes.

Next, Hamid talked at length about Arabian horses, telling us about the sheikh of the United Arab Emirates – the crown prince of U.A.E. The sheikh races these animals in Britain and in Gulf nations. They cost a couple of million British pounds apiece, plus expenses for trainers and shipping back and forth to Dubai. Prize money is perhaps ten percent of total operating costs.

The British races didn't pay much, so he didn't go there. They pay a million pounds for first prize, which the sheikh's horse won. That's not a lot considering how much is charged to compete. Hamid asked if we had seen the horse races on television. We hadn't; but he told us what we had missed: several miles of racing, in which the sheikh, his wife, and all of their children had ridden these expensive Arabian horses.

Hamid worked at different jobs, including overseeing the security and entertainment arrangements for the wedding of the sheikh's grandson, which David had attended the previous week in Fahaheel, Kuwait. There had been caviar, smoked salmon, and many other goodies. 6 buffet tables, all with the same spreads of food, were set up throughout several tents that connected from the beach to the hotel. Security people stood all around. 20 valets were hired to park cars. [Hamid confided that the only people who don't really enjoy such affairs are the people who run them, like him.]

David told him he had felt terrible when he saw all that salmon, because he was thinking of me. He didn't want security to see him taking any, because he thought that word would get around that he was a bad guest. He felt bad about me missing it but kept his thoughts to himself. It hadn't occurred to him that it might have been okay to ask for some for me. Hamid smiled; he said that asking would have been perfectly okay; he would have ordered some packed for me. I thanked him and said that I didn't feel bad about it because they had both thought of me. Hamid smiled again.

The whole time we sat in the restaurant, Hamid left the new driver from Sri Lanka in the car. We felt rather sorry for him. What if he was hungry? Was there dinner at home for him? Hamid said there would be, and that he had spoiled his predecessor by bringing him into restaurants with him, so he was not about to make the same mistakes with this new employee.

We were very interested to meet Hamid, and we had a great time with him.

He took us home and we arranged to go to Wafra the following week.

MSG-Laden Chinese Food in Salmiya

One evening we ended up in Salmiya after running an errand to an office building.

David decided he wanted Chinese food for dinner. We went to a restaurant that he noticed on a previous cab ride, within brief walking distance. Salmiya was hopping with Kuwaitis and Westerners eating out and shopping. A lovely cool wind was blowing.

We ate outside on the patio, choosing nothing that had chicken in it; this was our break from Abraq Khaitan/Abraq Shaitan cuisine. Shrimp and Asparagus Soup was followed by Hammour (fish from the Gulf) with Mixed Vegetables. We should have realized that there was trouble when we still felt hungry.

Our stomachs growled through the night, as if we were starving. We woke up the next morning feeling very hungry. After eating breakfast, we didn't feel much different. This lasted into the late afternoon. David said it was due to monosodium glutamate in the food – it makes things taste good, but salt also does this without the ill effects. This was unregulated Chinese food at its worst. They added the MSG to induce a continuous feeling of hunger, causing the customers to order more food and run the tab up.

Genius Meals

One Wednesday in the spring, we took our cat to the veterinary hospital in Ahmadi City. Hamid had lent us Partha's services for the afternoon. After that, we wanted to take him out for lunch. There was a small restaurant back the way we had come that looked okay. At first, it looked like just another lousy Egyptian take-out place, but we found that it was actually a sit-down place with tables both inside and on the side patio.

The menu offered a decent array of options; we had a lovely meal. I read through it, curious: it actually offered a "Genius Meal" – a hamburger with fries. Kuwaitis admire Americans, and imagine that eating American food will make them smart and efficient – like Americans. Mansoor told us this many times. We told him that this is not so, that it will only ruin one's health, but we can't tell this to all Kuwaitis. At least he listened…we hoped.

We ordered a Zubaidy fish (mine) fried and served with herb-garlic sauce and biryani rice, chicken kebabs, hummus, samosas for Partha, and lentil soup. Partha tried to stop us from feeding him, but we insisted. Hamid never took him out, and he was helping us with our wonderful cat, so we wanted to spoil our Sri Lankan friend a little.

We bagged the leftovers and went home – having forgotten to ask whether carrots were part of the "For Your Eyes" meal.

We took our cat back to the great veterinary hospital in Ahmadi a week later (Assim drove us there). She had scratched up her left ear until the fur was gone, so she got a lampshade collar to wear – poor little beastie. When that was over, we ate at that same place next door, where we had had great fish. They were out of fish – oh well. Still, it was a good outing, because our cat was okay and we ate something other than Abraq Shaitan chicken.

Here is the menu at the tiny eatery near the Ahmadi veterinary hospital. The close-up view shows an option labeled "Genius Meal." It's a burger and fries – the fatty food of foolish, unhealthy choices.

We ate outside in absolutely perfect weather – breezy and warm but not hot – and I saw 13 men march past our table, set up their prayer rugs on the desert sands, and bow in a long row to Mecca for a while, praying. After that, a nice Egyptian lent us his phone to call a taxi.

The Restaurant at Souq Sharq's Sultan Centre

In Kuwait City, in the Sharq District, at the west end of the sprawling, luxurious Souq Sharq Mall was a restaurant in the Sultan Centre store. The restaurant was downstairs, facing out onto the marina. It had inside and outside seating, and a choice of either eating from a buffet or ordering off of the menu. We always ate outside to enjoy the beautiful breeze.

The entrance to the indoor seating area; the buffet of lamb and saffron rice; the outdoor seating area at night.

The seating inside was mostly booths. The customers who sat in them appeared to be middle class or wealthy Kuwaiti families. The customers who sat outside included Americans, young single Kuwaiti males in groups, and an occasional single man.

We usually ate there just after shopping in the grocery store, and we would order off the menu. One of our favorite items was the Gulf Coast Shrimp, and another would be spicy fries and fried cucumber. It wasn't the healthiest of menus, but it wasn't the unhealthiest either.

This was where I learned a bit more about Muslim rules of food choices: halal means that the food is allowed, and haram means the opposite. Any part of a pig is haram, but shellfish is among the halal choices. Interesting – Jews say kosher and non-kosher, they also don't eat pork, but shellfish is forbidden to them. Muslims could not have alcohol, but Jews could, whereas Christians could have any of the above, yet Hindus tended to be vegetarians…enough. I was getting caught up in comparing food rules, but I couldn't help being a bit fascinated.

The Grill at Sultan Centre was a fun, casual place to eat. We couldn't read the name on the sign; part of it was in Arabic, part was a scrawl. We could see the Fish Souq next door, the Dhow marina just beyond it, and the yacht marina right in front of us. Arabian Gulf Street and Kuwait City were directly across the marina, so we could look south at the Liberation Communications Tower, or to the east, at Kuwait Towers.

Easter Sunday at Asha's Indian Restaurant

We had lost track of our own culture's holidays in Kuwait because we our calendar showed Arabic dates. So we had no idea that it was Easter Sunday until I happened to call Rola Al-Dashti to coordinate some woman suffrage work. As we talked, she wished me a Happy Easter. When the call ended, I told David we had to celebrate the spring holiday. He protested that he had to write an article, but I would have none of it. He realized that his fate was sealed. "I am very annoyed at Rola Al-Dashti for telling you it's Easter," he sulked. "Tough," I replied.

We had a lovely dinner at Asha's Indian Restaurant at the Marina Crescent Mall. The meal was delicious, with curried peas, basmati rice, and other spicy thrills. It ended, appropriately enough, with a carrot sweet – thus reminding us of the Easter Bunny, the spring goddess. The place was simply decorated and dimly lit, and had a view of the crescent-shaped marina for which the mall was named. The walls had lots of browns, and the seats were wood with multi-colored cushions. Some other seats – low, cushy living room chairs – were out on the connecting patio. We ate inside by a wall with a view of the whole room, at a table for two.

Inside Asha's Indian Restaurant was a beautiful dining area. It was dimly lit with lots of semi-private areas.

We chatted with a young Kuwaiti couple who were just married in December of 2004. They were honeymooning in the Indian Ocean when the tsunami hit, but not close to the area of disaster. Still, the bride's mother called them, frantic, only to hear that all was well.

The husband worked in civil aviation – it sounded like a government department of some sort. The wife worked as an attorney for a bank, handling its lawsuits. She wore no hijab, and seemed happy with her life. Both were dressed in tight-fitting, almost revealing,

Western clothing. The wife wanted me to tell her about different places in the U.S. that are worth visiting, and why. I talked her out of Las Vegas. Her husband had already visited 33 of the States, and now she was looking forward to going there. We exchanged business cards and chatted before leaving them to enjoy their dinner.

It was always fun to talk to people in restaurants. We did this whenever the opportunity presented itself. We found out and shared all sorts of helpful things, and enjoyed the conversations.

Indian Food in Farwaniya

Late in April, a few weeks after moving across the highway to Farwaniya and a week and a half before we were to go home, Mansoor came over to take us out for a last visit. He said he would miss us. (We still miss him.) We said that we still hoped to get him a McDonald's cap and a McDonald's book – a hard cover one full of color photos with the history of the corporation in it. (When I got home, I managed to buy the cap – but I still have it. We tried to locate Mansoor – no luck.) He said he would be delighted with that; he would wear it to work and everywhere else and make his friends jealous.

Mansoor drove us directly to Farwaniya, and took us to the outside of the new building that he had moved to with his mother and sister. We never went inside his new apartment. This was a taller building than ours. I forgot to count how many stories, but it had more than nine. He lived on the sixth floor, with 3 bedrooms, in the front and on the left. The building was newer than the one we lived in. We could see lights on in the living room of his apartment. He said he liked it there. It was a sand-colored building with decorative, mottled green squares of glass that formed bow windows up the middle of the front. We were glad he was happy there.

Down in front of the building to the left was a tiny new building adjoining the big apartment building. It housed an Indian restaurant, where Mansoor took us for dinner. It is so new that the owner hadn't had time to make any menus yet. The owner had gone to a great deal of trouble with the paint, the wainscoting-style wallpaper, plastering fake rose blossoms of many colors in rows onto the wallpaper. The ubiquitous and obligatory strings of tiny colored lights festooned the overhanging front roof. 2 televisions played the same Bollywood movie – a sad one with a metaphorical depiction of the rape of a married woman who then killed herself in time for her husband and 10-year-old son to find her. It ended with a Hindu funeral pyre.

The owner tuned in to the BBC News after that. He was very excited to have Americans in his restaurant, and insisted on visiting with us for most of the time that we were there, even though we didn't know him and had come out to visit with Mansoor. He told us all about himself and his family, and called all of his friends to say that he had Americans in his new restaurant! It seemed strange, because he was Indian, not a grateful Kuwaiti who loves Americans for ousting the Iraqi invaders. He didn't seem to want anything more than attention from us. He bragged that he owned 3 businesses in Kuwait, and worked as a mechanical engineer at Kuwait International Airport. His kids all had good careers, too.

The most entertaining thing about him was that he kept loudly telling Mansoor that Kuwaitis don't know how to work. Mansoor didn't even try to deny it! He also was sure he had seen me before, so I said that it must have been while I was out shopping in Farwaniya with my friend Fatin – she liked the Nooran hijab store there. He was a bit of a pest, though, calling everyone he knew about us, and he even followed us to the car after we had said good-bye to him. It was bizarre, and it reminded me of the celebrity-obsessed culture at home. It was much the same: we were being admired without having earned it. It impeded our ability to chat with the friend who had brought us out for a nice dinner!

We met one other person while we were in the restaurant: Mansoor's new bouab. This bouab is a Saeedi guy – not unusual – but much younger and healthier than ours. He looked like he was in his forties. He wore sandals and a long dark green-and-white striped dishdashah with an open, wide neckline and no head covering.

Mansoor told us that he was a lawyer, so I wondered why he worked as a bouab. Maybe Egypt had the same problem as the United States – a surplus of lawyers without enough cases. This bouab spoke English. That is all we learned about him before he went back to his building. Mansoor seemed to have gotten used to him, but he was quieter than Abdul Mohti. We could tell that he was not the sort of person who would enjoy being silly, which Mansoor missed.

The visit with Mansoor turned out to be a quiet one, thanks to our Indian admirer and to the fact that we would not see each other again. We let him treat us to dinner, because this was our last visit. He enjoyed ordering food for us, partly because he knew what we liked. That was cute – he had fun spoiling us – not because he was operating on the usual assumptions that people here have about what Americans like, but because he knew us personally and liked us for ourselves. We would really miss him personally, and being silly with him.

Chapter 8
Laundry - A Comedy of Inconvenience

What follows is the tale of woe – a comedy of inconvenience – that was the chore of doing our laundry in Kuwait. Be warned – if you travel, you may not be comfortable. But don't let that keep you at home. Travel is too interesting to skip the experience.

September 2004 – I find out that we are going to Kuwait.

So I found myself contemplating 5 and a half months in a foreign country with a looming logistical problem: laundry. Granted, we would be in a first world country – a wealthy one. Kuwait is, after all, a gas station nation. The U.S. had involved itself in Saddam Hussein's attempt at geographic larceny – the Kuwait War of 1990-1991 – for just that reason.

But this did not guarantee an easy way to keep one's family's clothing clean. Just because I had come to believe that life in a first world country entails access to a washing machine and dryer, that did not automatically translate into reality once outside the United States. It couldn't be that easy.

I caught myself glancing at our cat with envy whenever I thought about this. But we humans could not wear the same thing every day, and we do not have built-in cleaning systems to maintain our outfits. No – Scheherazade Cat was the only member of our family without such problems; she could wear the same things every day, and combine taking a bath with doing her own laundry.

I would have to deal with this unknown of keeping our clothes clean when we joined David in Kuwait. Hurray...

Laundry in Kuwait – Episode One:
We Assess the Problem

November 23, 2004 – a Tuesday. Which translates to a Thursday in the Islamic world.

Shortly after my husband and I got at least somewhat settled into our new apartment in Abraq Khaitan, it became clear that I would need to figure out how our laundry would be done. [Before you leap to the erroneous conclusion that my husband does not do household chores, I should add that he washes dishes, dries them, puts them away, and takes trash out. And...if there are laundry machines, he does laundry!]

The truth is, unless there are machines available to us, I won't let David do the laundry. The reasons for this are perfectly legitimate, and can be summed up in this manic mantra:

> Won't let David do the laundry. Can't let David do the laundry; he is a Kuwait War Veteran who was a U.S. Chemical Weapons Officer, so he was exposed to some of Saddam's secret recipe of toxins. His hands and feet have lots of dry, cracked dead fissures that bleed. Must do all of the laundry myself.

Of course, this means that I can keep track of it all – what is clean, how it gets cleaned, etc. And write up this tale of inconvenience.

Alas, there were no laundry machines available to us. The typical Kuwaiti apartment building is constructed of concrete blocks covered with smooth-polished tiles inside and out, and comes with a full bathroom in each unit plus a kitchen with no stove – which must be bought, along with gas tanks connected to hoses which look, well...frightening.

A hot water heater is connected to both the kitchen sink and, immediately on the opposite side of that particular wall, the sink and bathtub/shower. This water heater spurts scalding water into the kitchen sink immediately upon being turned on. All apartments get their water from a tank on the roof of the building, which is periodically refilled by a truck that has to be summoned by the bouab – the live-in superintendent.

There is no laundry room below the apartments. In fact, all that is below them is the ground floor – and no basement. Just as in Europe, Kuwaitis mark buildings with a ground floor followed by numbers on the upper stories. On the ground floor, one exits the elevators to find that, at least in our building, one is outdoors. Around the front of the building to the left is the bouab's apartment. Ours was an old South Egyptian man – Saeedi is the slang but not derogatory term for someone from that area – named Abdul Mohti. He had a small, two-room living space, half of which was occupied by some filth-caked mops in a shower stall with no curtain and no place to hang one. The other half was his sleeping and sitting room. His cooking facilities consisted of a hot-pot.

So...I held out a hope that Saleh, the Kuwaiti physician who had invited us to Kuwait with promises of a laboratory to run (which proved false) would help us out by letting us come over with our dirty laundry to wash, dry, and fold it. What a lovely fantasy!

In America, this would seem like a reasonable expectation, not a fantasy, so we could hardly be considered crazy for entertaining this idea. But we were not in America any more…

I had some past experience which had taught me to never EVER allow a stranger to do my laundry. In this experience, I had been a guest of a very nice French family who went on vacation to Ibiza, a Spanish island in the Mediterranean Sea. The mother hired out the laundry to a Spanish cleaning lady. It came back clean, but as a teenager, I was mystified as to how my new clothes could have acquired random white streaks on them. Could they still be dirty? I wondered. No…a year later I went to college, did all my own laundry, talked to other people about this, and found out (outrage!) that this woman had boiled the clothes with bleach! That settled it – in Kuwait, I would do my own laundry one way or another.

And why not?! Here I was in a country full of foreign servants – as in not Kuwaitis. Some spoke English very well, others did not, but most were Muslim men who would not even speak to me, so the mere idea of maintaining control over this process was idiotic.

I did not look forward to any of this.

Laundry in Kuwait – Episode Two: Our Friends Help Us Out

November 25, 2004 – a Thursday. Which means it's like a Saturday!

Ooh! Excitement! Saleh's wife Raidah has invited us over to meet her (well, I am going to meet her – David met her years ago), eat dinner, and, most important to us, use her laundry machines! We will go there on Thursday afternoon. Thursdays translate into Saturdays here, so it will be the weekend. All socializing must be done on this day, because it's the only chance for that in a religious and Islamic country.

Well – this is great! At least for the first round of clothes washing and drying, we will have this problem solved to our satisfaction. I can relax about this for a bit longer, and keep trying to sort this out on my own.

November 27, 2004 – a Saturday. Must get used to this feeling like a Monday.

What a bizarre weekend that was…must be the culture shock. Everyone else seemed to find each situation to be completely normal, which of course tips me off about the fact that my reactions are examples of culture shock. Oh well…emotional reactions are more memorable than bland ones, so I guess I'm learning a lot.

Yesterday, Saleh brought us to his house. It's a Kuwaiti McMansion – beautiful, spacious, attractive…and mostly off limits to guests. We saw what little of the house that visitors may see.

This house (previously described) was to become the site of much drama, intrigue, confusion and odd behavior, all to do with our laundry.

Like a typical Arab dwelling, it had a walled and gated front yard. This particular walled area had a pretty, wrought-iron gate. It was possible to see right through it to the front door, but forget just walking up and knocking – this gate was kept locked. I found this out when we got out of Saleh's car, and I went up to the gate. Clearly, door-to-door sales or other solicitation is no threat in this culture. Saleh led us inside through the side door, which is around to the right, in a little alley between the houses.

In that alley, which leads to the servants' wing straight ahead, was where the cars were parked. Saleh had one car and one jeep. It turned out that we were living just one district to the west of Saleh and Raidah's area, which is called South Surra and is mostly in a state of new construction. It's a huge area of cookie-cutter McMansions, all in different styles, made of stucco in shades of sand, pink and yellow. Pretty wrought iron decorative effects are part of many of them, while others have modern lines of windows. You could tell which ones weren't occupied yet by the lack of curtains – Muslims cover every inch of glass with curtains so that no one can see in. Which led me to wonder why any Muslim, given choices, would buy a home with walls and walls of glass…that would just lead to a lot of bills for curtains.

Raidah's house had smaller amounts of glass, with just one window on either side of the front door, and a couple of other windows in the living room. I noticed that those windows had metal covers in addition to curtains – something I had never seen before. It was like a rolling sheet of metal coming down at dusk as she pulled them down and locked them into place. No light could get in from the outside. I doubted that these things were bulletproof – just gaze-proof. She was guarding against nosy, inquisitive eyes, it seemed.

But getting back to the way we entered: we got out of the car and went in through a door that was halfway along the wall. Glancing up as we approached the building, I noticed that the house was 3 stories high, with the exception of the servants' wing. Inside, we found white marble floors and a staircase to our right. Ahead of this was another door, which could be locked if one wished. We went through that and emerged into a hallway which led to our right, and thus to the back of the ground floor. To our left was the living room, which took up the front left of the home. The front right was the dining room, which was a continuation of the front room, but up on a platform.

We didn't go in there right away. Looking to our right again, we noticed 3 expensive motorcycles parked in the back hallway that had belonged to their oldest son, Hanbal, who had died a year and a half earlier of liver failure. Since we knew all about Hanbal, we just looked glumly at the motorcycles and made no comment.

The hallway had 4 doors total, 2 on each side. The ones on the right led to beautiful bathrooms that appeared not to have seen much use: each one had lovely tiles, some with decorative effects, a big bathtub, sink and toilet, and no shower curtain. I supposed that people would wash their hair by sitting down, French-style, and using the detachable shower sprayer on a hose. No bath towels were in there – just some fancy paper hand towels.

On the other side of the hall from the first bathroom was a door that Raidah said led to Hanbal and Saidah's old room. At the back of the hallway on the left was a kitchen with every appliance that a competent cook – or chef – could wish for. 2 of Raidah's sisters were in there – visitors from Iran. Would they be joining us for lunch? No. Hmm…oh well. It was interesting to see them at least. They were tall, they had pretty faces, and they were overweight, looming over us quietly in their black abbeyas and scarves. They greeted us politely.

Seeing the upper floors clearly wasn't part of the tour. The bedrooms were up there, and without discussing or mentioning the idea, we sensed that this was the extent of our tour. David had, after all, spent a week here without ever seeing anything beyond the ground floor, and despite my gender, I obviously wasn't going up there either. But that, we were told, was where the laundry machines were. I didn't ask how our clothes would be cleaned, despite my worries…

We headed for the living room, and then the dining room. Lunch was about to begin.

We had a delicious meal cooked by Raidah, all fabulously spread out on her formal dining room table. There were many empty seats between us and Saleh and Raidah's sons, Mohsen and Asim, who appeared to help bring out the food and eat with us. I asked about the youngest boy, and Saleh said that Hussein was upstairs and wouldn't be joining us. Odd…must have had too much homework. Or not…I really didn't know what to make of his absence. I had only been in this culture for a week and a half, after all.

The meal was American, which came as a surprise. David and I expressed slight confusion and disappointment at not being able to try the food of Raidah and Saleh's culture, but then hastily assured Raidah that her food looked and smelled wonderful. She seemed satisfied with that, and replied "Next time" to the idea of trying Kuwaiti/Persian food. Raidah is from southwestern Iran. A lot of Shi'a Arab people live there. So we ate fried chicken, mashed potatoes, French fries (which Asim called Freedom fries, prompting me to lambaste the idiots in the U.S. Congress who had suggested this nonsense, thus wasting taxpayer dollars on non-work-related natter), gravy, and one Middle Eastern dish: tomato and cucumber salad.

After the meal we adjourned to the living room, one step down from the alcove-on-a-platform that was the dining room. A store-bought chocolate cake that tasted like cardboard was served, along with coffee and tea.

The bizarre part of the visit came when another visit inserted itself into that visit. During dessert, a perpetually grinning guy named Mahmoud K. Mahmoud showed up, unannounced. For him, life is all about viewing his shiny red car. Saleh just sent us off with him because he was a potential investor. What about our laundry, I wondered, as we were driven far south of there?

Too bad for now...the impromptu visit at this faraway home dragged inexplicably on and on. It got darker and darker, and David and I kept glancing at each other, wondering and worrying about Raidah and Saleh. We thought it was extremely odd behavior for someone to kidnap another person's guests for hours on end. What must they be thinking of and about us, and how inconvenienced must they feel? Finally, I stood up and politely asked him to please take us back to Saleh's house now. It worked; he did it. What a relief.

We got back there well after dark. I apologized to Raidah and asked her if this business of taking someone's guests away from them was normal here. She said that it could happen sometimes, but not all the time. We went back into the living room to resume our visit.

It was at this point that I presented Raidah with the gifts that I had brought for her: 2 coffee table books of American art. Raidah politely looked through both books as I asked her all about her life.

She was from southern Iran and her family members were Arabs; she had met Saleh when he went to visit the holy Shi'a sites of Iran and passed through her area. Her family did not approve of her interest in this doctor; they wanted her to marry one of her cousins so that her children would have the family last name. I commented that: 1. Saleh is nice – to this she said that her family considered this fact to be irrelevant, which did not surprise me; and 2. I pointed out that marrying one's cousin leads to children with an insufficiently diverse gene pool and thus health problems. Poor Raidah has lost her 2 oldest children, sons Hanbal and Mashal, to this exact result – both died of liver failure after undergoing transplants.

Our visit continued like this for a while longer, during which time she had her maid start to clean our laundry. Since the washer and dryer were upstairs, in a part of the house that we would not be seeing, Sarah the little Nepalese maid, took care of it. I worried about her using hot water – which would ruin the clothes – and Raidah promised me that cold would be used. In fact, David had to spend an absurd amount of time telling her in Arabic to use *only* cold water, and to insist upon it regardless of what she thought should be used. These were *our* things after all.

Our clean and dried things would be dropped off the next day, as it was getting late. I didn't bother to ask about or hope for the clothes to be folded – it was enough to get them cleaned and dried. Saleh's driver Abdullah, Sarah's husband, would return our laundry to us the next day in the family jeep. Secretly, I wondered if Sarah and Abdullah were really their names, or just something easier for the Kuwaitis to pronounce and remember. We weren't going to find out, and I wasn't about to ask such a probing question while our laundry was out of our control.

As it was, Saleh was focused on taking us out to visit a few more people before the visit was over. We met Asim Al-Tikriti and his wife Aiesha, and then Asim's older brother Fahad, and then returned to the first Asim's house with him. At last Saleh drove us home and the marathon of visits ended for the day.

Sure enough, our clothes arrived the next day, not folded, but cleaned and completely dried, stuffed tightly into our laundry bag. What a relief.

Round one of laundry dealt with – without some hideous experience of labor-intensive work, without bleach, hot water, and ruined, shrunken clothing.

Laundry in Kuwait – Episode Three:
No Such Thing as a Laundromat – Only Laundry Services

14 December 2004 – a Tuesday.

It had been a month since we had our things washed and dried; time to face the problem of doing laundry again. I am not the sort of person to procrastinate and avoid work, but this was a significant logistical problem. Keeping clean is crucial – we couldn't be seen in stained, sloppy attire, and we certainly couldn't be smelled in it. This is just our rigid sense of what is and is not acceptable, but we won't compromise on it.

Here we were in what was thought of as a first-world country – a wealthy nation – and I felt a threat of third-world work looming ahead of me. I am not the sort to join the Peace Corps and wash my clothes in a river while worrying about the crocodiles attacking.

We needed to get our laundry done. There are no laundromats in Kuwait – only laundry services. They mix different customers' clothes together, and they use hot water and bleach.

We had one-of-a-kind, colorful things, and we are picky, so even if we were rich, we wouldn't be able to just replace our clothes once they were ruined. I buy classic clothing that stays in style, not trendy stuff. It is difficult to find clothes that I like. Once found, I get very attached to each piece of clothing. I wear it for years until it is completely worn out, and I DON'T want to destroy what I have…especially not all at once, as it would be if I allowed anyone else to clean it – and then look for other clothes. I don't like what is on the market right now anyway. And Kuwait's stores don't seem to offer the same sorts of clothing that I buy for David – it's all tightly fitted stuff that he wouldn't be caught dead in. I wondered what was up with that…and I intended to find out, when I had time to read or ask about it.

When I do laundry, I wash everything together in COLD water with soap – NEVER with bleach. David also has bitter experience with laundry services, especially in this country. It went something like this: You tell them what you want done with your property, and whether or not they understand you, they just smile and nod and then use hot water and bleach, and it all comes back white-streaked with the colors all run together – ruined.

We had no machines of our own, so Saleh was going to help us go and buy some. Meanwhile, he and Raidah had that Nepalese maid named Sarah (if that is her real name) who can't read but speaks a little Arabic and a very few words of English…and a washer and dryer.

After having had our laundry at their house once – with David overseeing the washing – I wondered how we could possibly keep that up. The washing machine was downstairs at the back of the house, in the area where male visitors were allowed to go. They kept the dryer upstairs, so Sarah handled that, but she couldn't hurt the clothes by drying them. What we needed to do was supervise the washing, because otherwise Sarah would use hot water and bleach on the clothes. As I mentioned earlier, she argued with him about this – quite a stress inducer. David had to work hard to prevent her from doing so last time!

Anyway, our laundry was to be combined with another errand, both of which were to be taken care of by going to Saleh and Raidah's house. What could be simpler? Many things...

But wait, it got better – or worse, depending upon your point of view.

Laundry in Kuwait – Episode Three, Continued: We Learn that Demons Live in Dirty Laundry

Sunday night, Saleh had the little Indian guy who drove for him in emergencies bring us to his house in South Surra. That "region" was divided into 5 "areas." What we didn't know was that the house was in Salaam area. Good luck finding it, because all of South Surra is under construction, with huge open areas of desert and several mosques that are only half finished. People routinely get lost going anywhere in it, and I still needed a reliable map, so I did not have a clear idea as to how to get there. Ramatallah arrived in a pickup truck, so David jumped into the back with the laundry and a note to Raidah inside the bag with our plea to wash it in cold water without bleach...and a very real risk that Sarah would simply throw it out (we suspected that she could not read it or anything else...). I got inside the truck and we tried to go to Saleh and Raidah's house.

It seemed reasonable to think (but what do I know, I'm just a direct and logical American?!) that we would go inside the house and that we would see Saleh. Nothing doing – one weird thing after another occurred instead. We got there, and were promptly met outside by Sarah's husband Abdullah (that can't be his real name!), the regular driver for the Al-Hamdullilah family. He and Sarah ushered us along the outside walkway to the right of the house. We were left standing in the darkness for quite a while, between a high wall and the house, facing the white marble hallway with a darkened stairwell just inside. I did not let David go up it – he would not be allowed upstairs – but I knocked on the door that leads to the living room where I had previously visited with Raidah.

No response – it was locked. Odd though...voices could be heard from the other side of that door. I went back outside. Sarah was back, but we couldn't go inside. Ramatallah was gone with our passports, and Abdullah was going to drive us back now. What about the laundry? I took the note out of the laundry bag and showed it to Sarah, for all the good that might do. What was going on? Why couldn't we go in?! We were confused, and we called Saleh. He made sure that our passports were gone, then swore that he wasn't at home, and said that he was with his mother. We could hear him both over the phone and speaking inside a room in the house directly above us as he said all this. *What was going on?!*

David suddenly grabbed the laundry and headed for the street. Sarah was still holding the note and looking confused. I tried to stop David, gave up, took the note away from Sarah, and forced David to allow it back into the laundry bag. We let Abdullah drive it and us back to Khaitan. I was furious! I wanted an explanation of all this immediately, and to know how and when our laundry could be done. David wasn't sure how to explain it, but I didn't care – I was very angry about being confused, put off, and kept outside. Eventually, he did explain.

2 things were going on in that house: one was a religious gathering for women only, held by Raidah in the living room; the other was that Saleh's mother had come over. It was mostly because of his mother that we couldn't go in. Why? We are not relatives, and I am not a Muslim (David is, but he also believes in all 3 monotheistic religions: Judaism, Christianity, and Islam. Adopting that last one without inheriting it from his family is not good enough for strict Muslims, it seems.). Also, Saleh's mother has, off and on for 20-odd years, been claiming to be at death's door. This, combined with being non-Muslims and non-relatives, meant that we would very likely have brought demons into the house if we went in. To top it all off, Kuwaitis have a superstition that other people's dirty clothing contains demons, so both we and it were kept out.

Demons...I should mention that the Al-Hamdullilah family sees demons often. David has met this mother twice...well, been presented to her is more accurate. After each brief presentation, he was quickly ushered out of her presence. She seems evil and insane, he says. She wears a black chador, that long shroud-like cloth that women in Iran wrap themselves in whenever they go out. All you can see is her ancient, sinister face. She grinned at David, he grinned back, and Saleh rushed him out. That was it. A friend of mine (a girl from Iran, no less!) once said that people who say that they're going to die soon always live forever. This certainly works for my grandmother (she turned 90 this past summer). We're not afraid of her! She is fairly comfortable, lives happily with her pet Sheltie, and eats chocolate every day.

So our laundry was now in Saleh's car, still dirty. He said we could do it at his house, the same way as last time, and that he would take us to buy used laundry machines. How we would get them home and hooked up to the water supply I don't know. Saleh is a genius, but incredibly scattered. I was angry with him now, because the next night he did another weird and embarrassing thing. And he had absolutely no appreciation of this!

He got our Egyptian engineer friend's son to take us to an Amway presentation! It has a different name here in Kuwait – Biznas – but the basic scam is easily recognizable: a loud fat guy lectures in a cheap, cheesy-looking hall to an audience of immigrants who are hoping to get rich quick by peddling junky products such as household cleaning supplies…and stupid Saleh gave them 40 KD! We could have strangled him. Of course he fell for it – he's naïve and down on his luck – but it was rather embarrassing that he was the only doctor and the only Kuwaiti citizen in the crowd. I can't believe we got dressed up for this.

Laundry in Kuwait – Episode Four:
We are Introduced to a Travesty of a Washing Machine

17 December 2004 – a Friday…like a Sunday here.

Saleh took us out all day yesterday – to a cardiology conference at a hotel in Manqaf.

After that, we left for Saleh's house to do the laundry – which proved to be nothing but a huge fiasco – as usual. It turned out that Sarah, the Nepalese maid, had killed their washing machine by overloading it and burning out the motor (it couldn't agitate, so no more washing machine – great). Saleh had since bought other, cheaper, smaller, labor-intensive ones, and she killed them too. He drove to a vendor to buy another one, which cost 32 KD, and was hoping to stick us with that piece of junk. "No!" we said – it goes to your place. We don't want it. He was trying to get us to buy it, use it, and then have wet clothing all over our flat. We wouldn't do it; we were determined to wait until we had the money for a good, washer and dryer. Until then…it was off to his house.

Saleh persuaded us to come to this inconvenient, user-unfriendly country, so he could damned well help us with this! Sarah could dry our stuff upstairs – they had a standard, working dryer. Meanwhile, Saleh insisted on buying this horrible machine, he borrowed the money for it from us, and so now he owed us 32 KD. That piece of junk ended up in his house. I was so glad it was not in our flat! Saleh actually had the nerve – in the store's showroom, in front of the proprietors – to point out the separate spinner section of the machine and call it a dryer! How insulting – what do I look like, a common laundry slave?! Wives do not come with notices that say "Free Maid" – I would not work with one of these pieces of plastic rubbish. David was outraged by the idea, too; I could tell from the way he backed me up.

Here is how it works: the left ⅔ of it is a washer-rinser section; the right ⅓ is a spinner. You plug it in, and run its drain hose down into a hole-in-the-floor toilet (most Kuwaiti homes have one of these in their bathrooms, though we don't, and we don't miss it – plus the bathrooms have toilets as we know them, sinks, and bathtubs with shower hoses that detach from the wall). IF we were to take this monstrosity home to our apartment, we would have to run the hose either into the drain in the bathroom floor, or the tub. And then our bathroom would be taken up entirely with washing our clothing rather than our persons. No way are we doing that. You take the shower hose off of the wall, and fill the wash-rinse chamber with water. Add clothes and soap. Run. Drain. Wring out clothes by hand(!), then move them into the spinner. Run. Transfer the load back into the wash-rinse chamber. Fill with water, run, drain. Wring out clothes again. Transfer again to the spinner section. Run. Then Sarah takes the clothes upstairs to dry them.

Each load must be spun in 4 or 5 batches, because the spinner is much smaller than the washer-rinser, all while fending off Sarah to avoid hot water, bleach, or overloading the new machine and burning out its motor. What fun! Also, what a lot of work and time must be spent just to do all of this…it is certainly a major imposition on *my* time. I skinned the knuckles of my thumbs doing this job. I'll bet home laundry service exists in Kuwait, with foreign workers buying and using these horrible things to earn extra income. Sarah and Abdullah wanted to know how much it cost as they took it out of its box. I should have brought my camera…then I would have had a photograph of the idiotic, hateful contraption.

When he tried again to make me accept this thing – by pulling up in front of our building, getting out and opening the trunk of his car – I got so mad that I started crying. David got out and stopped him from trying to unload it. Saleh kept trying to persuade us, saying "See? It knows its place!" That was what set me off. Saleh caved in at that point, clueless and unnerved by my tears…the classic reaction of a man to a woman getting that upset. He took the hated machine and us to his house as agreed, and we promised in return to keep quiet and not to expect to see Raidah…not a hardship when you know that someone doesn't want to deal with you!

Now the truth came out as we approached the house: she was ill, feeling lousy this week, seeing demons, thinking that we would bring some into her house, and didn't want us to come over unless she knew about it in advance. Saleh wouldn't stand up to her and her moods – and now it sounded as though he had married a younger version of his mother! (His mother was obsessed with demons and jinn also.) We had limited sympathy or patience. He persuaded us to come to Kuwait, as I said before. The laundry options were few and absurdly complex, and we expected him to help us out until our collective incomes (both his and ours were intertwined in that asthma study) improved, thus allowing us all to get proper laundry machines. And then we wouldn't destroy ours…

Abdullah drove us home after I completed the long and laborious process of washing, wringing, spinning, rinsing, wringing, and spinning again while David worked on the laptop in the dining room. Hopefully, Saleh would give us our [dried] laundry back that weekend! It wouldn't be ruined – at least we knew that much. But it would probably be wrinkled – though it was too much to hope that Sarah would bother to fold it.

Laundry in Kuwait – Episode Five:
A Bathtub and A Space Heater
Double As a Washer and Dryer

9 January 2005 – a Sunday.

After a few hours' break from writing, I could say that our clothes were clean again. As for being dry, that was quite another story. I am most definitely a laundry snob, and I make no apology for it. I am also well aware that the planet is populated by many, many people – mostly women – who are consigned to a lifetime of doing their laundry all by hand. However, this knowledge did absolutely nothing to change my attitude.

This space has already been filled with a detailed explication as to precisely why that is. The latest idiocy was Saleh's offer to do our laundry for us. Give me a break – he would just give it to his maid, and she would ruin all of our clothes. No way – David tried to persuade me over the phone today to accept this offer, and I told him that there would be no compromise on the issue of laundry – my way or the highway, even if this meant doing it all by hand myself and feeling angry and resentful at Saleh.

My way or the highway – what an awful-sounding thing to say! I normally don't say that, because compromise is much better, but if I did that with the laundry, we would not have any decent clothing left! Besides that, Saleh really had some nerve encouraging us – no, begging us – to come to Kuwait and help him set up a health clinic, only to find that the person (Dr. Naziha) and the place (downstairs on the 1st floor) were not available after all, Dr. Naziha because she didn't want to pay for help, and the 1st floor because a beauty "saloon" was going to be there. [By the way, this error – beauty saloon rather than beauty salon – was repeated on signs all over Kuwait. Few Kuwaitis realized that they are having their hair cut in establishments that purported to sell precisely what was most vigorously banned in their country. Go figure.]

Really, I would rather have had a dryer – a real one – than a washer. I could at least finish the job quickly with a dryer. A washer would entail all kinds of picky problems, such as getting water in and out of our apartment. A washing machine is just not welcome in my home unless it is the real thing – not that travesty that Saleh tried so hard to force down our throats a few weeks back! So now I was trying to dry our stuff by hanging it all over the apartment, on kitchen cabinet doors, door handles, the shower rung, and with the space heater that Assim Al-Tikriti gave us after washing everything in the bathtub with liquid laundry detergent.

It was amazing just how much brown dirt came out of our socks, my black pants, and a few other items. Most laundry detergent sold at our local grocery store is powder, by the way, not liquid. Liquid is better – it washes out without streaking the clothes. Our socks I washed all together, though most of them were David's, and most of them white ones. It wasn't complicated, just tedious. I filled the tub with socks and lukewarm water, figuring that it was okay not to use cold as long as I was doing the laundry by category rather than all together. It was also easier on my hands.

Then I added soap, pouring it all over the clothes for each tub-full. I squeezed and lathered everything, then agitated the laundry by swirling everything around the tub a few times. Next, I let it soak while I dealt with other chores, thus giving myself a slight rest from leaning awkwardly over the tub. I had to mop the floor continually as I dripped around the apartment, just so I wouldn't slip and fall down and hurt myself. I dressed in panties and a tee shirt for the job, so that I would have the option of standing inside the tub to give some of the clothes a little extra attention.

This job meant soaking one's hands and squeezing out the water often. David said he would do his own laundry – but he wouldn't be able to do this. His hands had only just started to heal. He still had open cuts on some of his fingertips. Meanwhile, the poor guy had used up almost all of his socks and underwear, and needed a few clean tee shirts. So I was determined to clean up all the clothes myself. He was too busy working (he's a workaholic), and his laundry bag was getting really smelly. I washed that, too.

David told me he used to enjoy going to a laundromat to do his own laundry – he found it relaxing to clean and dry the clothes – but that was with, as I call them, real washers and dryers. Now he reminded me of an American woman named Carla that Saleh introduced us to a week or two ago at K.O.C. Hospital, with the idea in mind that she would tell us where to find a laundromat in Kuwait.

But there was no such thing. Assim Al-Tikriti called me twice, and talked to me at length about washers and dryers – he wanted to buy us a dryer and maybe a washer, because we helped him so much with his son's studies – he was out at Al-Ghanim and Panasonic researching prices! What a nice guy. And he told me that he has never, ever, heard of any laundromats in Kuwait. Really, that was what I expected. As for Carla, she married a Kuwaiti and went home to her mother with the grandkids in the summers. Seriously…she must have bought herself a washer and a dryer. She was not going to tell us about any laundromat anywhere in this country, but I would ask her just to convince David – and our infuriating friend, Saleh.

Apparently, Raidah was seeing devils again, and getting nightly visits in her dreams from Hanbal's ghost, so we couldn't go over to her house to do our laundry. I wouldn't let Saleh do it – or Sarah, the maid. The last time she dried our stuff, she didn't fold any of it. That's how you avoid wrinkles with wash-and-wear clothing – you fold it as soon as it comes out of the dryer, while it's still hot.

I told Assim about the devils; he seemed a little confused. "Devils?" he asked me, wondering what I was talking about. I really don't know, frankly. What kind they were was a mystery to me, and I wasn't about to bring it up in conversation with Raidah. When would I do that anyway, and how? Not as an opener, certainly, but I could only picture her getting outraged and insulted if I were to ask. I'll bet she wasn't seeing as many odd things as Saleh imagined, and that this was just his way of getting rid of us after bringing us to Kuwait.

Instead, he seemed to be monumentally unhelpful even with bringing his own clinical laboratory into existence. He also didn't want to share any profits with the Egyptian people who were helping with the iqtirah (business plan). Saleh may be a hero of the Kuwait resistance, but he still exhibited the racist prejudice that many Kuwaitis shared: he considered non-American and non-European foreign workers to be less than human, not deserving of high pay or positions of prominence in this society. Being a partner in a business enterprise is certainly a position of prominence, and these iqtirah-writers deserved it. They were qualified, expert professionals who had done what was needed to produce an iqtirah. The iqtirah is necessary for success. These engineers were just as human as the Kuwaitis and Americans.

Assim Al-Tikriti, on the other hand, didn't believe in soliciting help from people and then just taking it without helping them in return. We helped him with his son, plus we wanted to be friends with him and Aiesha, and he wanted to help us with our problems. He seemed delighted to have something useful to do for us, too. David helped the most, but I did a few things, too.

David came home and told me to accept the offer of a washer and dryer! I seem to have a problem of being a bit fearful of accepting help from others. I would have to get over it. I showed Assim how to go about choosing an Ohio attorney (not worth the money once Hussain got a better dorm room in my opinion, but at least Assim now knew where to get an acceptable lawyer if he really needed one). I gave car shopping advice. I gave moral support. I supposed it would be okay to accept something from Assim.

David was also very thankful that I washed his clothes. ☺

Ultimately, however, we ended up deciding not to get these machines; the space heater made a good dryer for a couple who would only be in Kuwait for a few more months. I just couldn't justify the expenditure if we weren't going to stay there, and I didn't want to stay.

Laundry in Kuwait – Episode Six:
Mansoor Asks for a Laundry Lesson

1 February 2005 – a Tuesday.

Mansoor visited us last night, and we chatted for a while. He never washed dishes in his home – women did that – so he was amazed when I mentioned that David washed dishes often. He did this often lately, because for a week I had had a pinched nerve in the left side of my neck, and he wanted me to be comfortable. Mansoor seemed to find David's sharing of household chores less astounding once he heard about that. He was sympathetic, wanting to lend me some sort of massage toy he has – probably one of those spider-like things sold in malls.

Meanwhile, his mom had gone to Egypt for a whole month, and his sister had gone to stay with another sister until her return, so he was all alone. Poor Mansoor – we told him to visit us often. And…he wanted me to teach him how to operate the washing machine! Apparently, the absence of female relatives had made the desire for clean clothing outweigh any Arab male conditioning to avoid housework. Okay…but it was one of those horrible things like the one that Saleh got us to buy – and I still wanted our 32 KD back from him!

Fine – I would show Mansoor how to use it, but I still considered it to be a washer-woman-slave's tool and not a real washing machine. Fatin had a real one – good for her, and for Manisha, her maid.

2 February 2005 – a Wednesday.

I spent the day at home doing more laundry, by washing things in the bathtub with liquid laundry detergent, rinsing them out, wringing them, and then hanging them up or drying them over our space heater. I only did this when I was home to watch them – I'm not stupid or crazy! I don't want to burn ANYTHING, not the clothing, not the building, not anything. I did the pillowcases, and they smelled great. But the sheets…that would be tough. I kept putting it off, reasoning that we bathed daily and at least the pillowcases were clean. I probably couldn't win, and would have go through this hassle in a few days.

5 February 2005 – a Saturday.

It's a very good thing that we were friends with a nice person like Mansoor, even if he did need laundry lessons. I gave him the lesson on Thursday. This, after going out with Fatin, one of Kuwait's many hard-working foreign professors. Mansoor's mother definitely had one of those horrible machines that we hated, and her family's entire bathroom was taken up with that and buckets of clothing, some of which Mansoor had disintegrated by leaving them in bleach for a few days. Well, they were snowy white now…and the fabric had lost its integrity. It was all socks and underwear. He was quite funny – wanted to wash the clothes of everyone in the building, he gushed, wildly excited over knowing how to do this chore.

Interesting…

Just wait, Mansoor, I thought, until you experience the tedium of waiting for the stuff to get fully dry. You'll get over the thrill of knowing how to take care of yourself fast, and want to get back to the times when you are free to go off and do something – anything – else.

We went out that evening with Saleh. We had "rescued" him during the day by paying his mechanic bill so that work could be done on his car, which wasn't functioning.

He thanked us, and promised to pay us back not in a week but insh'allah in 3 days – great! And he would pay us back for the horrible washer. That has been in its box for weeks, rather than being used by Sarah to wash the mountains of Al-Hamdullilah clothing! (It seemed quite likely that Raidah had gotten another new washing machine – a real one, not a travesty of a one.) Saleh knew that I didn't want the damn thing, and his family needed a washer. Apparently, Raidah tried to send it back to us once, all boxed up and driven by Abdullah, but Saleh found out in time to send him back home with it. [They called him on his mobile phone when Abdullah couldn't figure out which apartment was ours, and he told him no – don't EVER try to make us take that washer.] Raidah felt guilty about the whole laundry thing now. Good.

Meanwhile, I washed the sheets. It took hours of grunt work of course, but David didn't take any of it for granted. When he got into our bed later that night, he could smell and feel the difference. "Nice job on the sheets," he complimented me.

Laundry in Kuwait – Episode Seven: I Have Settled Into the Wretched Chore

26 February 2005 – a Friday. *Happy Independence Day, Kuwait!*

We spent two days and one night in Wafra Farms (not to be confused with Wafra the town, which is northwest of the oasis) as guests of our friend Hamid Al-Qasim – at last. [This means that David got his schedule synchronized with Hamid's.] We had a fantastic and fascinating time. There were many interesting people to see, some of whom are the elite big-shots of Kuwait, plus lots of beautiful plants and animals, and some interesting places. I even got to attend a real diwaniya!

Meanwhile, our laundry is done after much exercise gained from wringing everything out over the bathtub, and David's socks are once again all in pairs and stuck over the tops of the kitchen cabinets, drying overnight.

Laundry in Kuwait – Episode Eight: Our Cat Worships the Clothes Dryer/Space Heater

14 March 2005 – a Monday.

David managed to get back to K.O.C. Hospital today. Even more impressive, he managed to get Saleh there. This shouldn't be such a big deal, but it was. Saleh was supposed to pick David up at 6:30 a.m. Saleh was on duty today. Saleh was feeling sick and seeing demons and devils, so he called David and said he couldn't make it today. David was livid! With less than 2 months before we had to go home, the asthma study must go on. Saleh was supposed to be the physician conducting this study. (Eventually, he got his entire part of it ready in time.)

We had a quiet afternoon when David came home. I did the laundry – mostly socks and underwear – in the bathtub, washing with liquid laundry detergent, rinsing a couple of times to get the dust out, and then hanging up the clean, wet things. I dried them in batches on the space heater. All that remains are pair after pair after pair of David's white socks.

Our cat, meanwhile, had reaped the benefit of this chore by sleeping close to the heater, sometimes worshipping it by leaning in close to touch her head to it. She also sat on the floor next to it whenever she was awake. Funny creature!

Kuwait's winters are mild and chilly compared with Connecticut's winters, but they can still feel cold considering the fact that homes and apartments are typically not heated here. Every structure comes with air conditioning and fans, but not with heating. I can't say that this came as any great surprise considering the fact that Kuwaiti summers feel, according to David, like a blast furnace. He had timed our stay in Kuwait so that I would not experience this, because he thought that it would actually make me sick. Many Americans and Europeans, not being used to that level of heat, find it debilitating.

Laundry in Kuwait – Episode Nine:
Only One More Round of Laundry To Go...

1 April 2005 – a Friday.

Happy April Fool's Day! I love this holiday, and I love to April Fool people. I did it to David twice. First, I told him that while he was out, Raidah had called, wanting him to go over to her house and tutor her youngest son for a physics test. David just said that he wouldn't, and angrily turned back to the computer. Then I shouted "April Fool!" and he said I ought to have drawn it out longer, until he called her up, but I didn't agree. Still, he thought that that was a pretty good one, because Saleh was away and he often tutored his sons for school. The second time was when I told David that our landlord was raising our rent by 30 KD, and that the bouab had accordingly decided to raise his monthly demand for baksheesh money to 10 KD instead of 5 KD. I yelled "April Fool!" in time to dissuade him from calling the landlord. ☺

Today we were home, doing laundry, writing, and nursing our cat, whose mouth was much better after some minor surgery at the fancy veterinary hospital in Ahamdi City. She seemed happy, and was sleeping a lot.

Meanwhile, it looked like I was settled into the exact labor-intensive laundry routine that I had wanted so badly to avoid.

One more round of this and I could go back to the United States and do laundry in real washers and dryers.

At least I got something bizarre to write about.

Chapter 9
Let's All Go to the Mall - Souq Tours

Before I left for Kuwait, my mother told me that she saw an episode of *The Oprah Winfrey Show* that featured the malls of Kuwait. In it, shot after shot of upscale mall after beautifully appointed mall after luxurious shopping environment was played until my mother, who loves to shop, was happily anticipating my time trolling these monuments to consumerism.

She had forgotten, as usual, that I don't love to shop like she does. What I love to see is an interesting and unfamiliar place, and what I love to do is study it until it becomes familiar. I did precisely this, and I thoroughly enjoyed it, so at least she can derive that much satisfaction from my experience with Kuwaiti shopping palaces. The malls were everything that they promised to be – they contained things that I was not used to, they exhibited aspects that resembled American malls but with a Kuwaiti cultural imprint, and they contained the familiar.

They also granted endless opportunities for people-watching, which showed me the Kuwaiti people in their natural habitat, and also Americans and other foreigners outside of theirs. It didn't get old.

Mall Insecurity in Kuwait

David will often see a trailer for a really bad movie and say, "I'd pay NOT to see that." I recently said that when I saw one for a movie about a mall cop. It was just too stupid. But when you look at someone in an all-too-familiar job but removed from the surroundings that you are used to – a mall cop in a foreign culture and country – your perspective changes. Suddenly the mall cop becomes interesting.

The heading for this section is my little joke, left over from when I worked at a Williams-Sonoma store in a mall in Connecticut. The mall had a security force, but it wasn't helpful to the staff of the tenant stores. It seemed to consider its purpose to be the customers and only the customers, and so late at night when we closed the store, we wouldn't bother calling them to take us to our cars. I just broke the rules and parked close to the building, then followed my co-workers to their cars so that they would feel safe. We had a habit of referring to them as Mall Insecurity.

In Kuwait, that is exactly how they seemed: anything but secure. The mall security guys didn't wear uniforms, and they didn't look at all like cops. That was the first thing that we noticed. They wore dishdashahs, and carried walkie-talkies – thus identifying themselves to the general public as mall security officers – and prayer-beads. Kuwaiti mall security staffers are all men. They pace around, moving the beads back and forth, clicking away with them, looking more like mystery shoppers than substitute cops.

Perhaps this is because we were noticing the way the Kuwaiti mall cops looked, dressed, and behaved. They did not look intimidating. They can be seen standing around at various points around each mall, just people-watching. They look very benign. They have security vehicles with blue lights to drive around in, just like in America. But they look so…friendly. They seem just like regular people, not law enforcement patrollers. They don't even have night-sticks.

David and I felt a bit naughty as we smugly asked each other what they would do if they actually saw a thief – "Hike up their dishdashahs and run?!" We felt a bit guilty about it as we laughed at the absurd image that instantly conjured itself in our minds. In the unlikely event that a thief would materialize in a Muslim country, openly and obviously, the punishment would be severe. (I have been told by a Shia scholar that the punishment for theft is having a hand cut off.) This made the possibility of seeing such an amusing sight as a worry bead-swinging, dishdashah-wearing mall cop chasing said thief seem like a vague, improbable idea. Too bad – it would have been priceless.

American mall security staffers dress like state troopers. They look scary, both because of the way they dress, and because they look so forbidding – they rarely smile. They have night-sticks, and usually intend to go on to a police academy. They tend not to be seen just standing around – they are usually walking somewhere in the mall, or driving around outside of it. They work out at gyms. Some of them are women. The women may be a little smaller, but they are tough, and it shows when they speak. I met several mall security people when I worked at that mall in Connecticut, and I watched 2 of them chase some shoplifters who had raided a Victoria's Secret store. Another time, I saw another 2 of them confront a pair of shoplifters in a department store. They were scary to watch.

After analyzing these differences – and then realizing that the level of fear of being caught and punished in Kuwait far outweighs that of the same in American society – David and I just made that sound that we came to know and love since hearing several Kuwaitis make it: a tongue-clucking sound. People here make it when they disapprove of something: mothers, men, teenagers, everyone. It makes us laugh just to hear it, and is often accompanied by finger-wagging. We couldn't quite get it right, though. I suppose you need to be a native of this society to sound authentic.

Souq Sharq

The construction of the 10-year-old Souq Sharq mall was a reaction to the Iraqi invasion. Our good friend and neighbor Mansoor told us that before the 1990 Iraqi Invasion of Kuwait, Kuwaitis used to regularly drive up Abdaly Road and into Iraq to go shopping! This was for fun shopping, not grocery shopping. Just outside of Kuwait, a bit beyond the border into Iraq, is a township called Safwan, where Kuwaitis and others used to go to malls. Not surprisingly, they have completely lost their taste for the area.

Souq Sharq, seen from the parking lot, looking south; the promenade overlooking Kuwait Bay.

Now Kuwaitis can go shopping within the safety of their own borders, enjoying the convenience of a short drive. Souq Sharq is located within the limits of Kuwait City, and has lovely waterfront views on both sides: the parking lot has a promenade that overlooks Kuwait Bay, and the other side of the mall has its own marina, complete with a Starbuck's Coffee shop and a restaurant. It is the perfect retreat and hangout for the Kuwaiti citizen who wants to spend some quality time safely frittering away hours at a mall. Fatin took us there a week after I arrived. We had coffee at Starbucks, where we enjoyed the view of the marina and Kuwait City, seen from the north.

A panoramic view of the Souq Sharq Marina that I shot from the Starbucks balcony seating area.

The mall had a department store called Debenham's – British – at the eastern end, and a Sultan Centre store with a restaurant at the western end, across from the Fish Souq, which had matching décor. I saw familiar cosmetic counters in Debenham's: Lancôme, Estée Lauder, etc. Guess, The Body Shop, L'Occitane, and Kenneth Cole were some other familiar names. There was also one that was new to me, though there are branches of it in Manhattan: Zara. That store had floor-length skirts with a solid under-layer and a gauzy, patterned top layer displayed prominently at its entrance (these are usually worn by religiously dressed, hijab-covered young girls and women who are not yet married or newlywed).

The water clock at the center court of Souq Sharq Mall.

Also, Kuwait is, sadly, saturated with American fast food joints: McDonald's, Burger King, KFC, Pizza Hut, Cinnebon (called CinneZon in Kuwait), Starbucks, etc. David and I prefer to try Kuwaiti things that we don't see at home whenever feasible. Souq Sharq had a Starbucks upstairs in the Debenham's anchor store, and various fast food joints in the food court.

The Souq Sharq had some interesting features, including a huge water clock with lots of blue and clear glass. Getting a photo was complicated, because one must always be careful not to include any passing women in it. I commented about this to Mansoor as I took the pictures, saying that I would have to wait until no women were walking by, or they would say, "Don't photograph me!" – I said all this as I backed up quite close to a group of hijab-covered women, so they stayed out of the picture (insert evil grin here).

A hallway showing the levels and décor.

I wandered around taking photos. The top of the clock was decorated to reflect the history of Kuwait – pearling and boom-building. Around the clock were lots of plastic dolls dressed and painted to look like Kuwaitis from the old days, before oil wealth changed the country. Scenes with the dolls were all around the base showing men at diwaniyas, carrying water, and so on. After seeing that, I headed off down the length of the mall, taking pictures wherever I could without having any women get upset at me.

Mall security men wandered the hallways carrying worry beads and walkie-talkies while customers silently paced from store to store. I found a magazine stand in the center of the mall, in the hallway. It offered *National Geographic* and Marvel comic books, much to my surprise.

Doll display showing a game of damma; giant chess set with a mall security guy on the extreme left.

The day that we toured AlSadu House and the Kuwait National Museum, we hailed a taxi – or so we thought until we got in. It was just a car with someone who wanted to give us a ride for pay. This "taxi driver" was probably just an Egyptian who wanted to make a quick couple of dinars on the way to his regular job. He wore a shirt that read SHOWTIME – referring to the movie channel – and had lots of the company's brochures in his car. Sure enough, he worked for them. He was very nice, and we paid him 1.5 KD to take us into Kuwait City.

We stopped first at the Kuwait National Museum, but they were just closing up for the afternoon, and told us to come back at 4 p.m., when they would reopen everything. The driver came with us to check on this, and when we heard that, we told him we would pay him extra to take us to Souq Sharq – that made it 2 KD. He was so nice that he tried to talk us out of it, but we paid it anyway.

We had a little less than 3 hours to spend at Souq Sharq, so I got the camera out.

Hallway views of the interior of Souq Sharq Mall. The center of the mall, upstairs, had a food court.

After shopping in the Sultan Center store for some food and tea, I met David outside at a restaurant table, where he was happily enjoying a water-pipe and reading *The Arab Times*. I sat down with the groceries and read some of it; Claudia Farkas Al-Rashoud, the Californian journalist who married a Kuwaiti, had written the first of an eleven-part series on jinni, known in the West as genies. It was fascinating – it mentioned that the Queen of Sheba had had a jinn in her. I told David that he must buy the paper every day until we have read it all. He agreed.

Our waiter showed up and I decided to eat at the food bar, which is part dinner bar, part salad bar, and part dessert bar. The waiter was a short Philippino with wavy, gelled hair, foundation makeup, and eyeliner. He was very nice, and good at his job. David and Mansoor had noticed him before, with the result that we told Mansoor all about a certain aspect of Provincetown, Massachusetts and San Francisco, California. There was another gay foreign worker in Souq Sharq – all the way at the other end, in Debenham's. He sold cosmetics, and he had wildly spiked black hair, heavy foundation makeup, and eyeliner. I got a kick out of walking Fatin past his station on another day at the mall – after she promised me not to react.

Muslims seemed to be easily shocked and appalled by the sight of a drag queen or a guy who was gay but less obvious about it. Fortunately, however, religious Muslims didn't seem very skilled at spotting homosexuals. They have to live somewhere and have jobs, so I wasn't going to call any bigot's attention to them. If the government knew where to find them, they could be expelled from the country. Assim told us so when we mentioned this nice waiter. I scolded him when he asked for more detail about him. I said "Oh no – I'm not going to help you find him and ruin his life – he's not bothering anyone!" Assim backed off.

I went inside to get some food and came back quite happy, with a plate full of thick, raw carrot and cucumber strips, babaganoush (eggplant purée), hummus, fish with red bell peppers, rice, and lentil soup. What a nice change from the monotony of Abraq Khaitan's Egyptian take-out food! I didn't eat the soup – it turned out to be rather oily, prompting some jokes from David about how the food here must reflect the nation's major source of income.

After eating some fried calamari with red sauce, we left, because it had started to rain. We went into the mall to find a place to sit down until 4 o'clock, having noticed that 45 minutes remained. I noticed a Haagen Daas ice cream shop with some comfortable armchairs, and we went in.

As I looked through the menu, planning to have a chocoholic sundae, we heard someone repeating phrases in English at the next table. We both looked up, nonplussed, trying to make out what was being said over the din of the mall. It turned out to be three Turkish businessmen; the one with his back to us was practicing English out of a phrasebook.

As we asked each other what the guy was saying, the one facing us starting laughing until he turned red, and he couldn't stop. The third guy, who could also see us, looked up and laughed too, prompting the one who was using the phrasebook to stop and look for his audience. When he realized what was going on, he thought it was amusing, too.

The one who laughed the hardest had glasses and thick, white hair, and he was wearing a yellow tie. He invited us to come to his place in Salwa sometime for dinner. They were all Turks who had places in Salwa, where a lot of non-Kuwaiti, Middle Eastern professionals lived. We were delighted to meet them – we love Turkish food, and all 3 were very nice. The third man came over to me and asked me "Parlez-vous Français?" We chatted for a minute or so in French. Then we all traded business cards.

The Souq Al-Mubarakiya

On Christmas Day, David and I took a bus to Kuwait City. It was full of Indian workers – who live 8 men to an apartment and live on lentils, sending their pay home to their families. Suffice it to say that we seemed thoroughly out of place, standing up for the whole ride, hanging onto the bars with them.

We got off to a difficult start: the water wasn't working that day. It turned out that the tank on the roof of the building was empty. The bouab had frantically called for a refill on the double when this was discovered. David had gone down to see him and ask what was going on, telling him that it was his wife's birthday AND Christmas Day, so he had to take me out today and not on some other day. The bouab liked us; we kept giving him 5 extra KD with our rent plus farawla (strawberry) ice cream from Mr. Ali's sweet shop – 2 kinds of baksheesh (bribes)!

After the water was restored, David and I had our baths and showers and Christmas Day was thus saved. David gave me 2 beautiful cards: one from him and one from our wonderful Scheherazade Cat. I kept re-reading them – they were just the best, most perfect gifts! (I didn't need more "stuff" – those cards were exactly the sorts of gifts that I wanted.)

We drank some of the Turkish coffee with milk, and then took the bus to Kuwait City for 150 fils each. The people who rode the bus with us were very nice; they told us how to get where we were going. It was crowded, but we got seats and found the right stop, and were told which way to walk to the Souq Mubarakiya.

The Souq Mubarakiya was huge, both outdoors and in. The building had beautiful wooden doors that open out from each shop into a long series of halls. The best shops had food – dates, nuts, tahini, fish, dried fruits, etc. We saw a prayer beads shop, several elaborate musk shops, and endless shops outside, grouped by product, selling junk.

It was after dark when we arrived at Safat Square. This is a view towards the Souq Al-Mubarakiya.

The junk ranged from kitchen items such as flimsy juicers and awful china to suitcases, wristwatches, cheap, ugly bedspreads, and dishdashahs to abbeyas. We looked at abbeyas – I thought it might make a nice souvenir to take home and show my family and friends – and I tried one on that had beautiful black embroidery all along the edges. But for 56 KD, we decided that the vendor could keep it! It turned out that this was just the size. He was trying to rip us off, but it didn't work. He also offered me a veil to cover my face – a nekhab – but I wouldn't be caught dead in one.

A beautiful musk shop, framed by old wooden doors; a prayer bead shop with Kuwaiti guys relaxing.

David was quite upset that after looking for weeks in both cheap and expensive places, he was unable to find me a new, small, gold, pocket-watch. My old one was failing, and not because of the battery. I hate wristwatches and I love little, women's pocket-watches, but they are hard to find.

The upscale jewelry store on the edge of the souq.

After asking an Arab jeweler in an expensive shop where we might find such a thing – he made some calls for us and came up blank – so we gave up. I don't know why David thought he would find such a specific item in a cheap place – wishful thinking, I guess, but not realistic. It didn't matter; we eventually bought one several months later, at home.

Inside the original building of the Souq Al-Mubarakiya.

All things considered, I had a lovely time for Christmas and my birthday. I usually feel quite delighted to have been born on a day that most people have off, so that I am guaranteed a great time with David and whomever else I might want to see.

This year, the fun of Christmas and my birthday was threatened by – of all people – Saleh Al-Hamdullilah, who kept telling David that he wanted to take him to a cardiology conference.

David categorically refused to go, explaining that it was my birthday and Christmas, that he had to spend the entire day with me and not do the slightest bit of work all day. Saleh densely replied, several times, "Oh, but this is very important – Stephanie will understand!"

David just kept telling him no, but that made no impression until he added that Stephanie would cut a piece of him off if he didn't spend the day with me (I wouldn't!). At last, Saleh got the message and gave up. Insert another evil grin here.

We saw the Kuwait Liberation Communications Tower from Safat Square as we headed back from the Souq Al-Mubarakiya, lit up for the night. It was only open to the public once each year.

We wandered around the Souq Al-Mubarakiya until dark, then went out to dinner.

Al-Muthanna Complex – The Kuwait Bookstore

This was a boring mall, but that was probably because I was with people who wanted to go clothes shopping (a thing that almost always bores or frustrates me), because the architecture of the place was nothing but a large cube-like building with perhaps 15 or 20 stories, most of which we didn't see (probably offices), and because we spent our time in the basement.

The Al-Muthanna Complex probably pre-dated the Iraqi invasion. It had various clothing stores, which I paid absolutely no attention to, and a Baskin-Robbins stand in the hallway. I went to this mall with Aiesha and her 3 daughters. We ate some ice cream there. The mall was nothing special to look at; most of the stores were rather forgettable.

But it didn't matter that the place itself was nothing exciting. It had a fabulous bookstore, and I soon found myself in bibliophile heaven.

We all ended up in the bookshop, which took up half of the basement level of the mall. I found a few paperback novels – about sea adventures in the 19th century, and present-day U.S. lawyers and intrigue – and 4 showpiece books. Three were about Kuwait: one contains the Kuwaiti Constitution and lots of photos of the country, another is by an Al Sabah princess, detailing Kuwaiti clothing, Bedouin fabrics, weaving, and the third was about Kuwaiti booms (merchants' sailing ships).

Assim and Aiesha were delighted to find that Aiesha's grandfather was interviewed for that book. The last book was a belated Christmas gift for David, though I will certainly read it too: it is a photographic celebration of Mecca and Medina, the places that Muslims must visit when they go on Hajj. (David was delighted with it.)

I asked the bookseller about Scheherazade's *Arabian Nights* – all 16 volumes, in English. He said it could be special ordered for me. It sounded very, very expensive, so perhaps in the future I would order it, but not now.

It was not possible to see inside the bookstore from the hall; it was surrounded by displays of examples of recreational reading in Arabic, such as seen here.

That bookseller looked familiar to me somehow…and I think that I might have met him at the Mark Twain House in Connecticut years ago. Could he have been on one of my tours? I gave detailed tours of that 19-room mansion for several years. I should have asked him.

The man was sitting in a chair among the bookshelves, near the back, reading. He was in Western clothing, and had thick white hair and a beard. He was quiet and at home among books. Thinking back to the conversations I had in the basement of that historic house museum, I remember chatting with this guy about Mark Twain at the end of one of my tours. The planet seems small when you run into someone again on the other side of the world.

So, I would have to do without the epic collection of Scheherazade's stories. It didn't matter – I could just sit and read other books while my cat of the same name kept me company.

Where I Got My Books...Various Places

The entire time that I was in Kuwait, I kept collecting books on the country's history and culture, plus other, unrelated books of fiction to fill the hours of quiet when David was out with our computer.

Immediately after arriving, I got started. Fatin took us to first one mall, then another. I promptly found the Virgin Megastore in the Marina Crescent Mall, which was full of English-language books. On various tables toward the front of the store, I found a book about Dame Violet Dickson, who spent nearly her entire adult life in Kuwait. The fiction was around the corner, and was later moved to a balcony area upstairs.

Another source of books was much more limited: I found one book on Kuwait's environment – particularly, what the Iraqis did to it and how it was remediated after the war – in a pile at the end of an aisle upstairs in the Sultan Centre store of Souq Sharq.

Each museum that we visited offered another chance to acquire a book about the nation's history and culture, so I collected a couple more at the Tareq Rajab Museum, another at AlSadu House, and even one at the SAS Radisson Hotel at Messilah Beach, where the Al-Boom Restaurant was permanently docked.

I would also get a *National Geographic* sometimes, or just stop to look at a bridal magazine without actually buying one. That was when I discovered that Kuwait's Ministry of Islamic Affairs, also known as Awqaf in Arabic, had previewed each one of these before releasing them into the stream of commerce.

Each magazine had been gone over page by page with a thick black magic marker. All models wearing low-cut gowns had a thick line of black ink covering whatever cleavage the couturieres had not seen fit to conceal. One photo at the end of a *National Geographic* of a group of skinny-dipping men – who were all running away from the camera and into the icy waters of Alaska – wore black magic marker bathing shorts on their originally naked butts.

Apparently, Kuwaitis could not be trusted to provide their own mental filters as they perused a magazine, so Awqaf did this for them...

The Marina Crescent Mall

This was a beautiful mall in downtown Salmiya on Arabian Gulf Street.

It was probably one that appeared on Oprah's show one afternoon before I left for Kuwait. My mother told me about it; I don't watch daytime television. It didn't matter; I went there and walked around it several times.

The center court of the Marina Crescent Mall was full of chairs and tables and potted palm plants. The hall led in several directions to many upscale clothing and cosmetics shops.

The center court of the Marina Crescent Mall, outside the Starbucks and the French pastry shop.

It is actually in 2 sections that are connected by a bridge that spans Arabian Gulf Street, leading to a crescent-shaped marina, hence the name of the mall.

In the large section surrounded by streets, there is a huge center court full of tables and chairs surrounded by a fancy French pastry shop, a Starbucks (of course), and hallways that branch off to other sections of the mall. Looking up, one sees a dome. Escalators lead up and down from there.

The upper level is a food court with Indian, Asian, and other foods, plus the more familiar and less healthy McDonald's, KFC, etc. Also upstairs are some intriguing signs directing the visitor to the rest rooms, the marina, the fountain…and the prayer rooms. Throughout Kuwait, the devout Muslim can find places to pray if caught away from her or his usual prayer venue when the muezzin starts calling. I wondered about the fountain until I remembered the need for pre-prayer ablutions.

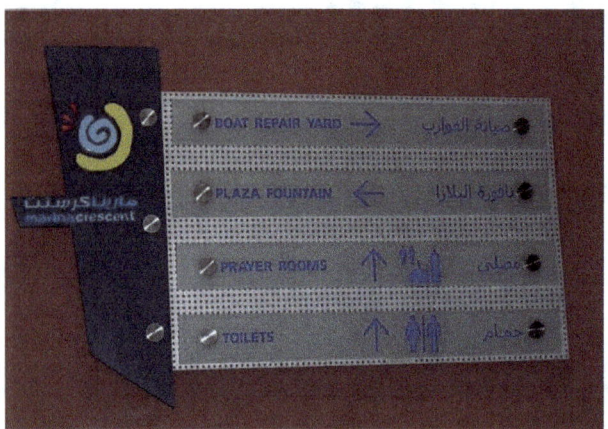

Sign directing visitors to various places around the Marina Crescent Mall.

Heading out toward Arabian Gulf Street and the bridge to the marina, one finds many high-end stores loaded with merchandise, including jewelry, Tommy Hilfiger, M.A.C., Hallmark, and so on. 2 halls converge facing the bridge, which had a grey curtain of sorts (made of a somewhat transparent fabric) to shield people from bright sunlight. A staircase led upwards to the bridge, and off to its right side was a coffee shop called The Second Cup – European, I was told. We never tried that one.

Turning back to look at the shops, with our backs to the bridge, we saw the Virgin Megastore to the right, full of books, games, CDs and DVDs. Before leaving for Kuwait I had learned that it would be pointless to bring our friends Fatin and Nuwwar any new movies on

DVD; all DVDs are coded somehow to play only for the continent for which they are produced. This probably helps the censors in the Islamic world to prevent uncut, original versions of our racy, free-speech-riddled movies from seeping into their culture.

This was the view out the shaded windows of the bridge connecting the sections of the Marina Crescent Mall. The structure to the left, which resembled a collage of sails, was a lookout point near the mall.

A CinneZon coffee shop was straight ahead if one still hadn't turned again, and Nuwwar and I patronized it once.

Going across the bridge, I sometimes saw other Americans, all people whom I did not know, walking by sipping out of Starbucks coffee cups with plastic lids, wearing jeans and polar fleece jackets. It felt odd to see them; I was becoming so thoroughly accustomed to the sight of Arabs, either in traditional or Western clothing. Suddenly the Americans stood out to me as oddities, even though I recognized them instantly.

Crossing the bridge, one arrives at a lovely vista showing Kuwait City to the left, with Kuwait Towers in the distance, and the Gulf straight ahead, with the marina down below. A balcony runs across the upper level of the marina, to a water-pipe restaurant all the way to the right and more businesses on the left.

A Kuwaiti man enjoys the view towards Kuwait City over the marina; looking to the right of him was the rest of the marina and a view – on the upper level – of the water-pipe place that David tried.

Down the escalator inside this section was a plaster fun house, where one could pay to paint the ceramics, and a beautifully appointed Indian restaurant where we ended up having our Easter dinner months later.

I went with David to the water-pipe place after buying the book on Violet Dickson at the Virgin Megastore. He hadn't tried one of those since the last time he had been in Kuwait 11 years earlier, so he ordered one. They have several names: argeelah, hubbley-bubbley, hookah, and water-pipe. They have coals and a scent, which can be ordered off of a menu. David chose strawberry, and I got a glass of fresh strawberry juice. I watched him try this with trepidation; David is 6 feet tall and a big guy; I am 5'5" – if he got high, how would I get him home, I wondered?

Here was David, puffing away and holding up the book about Dame Violet Dickson. The place was called Tche Tche's, and was full of people out for a chance to socialize. Alcohol is illegal in Kuwait, as in most Islamic nations, because of the concern that its effects would not wear off in time for the next prayer. Why then, I wondered, would these pipes be allowed? The effects were similar, it seemed. I never found out.

Sure enough, he had forgotten how to puff on the thing, and the Iraqi and Kuwaiti girls (one of each) at the next table started laughing. They very nicely explained how to puff without inhaling, and he took that in, but it was too late for this round. I steered him out to the street and took the next cab home before the effect got any worse. It was okay – he maneuvered on his own well enough to walk.

A Gold Souq

On a Thursday in late January, Fatin showed me her jewelry while we sat in the den after dinner. It was gold – all of it – in large and interesting styles that I didn't see in the West, with fake pearls and some tiny stones, mostly fake little red and green stones. Most it came from the gold souq in Salmiya. She intended to go back there to exchange some items.

She said she was waiting for Zahid to have time to go there with her, because she did not like to go among rude men without him. I wanted to go to the gold souq to buy some small gold earrings for myself, my mother and my grandmother, and I told her so. So Fatin said that she would call me and we would go there without Zahid. She doesn't mind going there with just me – I can handle idiots who stare. I either turn my camera on them, or look at them with a "what are you looking at, you dope?" expression. This would be fun.

Kuwaitis and other Arabs seemed to favor large, ostentatious styles of jewelry (my own strong sense of aesthetics was affecting my view, no doubt), and the things I saw in jewelry shops all over Kuwait reflected this.

The following Thursday, I went out with Fatin in the morning. We went to the gold souq in Salmiya, and I found lots of Kuwaiti gold earrings for my mother, grandmother, sister-in-law, and myself. Kuwaiti gold is 18-carat, 21-carat, and 22-carat, and always yellow. Other gold products are usually from Italy, but I didn't come to Kuwait for non-Kuwaiti products. We had fun shopping together.

The souq consisted of a rather small collection of shops. It was one alley that led off of an open-air parking lot. The alley turned left at the end and opened out onto a side street, with a small courtyard just after that left turn. All along the walkway were gold shops – many small ones. I saw a bracelet made of different colors of gold that depicted camels, and I found a pair of earrings that looked like little oyster shells. They were stamped in Arabic to indicate that they were made of 24-carat gold, Fatin told me. I bought those earrings because they reminded me of Kuwait's pearl-diving history.

A window display at the Gold Souq in Salmiya; the oyster-shell earrings that I bought, and their pretty box.

Hijab Shops

Fatin tells me that a head scarf is called a hijab and means, very generally, any type of head covering that hides ears and hair.

We went to a mall in Farwaniya, to the Nooran hijab store.

The hijabs were pretty, long, usually sheer rectangular scarves, some of which had embroidery, with solid-colored opaque things to go underneath. The opaque things matched the scarves, and hide hair, ears and earrings, while the scarves just dress up the woman's head so that she has something pretty on top. The opaque things are close-fitting, made of cotton, and have a hole for the face and another one for the neck. They must be awfully hot to wear in the summer, late spring and early fall.

I went with Fatin once to the place in Farwaniya with Zahid, another time without him, and to another hijab shop at Souq Sharq Mall, upstairs near Debenham's. As we looked at the merchandise in that shop, waiting our turn for assistance, I picked a long scarf up and tried to show her how Aiesha wore her hijab. Aiesha, a Kuwaiti, would take the scarf and drape it over her head with one long side and one short side, then wind the long side around and around until she could tuck a bit of it into the other side, thus fastening it there. Fatin, an Egyptian, would drape it evenly over her head, then toss each hanging side over her shoulder.

This, however, was an American who didn't usually put a hijab on. There was a small group of Kuwaiti women in the shop, and they were all wearing the full costume: abbeya, hijab and nekhab. They turned around to watch me when I started to show Fatin how Aiesha wore her hijab, and although I could only see their eyes, I could swear that they each had the same expression: "Oh, this ought to be good!" they seemed to be thinking.

Unfazed, I proceeded to try to wrap the scarf around my head as Aiesha did it.

Close, but no hijab – I hadn't gotten the proportions of short and long right. When I finished winding, there wasn't enough hanging to attractively tuck it in and finish the effect. I said so with a laugh, pulled the whole thing off, and took out my gold hair clip to smooth my hairstyle.

The Kuwaiti women turned back to their conversation, and I noticed that they were very polite – they didn't seem to be laughing at the American woman.

And why should they? I had described Aiesha as my friend, a Kuwait woman.

The Al-Dahi Malls

One evening, David and I went out to walk around Abraq Khaitan for a while, heading across the desert square to see what was over on the opposite side. As we neared a small shopping mall, we noticed that it said, in big red lettering, "Al-Dahi Comm. Co." in English and in Arabic.

We knew he was a big landowner in Kuwait, having met him over Liberation-Independence weekend. That was when his teenage children told me that he owned most of the mini-malls in Kuwait. Intrigued, we decided to walk around inside the mall. It was a typical place, with a large basement store that could be looked down upon from balconies on the other levels, which contained many small shops. The basement shop was full of people buying cheap stuff – very crowded. I don't like to shop in such places; you expend more energy politely pushing your way through large numbers of spaced-out people than you do enjoying the sights in them.

David and I walked around only the first level, and I went into 3 hijab shops. One of them also sold abbeyas, and I would have bought one as a souvenir if it hadn't been so long. I didn't want anything that dragged on the ground. The one I liked was rather pretty – all black with embroidery around the edges, for 7.200 KD, but it was definitely too long for me. I looked at hijabs, and found one for 2 KD in black with colored embroidery. It looked like it would match most of my clothes.

David was funny; he hates to shop and tried his best to ignore me when I called into the hallway to show it to him, then realized that I was wearing a hijab and got interested in it. He said I looked like an Iranian woman when I put on a hijab. It was just a souvenir, I reminded him.

These malls tend to have a similar design, housing an array of inexpensive stores. There are 3 or 4 levels above ground in the shape of a rectangle, with escalators in the center. The shops are all around the perimeter. Looking down at the basement, a bargain basement store covers that entire space. One can walk down a cement staircase to get there, usually. The Al-Dahi malls appeared to be all function and no aesthetics – basically, rent-producing machines. Apparently, they did a good job of that.

Photography would have been difficult, because everywhere I looked, I saw a woman shrouded in black from head to toe, usually without a nekhab, giving me a baleful look. I wasn't about to try to get a photo only to be upsetting one of them. They were just everywhere I looked, and I knew that they did not want to be photographed.

The Al-Jial Mall in Fahaheel

David and Saleh briefly entertained the possibility of setting up a clinical laboratory in a newly built mall in Fahaheel, which was near Manqaf, well south of our area, close to Ahamdi City, where the Kuwait Oil Company Hospital is. It never materialized, but we had an interesting day of it, meeting a nice Palestinian family who lived nearby; the husband, Thamir, was a chemist who knew Saleh. His wife worked in a perfume shop at this mall. We just heard, recently, that she died of cancer a little while ago, and that her poor husband was very sad about it.

The place was called the Al-Jial Mall, and it was a large box-like structure.

We parked and went in, and Thamir immediately took us into a store called *Faces*, which sells all kinds of famous brand-name perfumes and colognes. He did this because his wife, Nawrah, worked there, and since we had just met his children, now he wanted to introduce us to his wife.

The Al-Jial Mall in Fahaheel, Kuwait.

    She was beautiful and chic, with her hair done up in the same style as her daughter, who no doubt learned it from her. Both of them had lightly applied but lovely makeup on, and were rather quiet. Nawrah shook hands and greeted us, and let me take her picture with her husband. Then she sprayed me with some Carolina Herrera "Chic" perfume before I could say anything, so after that my pink jacket smells like that perfume. I liked it, though. She was about to spray David with "Chic" cologne (for men) when we stopped her, politely saying that he never wears any cologne. We all laughed.

Thamir and his wife in the perfume shop where she worked.

After meeting Nawrah, we went up an elevator to the 2nd floor and used the rest rooms. They were satisfactory – always good to know if you might rent space somewhere. Then we went to get the manager and see the space. It was my job to photograph the space, but I also photographed the manager, the management office, and many other areas around the mall, while avoiding photographing any women. The manager proved to be a quiet guy in a gray dishdashah with worry beads in his hands. He was very nice, taking us around the potential lab space, showing us first the annex, a small room down the hall from the bigger room. This could be the "contamination-risk area," David said.

The view out the windows in the space that we looked at; inside was unfinished concrete.

The bigger area was an unfinished room with a concrete floor and exposed ceiling – just like the annex. This bigger room had floor-to-ceiling windows across the entire outer wall, with a great view of downtown Fahaheel, including a big white mosque and other shopping areas. We thought it was very nice, and the correct size for a lab. David took down the postal address while I took lots of photos. Then we went back to the office to get a CD full of professional photos of the exterior and interior of the entire building – including nighttime and daytime shots.

A hallway leading away from the rental space; the manager in his office, where we picked up brochures.

Before we left, I insisted on walking around the other 2 floors and seeing the place. Thamir said he wasn't in a great hurry, and let us check the place out. I wanted to know which stores were there. I wouldn't have been so interested if we weren't looking at rental space there. The stores weren't any that I recognized or particularly cared to visit again, but they were nice. There were some hijab shops, of course, and I photographed the window display of one of them. David bought nuts in a candy shop, and then Thamir took us home.

Some views of the food court at the mall, complete with a woman in an abbeya buying something, and a boy in a dishdashah sitting among the games, waiting for his meal.

The mall had a movie theater. We never went out to a movie in Kuwait, because we were told that we would have to sit apart in some places, or else, if I went with just women, along the side, just like at a mosque. Men got the center seats, so it didn't seem worth the trouble to pay to watch a censored show while craning to see properly. At right, this was the window display for a hijab shop in the Al-Jial Mall. The scarves all came in different colors, were rectangular in shape, each with an embroidered design.

The Al-Fanar Mall in Salmiya

There was a beautiful mall in Salmiya that I visited while Nuwwar was home from college with her and Fatin. We were out doing last-minute shopping for Nuwwar to get her ready to go back to college in Cyprus. It had the most amazing windows, curves, and geese-in-flight statues suspended from the ceilings.

The grand escalators of Al-Fanar; a dense arrangement of tall plants gave the place a tropical look.

The Souq Al-Fanar with its windows and geese-in-flight statues.

The grand escalators of Al-Fanar; a dense arrangement of tall plants gave the place a tropical look.

It was called the Al-Fanar Mall, and I had my camera with me. Salmiya has so many foreigners living nearby – particularly Americans, Europeans, and British – mostly Westerners who don't care if they end up in some random photo, that I made full use of my camera.

When we were outside, I shot another photo of a mall nearby, but the photo turned out to be memorable for another reason: 2 cops were posing at the bottom of the image. The reason I took this particular photo was not to show Kuwaiti cops, but to show some buildings on a busy street in downtown Salmiya, an area where lots of Americans and Europeans live.

The cops were hilarious – one grinned while the other put his hands on his hips and gave me a stern look. Neither of them objected to the photo, but their joviality was totally lost on me at the time. Oh well. They didn't mind what I was doing, they were just hamming it up for me, and the result was a funny picture. So that ended well.

Clearly, this was not a high-crime area. These cops had nothing better to do than stand around in the sunshine, striking silly poses at tourists. They were both friendly – the one with his hands on his hips grinned and waved at me a moment later.

Downtown Salmiya, on a street full of shops catering to foreign professionals from Egypt, Lebanon, Europe, the United States, and many other places. We visited a currency exchange shop along here.

The Courtyard Marriot Mall in Kuwait City

This was the mall in Kuwait City where we met Rola A. Al-Dashti, Ph.D., Kuwait's lead woman suffragist. It had every high-end store a rich person's heart could desire and more, plus some fabulous cafés and restaurants. However, it was always very quiet, with few customers wandering through it. Perhaps this was because it was connected to a hotel, and perhaps it was because location is everything, and Kuwait City is a rather quiet venue.

After the day that we met Rola, I did not take out my camera in this mall. The guard was concerned that photographers would share their results with the competition, I was told. I decided to go back on another day, on my own, to see the beautiful house wares – dishes, cutlery, home furnishings – in one huge store at the end, and wander through a hall with Burberry's and other recognizable brand names. It was fun.

Views east and west down the ground floor concourse of the Courtyard Marriott Mall.

The exquisitely appointed cafés on the ground floor of the Courtyard Marriott Mall; Richoux, where we met Rola, is on the right.

I continued to wander around. I found a beautiful shop on one of the upper levels that offered custom-made abbeyas with matching hijabs. What was so special about them was the embroidery that could be added after tailoring the fit to conform to an individual customer. The only thing that confused me was how to actually wait on a female customer, as all of the people in the shop were male.

The point of being there was just to walk around and look, and the men who worked in the shop sensed that that was all I wanted. They had displays of swatches of embroidered cloth, which were all black with a variety of colors of thread (usually just one color), depicting floral patterns and curlicues. There were a few mannequins with abbeyas and hijabs on the perimeter.

That was the same day that I saw a quiet group of women who might have been customers at this shop. All were dressed in beautiful abbeyas – prettier than any others that I had seen since arriving in Kuwait.

Chapter 10
Ghosts, Jinni, and Superstitions

After a month and a half in Kuwait, I began to wonder about Kuwaiti folklore and superstitions. As it turned out, with a bit of prodding and careful perusing of whatever written material I could get my hands on, I was able to find out a few things. David was also able to supply some information, having spent nearly 3 years in the country as a civilian scientist immediately after the war, so at least I could bounce my curiosity and ideas off of him.

One night in mid-January, Kuwait had a severe dust storm. It lasted for several hours. The air in our flat smelled chalky. Our cat got up and walked around, yowling and sniffing the air. I made sure I had some extra Kleenex available when I went to sleep, but fortunately I did not have the attack of sneezing that I expected, and neither did David. It was just as we were going to sleep that the storm, which had been raging for a few hours, seemed to be at its chalkiest.

David told me that Arab people believe that jinni, genii, devils, demons, and other evil spirits come out during dust storms. [Keep in mind, though, that they believe that these things come out in calm weather, too.] I asked David if this was due to of the greatly decreased visibility caused by the storms, leading to more accidents and deaths when people crash into camels, vehicles, each other, etc. He said that this definitely had to have something to do with it.

Then our conversation turned to the Arabian philosopher woman, Scheherazade, for whom our cat is named, and her 1,000 tales. I brought this up because of the tale of Aladdin and the magic lamp with the genie who could grant wishes. When the genie comes out of the lamp, it appears as dust until the upper reaches of the dust take on a slightly human form, showing a torso with arms and a head. Sometimes the genie becomes a walking man with legs and hips to go with the rest, but he still starts off as a cloud of dust.

David wasn't so sure that this had anything to do with it, but I pressed on. Arabs are often worried about going insane, getting possessed by demons, or having everyday lives disrupted. People from all over the planet from many different cultures have fears like this, and stories and superstitions to go with those fears. Europeans, Native Americans, Indians (the ones from India!), Africans, South Americans, British and Celtic peoples...all can offer ghost stories without much memory-searching.

But I was still determined to convince David that there might be something to *Scheherazade's 1,000 Tales*, or *The Arabian Nights*. I told him that it definitely wasn't just that children's book that we can buy back in the States, the one with only 25 or 30 tales but with reference to there being 1,000 tales that Scheherazade told to her husband, the sultan, and her sister, Dinarzade, to make the sultan fall in love with her and stop him from marrying a different woman every day and then having her killed the next day. Instead of just this one-volume book with a few color paintings and many more black-ink drawings, there is – somewhere – a 16-volume publication that includes all 1,000 of Scheherazade's tales. I don't know who wrote it, but I wanted a copy if I could get one in English.

Where was I going to find that? I would have to start by asking my Kuwaiti friends. I can't count on them knowing where I could buy this – maybe it's only in Arabic, or only in a library. But none of these friends of mine might know – I am talking about something that is not their fields of study. I would just have to try. Whatever ghost or other stories they had to share would be welcome, I told myself.

No need to explain what a ghost is – people everywhere apply the same definition to that word. It's the spirit of a dead person, usually with unresolved issues. Without issues, it wouldn't stick around to haunt living people and freak them out.

We were in luck a few days later: our friend Assim came over for tea and told us a ghost story: he said that there is a haunted house somewhere in Kuwait – he would not tell us the address, much to David's disappointment and my relief. I am just superstitious enough that I don't want to go to a house where Kuwaitis have written "In the name of God, the Merciful, the Benevolent" and refuse to tear it down or visit. It is kept clean (by foreigners?), but left standing. (Assim also told us the many people believe that allowing the dirty laundry of others to be brought into their homes means inviting demons in – no wonder we had so much trouble over getting our laundry clean! A cultural superstition was why I was washing the clothes in the bathtub by hand.)

I also had a book about Kuwaiti history and culture. The part about jinni and devils and the evil eye reminded me of the information he had shared with me about those things. Assim told me that Kuwaitis worry that if someone with an evil eye – a jealous person who may not even wish you ill in any way, at least not consciously – if that person sees something that you have and value, bad things will start to happen to it. This will happen even with unconscious thoughts and feelings of jealousy on the part of the evil-eyed person. That is how superstitions work here. Kuwaitis need to think more positively, I suppose, but Westerners live in glass houses on this point – we have superstitions of our own!

David's Wartime Ghost Story

That same evening while Assim was visiting us, David told his best wartime ghost story. David has ghost stories from before he was ever involved in a war, so I think he can see psionic energy, but it is good to add this so that readers won't jump to the conclusion that he only saw ghosts because of post-traumatic stress syndrome, or some such excuse. As for stress, the fighting, such as it was in Gulf War I, was over when David saw these ghosts. Here is the story:

The story takes place on Abdaly Road, which leads away from Kuwait City and goes north into Iraq. At the end of the Iraqi Invasion, the U.S. military commanders told the Iraqis to get out of Kuwait by a particular time, or else. The Iraqis stayed until the absolute last minute, looting Kuwait City of property, including vehicles, and kidnapping Kuwaiti citizens. Only then did the Iraqi invaders comply with the order.

Their entire garrison evacuated the city, moving north on Abdaly Road toward the border town of Safwan. Approximately 30 kilometers out of Kuwait City, they were attacked by (mostly) U.S. and British aircraft. Using a combination of cluster munitions, napalm, air-to-ground rockets and mini-gun strafing, the U.S. and British military killed virtually everyone in the convoy – including the many kidnapped Kuwaiti civilians. This left a 10-kilometer stretch of the highway littered with loot, vehicles and corpses. Now the spooky part...

Days later, David's unit was assigned to patrol this highway of death and destruction. Every hour or so, he and a couple of other guys would get into a jeep and drive up and down this area, checking to make sure that no one was messing with the corpses or stealing anything (if indeed anything was there that might actually be worth stealing; it was all burnt). It was in the early hours of the morning, before sunrise and about 10 days after the napalming, that David and his comrades saw some people grouped around one burned-out jeep, walking back and forth and talking to each other.

David stopped the jeep and got out. When he walked over to them, he saw that they were Kuwaiti civilians.2 were men in dishdashahs and guthras, and 3 others were women with hijabs and long black abbeyas. He spoke to them in Arabic, having learned enough by then to be able tell them that civilians weren't supposed to be in that area. They seemed to understand him, but they continued to talk, both to each other and at David. They talked at him rather than to him.

When David continued to insist that they must leave the area immediately, they all simply sat down and made themselves comfortable around the jeep. They weren't hostile at all; they just placidly settled themselves onto the ground, smiling and quite unconcerned by the U.S. soldiers telling them to go. David didn't know what to make of this, nor was he sure what to do about it, so he told them that they would have to be gone in an hour, when he and his unit would make their next inspection tour of the area. Then he and the other 2 soldiers got into their jeep and drove away.

David figured that waiting an hour and leaving these people alone would be easier – and perhaps more politic – than prolonging a confrontation with a group of unarmed Kuwaiti civilians. After an hour or so, and after sunrise, he and the other 2 soldiers returned to that place. The 2 men and 3 women were all still there, seated exactly where they had settled around the same burned-out jeep an hour earlier...and all were in an advanced state of decomposition. They were 10-day-old rotting corpses.

Assim was thoroughly scared by this tale. We could see that he utterly and completely believed and accepted it as true. He did not deny it. I tried to cheer him up with my grandmother's tale of seeing her friend's ghost checking up on her pet cat, which my grandmother had adopted the day after her friend died in her sleep. Mrs. Molloy had come to make sure that her cat was okay, and my grandmother woke up in the middle of the night and saw her white, transparent spirit leaning over the chair where the cat was sleeping. When the ghost noticed that my grandmother was watching her, she vanished, almost as if she had broken some rule of ghostly visitation by being seen.

I thought that this tale would calm him down. He did, but not because he found it amusing; he just found it unconvincing. Perhaps a ghost story must be spooky and really frighten the listener to convince anyone that it is true. (He also didn't like cats – when he was little, a cat jumped at his face and scared him.). Assim then went on to tell us that there were Kuwaiti women who believed that devils kept impregnating them with bad babies. They got blessings from imams and mullahs in the hopes of exorcising the demons/devils/jinni.

A Wonderful Newspaper Series about Jinni

Jinni (plural of jinn) are known them as genies in the Western world. They are a separate group from ghosts, and they are alive. They have supernatural powers, can grant wishes, can cause terrible trouble, and can appear and disappear at will. It sounds to me as though they can teleport, just like one of the mutant superheroes in the Marvel Comics series of *The X-Men* – Nightcrawler, Kurt Wagner, the blue teleporter with a pointed tail and ears.

The reason I mention Nightcrawler is that an 11-part newspaper series on jinn ran while I was in Kuwait, describing the beings in detail. As I read each installment, I noticed many similarities between that mutant and the jinn. The series was written by an American woman, a journalist from California who had married a Kuwaiti and decided to live in Kuwait permanently. Her name is Claudia Farkas Al-Rashoud, and her series ran in *The Kuwait Times* (really part of *The Arab Times*, but published with local writers as well as regional news). Unfortunately, my stay in Kuwait ended before the last few installments, so I didn't have the chance to read each and every one of them, which disappointed me. They ran each week, starting on March 17th. David helped me to get each installment, checking the newsstands so that I wouldn't miss any of the series while we were still in Kuwait.

Jinni appear in many of Scheherazade's tales to the shah in *The Thousand and One Nights*, which were translated into 16 volumes by the 19th-century British writer Edward William Lane. Silly me – I had contemplated buying a copy of this while in Kuwait, and thought about it several times before the trip. I changed my mind after finding out how prohibitively expensive that would be when my friend Aiesha took me to The Kuwait Bookstore at the Al-Muthanna Mall, an older, not-trendy place in Kuwait City.

Claudia Farkas Al-Rashoud's series on jinn was enough to fascinate me about cultural lore, plus conversations with any Kuwaiti people who could be induced to discuss a topic that clearly made them very nervous. She says that genies – jinni – are not all nice like the one in Disney's *Aladdin* – they can be evil and frightening. Some are benevolent and will grant wishes and make life nice, as in the story of Aladdin; others are angry at being imprisoned and will seize any chance to hurt someone. Jinn are from all over the Middle East, northern Africa, and many parts of Asia. They appear in many different countries in Scheherazade's tales, in many different forms, and in many different personality types.

Ms. Farkas Al-Rashoud mentioned Harold Dickson's book, called *The Arab of the Desert*, and his comments about a thorny dark green desert bush called the ausaj bush. This bush is supposedly under the special protection of the jinn, and the Bedouin people believe that anyone who breaks a piece of it will be tormented forever by the jinn as punishment. To prevent this from happening, people surround the bases of these bushes with stones. Superstitions are fascinating but, while I would not push my luck by deliberately doing something that a superstition advises against, I would not live in constant fear of jinn or bad luck, either.

She went on to write that, in the times before Islam, the Bedouin desert peoples believed in Mother Earth, and in spirits – called jinni – which inhabited every tree, well, spring, stone, stream, etc. It reminded me of Wicca, the ancient religion of Europe, which teaches that there is a Goddess, also called Mother Earth, and mentions the four elements of earth, air, fire, and water. These ancient religions are not so different from one another – only geography seems to separate their adherents. Then the patriarchal religions came along. Now the descendants of these people are taught that their current religions are the only true religions, and that all others are false. And they fight about whose religion is legitimate instead of simply leaving each other and the subject in peace…

She called one essay "Jinn: Frankincense & Fire Shield the Soul," and talks about frankincense trees. Apparently, there is an ancient ritual of burning dried frankincense tree sap to exorcise jinn out of possessed individuals. This reminded me of the gifts of the Magi – the 3 kings who visited Jesus in the manger. I have always wondered, idly, but not actively looking for information on it, about a particular Magi gift. It now seems that the king of Arabia gave Jesus a container of dried frankincense tree sap, just in case he were to have trouble with jinn possession in later life…what an absurd thought, considering who the gift was for. The exorcism ceremony is called a zar, and some are still held in Kuwait.

The next week's jinn article talked about methods of warding off evil jinn. Iron is considered to be a universal antidote to jinn. The article includes a photograph of some nails just like the ones that we received as souvenirs when we ate at the Boom restaurant. Reading the Quran over iron nails and then hammering them into the wall of a jinn-haunted house helps drive jinn away, it says. A story about a Pakistani family plagued by jinn in a place called the Pink Palace talks about attempts by jinn to strangle people in their sleep, stopped only by praying to Allah and refusing to enter particular rooms alone. These jinn sound more like angry ghosts of ordinary people to me, however, because the Pink Palace was built over a former ancient graveyard. It is never a good idea to build over a burial ground – Americans have had trouble doing that over Native American burial grounds, too.

The following weekly jinn article discussed where to find them. With its distinctive Papyrus font, her story described a couple of places in the former Kuwaiti Neutral Zone (now part of Saudi Arabia), plus 2 others inside Kuwaiti territory. They are: Jebel Salam, near the northern, Iraqi border of this tiny country; and a place called Subaihiyah, on the edge of Burgan oil field, where Kuwait Oil Company struck its first oil, thanks in part to a dream of Harold Dickson which recurred 5 times. Subaihiyah is deserted, and has been since the 1960s, when the government constructed a new town for its residents. Some old wells, now filled with sand, are considered likely places for jinn. The whole area is rife with trees and other desert growth, suggesting an abundance of hidden water that would attract jinn to the area. One jinn, a black man, allegedly lived in a salt marsh called Maqtah. When Harold Dickson was alive, he wrote about hearing this tale. It was an unpleasant place, 40 feet across, smelling strongly of sulfur. Humans don't like the area, and it drains through a channel slowly out to the Gulf. The jinn liked to come out and sun himself when he thought he was alone.

Her next jinn article was full of tales by other women, because she had attended a ladies' tea party and all the women spent part of the time talking about jinn – just as many people sit around sharing ghost stories or war stories. They seemed to have scared themselves a little, talking about jinni in Saudi Arabia who cause car crashes, making drivers think they have hit and killed someone, then just stand around staring at them as they chant Quran verses and try to calm down. Evil jinni don't want anyone to crash their wedding or other celebrations, and will kill intruders, as friends of a dead man believe happened to him – but he took a photograph of the killer-jinn just before dying, so they published it in a magazine.

On the calmer side of the issue, the women try to "get a grip" on themselves (these quotation marks are not for quotes from the article – they are my own expressions) by also balancing the discussion with stories of good and benign jinni who live in Kuwait. People believe jinn are real, and that some are Muslims. One old man jinn prays at a family's well, while another scents them with incense. The old man appeared to have the ability to appear and disappear at will. I thought about the other jinn who lived in a sulfurous well. The blue mutant teleporter came back to mind.

David managed to bring me just one more of the jinn articles, which he had bought as he left Kuwait (his plane ticket brought him home a day after mine, because I was traveling with our cat on a different airline). This installment described a haunted house that Assim had mentioned to us earlier – it was haunted by jinn. The house had just been razed and another structure was planned. It remained to be seen whether or not the jinn would come back.

There were several great stories about Kuwaiti people who had dealt with jinni: a woman befriended a jinn who appeared in the form of a black cat, who promised to help the woman's family in return for secrecy about being a jinn. Things went well until the husband demanded to know what was going on – then all help ended. Another family had a different experience: they found that a family of jinni accompanied them out of Kuwait during the invasion, stayed with them, and returned home with them when the war was over. The jinni never did anything terrible to the human family – only silly, annoying things like tap the newspaper while people were trying to read it. The family concluded that, because of this, the jinni must be Muslims.

Since I left Kuwait and came home to continuous Internet access – a thing that I never had while visiting Kuwait – I have tried to obtain a virtual copy of this series on jinn. No luck; it seems that I would have to special order any books by Claudia Farkas Al-Rashoud, as they are only in print in a select few places, such as travel bookstores in Manhattan, or else Kuwait and perhaps elsewhere in the Middle East. It's frustrating, because I can't see the rest of the series of articles, which is what I really want. David and I found that, unless we were able to secure work permits – called iqamas – we would not be allowed to order our own phone line or Internet connection in our own apartment. So we had to rely on visits to friend's offices and homes for web-surfing, and buy newspapers at local stores.

An Odd Superstition and Divorce Story

What he said had nothing whatsoever to do with ghosts. It was about his divorce. And it was about his marriage. He had told me that he had been married for a year to a woman who was 20 years his senior, but I was curious about how it had happened. He had been 20 years old when he married her. She looked his age, but he knew how old she was. They fought a lot. His mother and sisters did not think she was good for him. Why then, I asked, did he marry her? His answer explained everything: as often happens with young people who are emotionally inexperienced, he had convinced himself that he just had to be with her. So they got married and were unhappy.

The divorce was the really interesting part of the story. He used to tease her during fights that he would divorce her, but he said he wasn't serious. Then he got sick, being unable to keep his food down for 2 weeks, and having terrible pains in his gut. His family took him to the hospital, and – he pulled up his shirt and showed me a long, vertical scar running through his belly button – the surgeon removed a section of his large intestine. Considering the junk food that he eats, soda he drinks, sugar in his tea and his cigarette addiction, I was not surprised.

What did surprise me was what the doctor told him when he asked how he had gotten sick. The doctor told him that his wife had tried to poison him by adding some of her menstrual blood to his tea or soda. He believed the doctor without question, and divorced his wife. She now lived with her brother.

Incredible; it occurred to me that Mansoor's mother must have put the doctor up to this to get rid of an unpleasant daughter-in-law. I ran this theory by David later on, and he agreed. He added that you could drink a glassful or more of menstrual blood and it wouldn't hurt you, but of course no one would do a thing like that. Arab and Muslim men are leery of menstruating women, so this must have been a great line to feed to Mansoor!

Some time later, I asked Mansoor about this theory, explaining that I had realized that his mother had conspired with the doctor to rid the family of this daughter-in-law whom she had not wanted. Was he angry with his mother about that? No, he said, and I believed him.

I also asked him whether or not anyone else knew this excuse, which wasn't even a valid medical explanation. What I was concerned about was the possibility that the story had been spread around and thus ruined the ex-wife's chances of ever getting married again. He said that no, he did not think so, and he had not told it to anyone. Well…good. At least she might someday find someone else more suited to her, and then she might be happy someday…maybe.

This was a fascinating instance of how a superstition could be knowingly used to achieve a specific result. With superstitions like that, who needed real witches and wizards?

Chapter 11
Invisibility Cloaks and Abbeyas

Despite the Harry Potter reference, I mean a completely different sort of invisibility cloak when it comes to functioning in the Arab-Islamic world. There are abbeyas – which Kuwaiti women wear – and there is a cultural and religious directive that demands a sense of social invisibility from women in Kuwait.

An abbeya is a black robe worn by Arab women to cover their clothing. It has a fastener in the front, does not cover the wearer's head, it has long sleeves, and comes down over the tops of the wearer's feet. It can cost anywhere from 5 Kuwaiti dinars (KD) to say, 1,000 KD. It all depends upon just how proletarian, bourgeois or aristocratic the vending establishment is, what sort of fabric is used to make the abbeya, and whether or not the garment is custom made.

If so – and I did see a shop that sold such beautiful work once – the woman is presented with swatches of black cloth (always black, the traditional color for Arab women's coveralls) with seemingly endless variations and colors of embroidered designs that can go on the sleeves, collar, and matching hijab (head scarf). Kuwaiti law does not require that any woman wear one. The choice to do so varies from woman to woman and family to family.

The invisibility factor is not in the cloak. It is much more pervasive than that. It is something that is deeply embedded in Kuwaiti culture: women are to be concealed from men as much as possible, even when we are in plain sight. I resisted every effort by any Arab man I met to make me seem or feel in any way invisible. Kuwait does not have laws on women's bodies about clothing, so I did not have to worry about that.

Of course I confirmed all this in advance. Before departing for Kuwait, I had bought a travel guide, one of the *Lonely Planet* guides to the Middle East. I read the entire section on Kuwait before packing a single thing. As soon as I saw the section on women's dress, I relaxed just a bit:

I could dress as I do at home, which is in long pants, long skirts, comfortable shoes, tee shirts and long-sleeved shirts, and with my long hair either down or up in a clip. No problem about wearing makeup, either – and I feel as though I haven't finished getting dressed without it. Once I had found this out, I was willing to visit Kuwait.

As it was, I felt surrounded and hemmed in just by geography: Saudi Arabia with its laws demanding that I wear not only an abbeya but a hijab and nekhab as well was right next door, and to the north was

Iraq, which was still a terrifying war zone. The only escape, as I saw it, was by plane. But I was okay in Kuwait; I could retain possession and control of my own passport.

One thing that I noticed about Saleh Al-Hamdullilah was that he was laboring under certain delusions where his thoughts concerned us, and that all of these delusions were fueled by wishful thinking. He made numerous attempts to induce me to adopt Arab dress and cover my hair. I would either laugh as I explained the various reasons why this would not be happening, or flat out tell him to just forget it if I felt pushed past the point of maintaining a patient, pleasant demeanor with him.

As long as observance of a custom is truly the choice of the woman who follows it, I support it – even wearing a full shroud of abbeya, hijab, and nekhab. If her family or husband demands it, or her government does so, I do not. I will always take the woman's side first, and her culture, nation's laws, and religion second.

Many times as I have studied a foreign society or met someone from one, either a man or a patriarchal-minded woman has admonished me to not feel outraged on behalf of any of the women whom I see being restricted and controlled, because it is not my own society. To them, I say this: that is the attitude of an abettor, one who stands by and watches silently, not interfering, as a bully inflicts misery on others for the fun of doing so.

I am a feminist, and I won't be quiet.

Connecting with Women - Silently

I would not be getting to know very many of the women in Kuwait personally, nor would I even be talking to them. One encounters so many people in the course of a day as one goes from place to place, and people have their own duties and agendas. This meant that finding out whether or not a woman was dressing in full Islamic costume would usually be impossible. What would I do when I met such women, then?

Nothing much – I planned to just smile politely, and hope for a smile in return. When I got close enough for that level of eye contact, I was not disappointed. People are the same everywhere.

Walking Around the Kuwait Oil Company Hospital

The day after I arrived in Kuwait, I found myself wandering around Kuwait Oil Company Hospital while David and Saleh did some work together.

The people in the hospital were interesting to me. At lunch, a bevy of Philippina nurse-trainees came into the cafeteria and ordered cheeseburgers and fries. David told me that the hospital provided housing for them nearby to supplement their low pay. Only one of the trainees was male; the women were all dressed identically in white shoes (not sneakers), tights, dresses with pockets, and wristwatches (complete, no doubt, with second hands).

Men in the hospital wore either Western clothing or dishdashahs, which were worn with either white or red-checked guthras. I saw only one Kuwaiti woman who showed her hair – a doctor in the doctors' lounge. She wore Western clothing, glasses, had long, beautifully coiffed hair, and attractive but heavily applied makeup. She smoked cigarettes with the guys. I sat at the opposite end of the room (away from the smoke) and read a Kuwait government publication detailing the pearling industry, and trade before oil was struck, and then moved on to describe Kuwaiti life since oil was struck.

There I was, dressed as a Western woman, with my hair twisted up into a gold clip, with pearl earrings, lightly applied makeup, and comfortable shoes. I stood out as I wandered around the hospital. That was okay; some women in veils and abbeyas smiled at me, and the chic Kuwaiti doctor in her lab coat was pleasant to me.

I can't forget the woman with beautiful eyes that were outlined by a heavy coat of makeup who wore a veil, which concealed the rest of her face. She smiled back at me as I entered the hospital that morning. "The American woman is not bad, she's just different from me," her smile seemed to say to me.

Diwaniyas – but not Harimiyas

David had told me – he was told by Kuwaiti friends – that Kuwaiti society is a very contrived culture, and that he would do well not to let on to new acquaintances here just how much Arabic he can speak. The reason for this is that Kuwaitis are well aware that their society is contrived, and are ashamed of it. So they don't want this to be understood too well by outsiders, nor do they want it to be done in too much detail. Still, I wanted to learn more Arabic than just salaam (hello) and šukran (thank you). I managed to compile a list, in the glossary.

It was late in November; I was home alone, because David had been invited to a diwaniya. A diwaniya is held in a diwan – men-only gathering room in a private house – and it is a lengthy evening gathering for men only, during which they all sit on sofas around the perimeter of the room eating snacks and drinking tea. I could picture this because we visited Fahad in his diwan (it was even labeled as such outside, on a brass plate). The room that we sat in at Assim's house was furnished in a more elaborate style, but the layout was the same: sofas around the perimeter of the room. At these social gatherings, men meet new people and talk, and sometimes during the course of an evening, deals may be struck or problems solved.

Women *never* go to these gatherings – not even professional women. This presents a significant obstacle to professional women in Kuwait who depend on social contacts in order to accomplish anything, as men certainly do. No wonder the Kuwaiti Parliament nullified the Emir's decree giving women the right to vote. Just as it was in the past in the U.S., Europe and elsewhere, men didn't want to share political clout. What they had was full access to the most fun and interesting aspects of life, with diwaniyas and the right to vote. Kuwaiti wanted to vote as well. Perhaps they could start attending diwaniyas – or create a new custom of harimiyas...

I wondered how I would spend my time in Kuwait. David could go anywhere, but I would have to pick my way carefully. I like mixed company far better than that of only women, because I can talk to many different people in the course of a visit, of both sexes and all ages, to avoid discussing only fashion and children. I like politics, history, culture, and women's studies.

What would I do here? Getting around was difficult, but where would I go? There were malls, but who could I visit? I couldn't "fix" Raidah, as Saleh seemed to hope – I could only be her friend, if that was even possible. There weren't very many museums, either. I hoped I would find something that I liked to do, or make some friends.

As it turned out, I had Fatin to visit on most Thursdays, when she was off from teaching at Kuwait University, Aiesha on Friday evenings, and I met Kuwait's lead woman suffragist, Rola A. Al-Dashti, Ph.D. So it worked out rather well – there were plenty of interesting women to interact with. And I made sure that David and I saw several museums.

Doctors in Hijabs

One night late in November, not long after I arrived in Kuwait, Saleh took us to Kuwait University Medical School to hear some continuing education lectures for doctors. These are offered instead of taking tests. We had a horrible bagged dinner (mass-produced for the doctors attending the conference) of fries and pastries with bitter cheese, tea, fruit punch, and cake. Medical students were studying all around us.

I looked at them carefully, especially the women. Some did not cover their hair at all, while others wore long, fashionable skirts made of denim or sheer cloth over a solid material, and had on equally fashionable head scarves. Bareheaded or covered, all of the Arab women looked very elegant, and many wore heavy makeup. This intrigued me; it seemed that all of them were determined to look appealing, and if one avenue of doing so were closed off to them by custom, another would be found. Then I remembered that Aiesha wore a full, black hijab and no makeup at all when leaving her home. I was curious to get to know her better.

One woman doctor gave a lecture about Islamic ethics in medicine. I noticed that she wore a hijab – a white one – and no makeup. While some things differed from the ethics of the West (paternity testing is only allowed for babies lost or abandoned at the hospital here!), most of it seemed the same, just dressed up with quotes from the Quran: informed consent, good bedside manner, patient counseling, genetic information, and treatment options. Also, all lectures began with this sentence: "Bi's-mi'llah, al rahiman, al rahim. = In the name of God, the merciful, the benevolent." Then the lecture would be delivered.

We were to go back the following evening to hear a Canadian doctor talk about science and fiction in medicine. And have that same awful meal! David liked it, though – the outing, not the meal. He used to work in the immunology labs there with Saleh 12 years ago, and he showed me where they are. Anyway, perhaps we would see the same wide-ranging array of veils, scarves, Gucci handbags, abbeyas in white, black, and some with beautiful embroidery again this evening.

It certainly was fun to observe all of the different styles of covering oneself that are employed by women in this culture. Some are simple and plain, while others are very chic – it seems to depend on the personal taste and style of each woman.

Lady... vs. Hey Lady!

One morning, David's friend and old scientific colleague, Dr. Alim, called me. He and his wife, Nadira, wanted to take me out to the historic sites of Kuwait, he said. (Hurray, I thought – I love to do things like that!) That wasn't all...he wanted to take me and David to Qatar, the United Arab Emirates, and Lebanon – an hour by plane, 18 hours by car. By car would mean passing through Saudi Arabia, and I was NOT willing to cover myself up from head to toe, so I didn't know about this idea. I never want to set foot in that country. How we would have time or money to do this, I wondered, but the invitation sounded nice.

Nadira, he told me, spoke Arabic and a little French. I speak English and a little French, plus a very few Arabic words, so communication ought to be interesting. Perhaps we would get some mutual practice speaking en Français. [We didn't; Nadira didn't know much French after all. Her high-school age daughter, Mahibah interpreted and chatted with us. We had a good time.]

Dr. Alim had an interesting habit of calling me "Lady" when he spoke with me.

This practice was part of the Arab practice of hijab: the men consider it to be an invasion of another man's privacy to so much as know the name of his wife, so if one of them does know her name, he tries to ignore it by calling her "Lady" and thus sound respectful of her. It bothered me, though. I did not want to be made invisible. I can't help it; this was NOT a part of Muslim culture that I was willing to assimilate into. Plus I can't stop hearing a tone of disrespect in it: "Hey – Lady!" called from across a street, or to show annoyance with a female stranger...a negative facet of my own culture springing, unbidden, to mind.

No Consideration for HIS Lady's Wishes

Last one night in the spring – after the last prayer call – Dr. Alim picked us up and brought us to his home for dinner. We met some of Dr. Alim's female relatives, who were visiting from Syria after 2 years. They were Dr. Alim's older sister, a plain-looking woman who showed not a hint of either hair or makeup.

Her daughter was a somewhat prettier woman in her forties, also well-covered, and her 23-year-old daughter was with them. This daughter was not married. She wore a pretty dark pink blouse that did a good job of shrouding her arms and neck and hanging down almost to her knees. She wore pants, nice shoes, and a hijab. All 3 women were very pleasant to me and smiled a lot, but I thought that Nadira understood much more English than any of them. As usual, Nadira's food was delicious, and I told her that she was a chef – she smiled happily.

Before we went there, Dr. Ahmed called me in the afternoon to – of all things – invite our cat! The invitation was really from the 2 little boys, Osama and Yaman. The family knew that she was a famous cat and a war heroine, and they didn't meet very many animals (I didn't think to ask why that was just then).

So we brought our cat on her first social outing ever, in her cat carrier, and she enjoyed herself. The SUV pulled up, and when David and I got in, I saw that the vehicle was almost full. The back area had an extra seat in it, and on it were Mahibah with her cousins, all smiling at me. Next to me was Nadira, along for the ride, and Dr. Alim's sister sat by the other window, behind David.

Nadira told me that she is afraid of cats when I got into the car, and I looked at Dr. Alim in surprise. He had obviously neither informed nor consulted his wife about Scheherazade's visit – his boys wanted the cat, so he included her, with no consideration for his wife's wishes or comfort! I apologized and promised to control my cat – the car had begun to move as soon I was in, so it was too late to leave Scheherazade home when Nadira told me this.

The boys had a great time watching our cat run around the apartment, checking the place out. Cats will always inspect any new environment when they first arrive. She looked in the hall beyond the curtain, but all 3 doors were closed. She looked at the kitchen, but I grabbed her and carried her in only partway, telling her that she couldn't go into that room.

She was smart; she went back out to the living and dining area and hid on a chair under the table cloth. The boys watched her, and called their friends from next door to see her. I kept warning them to keep the door closed. I held the cat for the neighbor boys to look at from the hall until the door was shut. Then the aunt and cousins told them in Arabic to keep the door closed.

We put out some water for the cat, and I let the boys look at her and follow her around until dinner, but then I figured that Scheherazade's hosts had seen enough of her. They are children, after all, and children tend to bother cats too much. She swiped at Yaman, the youngest boy, when he tried to grab her out from under the tablecloth, but I had cut all of her nails, front and back. She didn't hurt him, but he got the message.

Dr. Alim agreed when I said no more after a while – the cat was not a rag doll, and the kids must not bother her too much. She had a great ride home, staring out the window of the SUV at cars and houses as we rode along.

Dr. Alim seemed to have cut down considerably on calling me "lady." He was being polite by his cultural standards. I wanted to be called by my name. I had told him so and explained why. I had explained to him that in my culture, women feel sidelined and therefore insulted if we aren't called by our names. He listened carefully.

As this was not our first visit to this family, I had already seen Mahibah's entire collection of hijabs. She had shown them to me – all in pretty colors. Syrian women do not wear only black, as Kuwaiti women do. Mahibah impressed me – she had made the honor roll and won an academic award, so she had a photo of herself in full hijab, with a graduation gown and mortarboard cap on to keep for her parents.

I asked her how she felt when she began to wear the hijab, curious to hear her reply.

"I felt precious," she told me. Interesting. I bought her a pretty pastel blue hijab, and brought it to her the night that the cat was invited. She loved it! "I will not forget this," she said.

Dr. Ahmed did slip and call me Lady as we climbed into his car to go home. It was getting hot in Kuwait, so that even at midnight, when we went outside, I had to strip off my light sweater. It felt like an oven outside, even though it had been dark for hours. Dr. Alim was in a comfortable shirt – no jacket, no tie.

I realized that Nadira and the two older relatives from Syria would be joining us momentarily, and that they were shrouded in cloth, showing only their hands and faces, unable to strip any layers off. Everyone smelled scrupulously clean here; I had read that the Quran dictated perfection in keeping clean and well-groomed.

I commented to Dr. Ahmed that I felt sorry for his female relatives, because they couldn't take off any extra layers of clothing to keep cool. "Don't worry, Lady," was all he said. What else could he say? He ran the air conditioning.

My New Invisible Friend

Being invisible is mentally unhealthy, and can be dangerous as well. It cuts a person off from support systems, isolates her, and makes her more vulnerable to attack with less and less chance of notice, let alone rescue. I mentioned earlier that I had made friends with a Kuwaiti woman who wore an abbeya and hijab – all black. This was Aiesha.

Between Christmas and New Year's Eve, I had my first visit to Aiesha and Assim's place. First he took us out to eat at a fancy restaurant, because he hoped to encounter Hassan, his oldest son, home from college in the U.S. We never saw him, but had a nice meal. Assim was having a lot of trouble with that kid, and asked for our help with him.

After we ate, Assim took us to his house. We had been there once before, with Saleh, on the night that we had gone on a marathon of 4 visits. This time it was less confusing, and we went into their home rather than only going as far in as the diwan.

On the previous visit, I had seen Aiesha and spoken with her only a little.

She had been busy silently bringing in tray after tray of tea, pastries and sweets, and then taking the trays away once we were finished. On this visit, Aiesha told me that she considered it to be more respectful to visitors to bring out trays of tea and cakes herself rather than have a maid do it. She came out 4 times with trays that night: orange juice, then croissants, followed by cakes and tea – 2 trips at a time. was glad to meet her. She told me that she knew accounting, and could speak some English, but had forgotten a lot of it. No she hadn't, I told her. She smiled.

She had entered the diwan to serve these things, and then sat next to me quietly, not participating in the conversation, which was about setting up clinical laboratory studies. There was nothing that either of us could add, so I had turned to chat with her. I was glad; she was the first Kuwaiti woman I had had a chance to converse with one-on-one since meeting Saleh's wife, and she was rather different from Raidah in her demeanor. I was curious.

Aiesha did not meet people's gazes directly, or raise her chin upwards to be level with other people's…at least not that evening. As I got to know her better over the course of my time in Kuwait, we had many visits, usually on Friday evenings, and always – despite the fact that Aiesha had her own car and a driver's license – with Assim driving me from my place to hers. Aiesha met my gaze directly after that. Perhaps being in what her culture deemed men's territory – that diwan – was why she wasn't behaving as an equal to men.

When I had a real visit with Aiesha that next time, I found that I liked her a lot, and I wanted her to visit me. Assim kept coming over to our place, but I thought that I would love to know Aiesha better, too. When I asked Assim about the possibility of her ever coming to visit me at my place, so that I could serve her tea, he said that he would not allow her to come to my area. Why? It was nothing personal about us, he hastened to assure me. The problem was that he considered it to be unsafe for her, with all those foreign workers and construction around us. Because I did not go out walking without my own husband, and because Assim always chauffeured me to and from his place, I didn't feel particularly safe in Abraq Khaitan either.

So I accepted this arrangement without further question, and never found any reason to reconsider. The only drawback came in January, when Assim went to Florida for 3 weeks. That effectively cut off visits with Aiesha until he returned, though we did talk on the phone.

Aiesha had earned her M.B.A. at the University of Pittsburgh after she and Assim were married, and after they had 2 or 3 of their children. All this while doing all of the housework and child care, I realized (though also with the household amenities that Americans are used to, such as a washer, a dryer and a dishwasher). She taught accounting in the community college in Hawali…and while she was raising 6 kids! That is a lot of work. There must be some servants helping with the housework, I thought. It turned out that she had one live-in maid on the premises, who was from Indonesia, was Muslim, and had a 2-year contract.

The 6 children were: 20-year-old Zahra, who was studying for a Bachelor's degree in pharmacy – all in English – at Kuwait University; 18-year-old Hassan, who was attending a university in Ohio, and causing endless trouble and worry to his parents…he had Type 1 (childhood) diabetes, and he was very lazy about doing his homework, and rude to his parents; 14-year-old Hamid and 12-year-old Abdul Malik, who attended a private American school; 6-year-old Karidah; and 4-year-old Safa'a. Assim's mother lived downstairs in her own apartment, and Zahra's room was down the hall from her grandmother's room. Hassan had a huge room all to himself upstairs, next to a room shared by the 4 youngest kids, and both rooms were across from their parents' room.

I had liked Aiesha when I first met her, I still liked her, and I wanted to visit with her again. Not yet realizing that it wouldn't happen, I hoped Assim would drive her over to our place soon, because our place was hard to find and I wanted Aiesha to know how to get here. He misled me at first, perhaps not wanting to offend us, saying that once she had been there she would find it again on her own and come back. I hoped so – and I knew that she had her own car and a driver's license, so I foresaw no reason why not.

A Deliberate Lack of Assertiveness

A week into January, in the late afternoon, Assim brought me to visit Aiesha. It was fun – and I met their oldest daughter, Zahra. She was about five feet two inches tall, had glasses and perfect teeth, a pretty face, and, of course, a hijab. All of her hair was hidden from view – all. She also wore no makeup, just like her mother.

When I arrived, Zahra had just returned a little while earlier from a dentist's office, having taken Abdul Malik to have some work done. He had seemed okay during the procedure, but after he got home he started crying. Aiesha was busy with Safa'a, who was taking antibiotics for an ear infection. Zahra and I went into the kids' room to see why Abdul Malik was crying. The 4 younger children shared this huge room; it had 2 sets of bunk beds, one for the little girls, and another for the older boys.

I went up to the top bunk bed, where he was sitting up against the wall, moaning. I asked him to open his mouth and show me. He did; I was amazed and disgusted. He showed me his lower teeth – what remained of them. His front two bicuspids – the teeth just after the canines and before the molars – were gone, and all that could be seen were two holes in his gums. The teeth had been extracted that afternoon, after school.

He said his jaw hurt – no surprise there. I questioned him about anesthesia. What had they done for him about pain? Novocaine? Nitrous oxide? Anything? Apparently he had been given painkillers just for the procedure. So when he came home, the anesthesia wore off. Then he started crying. We didn't blame him. I told him that they should have given him some pain pills for later on. I told Zahra that it wasn't her fault; that they probably figured that they didn't have to be accountable to a big sister. She said she knew, and smiled.

Zahra smiled ruefully and said, "This is Kuwait – what can you expect." I knew that health care in Kuwait left much to be desired. Private hospitals were just glorified hotels, staffed by foreign maids/nurses. The government pays for Kuwaitis to fly out of the country and be treated elsewhere if a specialized treatment is necessary for any of its citizens and unavailable.

I went back out to the living room and told Assim and Aiesha that their son needed to be taken to a doctor immediately for something stronger than over-the-counter drugs. He needed prescription pain killers for a couple of days, as this was obviously oral surgery. Assim and Zahra took him right out for it. He came back still hurting, and hid upstairs in one of the big empty apartments until he felt well and calm enough to go back to his room. Poor Abdul Malik!

That ended well enough, I suppose. We moved on to the purpose of the visit, which was to see Zahra and have a long, fun chat for about 4 hours. She told me about her studies, including the fact that she did not really love studying pharmacy, but that she didn't have much choice. I wanted to know what she meant by that, and what she would prefer to do.

Zahra told me that there weren't many choices of subjects to study in Kuwait. I had gathered that from our conversations with Hassan, and with Assim about Hassan. Those discussions had revealed that the Kuwaiti government was very particular about which major fields of study it would grant scholarships for. This meant that if a student was fascinated by a subject that was not on the government list of accepted choices but had won a scholarship to study in the States, that student must select something else. Also, if a student attended Kuwait University, the choices were limited to whatever fields of study were offered there.

Zahra said she would really have preferred to study engineering, as several of her friends had chosen, but that she saw little point in doing so. Why? Because upon graduation, women engineers in Kuwait faced a much lower chance of being hired than men. Apparently, her friends were willing to take this risk rather than study for a profession that didn't thrill them. And, apparently, Zahra could face a lifetime of working in a profession that didn't thrill her.

I couldn't face that, and I told her that I had taken a risk, too: writing and editing.

As we talked, the subject of how Nuwwar looks and dresses surfaced. (I made it surface, subtly enough.) I wanted to hear the opinions and reactions of Zahra and Aiesha on the issue of covering oneself or not covering oneself, so I told Zahra about the fact that Nuwwar looks the way she does – heavy eye makeup, long black straightened hair with bangs of varying lengths, tight clothing – and has politely told her stepfather not to bother her about wearing a hijab, as it is simply not her choice.

Aiesha clucked her tongue as I told this tale – she had heard it all before on previous visits, but what I was trying to learn was, did she disapprove of Nuwwar, approve of her, simply accept her, what? I was so curious to know how Arab women who cover themselves view other Arab women who do not cover themselves.

Zahra had an interesting response. When I told them that Nuwwar told me that she thinks as they do about waiting for her husband, and that she had never had a boyfriend yet, Zahra told me that there are girls who wear hijabs but date and have sex, so why bother wearing the hijab at all?! Fascinating. Aiesha even said that what matters is what goes on in a woman's mind more than how she dresses. I was pleased to hear it.

They wanted to know what my summer dresses looked like. I described them – sleeveless dresses with a jewel neck, and no spaghetti straps. The skirts come down past my knees to the mid-calves of my legs. The shoulders look like clothing with sleeves that were simply never added. I also had summer dresses with sleeves, but I hadn't brought any to Kuwait. Instead, I brought sweaters to hide my arms in case I went into a chilly, air-conditioned place.

I told Zahra I would bring my wedding pictures next time so she could see my bridesmaids' dresses. We had a nice, long, lovely visit, and they wanted me to come back soon. I brought Aiesha some of the candy that I had brought from America and been saving as a present. It was coconut covered with dark chocolate. She said she loved that kind.

After a while, Assim came in with a tray of tea and spinach buns, and sat down on the sofa next to Zahra to eat his food. He asked me if he was bothering me, which I thought was rather odd. I told him so, and added that he ought to be able to sit down and eat in his home. He explained that he knew that most women liked to sit by themselves for a visit. Yes…well, I reminded him that I am used to mixed company, and I like it. So he sat with us and ate.

Hassan appeared and told me that Zahra had lost her English after spending so much time in Kuwait. I didn't think so – she was fluent! She laughed and said that Kuwait University classes are all in English, so of course she can still read, write and speak English.

Aiesha taught accounting in Arabic, so she practiced it less, and was glad to have an American visitor to practice with. Her 2 younger boys said that she wasn't fluent, but I corrected them: they were confusing fluency with perfection. Their mother could carry on a detailed conversation with me in English without an interpreter – she earned her M.B.A. in the United States, after all – so she was fluent. Her English was not perfect…she made some mistakes…but she didn't need help communicating.

Thus far, from what I had been able to observe about Aiesha, she chose to be a quiet, observant Muslim. I was now seeing her at ease in her own territory – the harim – her part of the house. She seemed more relaxed, and met my gaze directly. So did her oldest daughter, I noticed. They were not, however, what I might ever have called assertive. It appeared that a deliberate lack of assertiveness was, to them, a sign of being a dutiful wife and daughter. Their demeanors and appearance practically announced this, and bordered on passiveness. I wanted to learn more.

An Invasion of Privacy to Ask How Women Are...

A week later, I had my next chance to visit them.

Zahra was glad to see me again. We had a lovely visit, and Zahra wore a white hijab. She was wearing a pink exercise suit, and she and her little sister, Karidah, matched. Safa'a was wearing a shirt with pink roses all over it, and wanted to see my wedding ring, which is all roses, in yellow and rose gold.

Zahra had 3 weeks' vacation. She was very happy to be able to relax. She was also looking forward to going out shopping with a friend. Assim wasn't sure that this was such a good idea – it would mean letting his 20-year-old daughter go unchaperoned around a mall. I was surprised; I told him that she was obviously a good girl who would stay with her friend and ignore all the guys. Zahra told him that she would go during daylight hours. He said she could go. 2 girls alone at a mall – 2 college-age girls – seemed unremarkable to me.

A Western parent would have thought, oh, she's 20, she is a legal adult, and left it at that. But for Kuwaitis, an unmarried daughter must get permission to go to the mall. An unmarried daughter in the Islamic world is not treated as a legal adult, although 21 is the age of legal majority in Kuwait. I mentioned that I had gone shopping with 21-year-old Nuwwar, Fatin's daughter. Assim said that of course Nuwwar was allowed by Fatin to take off into a mall with just me, a married woman 14 years older than she – I was considered to be a chaperone.

Zahra wanted to see my wedding photos, which I had brought but almost forgot to show her. She enjoyed them. I wondered if she knew what sort of dress she would like when her time came. She said she would just see what was for sale when she was ready. Hijabs were discussed again, and Zahra said what I am sure she was raised to think: she considers herself to be a jewel, to be looked at only by family and her husband. Aiesha told me that her daughter was 9 years old when she started wearing a hijab; Zahra corrected her and said she was 10. No great difference. So that would happen to Karidah and Safa'a in just a few more years.

Assim sat with us after a while. I asked the family about something that Mansoor had told me earlier in the day. Mansoor had told me that it is considered very rude in Arab culture for any man to ask another how his sister is. Asking generally, "How is your family?" and referring to no particular member is okay, but knowing a sister's name is bad, and asking about her by name can enrage the Arab whose sister is referred to. Mansoor told me all this, but was at a loss to explain why this is so.

Assim told me why. It is simply considered an invasion of privacy. Arabs can never ask about the well-being of each other's wives, sisters, or adult daughters. If they do, the expected response is a wild rage. It is okay to ask about a little girl – she's cute, how is she, like Safa'a, for example – but forget it once she starts wearing a hijab.

She's too old for that, and privacy is invoked as soon as she puts on the hijab.

Assim would not get angry if David said, "How's Aiesha – tell her I said hello." Western etiquette directs both men and women to ask about the whole family, either collectively or individually. We have no taboo about inquiring as to the well-being of a person of the opposite gender. If we have met that individual, we are expected to ask about her or him. Not asking, we have been taught, appears rude and inconsiderate. Assim knew this, so he wouldn't take offense. He had, after all, spent years studying in the United States.

Out at the Mall with Aiesha and the Girls

Another week passed, and Aiesha invited me to go out to a mall with her and her daughters – all 3 of them. Assim came to pick me up, and he conveyed Aiesha's worries that I might find this invitation to be silly or frivolous. I was surprised; it was the most normal of invitations. Zahra wanted to look for new clothes for Eid, and that sounded like as good an excuse as any to go out for a visit. Aiesha also hoped to find something new for Karidah and Safa'a to wear. They ultimately didn't find anything that they liked, but we had a nice time.

Aiesha drove us in the big black SUV. She and Zahra did what Kuwaiti women do when they go out to the mall: they dressed up. Aiesha wore a long black skirt, a black hijab, and a white suit jacket with thin criss-crossed stripes all through it. Zahra wore a long skirt with dark pink, brown, and black in it, a brown suit jacket, and a beige hijab. She said that her dad had bought the skirt for her in the States. Next to them, I was quite casual in a bright blue shirt, matching cotton sweater, black cotton pants with pockets, and Teva sandals with black socks that had a cat pattern on them. I was also the only one with makeup on, and my hair was uncovered, of course. What a contrast. We visited the Al-Muthanna Complex.

Assim had explained earlier that Kuwaitis like to show off whenever they go out. This explained why Kuwaiti people bother to dress up to go out to the mall. It amazed me to see all this effort in a culture in which dating was forbidden. Girls and women with beautiful makeup, high heels, and long, flowing designer clothing trolling the malls, while guys walk around in designer sneakers, jeans and shirts or dishdashahs with gel in their hair and stare at them. But they are not supposed to approach each other; that is haram – bad.

We ate some ice cream and chatted. I asked Zahra about summer jobs, because she had 3 weeks off in the winter and 3 months off in the summer. American college students usually get jobs during both school breaks and save the money to spend during the academic terms, so what did Kuwaiti kids do? She told me that there was an office for Kuwaiti college students to put their names into for the purpose of getting jobs. The office matches them up with jobs related to their studies, but those jobs tended to go to older students, so Zahra was turned down this time.

What about going to the local mall and applying at some book or clothing store? It doesn't work that way, she said. Why? Foreign workers get those jobs. They keep them year-round, so there are no seasonal openings. Oh yeah, I thought, glancing back at the Indian worker who had sold us our ice cream. Kuwait is serviced by an entire subpopulation of expatriates who wait on the Kuwaitis. How is a college student to feel independent, then? Forget it – mom and dad pay for her entertainment, not the student.

We went back to their house, with Aiesha pointing out one of the 4 remaining sections of the old wall that used to surround Kuwait City. When we got back, Aiesha served tea with milk, and honey croissants.

She and Zahra told me that while in the States during the 1990s, they were afraid to identify themselves as Kuwaitis, and often claimed to be from some other Middle Eastern nation. Why? Because they thought that relatives of soldiers who had died in the Gulf War would resent and dislike them just on general principle. I told them that their fears were most likely unfounded, and that the attitude had been predominantly feeling sorry for Kuwaitis that their home had been attacked, and glad to have had something to do with kicking the invaders out.

Assim and Aiesha kept telling me and David that we were now like a sister and brother to them, and Aiesha told me that I was her best friend as I left last night. Part of me was delighted and flattered; another part of me was suddenly very curious: what about her other friends? Did she have any? I had just gotten to know her. This was a bit odd. Was her social life that limited that she could not talk to any other women her age? Why? I would have to wait and see.

No Visit with Assim Away

We didn't visit while Assim attended a faculty conference in Florida – and he was gone for over 2 weeks. But it was at least 3 weeks before we had another visit. So, with the exception of phone calls, we were cut off. By the time we visited again, it was March, and David and I had already had our fascinating weekend at the Wafra Farms Oasis.

This gave me a lot to describe to Aiesha. I told her about meeting Faisal's wife, that she had avoided being photographed, and had given up an intellectually satisfying career at his behest. I told her how much I abhorred the idea of being invisible. I love the fact that my culture does not stop me from being seen, noticed, and remembered for who I am, photographed and, if I do something truly interesting, noteworthy and useful in my life, identified in history as myself, with my face visible to the world. This is not possible for Talibah and many other women – but there are devout Muslim, Kuwaiti women for whom it is possible. They had their photos in *The Kuwait Times* and *The Arab Times* every day.

Aiesha didn't do this to herself. She didn't mind photographs, as long as she put on her hijab. After that, she would go out into the world to do things. Assim did tell me not to show those photographs to other Arab men, but that it would be fine to show them to my family. [This attitude is typical here. Mansoor told me that if he has to take his sister's civil I.D. card someplace, he holds it out for officials to copy the written information off of, with his thumb covering her photo. He would only let them see it with a compelling legal or medical reason.]

I told Assim that I was annoyed that Aiesha's entire vacation from teaching had gone by before I could visit her again, thanks to Assim forbidding her to come to my place, and my inability to get to theirs. What about the week and half after his return, before school started again?! He actually had a plausible excuse: Shi'a Muslims have a 10-day period that fell just then in which they don't go out to see anyone. All I could think was: how convenient.

Next, Assim told me, lamenting the fact, that Aiesha has no friends. Of course not – she is intelligent, but when she did find a friend, he always found some problem and then forbade her to see the person! I had asked her about this, and she had described being friends with a divorced woman who went to the mall with her a few times, only to have Assim object that she was a bad influence because she was divorced, so Aiesha had stopped seeing her. They had also tried being friends with a married Kuwaiti couple, but Assim had put a stop to that as well – because the wife didn't wear a hijab. Assim seemed to be deciding everything for her – who she could see, how, on what terms, and when.

Well, the friend-cop was back, and Aiesha and I could visit again.

An American Woman Plays Car Mechanic in Kuwait

One evening at 8 o'clock, Assim brought me and David over to his and Aiesha's house for a visit. David caught up with some research and writing on their computer while I chatted with Aiesha. By this time, I had met Rola Al-Dashti, Kuwait's lead woman suffragist. Aiesha looked at my letters for the Kuwaiti suffragettes, and thought that they would do some good. She also told me that Rola had brought her petition to their home, and that she had signed it, but that her mother-in-law would not.

Aiesha gave us tea and cookies, and then I rode with her to pick up Hamid and Malik, who were on spring break and visiting a school friend in Mishrif. When we set out, Aiesha and I were in her 1995 white Mercedes sedan. [It was a lovely car, but Assim later told me that it is no longer considered attractive in this show-off culture, because it was not new. This seemed crazy to me – the car was in beautiful condition, and its engine ran well.] There was a problem with the car; its front windows didn't work. Aiesha said that this was a nuisance at gas stations; she had to open the whole door to pay for gas – Kuwaitis don't pump their own gas, apparently. I checked the switches as we rode along, and got out the owner's manual from the glove compartment to look up the fuse box location and see which fuse controls the front windows.

Aiesha was amazed when I told her that I used to do this with my own second-hand Mercedes at home in the States. I was equally fascinated to hear about how a woman in Kuwait must handle even such minor car trouble as blown fuses – they let their husbands handle it, of course. When she and I found the house, I got out with the manual, in the dark and in a tee-shirt, and asked her to pop the hood open, telling her (I actually doubted that she knew where it was!) that the lever should be down by her left knee. She did it, and I opened the fuse box, shined my pocket flashlight in there, and found that fuse #25-G was burned out. The metal was worn through, providing no electrical contact for the current.

Not a complicated thing to do at all; this was not something that I would pay someone to do, nor would I wait around for some man to do it. The next thing to do is go to the parts store at the Mercedes Benz dealership and buy fuses. They are inexpensive, and the car owner can install them – for free – by turning off the car and snapping them in. I explained this to Aiesha. She said that she couldn't go there, because there are all men in the parts store. It is just not done by Kuwaiti or Arab women. I took the owner's manual upstairs and explained it all over again to Assim; he said he would do it.

My Attempt to Go Car-Parts Shopping...Nixed.

Not long after this visit, I was out at the Kuwait Ministry of Animal Health with our cat. I noticed that the Mercedes Benz dealership was right next door, and I could see the parts store from the entrance when I arrived. When I was finished, I calmly mentioned to Dr. Aziz, the Egyptian virologist who worked in the labs, that I was going to go over there and get fuses for my friend's car, because her front windows didn't work.

The reaction was almost comical; Dr. Aziz gave me an odd look, as if I had just announced that I was beaming up to the International Space Station – or something equally improbable. I realized that I wasn't going to be able to just walk over there, but now I was fascinated to see what he would do next.

Dr. Aziz did not want me to walk anywhere to do any other errands. When I announced my intention of also going on foot to Al-Ghanim for an ink cartridge for my computer's printer (it was just across the 2-way street from both the car dealership and his office), he looked at me strangely and ran off to ask a colleague to give me a ride there and home. He didn't have a car.

Going to buy fuses for a car is something that I have done many times in the U.S. It is something that is perfectly normal for an American woman to do that – but it seemed weird in Kuwait. Apparently, Kuwaiti women never do this. I got a kick out of seeing what these guys would do and say when I told them my plans.

They got the Indian veterinarian to drive me home.

Kuwaiti Men Don't Do Chores

On a Tuesday evening in mid-April, David and I visited Assim and Aiesha.

I noticed that Assim was in the habit of sitting down on the sofa grandly and then asking Aiesha to bring him drinks of water, tea, etc. Aiesha did it, informing me as I watched with an incredulous expression, that she gets more points whenever she does this. I didn't ask where the points come from...probably Assim and Allah. Assim told me that the drinks just taste better when Aiesha brings them to him. How does he cope when she isn't there to bring them? I asked him. He gets them himself, but he doesn't enjoy them.

Later, at home, I asked David whether he enjoyed tea more when I prepared it for him and brought it for him, well aware that this was a loaded question. Predictably, he gave me the ideal answer: yes, but because it is a gift from me, unasked for but freely given with the intent of pleasing him.

He does not expect me to drop whatever I am doing to bring him things on demand; he would feel ashamed of that. And...he can earn points as I do if he brings me things, with the same sets of reasons on our parts. This is not part of the equation for Assim and Aiesha.

Aiesha's Wedding

One April afternoon I called Aiesha and learned something interesting from her about Islamic weddings. Elaborating further about her own wedding and answering my questions about another, upcoming one, she satisfied my curiosity about the practice of either allowing a bride to be seen or hiding her, as the circumstances may warrant.

To adequately tell this story, I should begin where she did: with the engagement. For that, a party was held at her house in January of 1984. At this party, Aiesha wore first one and then another elaborate dress – one green, and one orange. She had her hair curled, she wore makeup, and she looked beautiful and picture-perfect. She usually wears a hijab and no makeup, and as this story unfolded, she told me why. It was interesting. She said that the best time of her life as that 6-month engagement period.

Dating was not allowed until then, so she and Assim had their first date after this party. Unfortunately, they were full of party food when they drove off for it – one photo shows them getting into Assim's car for the date – so they had no idea what to do for the date. This is where the story gets amusing: at a loss for ideas, Assim drove around, parked, and they sat talking until a cop appeared wanting to know what they were doing. They explained their situation and he left. All other dates went much more smoothly, with no nosy cops.

Fast forward to June 27th when they had their wedding...dating was over, it was time for the marriage to begin, and everything was ready. Brides in Kuwait are paid dowries by their husbands – it could be 5,000 or 15,000 KD – it varies. The Kuwaiti government might get involved, too: If a Kuwaiti national marries another Kuwaiti national, they are given a grant of 5,000 KD.

This is only done if BOTH the bride and the groom are Kuwaitis. The motive is to confine the country's wealth to an elite group of "genuine" Kuwaitis. The money is used by the bride before the wedding to buy household items. After the wedding, friends and relatives may throw a bridal shower and additional gifts may pour in, but most of that gets taken care of in advance. The ceremony was held at Aiesha's home, and after that she and Assim drove to his family home for the reception party. They still live there today.

Aiesha married Assim in 1984 with a small family party at home. The reception was held in the Al-Tikriti house, just downstairs from the apartment that they now live in, with the men in the diwan and the women in the harim. Assim came into the harim and sat next to Aiesha for a while among the women, and Aiesha went and sat next to Assim for a while in the diwan.

What I had not learned when Aiesha first described this celebration to me was that it is usual for a groom to go and sit among the women, but it is not usual for a bride to go and sit among the men. Why then, did Aiesha, a devout Muslim, do this?

She explained that this was because all of those men were her and Assim's relatives – no friends, no non-relatives or other outsider men were in that room. She sat among them because she was a new relative to her in-laws, and they were expected to know her. To do this, and to be properly welcomed to the family, she had to be seen in a formal way, to mark the occasion and let them get used to her.

If the wedding had been celebrated in a grand fashion (i.e. not at home), the women would have been celebrating at one hotel and the men at another. The groom would have stayed away until late in the party, and then come to the women's party to sit with his bride until it was time to leave. The bride would have stayed with the women.

When Aiesha visited the men, she sat with Assim keeping her 2 white hijab cloths hanging over her face and she hung her head. Looking at these photos, I found myself full of questions, and Aiesha willingly satisfied my curiosity. It was fun for us both.

First, there were the wedding clothes. Assim's outfit was just what I had learned to expect: he wore a white dishdashah, a white guthra, and a black bisht with gold trim. The bridal gown Aiesha wore was unremarkable in terms of cultural difference, but beautiful.

What was noteworthy was what she wore on her head: not a hijab like she wears every day, but a hijab nonetheless. It consisted of 2 pieces of cloth draped carefully over her head – one of plain white satin, and one of white lace to go over it and decorate it. Underneath, I could see that her hair was somewhat visible, and beautifully curled.

She also wore makeup, something I never saw her do. She hung her head as she smiled out from under it, sitting with Assim in the men's diwan. What a contrast to my photos, in which I wore only flowered and beribboned barrettes in my curled hair, and I gazed and smiled straight into the camera with my chin up!

Of course Aiesha and I took this apart in detail. Why did we pose the way we did? In a word: jealousy. Kuwaiti men are socialized to be jealous of their wives. Okay, I thought, so are Western men. We needed to discuss this further to understand the difference.

Aiesha went on to say that Arab men's jealousy makes them upset if men other than husbands and relatives of a wife see her hair, and see her wearing makeup and looking as beautiful as possible. They want to be the only ones who enjoy that sight. Cindy Lauper's version of the 1920s song *Girls Just Want to Have Fun* came back to mind: "Some boys take a beautiful girl and hide her away from the rest of the world. I want to be the one to walk in the sun…" So to please her husband – to avoid displeasing him – she must be invisible.

I told Aiesha that Western men want other men to see their wives, because they feel proud when they have a beautiful wife. Jealousy figures into the equation only if another man is so foolish as to make advances toward someone else's wife. Then that man is in trouble…

Assim later told me that he thinks that Aiesha carries this idea too far, and that wearing makeup – enough just to look well-groomed – would be perfectly fine, including whenever she leaves the house. But she won't.

A Real Wife-Beater

Aeisha took me out alone for coffee one evening – just the two of us – a girls' night out. Her 2 boys made nuisances of themselves for half of it, calling us several times on her cell phone until I grabbed it and turned it off. Aeisha gave me that shocked and delighted look when I did that. We were trying to talk, and her 12-year-old son kept calling to ask for pizza, lattes, etc. – any excuse to interrupt. Aeisha didn't know what to do – so I turned the phone off.

Before we into one of the ubiquitous Starbucks coffee places, she paused in the parking lot, with the car sealed shut – except that the sunroof was cracked open for air. The evening was dark and starry, and the air cool and comfortable. In a halting voice, Aeisha confided a secret to me: Assim beats her. Not often, perhaps every couple of years, but he beats her. I stared at her. I wasn't what one might call astonished by this revelation. Assim showed many of the signs of being a wife-beater: blatant disrespect, a lack of appreciation, taking things for granted, expecting and requiring to be waited upon hand and foot, interrupting our time together…

I had to say something. When does he do this, and after what behavior on his part? After being extremely frustrated about whatever is going on in his professional life, or with their distressing oldest son, she replied. She wanted some advice from me: was there anything she might do to prevent him from hitting her – any way of modifying *her* behavior that might make him decide not to hit her? I looked at her for a moment, unhappy. There was no way that I was going to encourage her to behave in a submissive manner. Aside from being opposed to letting a man feel entitled to see a woman abase herself before him, it is common knowledge among sociologists and women's studies experts that this just increases the physical abuse.

So I told my friend that no, I didn't see how she could have caused the behavior let alone prevent it in the future. I told her that the abuse was completely her husband's fault, caused by his own feelings of inadequacy and low self-esteem. Telling him off would give her better protection that submissive behavior, I added. Stand up to him by demanding that he not touch her unless he wants hugs. Then walk off and wait for him to calm down, ignoring him until he does. Since she couldn't get away, it was the best advice I could think of. She listened to me gravely, and we went inside for coffee.

It was weird sitting in a Starbucks after that, surrounded by elegantly-attired college women texting on their cell phones with all the comforts of a first-world nation amidst a medieval-minded culture. Relations between the sexes in Kuwait lag sadly behind the physical comforts that the place is able to afford its citizens.

The Guilty Party Feared Exposure

So I now knew the true reason why Aiesha had no friends: Assim feared that she would confide in them, thus exposing him as an abusive husband. I still hadn't forgotten the evening that he had sat with us, counting every 10 minutes and loudly announcing each interval, timing our entire visit! It was like sitting with a 6-year-old brat.

Sure enough, Assim was in a bad mood when we got back. He was annoyed that we had been out so long, he exaggerated the time that we had been gone, and demanded that Aiesha go right out and get Karidah and Safa'a from a party. It was the first time that they had been to that person's house, so he deemed 5 hours to be too long – even though it was a party. Aiesha said nothing, but went right out and got them.

I was disgusted with Assim, and before she left, I asked why he hadn't gone to get them. I just wanted to hear what he would say. "Because, that is a woman's role!" he said, raising his voice a bit. I just looked at him in disgust, then suggested that he not go in, but could have pulled up outside and called on his mobile phone for the girls to come out. Still not acceptable…he was surly to his wife for the rest of the evening, speaking unpleasantly to her in Arabic whenever she went into the other room.

An E-Mail Account

When Aiesha was back, I signed her up for a free e-mail account, and entered her new e-mail address into my own e-mail account. We were thinking about how to communicate when I was back to the United States. I tried to keep it a secret, and gave Aiesha the piece of paper with the password on it. I told her not to let him have it, or this avenue of uncensored communication would promptly be lost to her. He got it shortly after I returned to the States.

The Evidence Continued to Mount

In late April, with less than a month to go before our departure, I got another nasty surprise: Assim admitting to cheating on his wife. This was in the jeep on the way home.

What upset me most was the fact that I can't stand to see another woman unhappy and trapped with a male chauvinist of a husband yet utterly incapable of changing her life. That was the case with my friend Aiesha. I could see what was happening to her. She was definitely depressed, and despite being a well-educated, intelligent person, she was also a woman in a closed society who was unable to control her own life.

Laws and selfish men are all that is needed to produce a situation such as this one, and both conditions were present. The old saying that "the lady doth protest too much" can apply to others than ladies, and it applied to Assim. He made too much of a show of proclaiming that he was a great husband – a nice husband – a nicer husband than most others…and he wasn't.

Assim shouted at his wife whenever she went into the bedroom for a moment during our visits. The shouting was all in Arabic. He had become comfortable enough around me to shout in the living room also. The timing, along with the harsh tones and unpleasant expressions on his face gave him away – he was criticizing her management of their children, while not contributing a fair share of caring for them.

Apparently, he preferred to pay for things for them but not do much hands-on care-giving. He told me that his wife should have saved lots of money from her job after several years of teaching, but with 8 people to feed and clothe, she found a lot of her money going out as fast as she earned it. He paid for some too, but whoever shops, pays. Aiesha found herself buying more milk and juice every couple of days.

As an accountant who graduated with honors, she had calculated the numbers on this for him. It seemed to make little difference. He wanted her to have some savings for an emergency, or in case something happened to him – logical and reasonable even though impracticable.

Assim was in love with sharply defined gender roles – but not his wife. The Friday evening coffee shop visit was illuminating, to say the least. The nastiness began after Zahra was born, during Aiesha's second pregnancy. She felt queasy and tired, and had difficulty holding Zahra. When she asked Assim to hold their baby, he was outraged, and said that this was women's work, and never to ask him to do any of it again – in a harsh, unfriendly tone.

Thus began a stressful existence for Aiesha. She never knew when her husband would yell at her or find fault with her, which he did often. He complained bitterly (to me!) that she didn't wear makeup around the house. When she showed me her makeup, she told me that Assim is so unpleasant – refusing to smile at her or confide in her – that she decided that he doesn't deserve the effort of applying makeup. She couldn't wear it outside of the house anyway, so she only wants to go to the trouble of putting it on if he is going to be sweet to her and share his thoughts with her – which he doesn't.

Aiesha told the children, when they misbehaved to behave properly, but she received little backup from their father. Assim seemed to believe that if his children misbehaved, it must be entirely the mother's fault, because he imagined that child-rearing is entirely up to the mother. His own mother reinforced this nonsense by saying that voting would take a woman away from her traditional role as a mother. A brow-beaten mother, however strict, will not be respected and obeyed by her children if they see their father and grandmother undermining her.

I Give Assim a Taste of His Own Medicine

I am clearly not afraid of my husband at all – far from it; we are best friends. Not so with Aiesha and Assim. She sat cowed on the sofa, never daring to tell him off if got obnoxious or unpleasant, and I saw a happy look on her face when I told Assim to back off while we are visiting. This happened when he wandered through to the kitchen, accusing his wife of distracting me from my Internet research.

I said, "no she's not," and he "sure she is!" so I got louder and said, "NO, she's NOT!" and then forced him to listen to me saying that Aiesha was actually keeping me from getting stressed out at the parsimony of contact information on the websites and the slowness of the connection in looking the stuff up. Assim gave up for a while.

A little while later, he looked at a *Hello! Magazine* that I had just given Aiesha, and went on and on about how UGLY he thought Camilla Parker Bowles was. Why did Prince Charles marry her, he wondered, rather than Camilla's much prettier daughter? Are you kidding, I asked him? Charles has loved and wanted Camilla for over 30 years – on the basis of their compatible personalities. This idea was utterly incomprehensible to Assim. Looks win over compatibility with him, even if this attitude leads to unhappiness.

This was invitation enough for me to pull Assim's chain. I pointed out that I find bald men are unattractive – and Charles was losing his hair – so why marry them? Really, Assim, if looks alone were all that we were to go by, there would be many rejected men out there. That struck a nerve with him – he was losing his hair in both the front and back. I loved it – why should Aiesha have to look like a supermodel for a husband who is going bald and won't smile at her, confide in her, or talk pleasantly to her? She shouldn't, of course.

Assim was really funny – he had a fit, insisting that 95% of all women think that bald men are attractive – but Assim was no telepath. Next, he pointed out a bald newscaster with an ugly face and insisted that I ought to think he was handsome. I didn't.

Just to add a familiar gesture to my opinion, and to rub his nose in it, I made that Arabic tongue-clucking sound and wagged my finger after I said that baldness in men is unattractive. That drove Assim crazy. (Insert evil grin here.) David will never go bald, I gloated to him, further rubbing his nose in it. The look of delight and appreciation that I saw in Aiesha's her eyes made it well worth it.

At one point I asked her, when Assim wasn't there, about divorce in Kuwait. Her reply was, "It's all by the man." I thought so. Women cannot demand a divorce if they are unhappy, and as for battered wives, Mansoor answered that a long time ago: cops would ask a wife to show some marks such as bruising or scarring before they will even listen to such complaints.

Of course the whole visit couldn't be taken up with Assim. Aiesha served me tea and 2 small saffron cupcakes, gave me some saffron in a small plastic box that she had bought on a trip to Iran. I thanked her profusely – saffron is the most expensive spice in the world.

Assim DID Want Another Wife

Assim drove me home a little while later, and that was when he told me that if he were "man enough," he would get another wife. He told me that "this was just between [me] and [him]" – in other words, keep his thoughts secret from his wife. If it comes up, I won't do it, but I won't bring it up without a reason, just to upset her. I would not keep this guy's secrets, but I would keep hers. I decided to obtain an absolute clarification of his choice of words. I asked whether if by "man enough," he meant "rich enough." He admitted it. I told him that I hoped that he NEVER became rich enough to have multiple wives. He was, after all, telling a woman that he wished for multiple wives, and so it would be absurd of me to support him. He didn't debate the point.

The real crowning admission from him came just before I got out of the car: he "does have fun" without his wife knowing about it. Translation: he cheats on his wife. It didn't sound as though he bothered with the Shi'a custom of a "temporary" marriage. Assim added that "the reality of life" is that most men are horny bastards. How silly of me – I thought that most men were just horny without being bastards. Horny guys *could* work off all their excess energy with their wives…the idea is not inconceivable. Assim's justification for his fantasies about having 2 wives was expectedly obnoxious: men are horny, and "variety is the spice of life."

I said that did hope that he always had enough money to pay for the family he already had in comfort, and I told him so, but at the same time I hoped he never can have another wife while Aiesha is his wife. After all, I am a feminist and no patsy – I *will* take the wife's side in such instances, no question about it. Assim was unconfident in his work and ability to make lucrative investments. So he dumped his frustrations about himself on his poor wife. After all that I had discovered about him and his personality, I just didn't respect him anymore.

What would happen to their daughter?

Zahra was 21 years old; soon they would likely search for a husband for her. I wanted to see her one more time to say good-bye. Assim knew this, but not why I wanted to talk to her again. I intended to advise her about choosing a husband, and about why she must value any opportunity to vote. Voting is a way to have a voice of her own and to control some aspect of her life, something that she ought to grab at any chance for. She should demand – yes, demand – a husband who comes from a family with monogamous parents, and find out his true views on the matter before agreeing to marry him. Don't wait until the engagement period. She must insist on never sharing her husband, and on not having sharply defined gender roles – or risk a lifetime of unhappiness.

Assim has talked to me (always in the jeep) about Islamic extremists: some Muslims just read the parts of the Quran that support their own agendas without reading the parts that don't, and without considering the whole book. They then live according to their own agendas, making horrible jihad wars on non-Muslims and trying to force others to live with the damage that they do. I had heard it before, of course.

He should apply that to his own life, I thought, because that was exactly what he was doing: taking the parts of the Quran that suit his own agenda with no regard for the happiness of his wife. Aiesha is not stupid; she is cowed around him, afraid, but she knows what he is up to.

This is why I was so upset about my latest visit to them – Aiesha was stuck with a cheating husband. She couldn't possibly get a divorce, so her life was a permanent hell. What about Aiesha's chance to be happy and have the kind of life she wants?

Assim must realize on some level – even if he doesn't wish to acknowledge it – that this is exactly what most women want more than anything else in the world. He was so selfish (and apparently also so horny) that he was absolutely unwilling to give it to his wife. He wanted to please himself much more than to please her. He believed that this was his right, and that women should just be ready and willing to please their husbands regardless of how bad they felt. He often kept me listening to him for almost an hour when dropping me off at my building, ranting on and on about how his wife wasn't a touchy-feely cheerful happy companion who wants to sit beside him on the sofa in the evenings. Then he stupidly told me he was sleeping around behind her back. I'm glad I had the nerve to tell him that bald men are not handsome.

David listened when I went in, and said that his respect for Assim had just taken a dive.

Quranic Guidelines on Wife-Beating

A few days before we were to return to the States, on a Friday afternoon and evening, we visited first with Fatin and Nuwwar – they came over to our place for a while just to talk – and then in Aiesha's living room. We had a great time, first Nuwwar and me, chatting in the bedroom while David and Fatin talked science in the living room, then

Aiesha and me, with a brief appearance from Zahra. These were our good-bye visits.

When I saw Nuwwar, I could see that she still looked the same: gorgeous. She wore a close-fitting, sleeveless black shirt with long black running pants and sandals, and her hair was still long and black with bangs. Her makeup was pretty. I took a lovely portrait photo of her and printed it right away, then gave it to her mother. Fatin was very pleased with it.

Nuwwar looked at the Quran with me, at the part that mentions "striking" a disobedient wife. It looked to me like it advocated wife-beating, but she read the Arabic translation next to it and insisted that it wasn't so. Okay, I said, but I wasn't convinced.

I told her that I wouldn't abandon my own religion and culture and switch to Islam, and that many people had suggested that I do this – including her mother. This was after Nuwwar told me that in the Greek part of Cyprus, where she attended college, many people had suggested that she switch from Islam to Christianity, calling her religion "retarded." I was pleased to hear that Nuwwar is on my side with this point: people shouldn't suggest that others switch religions, and they shouldn't be saying that their religion – whatever it is – is better than someone else's.

Nuwwar told me about her boyfriend: he is Greek, an atheist, but a member of the Greek Orthodox Church. She would break up with him when she finished her degree and left Cyprus. They had religious debates, but these debates didn't make him any more religious or likely to devote any time to prayer. The most that she will get out of this relationship is social interaction with Western men – part of the search process for her future husband, I suppose.

A Last – and Unveiled – Visit

Assim came to get me at approximately 9 p.m. at the end of April for my last visit with his family. By now, all veils were off: his, hers, their daughter's – literally and figuratively.

Aiesha was waiting there, with no hijab, wearing one of the blouses that her husband had bought for her on a trip to America. She gave me cake, and I told Aiesha that I would miss her. Zahra appeared suddenly at 9:30 p.m., bouncing into the room in her pajamas, saw me, and stopped short. "Is David here?" she asked anxiously. "No," I said. "The coast is clear – no need to bolt for a hijab." That was funny, because this effort at reassurance provoked an immediate and effusive spate of assurances on Zahra's part that running back for one was absolutely no inconvenience at all whatsoever. "Yeah it is," David said when I got home and told him about it.

Zahra had to go to bed at 10 p.m. so that she could get up at 6 a.m. the next morning and get ready for school in time for an 8 a.m. exam. I knew she would ace it. She and her mother both had shoulder-length hair that they keep pulled back into short ponytails, with a slight part in the middle. Their hair looked plain but interesting, because the parts in it looked unintentional rather than like hairstyles that they meant to keep. I commented that mothers and daughters often have similar hairstyles, probably thanks to both DNA and interaction with each other.

They agreed, then told me something interesting about Islam: the washing that Muslims do just before prayers – ablutions – includes parting their hair and wetting it in the middle, so that is how their hair came to look as it did. Their hair became trained to grow that way over time from all the ritual washing and parting for prayers. Aiesha and Zahra subordinate fashion to religion. It was interesting.

Hasan and Mohsen were there, first using the computer, then studying together in their room. I scolded them both some more for interrupting their mother's coffee shop outing with me the week before, emphasizing that their mom is not a servant, she's their mom. They knew, and admitted that they knew. No emergency, don't call, I said, adding that I was the one who shut off the phone on the sixth call. Aiesha looked pleased that I told her boys to respect their mother and not bother her on her few and far between social outings. David was sure that I had done that family a lot of good when I told him about it.

While Zahra was there, I told her that I was worried about her, because I thought that her parents might start shopping around for a husband for her by the end of the summer. She said not to worry; she wouldn't be willing to get married for a couple more years. I guessed correctly as to why – pharmacy school was 4 academic years and one applied year, and Zahra wanted to ace all 4 academic years. When she could relax a bit, she would be willing to get married and focus her attentions elsewhere. Still, I insisted on advising her about husband shopping. Get a guy whose parents are monogamous, so that he won't have been raised with a bad example right in front of him, and then insist on never sharing him. No problem, she said. Also, get one who doesn't insist upon sharply defined gender roles. She and her mother said that guys lie during the marriage marketing phase, but that they would make an effort.

A bit later, Assim asked for my advice on how to address women who are strangers to him. It seemed that he had been calling waitresses – especially in the U.S. – "sweetheart," "dear," "honey," etc. He actually believed that they liked it! I told him differently; they are being friendly so that they will get a tip, but when they meet each other in the back room, they were laughing at him and saying that he was a rude male chauvinist who should be lavishing all of these terms of endearment on his wife and not on complete strangers. He was amazed and astounded to hear all this. I added that it was a public insult to his wife, whether or not she was with him, but worse if she was with him at the time. Aiesha loved it.

Aiesha hugged me tightly when it was time to go. I told her to stand up to Assim, and to find time to e-mail me. She said she would try, but she seemed to feel hopeless about it.

When I rode back with Assim, I told him never to ever let the kids see him criticize their mother. If he did that, then he should not wonder why they didn't respect and obey her. He cannot expect great behavior from them when she orders it if he undermines her authority rather than backing it up. Parents must present a united front to kids, I told him. He agreed.

Then he went on and on about how much he will miss us, how he has become used to our company, etc. He said that they might visit us in the States.

A TV Interview with Varied Hijab Forms

Late in March, I saw an interview on BBC World about hijabs, nekhabs and abbeyas. It was conducted by a British woman journalist with 6 Muslim women in Giza, Egypt. One woman was from Libya – unmarried, a corporate executive, dressed in a black business suit. At the other end of the extreme was a twentysomething-year-old Yemeni woman with no makeup who wore a nekhab and was totally shrouded in black.

Next to her sat a beautiful, chic woman in bright blue, wearing a fashionable hijab with a matching set of long voluminous blouse and pants, plus expertly applied makeup, and showing a gorgeous long curl. She was from Saudi Arabia.

She didn't like the Saudi law that demands that women dress as the Yemeni woman does, while the Yemeni woman was free to choose her outfit. My favorite statement was the one by the Saudi woman, who said that her face is her identity.

It's all about choice, these women said, including the older Egyptian doctor in modest Western clothing with minimal makeup and short hair. I wish I could have spoken to the young Kuwaiti feminist in the short shirt, however. She looked beautiful with her long straight hair and makeup, her clothes were fine, but her body language needed work – she sat in an angry pose with her arms crossed over her chest, looking upset.

Friendly, open-minded body language is necessary for feminists who have a hard and long list of problems to fight against. It is a tough thing to maintain for young ones who still feel a lot of anger, as young people tend to feel intensely.

She told an interesting thing in the interview: her mother called an official with a question about a municipal service in her area, and he actually wanted to know whether there was a male relative to speak for her! How infuriating – we don't want a go-between.

Hijabs, Hijab-Shopping, and Veiling

One day in mid-December, Fatin took me out for an entire Thursday. I met Zahid.

Zahid came home for lunch, and drank tea with us in the den while we finished our movie. Then he took a nap. He was quiet, and he only spoke Arabic, so he must have been bored while Fatin and I chatted in English. We did include him in the conversation – Fatin translated the general plot of the movie for him, plus some other things.

Zahid was Syrian, with dark brown hair and eyes. He kept his hair very short, but Fatin had been on his case for a couple of weeks to get a haircut. He had a beard, too (short, of course). He was a few inches shorter than Fatin. She told me that they were very, very distant cousins – not that it matters much, because they wouldn't be having children.

She wore a hijab to please him whenever she left the house. She was always religious, but she never wore a hijab until after Zahid joined her in Kuwait. She was spoiling him in a bad way, I thought. Still, as they shopped for more hijabs for her that evening in a mall in Farwaniya, I told her that she was a very chic Muslim, and she was very pleased.

It was funny watching Fatin shop for hijabs – pretty, long, rectangular scarves with solid-colored opaque things to go underneath. The opaque things match the scarves, and they do the job of hiding hair and ears, while the scarves just dress up the woman's head – preventing a "geek" look.

These opaque things are close-fitting cotton head coverings have a hole for the face and another one for the neck. Fatin needed my assistance as a model – to see if the colors matched, and whether or not the ears were effectively hidden by the whole ensembles. My white pearl earrings served as the litmus test; if they couldn't be seen, the hijab was acceptable.

Even funnier, a woman with a hijab, a veil over the lower half of her face, and a long abbeya – all in black – thought I was planning to adopt the hijab for myself. She came up close to me, saying in English, "here – this is how to put it together," and arranging the whole thing properly on my head.

I thanked her and explained that I was just modeling it for my friend, so that she could see how it looked without taking hers off, as I was the only bareheaded woman in that shop. I ended up buying one of the pretty outer scarves – black with huge, pink hibiscus flowers with green leaves – for 5 KD (for a souvenir). I refused to acquire one of those horrible opaque things, though. It would squash my hair flat and ugly.

For a moment, Zahid got hopeful that I was going to adopt that odious custom. No, I told him. It was possible that I would go to Iran with David for a short trip. The only way I would wear such a garment was if we visited Iran, and I really didn't want to go. And I told him that I would not ever visit Saudi Arabia because of the law about the full-body veil for women. I told him this knowing that his mother in Damascus wore that exact costume whenever she went out to the grocery store. I was quite unapologetic about choosing not to wear a hijab.

One noteworthy thing from our conversation, though: Fatin told me that Zahid's mother, who lived in Syria, wore a nekhab over her face when she goes out of the house to shop. She didn't go out much, though. Zahid had expressed a wish that Fatin wear one in the house, just to see it once.

Fatin thought that was cute (had she lost her mind?!). She never used to wear a hijab, and even now she only does it because (she says) she is older. Her daughter is the same way – she plans to wear a hijab when she is older, but not while she is young. Fatin said that she wouldn't start wearing a nekhab – and I guessed correctly when I protested that they must be considered a safety hazard in the lab. In fact, they are banned for that reason...but the university looks the other way for students, because boys are there, too.

Virtuous Un-Veiled Women – All Over the World

Comparisons between 2 very nice, very good Arab girls I knew in Kuwait: Zahra and Nuwwar. Zahra wears a hijab and no makeup when she leaves her bedroom to greet visitors in the living room, while

Nuwwar wears heavy eye makeup with her long, black hair fully visible, and tight, somewhat sexy clothing. They look like total opposites on the outside, yet on the inside they are not so different: they both consider their bodies to be for the sole enjoyment of their husbands.

Granted, Nuwwar was a 21-year-old college student, and as of New Year's Eve in 2004 had no boyfriend let alone husband, but this is beside the point. [By the way, she was also the goddaughter of David, and by association, of me as well.] What matters is not how a women dresses, but how she thinks and lives.

Sadly, fewer men than women seem to realize or even understand this, so entranced are they by the sight of a beautiful woman, and so judgmental are they of a woman's choice of whether to show her hair or to cover it. I myself have been stared at balefully by many a food vendor while David and I ordered take-out meals.

Why don't more men realize that just because a woman considers it perfectly okay to show her hair and face, that it does not follow that she would sleep with any and all men who might ask?!

This is the impression I get when I find out that mullahs and imams and religious-minded Muslim men won't shake hands with a woman who is a non-relative because they might get turned on. It's as if one will end up watching a devout Muslim male's ability to think sink from his brain to his crotch in a nanosecond.

Wearing an Abbeya – but Only to the Old Souqs

Nuwwar told me that she wears an abbeya to old souqs – because the floor-length abbeya hides her shape, and cuts down on the nuisance-factor presented by obnoxious, flirting guys. Young men her age acted like total babies in malls, she added, and were even worse in souqs. I had seen it while out with David, but I saw much more of it when I was out with Nuwwar, because we were 2 women alone.

At the mall with Nuwwar, there were whistles, cat-calls, silly suggestions…as we walked down one section of the place, Nuwwar was sipping her coffee when a young Kuwaiti said to her: "Ooh, I'm thirsty – can I have some?" We laughed and didn't respond. What did he expect her to do, share it by French-kissing it to him?! How stupid – no intelligent girl would respond to that!

Hissing from the Shadows

Women who veil do it to make the men around them more comfortable, both in thought and impulse. They also do it to make themselves more comfortable by shielding themselves from those same thoughts and impulses. And finally, they do it to feel "pure" – untouched by any but an authorized male. This means husbands, of course.

The signs of it are everywhere, especially in the way that women dress. That is always the first tip-off as to how a culture views and treats the women in it. The women in Kuwait are, as often as not, veiled in some way. Why? To make men more comfortable. I won't do that for any man. His thoughts, his impulses, and his actions are all his problem and responsibility. I will not shroud myself in cloth – especially in a hot climate – to make men feel more at ease.

The men there hissed at me from the shadows as I walked through the town with my husband. I knew that this was because I would not make myself unattractive or wear a veil. To do that would show a disgraceful lack of self-esteem – and that's my own culture speaking to me. I wore long pants and shirts with sleeves in Kuwait – but that was as far as I was willing to go in terms of dressing modestly.

What was this hissing? In the West, if men make a noise at a woman because of her appearance, they hoot, whistle or call something out about her appearance. It leaves no doubt that such men are both ill-mannered and consider the woman in question to be attractive. In the Islamic world, they hissed. I was intrigued.

After questioning every Muslim woman I befriended, I had it figured out: men hissed at an attractive woman to say that they were angry with her for not shrouding herself in a veil and thus concealing her attractiveness from them, because that attractiveness was a turn-on and therefore a sinful thought. Why was it sinful? Because I was a woman who was forbidden to them – married to someone else and not them. To even have such a thought about me was sinful, and the fact that they had such thoughts was – to their way of thinking – my fault.

No, it wasn't. This was the clash of the cultures that I experienced whenever I went outside, which was mostly after dark, and only with my husband, who had me walk ahead of him. As long as he knew that I was safely in view of him, and that no one would bother me and I would always be there, he was greatly amused by all this. Another culture clash: Western men are proud if they are connected to a beautiful woman, and flattered by compliments or jealously from other men. David was having a great time! Granted, he appreciated the inherent threat and guarded against trouble, but he was getting a constant dose of ego gratification.

Okay, so I thought it was a bit funny, too.

Naming Customs: Invisible Daughters

Whenever I noticed girls not being appreciated, I felt angry.

It should come as no surprise that Kuwaitis prefer and favor boys over girls, sons over daughters, and ultimately men over women. This is not unique to Kuwait, and scarcely any culture on the entire planet is exempt – including, on occasion, my own.

In the West, most people who have daughters are thrilled to have them – even if they might also have wished for sons. Perhaps they want some of each gender, but some actually wish for just daughters, and there are even television shows and movies that feature families with daughters and no sons, in which no indication of dissatisfaction about this is ever given.

Not in Kuwait, and apparently not in neighboring countries – but I shall stay on point and focus on Kuwait. In Kuwait, when people have children, they call the parents Umm (Mother of) and Abu (Father of) Child'sName. Regardless of the offspring's gender, parents do this. If the firstborn proves to be female, there is usually still a sense of pride – after all, the couple has just proven to the world that they can reproduce. But after a little while, they try again and hope for a boy, because if they get one, they will immediately switch from being Umm and Abu Daughter'sName to Um and Abu Son'sName. Unless and until they manage this chancy feat, they will feel a bit inadequate. And they would never, ever switch from calling themselves Umm and Abu Son'sName to Umm and Abu Daughter'sName.

Our good friend Mansoor was the 5th of 5 children, and the only son. His mother was married to a man before his father, she had a daughter, and then the man died. She remarried, had 3 more daughters, and then Mansoor. At last! Big celebration! A son! She had previously been known as Um Farah. No more – now she was Um Mansoor. This was a demotion for her. This was the divorced sister who lived with him and his mother, by the way. I felt awful about her when I heard that. Bad enough to have had a failed marriage, but to have felt like she wasn't what her parents really wanted in the first place must have been a very bad start.

I asked Mansoor, "Didn't Farah feel bad about her parents' attitude, and about no longer being referred to as they introduced themselves? All her life it was Umm Farah, and then suddenly it was Umm Mansoor, like she was never very important to them, and as though they weren't proud of her." He admitted that it was true, that Farah felt terrible. She was the one of his sisters who was divorced, living with him and his mom, sharing a room with their mom, and sad because her ex-husband, a Saudi, took the kids away after they had been divorced for 7 years (Kuwaiti – and Saudi – divorce law gives the mother the kids until then, and then allows the father to summarily take them home, whether the mother and/or the kids like it or not).So Farah's life had been one major disappointment after another, it seemed.

Kuwait is a first-world country. Money helps significantly in improving the lot of women in particular. But money can only help so much. The greatest boost to females is a sense a value from the family – of being listened to. Education for females is a by-product of that. Granted, money assists in making education accessible, and it has in Kuwait. Attitudes of the family go a long way toward accomplishing this, and perhaps longer than money.

When I saw that our host at the Wafra Oasis did not appreciate his daughters, I wasn't just disgusted; I was angry on their behalf. I am an only child, and my parents always assured me that they preferred a female child, and were not concerned with passing on the family surname by having a son. My paternal grandfather once asked my father about that in my presence; I was 9 years old. My father replied that they were not going to have any more children, and my grandfather dropped the subject.

Which brings me to another interesting facet of Kuwaiti culture (not unique to Kuwait, I might add): Kuwaiti women do not change their last names when they get married. They stick with what is on their birth certificates for their entire lives, married or not. I like it.

Why should I file paperwork to change my I.D., my banking information, whatever else there might be to change, and then find that my academic degrees have names that do not match my name?! It's insane – and grossly inconsiderate to expect such a thing. I love my last name. Then I learned about the courtesy title Ms. – for feminists, professional women, and for women who just wanted their own names (that entire list describes me). Problem solved.

But there was more to learn about Kuwaiti naming customs. I talked to Aiesha and her daughter Zahra one evening. How did Kuwaiti naming work? Well, they were happy to answer if I would tell them about my own culture's naming customs. Kuwaitis name children like so: NewFirstName Father'sFirstName PaternalGrandfather'sFirstName NextPaternalAncestor'sFirstName Al-Tribe'sName...and so on. (I wondered how many male ancestors' names they could fit onto a birth certificate. Probably more than on a civil I.D. card, I thought.)

Interesting, I said. Is that just for a boy, with a NewSon'sFirstName and then add all that on, or it is similar for a daughter? Oh no – it's exactly the same method for a girl: NewDaughter'sFirstName, then the Father'sFirstName, followed by the PaternalGrandfather'sFirstName, after that, following the male line, the NextPaternalAncestor'sFirstName, and finally the Al-Tribe'sName. The mother's tribe name goes unacknowledged, and the daughter gets no other female names. It was what I had expected.

Then Zahra asked me how it works in my culture, so I explained it: In the West, people almost always use the father's last name. Whenever the mother's last name is used, the first thought is that the parents never got married, and perhaps the father just abandoned both the mother and child when the pregnancy was discovered. Not so much anymore, however: feminism has changed this.

David and I knew a married couple with different last names who had a daughter. They had decided that if they had a daughter, she would get the mother's last name and if they had a son, he would get the father's last name. So the girl was carrying on a matrilineal tradition – a new tradition. That's how traditions start…someone decides to do something new. Zahra and Aiesha were intrigued. It was fun having their curiosity turned back on me, just to see what aspects of this piqued their interest.

So what was my full name? Stephanie Carole Fox. Carole is my mother's first name, and Fox is my father's last name. My mother filed paperwork to change her last name to Fox. Zahra asked why I didn't have Paul for a middle name. Because I'm not a boy. If my parents had had a son, his name would have been NewBoy'sName Paul Fox. But according to our French ancestors' naming customs, a daughter got her mother's name as a middle name. If I had had a little sister, they would have chosen some other female relative's first name for her middle name, and thought of a first name that was hers alone. Zahra was intrigued.

Next, I asked her about younger siblings. She told me that for Kuwaitis, every child in the family, both male and female, had the exact same sequence of names added: Father'sFirstName PaternalGrandfather'sFirstName NextPaternalAncestor'sFirstName Al-Tribe'sName. No variations.The custom was monument to patrilineal male ego gratification. To be fair and balanced, so are names like William Stratton IV and Henry Jones III (see *Silver Spoons* and *Indiana Jones IV*).

To top it all off, Aiesha told me that Assim had named all of their children but one: Abdul Malik. Why not him also, I had to ask? Abdul Malik was born in Pittsburgh, and Assim wasn't around when the hospital officials came to her room to prepare his birth certificate.

American hospitals won't release a baby unless and until that is completed, so Aiesha got to choose, and I could tell that she had enjoyed it. Assim did not make a fuss for who knew what reason – perhaps logic. So despite being pregnant and in pain giving birth, it seemed that a Kuwaiti woman could not count on having a say about her child's name.

No wonder girls weren't valued in Kuwaiti families – except as a commodity...

Ogling the Professor as She Lectures

Fatin told me that when she is teaching, she hopes every term that only female students will sign up for her classes. That happened last term, and she was really glad. Male students stare at her while she is up in front of the class lecturing, looking at every part of her body, and she absolutely hated it. She already wears a hijab, but she said that these boys make her want to put a bag over her whole body.

She added that it's extremely rude and disrespectful. Kuwaiti boys are just not socialized to consider the feelings of others around them, particularly women. Fatin dresses in a skirt suit with panty hose and high-heeled shoes, and a pretty scarf over her hair with her bangs showing in front. The scarf also has an opaque layer underneath, a hood-like thing that conceals every bit of hair. It must be a sweaty, uncomfortable thing in the summer.

Saleh's Attempts to Induce me to Veil - Useless

At the beginning of February, we heard a report on television – on Al-Jazeera News, which broadcast from Dubai - about a shootout in Salmiya, Kuwait. The BBC News channel reported this – in error – as being the work of a Kuwait-based branch of Al Qaeda, saying that the group's religious leader had been arrested and his brother killed.

However, Mansoor got the real scoop at the airport, where there was an excellent truth-telling grapevine: it was hashish dealers. So why all the coy lies by the press? Possibility number one: the press has been lied to. Possibility number two: the press has been bought off by government leaders with agendas to pursue.

The effect of these lies on gullible Westerners, be they Americans, Brits or Europeans, is that they often just believe the news. Americans were NOT targets in Kuwait. Kuwaitis actually liked us. David, among other Americans, was one of the soldiers who made the Iraqi invaders leave and stop terrorizing Kuwaitis, after all. No...this was about the police confiscating (and perhaps selling) the hashish, and arresting the dealers.

Saleh, however, tried his best to convince David that the shootout meant Al Qaeda and that we as Americans were therefore targets. This was in his car on Monday morning, going to K.O.C. Hospital. It didn't work; David didn't buy it thanks to Mansoor.

Then Saleh said that David should let me believe that it really meant Al Qaeda even though it didn't, because then I would wear a hijab. Oh – so now the real truth was coming out. Saleh seemed to like me less and less lately because I just wouldn't turn Arab and abandon my own culture. This, after telling me that he and Raidah didn't respect those who do so!

Later on, quoting a detail from the report, he mentioned that a black car had managed to successfully flee the scene, so more alleged Al Qaeda operatives were still unaccounted for. Saleh came up to our apartment and said to us: "You must watch out for a black car!"

I just laughed and told him that it was too late – Mansoor had told us that it was just the cops and hashish dealers shooting at each other. Saleh looked crestfallen. I thought it was hilarious. David, to his credit, refused to lie to me, to attempt to confuse me, or to force customs that I find offensive upon me. That is because David is just the best guy in the world.

Women in Abbeyas at a Mall...and Me, Visible

One lovely afternoon in April, I left Rola's office in Kuwait City and went across the street to walk around the Courtyard Marriott mall, just because it was new, beautiful, upscale, and not a place that I was likely to have time to look at again.

I saw several women my age walking around – shrouded in black veils and abbeyas. They appeared to be very wealthy and comfortable, and thus free to walk about a mall for hours. (Servants could run their homes.) I also saw a store where custom-made, embroidered abbeyas with matching hijabs could be ordered. The abbeyas were extremely expensive; apparently, anyone who purchased one would be satisfying her predilection for fashion in the only part of her wardrobe that her religious strictures allowed – the rest was hidden.

If they wore Gucci or Versace underneath, it was all lost on the viewing public. They would wear the best over-garments that their own culture could sell while shopping for world-famous designer labels that would be worn underneath. It was odd knowing that there were fantastically wealthy women here who had to hide themselves while enjoying such things.

The wearers of these costumes looked out at me from behind their nekhabs, and I thought about how wealthy they are, but that they cannot enjoy that wealth except behind closed doors at home. David later told me that they think their own lives are great, but that they also envy women like me. I wouldn't trade places with them for all the money in the world. I love my freedom, and I know that it is cultural as well as legal. But I know that they wouldn't trade either. They are choosing to follow their own customs, and love their anonymity.

Walking the Walk

After eating dinner with Mansoor at Haitham Restaurant one evening, we all went across the street to the jamiya (grocery store). Mansoor insisted on accompanying me throughout the place as a sort of chaperone/bodyguard. Although this was not the only time he did this, it was funny. [David and I tend to go our separate ways while grocery shopping, thus each seeing whatever we wish.] It was sweet of him to want to watch out for me and protect me from the rude men who like to stare at a Western woman.

We chatted as I looked for groceries and house wares. The most interesting thing he said was that I don't walk at all like a Kuwaiti woman.

"How do they walk?" I asked him.

"Slow and sexy," he answered, trying briefly to imitate it, then giving up. [Mansoor certainly was no drag queen; that was obvious. I would not have attempted to explain the concept to him.]

I looked around carefully as we shopped, and saw that it was true. They all moved about, unhurried, so that they could be seen and admired, covered in abbeyas and hijabs as they were. They were using the mystery provided by their covering to give off an attractive appearance – one that would require imagination by the observer. I told Mansoor that I walk to get from one place to the next. Then I added that I have always walked that way. I impress David with conversation, a bit of makeup, pretty clothing, and hugs and kisses, not by simpering about.

Still, I found myself asking David later, after listening to a Mansoor comment on how scintillatingly Kuwaiti women move, whether I seemed particularly feminine to him. Western women do come across as more independent. David immediately said that yes, I do seem very feminine, but that his expectations are not those of Arabs.

Arab men seem to feel more of a difference between themselves and women, and to wish for it more, than Western men do. David is content that we are different, in dress, physical makeup, and our thoughts.

Human Trafficking in Our Building!

Late in March we heard some rather sensational news about events in our building – 8 Bangladeshi prostitutes were arrested and evicted from the 7th floor! Neither David nor I had had the slightest idea that the police were here – maybe we weren't home at the time. David says that the police import these women and use them until something goes wrong. Then the women take the brunt of the trouble and are sent to jail – stuffed into a filthy cell together – and summarily deported, while the men who set them up here go unnoticed.

At least one bad thing that happens to the victims of human trafficking happens to the men who enjoy those same victims: AIDS and other sexually transmitted diseases…justice.

When Mansoor's mother heard about all this, she got upset and demanded that he find a new place for the family to live – immediately. She wanted nothing to do with a building in which prostitutes were living and probably working. I honestly can't say that I blame her – not with her grandchildren coming to visit her.

Mansoor also said that she didn't like this apartment all that much, because she and Farah had to share a bedroom. He called some people he knew and asked them to please quickly find him a 3-bedroom apartment in either Khaitan or Farwaniya, and the friend found him one in Farwaniya. Both areas are equally close to the airport, where he works, which is why Mansoor had moved his family to Khaitan.

So they would leave in 5 days. The landlord didn't know yet that his most helpful and favorite tenant was leaving him. Mansoor promised to visit us. We shouldn't have been so upset; we were leaving in 6 weeks.

But we would miss him! Farwaniya was just across Airport Road, but Airport Road was a highway. He would still visit the bouab, he said, and teach him to read and write Arabic. I thought that once he met new people in the new building, maybe he wouldn't. Maybe he would be too preoccupied with networking at the new place.

All Those Invisible Rule-Followers

The woman suffragists of Kuwait had something to do that mattered, but when a government runs on wasta, that society is set up to demand so much dependence on conformity and blending into the background, people inevitably feel that there is little point in doing much that does not fall into preconceived rules and modes of thought. The feminist of Kuwait were not invisible women. The invisible ones suffered, partly because they would not act out, and partly because of the pressure to blend in and disappear.

Rules are very important in Kuwait. It is a Muslim country. One day when Fatin and I were looking at photographs, we got to talking about rules and following rules. She said that if a person doesn't follow ALL of the rules of Islam, then that individual will not go to heaven. Really, I said, that seems a bit far-fetched. I think that rapists and murderers can forget about heaven, but if a Muslim skips a prayer or two, and works instead, or does something to help others instead, then that Muslim will still go to heaven. Fatin did not agree. What could I say then, except that I guessed she is a total rule-follower, and I am not.

The alarming aspect of this rule-following line of reasoning is one that I saw repeated in news items and in conversations throughout my time in Kuwait: it is the idea that one may break rules with abandon – beat one's wife, commit a rape, even kill someone – and the slate can be wiped clean by a trip to Mecca. Those are the rules. The problem with this is that wiping one's slate clean does not make a good person – or a safe one.

Also, following rules can make life very steady, dependable, and BORING. Nothing special is likely to happen to you if you focus on toeing the line – whatever that line happens to be. Here, it was a schedule of 5 prayer sessions per day, from dawn till dusk – 2 prayers, then 4 prayers, then 3 prayers, then 4 prayers, and finally 4 more prayers. On Fridays, it is hoped by the imams and mullahs that Muslims will go to a mosque for midday prayers, where the Awqaf will then have an opportunity to dispense more rules to the obedient public. This will keep an entire society in line, doing the busywork of following rules, paying close attention to those rules, too occupied with the rules to notice when the rule-makers don't follow their own rules.

This situation also has the effect of making the rule-followers invisible. When you obey the rules, you disappear from the radar screens of the world. You blend into the background, and you become less and less noticeable. This is fine if you are a sociologist, but I was a visitor. I did not set out to be invisible – even to observe. Invisible people are ignored and their wishes are deemed to be of low priority. They take a back seat to life. Kuwaiti society requires this sort of behavior of its female citizens. No wonder they didn't vote yet; for too long they had quietly taken back seats…or side seats, as in a mosque. They pray on the perimeters in mosques.

Madame Dr. MyHusband

One afternoon, David wanted me to bring the cat to the Kuwait Department of Animal Health and sit with him while Dr. Mohammed Aziz gave a lecture, so I did, where Dr. Aziz proceeded to give a nearly 2-hour-long lecture on animal vaccinations. I was the only woman in the room, sitting to the side with David and the cat in her carrier.

When at last it was over – and I could tell that Dr. Aziz really knew his subject well – people got up, took some food, and chatted. I was asked to tell the heroic tale of our cat and the bombs on Failaka Island. The veterinarians were interested in our famous cat…and her medical problems. They offered various suggestions for tests and treatment, which was why she came.

I complimented Dr. Aziz on his presentation. "But it was in Arabic!" he protested. I told him that I had read the PowerPoint slides, which were all in English. When he called me "Madame Dr. David," I gave him my business card and told him not to call me that. "Why?!" he asked. "Because it sounds as though I have no identity of my own," I answered. It sounded too much like being called Mrs. Haines, a Western form of invisibility to which I am morally and philosophically opposed. He got the idea. I also told him that I don't want to be invisible. That cleared things up for him. He was really nice, and very happy that I offered to edit his presentation; it needed it. Scientists reuse their lectures, and his needed to use this one again.

Interestingly, Kuwaiti women do not change their last names when they get married. They find the Western custom of doing so odd. Instead, men in Kuwait tried not to know their names. Either way, both American and Kuwaiti customs were trying to mask our identities – to cloak them.

It seemed like such an irony that Arab women keep their own last names when they get married. I like that custom. I realized that Arab men didn't actively intend to demean me, but I insisted that they call me by my own name. I was glad to know about Kuwaiti and Arab customs, but I want my identity – it is an important part of me. The Kuwaiti custom seemed like another version of my own culture's attempt to make me invisible: Mrs. Husband'slastname (American) or Madame Husband'sfirstname (Kuwaiti).

I refuse to be invisible.

Chapter 12
A Day Off From Men

Kuwaitis have a winter tradition of setting up tents in the desert, north of Kuwait City, and spending the first day of their weekends in them. [This means Thursdays, as Muslims worship on Fridays, so their weekends run on Thursdays and Fridays, leaving just 3 workdays per week in common with the Western world.]

The tent floors are covered with red-and-black patterned woven carpets and have cushions set up all around the perimeters to sit on. The men and women keep separate tents, with most of the children staying with the women. Boys over a certain age go with the men, however. The maids, all from foreign nations, have a tent next to the women's tent, but with one wall missing, probably to discourage lingering and socializing amongst themselves.

Outside the men's tent.

There the similarity with ancient tradition ends, and modern life blends with the general atmosphere of desert nomad life. Electric wiring and bright lights are visible throughout each tent, as are loudspeakers, which blast prayers into each space as loudly as possible…until the superintendent of the park is called in to lower the volume. Plastic chairs and tables are set up in the middle and in some corners of the tents.

Inside the women's tent just before dinnertime.

Outside, nearby and presumably placed at regular intervals throughout this temporary park, are small rest rooms with flush toilets and sinks. Each family must bring their own toilet paper, watering cans (Middle Eastern people prefer this cleaning method to toilet paper, but keep both available), and soap.

Towards the center of each tent, a small, low-to-the-ground stove is set up for brewing tea. It is made of brass, long and rectangular, and appears to contain heated ashes in its well. The teapots, made of cheap tin or steel, sit inside. Around it are grouped various dishes of hot entrees, sides and desserts.

A tea-brewing area in the women's tent. Tea-brewing area seen from the side.

The women potluck it; the men have their meal catered. This is what the women call a day off from men. I wondered what they meant by this, as they were clearly working awfully hard at having time away from the men, while the men simply bought their way out of any work to do, until I spent more time watching married couples interact in their homes: the husbands expected to be waited on hand and foot by their wives, interrupting any attempt by their wives to socialize for an hour or so on their own. It is as if the men stay as children but the women do not.

I attended two of these tent gatherings with David – or, rather, at the same time as David. He went to the men's tent while I went to the women's tent. I should add that I am glad to have attended at all, and to have had the opportunity to see how this culture functions, because I remained very much an outside observer, in love with my own culture's way of life, and not won over to this one's. I am intellectually curious, but also a feminist who does not like to feel segregated and excluded from something more interesting and less restrictive.

That is precisely the sense I got from being in the women's tent. I expected it, and I sought the experience out when it was offered to me, because travel is an adventure, but the most important thing I took from away it was a profound love of my own culture, which sees nothing wrong in mixed-gender gatherings. This experience became an exercise in reminders that when genders are segregated, men have more luxury, fewer chores, and greater freedom to do and discuss whatever they wish, while women do not.

We attended our first tent party in late January and another in February. After that, I had seen enough. For me, the point was to learn something new, and I had done that. I had also been treated with politeness yet as an outsider who was not wanted on any permanent basis. Once I had gotten that sense, the feeling was mutual.

Here are my impressions of the first tent party that we attended:

The Al-Hamdullilah (their real name means warrior, but I have given them this religious, Allah-thanking-and-praising pseudonym) clan tent party took place all day on Thursday, the 30th of January, 2004. It was held out in the desert on some tent grounds that included a manager and decent rest room facilities north of Doha, overlooking Kuwait Bay.

A cousin of Saleh's gave us a ride. David met him outside, with his red cotton sweater on. He told the cousin, a man in his 20s named Mohsen, that he would be wearing it – and as no other Americans lived in our area, a tall one looming large in a red sweater would be easy enough to spot. That he was.

Mohsen Al-Hamdullilah worked in a bank, he told us, but doing precisely what there we could not ascertain, due to his rudimentary English and David's good but not perfect Arabic. It didn't matter – he was very nice, and with great difficulty, bother and hospitality on his part, found David. Then he drove us 40 minutes to the camp. (Our place in Abraq Khaitan was usually hard to find.) He took us directly to the men's tent, which proved to be perhaps one-sixth the size of the women's tent – could there have been more men's tents, perhaps a group of little ones? I wondered, but didn't worry about it. David told me later that there was a bigger tent for more of them.

We rode with Mohsen north, on a highway, and as we went along I noticed a sign for Abdaly Road branching off to the northwest. David had told me about that highway, which had become a highway of death and haunting at the end of the Gulf War...

The car continued north.

When we arrived, it was dusk, and I could see the coastline all lit up, with Kuwait City on the far left, and Shuwaikh (where Kuwait University is) towards the right. There were many white tents of varying size lined up at the camp. Many of them were arranged in rows forming a square, but there were other detached rows as well. There was also a high enclosure for geese, which were closed in by a wire fence. Unfortunately, I did not get a photo of that, as I was out of the tents only to carry 2 containers of food to David.

There was also a tent just outside the women's one that was open on one side, and looked rather chilly – winters here may lack snow and sleet and, for the most part, rain, but it still gets cold at night. This tent was for the servants. The Al-Hamdullilah family members had brought their maids with them to cook and serve food at this all-day affair. [Raidah, however, informed me that she had given Sarah the day off.]

So there in the chilly breeze were a bevy of Nepalese and/or Philippina maids, all wearing hijabs at the behest of their Islamic employers, and finding relief from the cold in entering the women's tent to serve more food. They are well paid so as to make their stay far from home and status as servants financially worth their whiles, but I could never be a servant. Neither could David – we said so to each other as we stood outside that tent while we waited for Saleh and Raidah to lead us to their jeep at the end of the party. Actually, for some Al-Hamdullilahs, the party lasted overnight – they were camping after all, recreating the lifestyle of their ancestors.

The men's tent, like the women's tent, had a floor covered with Persian carpets, and its walls lined with cushions, forming a continuous sofa on the floor edges. To the right were some water-pipes – argeelahs. In the center, just behind the pole that held up the middle of the tent, was a low table with tea and coffee pots, cups, and a few other items necessary for such drinks. Shoes were removed before entering – I was glad I had worn my Teva sandals – they have velcro straps, and are easy to take off and put on in a hurry, something that we had to do a lot of here. [I don't wear anything too beautiful or perfect without a high holiday or a special occasion such as a wedding to dress up for.]

Saleh greeted us in a snow-white dishdashah and white guthra, and let me take his photo – he looks great in all white, and prefers it even in the winter, saying that he is usually too warm to wear darker colors. He looks like an Arab Santa Claus, with a white beard and white hair, a little bald on top, and brown eyes that seem to be outlined. Sometimes they really are outlined – with kohl, a dark powdery substance that Arab men have worn around their eyelids for centuries to reflect sunlight away. Fascinating to know what they did in the bright desert light before the invention of sunglasses...

Saleh pouring tea inside the men's tent. David settled into the men's tent for a chat.

At first, both David and I were ushered into the men's tent, and I took some photos of the place, inside and out, and of the people there. I even got one of Saleh and Raidah's youngest son, Hassan, who I had not met before. He is 13 years old, quiet around adults, and polite.

I was settled for perhaps a couple of minutes when I was ushered back out and into the car, whereupon Mohsen drove me around the group of tents, turning just one corner, and then let out and sent into the women's tent. Good – another couple of minutes with a bunch of guys talking business and switching to Arabic would have gotten monotonous.

The women's tent was decorated much like the men's tent, but was at least 6 times the size of the men's tent, and had a small, concrete area just inside the doorway where everyone had removed their shoes. I did the same, and found Raidah right away – she called out to me, and I rushed over to her for a hug and kiss. She was glad to see me again, and demanded to know why I hadn't been calling her. I told her why not: Saleh had forbidden it. He had told us that she wasn't feeling well, what with her diabetes and whatnot, and to let her rest undisturbed. I always asked him how she was and told him to say "Hi" to her for me. She seemed satisfied with that, and the visit got underway.

Looking around the women's tent, I noticed that there were regular tables – regular in height – in the center and off to the left side near the doorway. Food and drinks were on the center table, and some heating facilities for the food were over in the corner by the doorway. A small, low table was over to one side near the center one, on which tea and coffee services were arranged. At the back of the tent, several women had prostrated themselves on prayer rugs, bowing towards Mecca – and in so doing demonstrating which direction was southwest.

These human compasses continued praying for quite some time, and Raidah joined them (albeit in a plastic chair) after giving me two plastic bowls of malakh (lentils with lamb) and two plastic, rectangular dishes of salad made of cilantro leaves, yoghurt, potato and thin croutons. I carried a serving of each of these things to David in the men's tent, and found him enjoying a water-pipe – without getting sick on it this time. The men seemed a bit startled to see me back again. I made David get up from his pipe to take the food from me – I wasn't about to unfasten my sandals – more cultural differences for the Arab guys to observe, I guess. Western women don't wait on their husbands in inverse proportion to men doing so for them – it's about equal for us.

After a while, some of the men came in to visit and eat. These men were the brothers and husbands of the women present. David was also allowed in to sit with me. Because of this, the women never took their hijabs (head scarves) off. As long as a man who was not a blood relative was present, a woman would keep her hair covered. Saleh's cousin Athir came in to see his sisters, because he has several of them, and his mother, a huge diabetic, smiling grandmother with a cane.

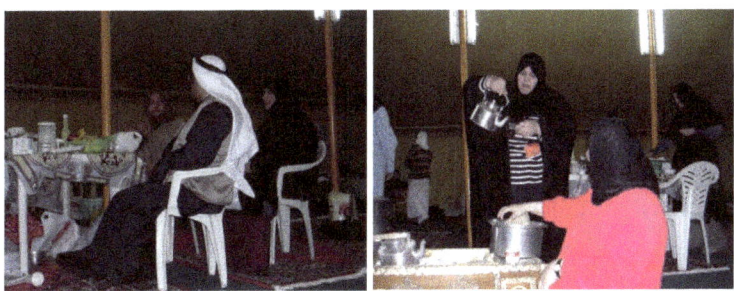

Athir visiting his sisters near the snacks. Raidah pouring tea; plastic tables and chairs behind.

Everyone seemed to have a good time. I did not know who prepared the food, who paid for it, how it was brought in, or much about how the tent party was assembled and produced at this point. It was only during my second visit to the encampment that I would find all this out. For now, I just met everyone and felt some mild culture shock, while enjoying the adventure.

We rode home from that party with Saleh and Raidah. As we headed down the highway, west at first and then south, Raidah pointed to the left (we hadn't gone far yet). There was a huge cemetery there. She told us that her sons Hanbal and Mashhur were buried there. Poor Raidah. Both boys had died in their 20s of liver failure after at least 2 transplants each (all done in Pittsburgh, Pennsylvania), first Mashhur, then Hanbal, who had been the oldest son. Both boys had been married, and Mashhur's widow was now stuck raising their little boy alone. I was glad that their other 3 sons were healthy; she could keep them and not be sad yet again.

The second tent party that I experienced was very different. Arriving and departing included some human interactions that revealed more about Kuwait and Muslim culture than I had previously seen, as did the time in the women's tent.

A word or so about marriage: wanting to be happily married to one's best friend is not un-feminist – it's just normal. Wanting what one's culture prescribes is another matter entirely. I don't want all of that – the children, the job in the cubicle, or a group of celebrity-watching, sports-loving friends. Here in Kuwait, I would find out what Kuwait's culture prescribes: children, segregation, religiousness, full shouldering of household chores while the men do none of them, and maybe but not necessarily a career.

I came to the Arab world and Islamic culture knowing quite a few things in advance about how women here are treated, and hoping to learn more. I also hoped to find something likable about this culture. I did not have much luck at this. I majored in women's history in college, and minored in women's studies. Why? I like history, and men are easily referenced in any encyclopedia, whereas women take more effort to learn about. This has translated into a lifetime of comparative thinking and observation, especially when I travel, but at home also. I am endlessly curious about the differences in the lives of men and women wherever I go.

This time, I managed to find out where it was that we were going, so I had a clearer sense of place as we went to and from the encampment. It was in the desert, well north of Kuwait City and to the west, overlooking Kuwait Bay. I went outside early in the evening and looked around, and could see the lights of the bay and the general shape of the landscape, but unfortunately my camera failed to take any decent pictures to illustrate this. Night photography was attempted, but with no success.

The Al-Hamdullilah family tent parties run not only all day on Thursdays, but into the late evening and on into the night. As I described it before, they had plenty of food, with their foreign maids to serve them, and a good hamman (rest room) inside a plywood box of a room, complete with soap for the sink and toilets with Kleenex. They rent 2 large tents, one for the men, and one for the women. There was also a tiny tent off to the side of the women's tent for the servants. Again, the loudspeaker system piped prayers into each tent.

Thanks to some conversations with our friend Fatin, I know the reasons behind this segregation: to mix the sexes would be un-Islamic. After all, we look and smell different from them. The only natural choice for a Muslim woman is to want babies – lots of them, and preferably boys. (If I did want babies, and I don't, I would want girls, and largely out of gender loyalty.) I don't know what Muslims imagine to be a woman's reward in heaven – I would ask Fatin – but for men, it is 77 houri (virgins). Why 77, I wonder? It was another thing to ask about.

Really, this culture galls me and fascinates me at the same time. This is why I hear stories about American women leaving husbands who have to work here to earn a living, and going home to the West. I am not like those women – I am morbidly fascinated by inequality and I want to get a close-up view of it and then scrutinize it. Also, I want to be with my husband, wherever he goes.

We were enjoying our time in Kuwait, after a fashion, but I certainly won't spend my life in this culture. It is interesting to realize that Kuwaiti women are raised to accept life as it is and not complain or make a fuss if they are unhappy. This is the opposite of my upbringing, thanks to a century and a half of feminism in my culture. "No wonder Kuwaiti women could not vote!" I thought [that was still so while I was visiting].

This second tent party in the desert actually made me angry while continuing to fascinate me. It was not the women who angered me. It was the men, but mostly our good buddy, Saleh.

Saleh's behavior on the way to the tent party was obnoxious in the extreme. He doesn't realize that we would know what he was saying, but David's understanding of spoken Arabic has improved over the past few months to the point where he knows what Arabs are saying even if they talk fast. That is what Saleh was doing in the SUV on the way: talking fast, and at his normal rate of speed. He picked us up with 2 other guys in the vehicle: one Iranian engineer, and one Iranian imam (Shi'a), who can speak Arabic. The Al-Hamdullilahs are all Arabs, including the Iranian ones; many Arabs live in southern Iran.

The imam – that is a cleric from Iran who wears a turban – was clad all in white and sitting in the front seat of the SUV. As soon as I saw this guy, I knew that David would be unable to discuss any business with Athir Al-Hamdullilah (that was Saleh's cousin who wanted to do this at the tent party – Saleh had agreed to this!) and with Saleh. Here was his out! We were learning all of his work-avoidance tricks.

Our friend Mansoor saw us get into the SUV. He told us what he observed the next evening, when we went out for dinner and argeelah pipes:

David and I came out in a hurry, because Saleh was 45 minutes early. Because I was closer and smaller, I opened the back door of the SUV and started to get into the back seat, next to the engineer, in the middle. As the smallest-sized person, the middle seat is where I was raised to think that I should sit – because this is the polite thing to do in MY culture, the only set of rules I yet knew. I had no idea that it might mean problems of any kind in Arab and Islamic culture, but I might have guessed. David crammed himself in after me, and Saleh stepped on the gas pedal.

What I did not see as I got in (nor could I have seen, as I was facing the seat and climbing into it) was the look of shock and horror on the imam's face as he turned and watched in disbelief as I settled into the middle seat. Mansoor saw it, and almost laughed himself silly on the spot. As a Sunni Muslim, he tells us that he finds this sort of thing unnecessary and irrational. [I now suspect that it is not about Sunni or Shia differences at all – it is about secular vs. religious thinking. Saleh is very religious, while Mansoor only wears traditional dress once per year, on the one day that he goes to the mosque.]

David caught a glimpse of the shocked gawk, felt great amusement at that, and gleefully followed me into the back seat. Off we went. David was not about to cater to this behavior, but he also derives much entertainment from shock and outrage in traditional, religious people from any culture. He also knows that I find sexism insulting and personal, and has no argument with that.

As we drove, the imam, speaking Arabic, started asking Saleh about me: why was I in the middle seat?! Don't we all realize that this is haram and kharban (bad in a religious way and bad in a general, secular way)?! The engineer, a secular guy, said something about how this must be normal for us – we are Amrikis (Americans), after all. Then Saleh chimed in: Yes, but Stephanie must know her place. [David, unbeknownst to Saleh, is fluent in Arabic, and he understood this rapid exchange. He told me all about it later.] David did not find Saleh's reply amusing. I cannot be responsible for the religious comfort of every Muslim man that I encounter. No wonder, I realized, that so many Muslim women kept to themselves when they traveled, not mixing with the people of whatever culture they were visiting. At least I was mixing and learning.

At the time, however, I had no idea about any of this. David could hardly have told me what was going on then and there, so the ride continued, calmly for me as I chatted politely with the engineer in the back seat, and awkwardly for the Muslim men. It all seems funny now – especially what happened when we arrived at the tent encampment:

Saleh stopped the vehicle near the men's tent, and we all – except for the imam – got out. I looked back, and the imam was fumbling with the lock on his door. Oh, I thought, not understanding what his problem was and acting on a lifetime of waiting on older people and trying to make them more comfortable, the poor guy is stuck! Something must be wrong with the lock on his door.

I walked over to him and tried to help him out, pressing the door handle and tugging on it. "Saleh!" I called out, "Something's wrong! Your friend can't get out of his door!" He waved dismissively and stepped towards the tents, saying, "Don't worry about him – just leave him there." I thought this was a bit odd, but took his advice, as I needed to be walked through the maze of same-looking tents to find the women's tent. The men's and women's tents were a bit apart from one another; it must be difficult to reserve adjacent tents for each family with all the demand placed on the park.

On the way back, the cleric was not with us. No prizes for guessing why not. And although the men had catered food that none of them had to lift a finger to prepare, it did come at a price: listening to that fool drone on, and on, and on, and on, taking up ALL of the time allotted for chatting and/or conducting business-related conversations. So I was right – Saleh had his out, as Athir confessed to David that such talk would not be possible that night, because the mullah (imam) had used it all up. The engineer rode in the front seat, and Saleh's 16-year-old son, Mohsen, rode with us in the back.

Mohsen is so much Saleh's son: he tried to sit in the storage area in the back, under the hatchback opening to the SUV. Saleh wouldn't allow that – he thought it wasn't a safe place to sit, and ordered him out and into the back seat. It was rather amusing when David jumped out to let Mohsen have the middle seat…as our culture dictates that kids should take the least comfortable seat. No, Saleh didn't want that, and he shoved David back in, hard, insisting that Mohsen sit by the window. No, no, no, David must shield his young, teenaged son from the woman, keeping the sexes segregated as much as possible.

I thought back to our previous ride home from a tent party. Why was I seated next to one of 13-year-old Hassan's friends, a kid who calmly ate junk food out of a bag all the way home? Why wasn't that a problem? Mohsen told us why on another day, when we went out in the same vehicle: boys who haven't yet had a wet dream are believed not to fully realize everything necessary to get turned on when seated next to a woman, so that's okay. Oh. [Mohsen didn't say it like that – his English is not that good, and he is a kid, but he did manage to say something about realizing things and fluids. That got the message across quite effectively.]

During the party, I saw nothing that made me feel particularly attached to this culture. Granted, little children everywhere are equally annoying, but this culture expects me to find their annoying behavior sweet and alluring. I don't, nor will I do so in the future. For example, Kalila was sitting across from me when a little boy went outside, climbed into the driver's seat of the nearest motor vehicle, and began beeping its horn – nonstop. She thought that that incessant, obnoxious sound was adorable – and expected me to agree with her! I didn't, and told her it was horrible and ought to be stopped. Fortunately, the little brat got tired of beeping and the sound ceased.

There was a little girl who was visiting from Egypt; she insisted upon grabbing the cane from sick grandmother and running around with it, waving it at anyone and everyone. When her mother tried to take it away and give it back to its owner, screaming and howling ensued. The brat got the cane back. The grandmother was thus confined to her sofa, unable to leave. At least she didn't have to go to the bathroom. Kalila wondered why I don't want children – who will I have when I am old? Not children, I told her: friends would be who I would have. American children don't live with their parents when they grow up. They move out, often far away. Only the rare lucky ones get to stay in their own homes and have their children pay attention to them, or even have those children living close by. I do not hope to be so lucky.

It didn't get much better as the tent party continued. Raidah arrived – despite my hopes that she would just stay home – and demanded that, because I am a lawyer, I arbitrate a family argument between herself, the grandmother (who spoke only Arabic, which put Raidah at a slight advantage), Kalila, Amel, and others. At issue was an Al-Hamdullilah family heirloom, a necklace that was 200 years old and made up of many fascinating stones. How interesting – what's the problem? The grandmother had bought it from this woman across from us and given it to her daughter, Kalila, and Raidah hadn't seen it since. Oh. Raidah wanted it. Oh. Alternatively, she wanted to break it up and share it among all of the women in the family. I thought to myself, "That would ruin it! One can't inherit everything." And Raidah was an in-law to the Al-Hamdullilah family. Why should she get the heirloom? She didn't even have any daughters!

Not being willing to embroil myself in a family argument, I made my escape as soon as possible – to the other side of the circle and then the tent. I simply said that I don't think taking a family heirloom apart is acceptable, and that I saw arguments over this necklace in the future. Then I went away. Kalila had the maids bring me tea – I was cold – but I just could not drink it. It was absolutely vile – like a thick cross between tea and coffee, and no milk was available. I was cold the whole time I was at this party.

I took out my camera and shot some more photos just to have something else to do. "Don't take my picture, Stephanie," said Raidah, as I sat across from her trying to keep occupied. "Okay," I said, and put the camera away, but not deleting the 2 photos I had managed to acquire of Raidah. They were better than the other ones already I had of her. Thanks to that request, I am not showing them here. This visit was not going well.

I managed to sit with Mona, another one of Kalila's sisters, and to my surprise she took off her black hijab. All of the married women shroud themselves in black, gray, brown, dark blue, etc. and I begin to feel homesick for the sight of a woman's hair. Mona's hair was pretty enough – long, with bangs. I told her that her hair was pretty. "What does that mean?" she asked me. "It is attractive to look at, beautiful, nice, etc." I explained, wondering but hardly caring whether or not I might have offended her in some way. I really don't want to go to another tent party, I thought. They didn't seem to want me around unless I would participate in a girl-fight, which I wouldn't do.

The teenage girl with the colorful, chic hijab (black with a colorful dark blue design of thicker thread on filmy fabric) was fun to talk to. She told me about interesting things to see and do in Kuwait. She liked to visit amusement parks, and described one to me in detail.

We ate our enormous spread of potluck food, and they insisted that I take a can of Pepsi home with my share of leftovers. I am, after all, an American, so this disgusting fizzy drink must belong in my home! They quite forgot that the last time they saw me at their tent party, I wouldn't drink any of it – just water. Like almost every other Kuwaiti group that I met, they thought that American foods must be great, and wanted to include the worst (most unhealthy) that we had to offer in their diets. It was astonishing to them to find that an American didn't like soda.

The Kuwaitis' food was delicious. The maids served it on the floor, laying out a long plastic sheet, slightly thicker than the plastic wrap used to store food, and not at all clingy (since the food is being served, not stored). And where did all this great food, which comprised a delectable, full-course meal, come from? The women, of course. They had no day off – despite the fact that Thursday is meant as a day off. It was spent preparing the food.

Wonderful rice and saffron puddings with pistachio nuts.

What did we eat? Green beans with tomatoes; cucumber and tomato salads in yoghurt; chicken over rice cooked with saffron, fried onion and garlic and golden raisins; lamb over more basmati rice with and without embellishments; flatbreads; creamy rice and saffron puddings.

At this point, one of the women asked me what I had made, and I felt bad; I had no stove, and had not known that the women expected me to bring something, so I had been unable to contribute to the spread now laid out for us. I explained, the questioner nodded, and that was that. It intrigued me to know that the men were now having other food, of a quality comparable to a 4 or 5-star restaurant, catered and served to them. They had done no work to get it ready – just a phone call and it was brought. They imagine that the women have a day off because they didn't have to cook for the men, or fetch anything for them – not tea, not a snack…nothing.

Interesting, I thought. But to my way of thinking, that is NOT a day off. I don't want a break from David. In fact, we don't like being separated at parties. That does not feel festive at all. Going out together for a social occasion feels festive. Being together for a fun event feels festive. Being separated feels like a punishment. Why do I feel and think differently? My American husband does chores, doesn't expect to be waited upon, and even waits on me sometimes. We wait on each other. So there is no need for a vacation day away from one another. I didn't say anything to the Kuwaiti women, however – I just observed them some more.

Family here means that men can choose their wives, but women can't choose their husbands. If a woman turns down a marriage offer, her family asks why – does she have a boyfriend? If so, she is a bad girl, a disgrace to her family. If not, she should just accept the guy, even if she doesn't like him, because she has little reason to think that another offer of marriage will ever be made to her again. If she can't get married, she won't have her own home, because living apart from the family is kharban and haram. She must marry and have children, preferably sons, so that she can live with one of them when she is old and rule the house, overriding the poor daughter-in-law, who won't be able to rule her own home. Widows live with sons, who won't let them remarry. Why? The sons don't want to be replaced as the man in charge of their lives.

Observing this culture had led me to ask about the reasons behind people's decisions, and this was what I had found out. Women could be forced into one path or another: marriage or living with their parents and brothers forever.

The party improved a bit as the evening wore on, however.

David arrived, and sat next to me with his arm around my shoulders, and someone took our picture with my camera.

David sitting happily with me. Dates, pits removed, stuffed with pistachio nuts.

He stayed for a while, chatting with Saleh and Athir, and we met a couple who had delayed their wedding because of a death in the family. (Better to have that happy time after the sad one was a bit in the past, everyone thought. That made sense.) The future husband had come into the women's tent to sit with his fiancée for a little while. They seemed happy.

Fascinated as I was by all that I was learning, I was not enjoying this culture. Men – and that included David – love visiting it, because it favors them, catering to their comfort and convenience (plus it provides many business, scientific and technological opportunities). This culture benefits men by disbenefitting women. That is my complaint with life here. And Mansoor loved us and wanted us to stay in Kuwait forever! I told him how I felt. Yes, we loved him, but I was unhappy there. Never mind, he said, you can sit with the men and see whatever you want, just stay here. If he said visit, that would be different. I could visit the friends we have made here – as long as I don't feel trapped in this restrictive, segregated culture. I want to live in my own culture most of the time.

David tells me that no one is asking me to abandon my own culture and to adopt this one. That's just not true. Saleh did that, saying that I "must know my place." My "place" is not a back seat to life, happiness, enjoyment, or anything else. Saleh wanted me to move to Kuwait, stay there, accept everything about it, have it applied to me, and like it. That was what got me so upset about the whole idea. It was represented as a visit until I arrived, when suddenly it became pressure to remain permanently regardless of my wishes. I told David that I would not be attending another tent party. He could go alone to talk business in the men's tent. I had seen enough, and would read, write and watch movies at home.

A few days after that second tent party, Saleh stopped by to chat with us from his car, with the motor running. He was on his way elsewhere, and just needed to ask David something quickly. Then he wanted to talk to me about Raidah. She was insulted that I got up and left her at the tent party to go sit with and talk to other people. What was I supposed to do, stick around and take sides in a family argument about a necklace? Not me – I got away from that situation – it was nothing but trouble getting out of control fast. Saleh couldn't insist on that point, but then he said that she was worried that I wasn't her friend anymore, and that I was abandoning her for other relatives, as if I would rather make friends with them.

This is insane – I just wanted to talk to some other people. You don't go to a party and ignore everyone in the room while you lavish most of your attention on one person. I talked with many different people of all ages, and one Moroccan woman – in French. It was nice to practice it a little. We chatted about her country, and I found out that it snows in the mountains there! Fascinating...that country is in the

Sahara desert, and the equator is close by, but it snows at high altitudes. She was very nice, and smiled and accepted me.

When I mentioned the imam, Saleh told me what went on – what was said in Arabic during the ride to the tent encampment – with that mullah that he brought in his SUV to the tent party. The parochial-minded mullah had told Saleh, whining in a tone of absolute horror, that he had never ridden in a car with a woman outside of his own family before, much less with an American woman. He had never been this close to one before, and he was obviously disconcerted by the experience. That was why he stayed in the vehicle after the rest of us got out at the tent encampment. He had locked himself in deliberately! And then, he asked Saleh to just let us go on ahead and away from him. All this, just to avoid spending any extra moments in close proximity to me – a woman.

I had thought that he was having trouble with the lock on his door, and had wanted to help an old man to be more comfortable, and he was trying to put as much distance as possible between us. Another clash of cultures, another lesson in human interaction…this culture was proving itself to be infinitely the exact opposite of everything I knew.

I'm very glad I went to Kuwait. The food was delicious, the artwork was new and beautiful to me, and I learned about the people and how they think. Learning how other people think and why they do what they do is what makes travel worthwhile.

A couple of months later, I read what happens to the camp grounds at the end of the tent party season: the entire setup is disassembled, packed up, and put into storage until the next winter. It was from the "Day by Day" report in *The Arab Times* on April 5th, 2005. My journal entry for that day summed it up as follows:

In just a few short sentences, the writer bemoans the state of the Kuwaiti desert at the end of tent season and chastises the users and the government for failing to leave the desert in pristine, clean condition. Kuwaitis set up tent encampments for winter months, which they (like the Al-Hamdullilah family) spend weekends in, enjoying food, tea, and each other's company all day long. When the weather begins to heat up in the spring, these encampments are dismantled. A landscape littered with trash and portable toilets was revealed when the tents were removed, prompting the writer to say that "[c]leanliness is one of the important teachings of Islam, and reflects the genuineness of our belief." That is certainly a clever environmentalist pitch to aim at this society. I hoped it would work.

Chapter 13
Additional Wives – The OTHER Women

Additional wives, mistresses, affairs and trysts exist in Kuwait, and exist in Islamic society. Surprise, surprise…well, not really. Of course this is the juicy bit of dirt on this culture that any women's studies reader would be disappointed not to find in this travelogue. Well, it's in here, but it is common knowledge that these roles exist in every society, not only Kuwait.

So what's different here? The labels and the perceptions behind them. Yes, there are feminists here, both male and female, who don't approve of anything less than monogamous relationships. But this chapter isn't about that fairy tale. If it were, this would be a boring book.

This is where one can read about second wives (then just add numbers third and fourth if the man is rich enough to support them all in equal comfort), siqeh (temporary marriages), and even less formalized methods of fooling around behind a wife's back (read: mistress, girlfriend, affair, tryst, whatever). There are also those who wish for but, for whatever reason – money, usually – do not have, more than one wife.

The first thing I did to satisfy my curiosity was ask my husband about it.

Not that he knew much, but I decided that he was as good a person to start with as any. At least he would speak frankly with me, accept any question I wanted to ask, and give me a starting point with which to sum up my thoughts and questions for future conversations with other people.

We had this chat in early December, not long after I had arrived in Kuwait and gotten over the jet lag from the journey. We were out walking in the neighborhood of our apartment, which was located in an area (segments of Kuwait are actually called "areas") under heavy construction and populated by many foreign workers from Muslim nations.

David told me that they are mostly from Pakistan and South Egypt, don't speak English, don't know much about any culture other than their own, have little or no education, and work for a pittance, living away from their families, sending much of their pay back home while living several guys – no women – to a small apartment on lentils.

We were on a routine errand, to exchange some U.S. dollars and Iranian riyals for Kuwaiti dinars at the Bahrain Exchange of Abraq Khaitan. We liked to call our area Abraq Shaitan for a joke, because the area was such a mess, with cement blocks and creepy shadows on almost every block. "Shaitan" means devil in Arabic.

As we walked there, I asked David about second wives, because apparently many Kuwaiti men have them. Why is this, I wondered? Being one sounds awful, because (among other reasons) it is considered very bad form for any man to talk about his second wife, or for another one to ask about her. But I could ask – women can ask about women. And I vowed not to let social barriers that were designed to aid and abet in polygamy stop me.

After running various ideas past David, I discerned that a second wife is a trophy wife – just knowing that he has her boosts a Kuwaiti guy's ego. He contributes to her financial support, while he supports his first wife outright.

Some households do have double incomes, but that is beside the point. So the second wife lives separately from the husband, who lives with his first wife and their kids. The Kuwaiti women do know when there is a co-wife, and they don't like the idea. I was to find this out as I talked to them, and as I found out about individual families.

I knew I was starting off with a limited understanding of the situation, and I wanted to know all about second wives in this culture.

It fascinated and angered me at the same time. I love my American husband – most particularly because he's all mine. No way would I share him! That sounds naïve, though. I guess the reason I feel good about David is that he is convincingly only interested in having one woman. He told me that his Arab business and science acquaintances offered him meetings with women – obviously for sex – and he said no.

It wasn't until late December that the subject of other women in Kuwait came up again.

A Cheating Husband – What a Shock...

We had invited some scientists over to our apartment for a meeting, and as we were all sitting in the dining room discussing the work, the Jordanian biochemist quietly informed me that he was leaving soon to go see his girlfriend. This was the same guy who had previously told us that he was married and had 2 kids with his wife – and that being with his wife had been more fun before they were married, when they were just dating. What a great guy…

Of course I reminded him that he had mentioned to me that he has a wife, whereupon he just looked proud of himself. I gave up on talking to him at that point – what more was there to say? It was abundantly clear to him that I was disgusted with him. What did he expect, telling a woman that he was cheating on his wife, congratulations?! He went into our bathroom just before leaving, and when I went in there, I was absolutely livid: he had used the little hose that Middle Eastern toilets have next to them, and sprayed our whole bathroom, soaking half our supply of toilet paper. I took it as a comment about women, an insult.

So...here was blatant evidence of men in Kuwait having affairs and second wives. David says it is almost expected here; that Arab men at diwaniyas can't understand why he isn't interested in fooling around with someone behind my back! In the West, we are not shocked, because we are not naïve, but do look at extramarital affairs with scorn, disgust, and anger...and with sympathy for the wronged spouse, be it the wife or the husband. Here, there is a glaring and obnoxious double standard: men are practically expected to have 2 women in their lives, while a woman is viewed as a terrible person if she has more than one man in her life.

It was the usual double standard that one would expect to find...

The husband was leading a double life, while the wife dutifully kept house and raised the kids, having become boring, perhaps by being easily attainable and accessible.

Evidence of Multiple Wives at Last

What got me thinking, and not for the first time, was something that Aiesha, my Kuwaiti friend, mentioned to me: her mother-in-law, Assim's mother, was the 3rd wife of his father. This was qualified with the information that Assim's father's first wife had died before he had married a third one, but I still asked them both how anyone would be willing to become a second [or third or fourth] wife. We were talking about concurrent wives, not consecutive ones! All the explanation that Assim and Aiesha were able to offer – and they actually seemed hard-pressed to think of a suitable one – was that some people are obedient and don't question much.

Aiesha does have a spine, though. She said would not allow Assim to get another wife, but fortunately he said doesn't want one. I didn't know whether or not I believed him, but at least his wife came out and directly said no to the mere idea of it. He would tease her about the idea, though...telling her sometimes that he might get another one. She wouldn't respond by telling him that she might start collecting more husbands, however; it just isn't done. I would waste no time in doing that if my husband pulled that sort of nonsense.

During a different visit, I had an unplanned opportunity to talk with Aiesha – alone downstairs, as we looked at old photos in the grandmother's harim, around the television – to ask about second wives. More data was suddenly available to me about them. Assim's mother is a widowed second/third wife. His father had another wife when he married his stepmother.

Why? 2 reasons, Aiesha replied: he wanted more sons to pass on his last name, and more sex. Apparently, Fahad's mother was Wife 1, Assim's stepmother was Wife 2, and Assim's father thought he was all set when Wife 1 suddenly died. But he wanted and could afford 2 wives, so...he got married yet again. Wife 2 lived across the street in a house identical to the one that Wife 2, had, and thus Wife 2 became Wife 1 and Wife 3 was really Wife 2 when their marriage took place...how's that for complicated?

Aiesha went on to explain what men might be thinking when they took on additional wives: when an older wife could no longer accommodate a husband who wanted sex, she would not be thrown away, but a new one would be taken on to handle these desires.

I still didn't understand what would attract the new wife to her role – money, perhaps, and a father pushing her to accept – but here was data on what the man was after.

It's All About Sex! No Surprise There...

Fatin has said that this is normal. She phrased it as if it were natural and right by echoing that the first wife isn't simply thrown away. What I didn't understand was, how can the first wife accept this? Doesn't she feel outraged and insulted? Fatin and Aiesha both describe this as though it is just fine, but what about a day when their husbands decide that they are getting too old for them, and start looking for new wives? Will they still feel this way when this hypothetical situation is a real part of their own lives?

David suggested that I ask Fatin this question. She has said that uneducated women are more accepting of this than educated women, and more willing to become second wives. There is nothing social about it; women do not solicit their own marital arrangements.

Fatin sounded very self-assured when she said this. She herself holds a Ph.D. in biochemistry, and Aiesha has an M.B.A. They seemed quite unconcerned that such a thing might happen with their own husbands, simply because they are educated women who would not marry a married man.

But what if their married men look for more wives, settling for uneducated girl toys and son-producers in the future? Then what? I couldn't really believe that this would be okay with them. Fatin had told me that she would only accept a husband who had never been married before when she was looking for Zahid, even though she had been divorced. I just couldn't imagine her accepting the idea of Zahid taking another wife.

I realized that I was worrying about the happiness of other people as though such problems are imminent and certain when they are not. I couldn't help thinking about it. I also learned that Aiesha NEVER had a chance to watch ANYTHING of her choosing on television. The reason was that Assim and the children took it over utterly and completely – especially Assim and the boys, so that they could watch soccer. Aiesha just buys books to read for her entertainment.

Now I saw why she couldn't watch *Sense and Sensibility* (she said she would have enjoyed seeing the beautiful dresses on the women). No one would try this with me. David says that I have too strong a personality to be shunted aside like that. I'm so glad.

What if...her husband ever wanted another wife?

Nuwwar supposedly had her first boyfriend. Apparently, Fatin intended to leave the choice of a husband entirely up to her daughter – no arranged marriages. Fatin told me that Nuwwar announced that she doesn't want an Arab husband, that she will move to London, England and get a job, but that she wanted a Muslim husband. A non-Arab, non-Shia, Muslim husband – good luck! They do exist, but the current boyfriend was not Muslim, and showed no sign of converting – Nuwwar said that she would have to dump him when she finished college.

While we were discussing it, I asked her what she would do if someday Zahid decided to take another wife, just for more sex and to have sons and pass his last name on. At first, she refused to give a straight answer, saying that he would never do that. That was not my point, I persisted. IF he did that, what would she do about it? "Good-bye Zahid," was her answer. It was Fatin who kept explaining that Islam allows a man to take another wife when the first one gets too old to accommodate him sexually. But the truth came out – Islam or no Islam, she wouldn't put up with such disrespect and a lack of appreciation!

An Economic Explanation

I didn't have to wait long for my next chance to discuss this morbidly fascinating topic. David and I were invited to a New Year's Eve party at the home of a nice Egyptian family in Salwa, an area where many Egyptian, Turkish, and generally well-educated, professional Muslim foreigners live. It is not legally possible for a non-citizen to own property in Kuwait, so people who might otherwise be able to afford to own their own homes simply rent nice ones and decorate them as if they were going to stay forever – wall-to-wall carpeting, wallpaper, paint, etc. This home was no exception.

The family included the parents – the husband was an engineer and the wife a high school gym teacher – their adult son, also an engineer, their 16-year-old daughter, a fluffy calico kitten, and their older married daughter, who came over with her new husband. They were expecting their first child in another month or so. The other guests, aside from me and David, were the best friend of the wife, who spoke no English, her husband, who was a professor of English, and their 2 daughters, one adult and one college student.

It was the college student, Manaal, who spoke with me about other women. She was a lot of fun to chat with; she spoke English just like a television newscaster, with an American accent. She did not approve of men having multiple, concurrent, romantic relationships. Manaal and I got along quite well, and she told me all about something that I had wondered about since chatting with Aiesha and Assim that afternoon: additional wives. This, from a girl who had (as far as I could tell) monogamous parents.

At the New Year's Eve party, Manaal had a few more explanations for additional wives. I was glad, because not knowing what goes on in the minds of men who take more wives and of women who become additional wives was just eating me up with curiosity. One reason was economic. A woman with a dead husband and several children left to raise might decide to marry a married man. Another reason for a willingness to share a man – on the condition that he spend equal time with each wife, just as the Quran dictated – was to widen the gene pool. But now that the gene pool is widened, the theory goes, this should have stopped. Apparently, the Prophet Mohammad only intended this to go on during his lifetime, but some Muslim men just love this idea and so keep that phallocratic tradition alive to this day.

Manaal was not advocating the concept of additional wives – just addressing my curiosity. We had a good time that evening, and talked about many things. This was merely the most controversial thing we thought of to discuss.

A long time ago, I was admonished never to talk about religion and politics.

I looked at the older girl who advised me against this, incredulous, and said: "But there is nothing else that is nearly as interesting to talk about!"

She looked surprised, but had no answer for this.

We were in college – at a feminist, liberal arts place. It was the perfect environment for encouraging discussions about religion and politics.

I'm very glad that I challenged her, and continue to do so, because if people stop doing that, nothing will ever get better in societies that treat women as second and unequal.

Which Wife Gets the Better Deal?

Apparently affairs and additional wives are standard in this society. David says that he attended Salman Al-Hamdullilah's wedding to his second wife over 10 years ago, but that it is considered bad manners to mention the second wife. Loyalty goes to the first female, and then whatever is left over goes to the other ones. I knew that the Quran dictates that all wives must be treated equally in money, affection and the husband's time. It also dictates that a man must not take on any additional wives unless he is willing and able to do that, but I came to understand just what I had suspected: no woman wants a co-wife.

Another thing to keep in mind: the Quran was written by men from the point of view of men, and is addressed primarily to men. It repeatedly puts women second to and below men. At this point as almost any Muslim reads this, I expect an outraged objection – a charge that I am insulting Islam. I keep up with Middle Eastern news, and the moment that any criticism of the religion or religious decision-making crops up, a defense mechanism kicks in: "You are insulting Islam!" This is the ploy that its defenders use in an attempt to deflect all criticism.

Economics Again...and Another Idea as to Why

About a week after this party, our buddy Mansoor came upstairs for another visit, and I made him a cup of tea, hoping for another chat about Kuwait. I was not to be disappointed. He loved any chance to hang out with the Americans. He was willing to answer our questions about Kuwaiti culture, never taking offense at our ignorance. He seemed delighted by our curiosity, in fact. His English, though not perfect, was so good that communication was easy. Any chance he got to help us out, he took. He just loved Americans.

I asked Mansoor to talk to me about second, third, and fourth wives. Why, I asked, would any woman be willing to become an extra wife? Being wife number one sounds much better, and being the one and only wife sounds best. Well, Mansoor answered, men realize this, so if they do take extra wives, they never mention their other wife while talking to one of them. Why? Jealousy: it is only natural for a woman to be jealous of another wife. If a husband with multiple wives gives money to one of them, he must give the same amount to each of the others. If not, he will not be thought of by Allah as a good husband.

So, why become an extra wife? I asked. An older woman, such as someone in her thirties or (gasp!) her forties, who has never been married before, might be willing to marry a married man and put up with sharing him. I told Mansoor that as much as I had wanted to get married, I had never wanted it so badly that I would consider a man that I could not have all to myself.

Mansoor listened with interest as usual; he was divorced, and was only ever married to one woman.

The Islamic Heaven Fantasy

We went out one evening with Saleh, to a meeting with his cousin, a Kuwait TV lecturer and businessman. His face was well known.

I took advantage of the opportunity to ask Saleh about the Muslim heaven fantasy – every religion has its own mythology after all, complete with a fantasy for the afterlife. I wanted the precise details of Islam's afterlife fantasy. [No need to bother analyzing an Islamic hell – it's the same misery that Christianity predicts.]

The number 77 for houri (virgins) in heaven was incorrect – it was either 40 or 70; he wasn't sure – and he wasn't sure what women got. He told me that Raidah wasn't pleased about the virgins. How are women supposed to enjoy heaven if they know that their husbands are off playing around with other women?! I for one have yet to hear of a version of heaven from any monotheistic religion that I would look forward to settling into for eternity. [Mark Twain didn't want to fly around on wings singing hymns and strumming harps forever, and his wife just didn't want to go there without him.] Too many issues remain that simply aren't dealt with by monotheistic religions.

Now for the creepy part of what he told us that evening: Saidah, Hanbal's widow, who I met just before David and I got married, was back at Saleh and Raidah's house to settle Hanbal's estate. She had been living with her parents in Iran, and had taken a ferry across the Gulf to Kuwait. At last they would settle the estate. Good. What was creepy was that because Saidah wanted to stay in Kuwait, Saleh was thinking of foisting her off onto Mohsen, his next son. Ugh – require that he marry his older ex-sister-in-law?! Disturbing as it sounded to me, it is socially acceptable in Islamic society, because the Torah, the Bible and the Quran all tell stories of brothers marrying and sleeping with their dead brothers' wives. [Henry VIII of England did that, though Catherine of Aragon's marriage to his brother was allegedly never consummated. No wonder he reformed the Church of England to escape from his first marriage.]

What if Mohsen and Saidah didn't want to marry each other? I let Saleh see my reaction. David said it was normal here, and none of our business, but I didn't care. Maybe I could visit Saidah; it would be nice to see her again. She stayed in my house in Connecticut for a night when I was engaged to David. She and Hanbal and Saleh had driven up from Pittsburgh, Pennsylvania to visit. There wasn't room for 5 people in the Farmington place, so we girls went to my parents' place. Saidah played games on the extra computer, and I did some work. She ran and hid when my father got up for a glass of juice – no head scarf. [He gets up at midnight every night for juice. He would not have looked for us, but she dashed out of sight anyway.]

There was one definitely funny moment that evening. When we were finished discussing business with Athir, his secretary brought us tea – with milk – and we had nuts and pistachio sweets and chocolate. Saleh, a diabetic, found a dish of mints and was eating them up like there was no tomorrow. He encouraged me to have one. No thanks, I said, mints make me sick to my stomach. Saleh, you're a diabetic, don't eat so many of those, I said. He grinned and kept eating more, being silly. That is usually how his sugar-shock attacks start, leaving him incapacitated for a day or two. We didn't have time for that. He tried to distract me by pointing out nonexistent distractions in the opposite direction, but I knew what he was up to and snatched the whole dish, carrying it to the office kitchen. We all laughed until we cried.

3 Times a Day...Like Meals

On a Thursday in mid-February, I spent the whole day with Fatin, at her place. She came over to pick me up at 10:45 a.m., but we didn't leave right away. She and David started going over their latest scientific abstracts. After that, we left and headed straight for Sultan Center in Salmiya, which is just north of Salwa, the area where Fatin lives. She wanted to do her grocery shopping, and I could think of a few more things to buy. Then we went to Fatin's place, and stayed there until past 8 o'clock. This afforded me an opportunity to observe Fatin's husband, whom I had not met before this trip to Kuwait. They had only been married for a year or so.

Why did the visit go on so late? This was done despite the fact that she and Zahid and Manisha were slated to eat dinner at Fatin's brother's place even later that evening. Why? Fatin and Zahid had prayers scheduled, and kept disappearing into their bedroom to carry them out. To begin with, after Fatin and I had been sitting in the den for only a few minutes, she set up the television with the Discovery Channel – apparently this one Western channel passed Zahid's inspection – and announced that she had to go pray now. I informed her that I had anticipated this and had brought a book, and showed her *Kuwait by the First Photographers*. She nodded her approval and disappeared.

A little while after Fatin finished praying, Zahid appeared, and Manisha announced that lunch was ready. We went to sit at the dining room table. The food was very good: fried chicken, some spicy, some plain; macaroni with tomato sauce; tiny herbed lamb burgers; cucumber and tomato salad; and Manisha's homemade chapati breads. During lunch, we talked to Zahid. He understood but didn't speak English, and he was very serious.

He understood the joke – all in English – about the best time to go to the dentist: tooth-hurty, is the answer. He even smiled. It was interesting to watch him and see how he reacted to whatever we did or said, knowing that he is the same age as me, and that his mother, who lives in Syria, wore a full abbeya, hijab and nekhab whenever she left to the house to buy groceries. Zahid is the reason why Fatin has taken to praying regularly and wearing a hijab. (She was always a believer in Islam, but she didn't used to be so observant about the rituals.)

Then we talked about politics. He told me, through Fatin, that he thinks that Americans want to attack Syria so they can get at Lebanon. Interesting – that is allegedly what the assassination of Lebanon's beloved Prime Minister was all about.

Fatin asked me about American tax money – so it was being spent on these military campaigns. Finally, I told him directly that we Americans, as individuals, do not wish to attack people and places around the world. We want to just leave Syrians alone and in peace. I don't want Zahid's family bothered or attacked. He seemed to appreciate this. Then Fatin said that there is no freedom of speech here. I know, but I privately thought it was rather significant that she and Nuwwar had just voted for a new president for Egypt – they have some say, but apparently are not supposed to criticize their government beyond the polls.

After lunch, including Fatin's homemade baklava, and resetting all the channels on the television (a repair person had unset them), Zahid disappeared. He had been blocking access to any channel that he considered un-Islamic. (Fatin explained this to me on a previous visit. It is done with her full consent, except that when Nuwwar comes home, Fatin requires him to un-block whatever Nuwwar likes. She won't allow him to regulate her adult daughter. He's only a step-father to this grown woman.)

That left me with Fatin and Manisha for a little while. Fatin was keeping me partly so that David would spend time writing an abstract for her to take to work – he always does the writing. This was why we were sitting there, and I was waiting out 3 rounds of prayers! Whenever the muezzin started moaning in the distance, she would disappear. I came to think of these calls as a command, later verbalized very neatly by both me and David: "Allahu Akbar – Get in here and pray! Drop and give me five bows to Mecca! Allahu Akbar." That was my idea – drop and give me twenty – David just made it funnier.

No wonder not much gets done – everything is subordinated to a prayer schedule. Still, I thought it might be nice to tour the Grand Mosque – it looked spectacular, just as St. Paul's Cathedral and Westminster Abbey in London are worth seeing. I knew enough to take off my shoes and bring a scarf for my hair if I went.

I guess it's all in what you're used to. This brings me to another subject that promptly came up: sex. Fatin brought it up, saying that Islam was sent to the part of the planet that needed it most, meaning the Middle East. She informed me that men in the Islamic part of the world had an abnormal libido. I had to take her word for that. She continued, saying that before Islam, some men might have had up to 40 wives!

Then along came Mohammad the Prophet, who told them that 4 should be the limit, and that even so, it is really better to have just one wife – this from a someone who had more than 4 wives himself. Fatin than told me that this was all because the men here needed sex 3 times a day. "Really," I said, "3 times a day, just like meals?" She looked at me seriously and, not wanting to appear to be making too much fun of sex-obsessed Arab men, I informed her that the Western cultural standard is for men to *hope* for sex 3 times a week. Our conversation then moved on to other things.

She also told me – in the car when we were alone – that Zahid had assured her that when he was dead, he would reject the houri. He would just wait for his chance to be with her. That seemed fair, considering the fact that the Islamic heaven fantasy lacked an equivalent for women. No gorgeous men on hold for a woman, waiting to cater to her every wish, whim, and sexual need.

It is an imbalanced fantasy, and it does not acknowledge a sex drive in women. Why not? Because men had written it, and those men could not handle the idea of a woman – especially one with whom they had ever had in that way – wanting another man. By then I had understood that Islam had a built-in mechanism for granting men more sex, before and after death.

Gossip: Mansoor has a Girlfriend...Maybe

In early March, we had an odd conversation with Assim. He was curious about Mansoor. The previous Thursday, when Assim brought us back from the vet's office, he had seen Mansoor getting into his car with a Philippina girl. The girl was wearing a tee shirt, a tight mini skirt, platform sandals, and had her hair up. I had spoken to both of them then, telling Mansoor that the cat was going to be okay, and he introduced me to the girl. Her name was Leah. She worked at the billiards hall where he played with his friends in Farwaniya. Great, David and I thought; maybe poor, lonely Mansoor has a girlfriend. Or not – we didn't know, and since we couldn't imagine that Mansoor would have been doing anything wrong, we had no intention of checking.

Well, married, comfortable, conformist Assim was curious about this woman, too. He wanted to know what I had found out. I told him what I knew. David and I listened to Assim say what he imagined was the case: that Mansoor had Leah for a girlfriend, and that he had had her in the apartment while his mother and sister were away. Assim said all this in a tone that suggested that Mansoor had been committing a crime of some sort. They're back, I corrected Assim. Even worse, Assim continued, parading this girl in front of his mother and sister! I doubt he did that, I said, and by the way, his sister is my age and divorced. Still, Assim retorted, that is terrible. And so on...apparently Assim thought that Mansoor should just be alone and lonely, while Assim had Aiesha. The next time I talked to Assim, I intended to make sure that this subject came up again, then tell him that he seemed unjustifiably smug about it.

It all seemed most unfair and unreasonable to me and to David. David said that this culture was very grim and unforgiving. I mentioned that this culture and the Muslim religion seem to remove everything that makes life worth living from reach. David actually conceded that point – although Christianity and Judaism make an effort, Islam does the most pervasive job. This is NOT a compliment. Religion should guide people, not take all the joy out of life.

The Quran Demands Obedience
...of One Half of Humanity

I looked at a copy of the Quran that Saleh Al-Hamdullilah left with David. While I had no intention of reading it cover-to-cover, I was curious to see what it said about legal affairs, marriage, killing, and other religions. "Legal affairs" as a topic seemed to cover all of the other items that I looked up. For marriage, it demanded that wives obey their husbands and condoned wife beating if they disobeyed – hardly a selling point for Islam as far as women are concerned. For killing, it said that one may kill to avenge a murder, among other things. Other religions count for nothing in Islam. Judaism and Christianity are considered to be superseded by the Quran – just throw out your old Torahs and Bibles, folks – the Quran is all you need!

As I have pointed out earlier, a general reading of any random passage in the Quran shows that the main audience that it addresses is male. Women are to listen on the sidelines, as in fact they do at any mosque. Prayer rug arrangements certainly reflect this: men are front and center, while women get the side and back "seats" – on the perimeters.

Not-Funny Phone Pranks

That same evening, David arrived with Saleh at midnight, just as Assim brought me home, so I chased Saleh down before he could drive off. He and Assim stood outside chatting about their sons in Ohio for a while. Then they each went home.

During this conversation, the bouab was sitting outside watching us all. David decided to call Mansoor; he hadn't communicated much with us or with Abdul Mohti since he moved away. We got him on the phone, and he promised to visit us the following night or the next. He would come tonight, as it turned out, and take us out for Indian food in Farwaniya, and show us his new apartment building. He is sorry that we were going home to the States in a week and a half. He also told the bouab that he would visit him, too. So he still wanted to see us! He arrived a few minutes after that call, while Assim was still there. (I did not encourage any questions about the woman from the billiards hall.)

Mansoor kept me talking a bit more while David said good-bye to Assim. The bouab was funny; he seemed worried that I was chatting too much with Mansoor, and kept gesturing for me to wrap it up. David thought that was hilarious when I told him about it. As we stood there, Abdul Mohti called his wife in southern Egypt and put me on the phone with her. I wondered what he was up to; at first there was nothing but a shocked silence on the other end of the line. At first I thought that he had made a little [!] error in simply calling, waiting for an answer, and then handing a strange woman his telephone. His wife must have been shocked – her husband lives 2 countries away from her for a long time, and then she heard this strange woman's voice.

Then I realized that he was playing an awful joke on her. I handed it back to him and glared, gesturing for him to explain to his wife who I was and why he was having me talk to her. He realized the problem and did it, and then I took the phone back. Now his wife was willing to chat – which was funny too, because she had to speak in Arabic and I had to use English. I told her that her husband was a nice man, and that I was sorry that he had to live so far away from her. Her tone sounded friendly when she replied, but I don't know what she said, and she certainly doesn't know what I said either. I can only hope that the men translated the truth.

It must be awful for a woman from a very poor family to wonder, as her husband moves far from her in order to earn and send enough money to survive on, whether or not he is being faithful to her. That is the lot of many women in the Islamic world – a separation from their husbands due to economic circumstances, while not knowing when or if they will ever again live together as a couple, with no one else in their husband's life. Too many women must live with the knowledge that prostitutes and venereal diseases may affect their lives, their marriages, and their health.

Why Wives Have Shorter Work-Days

We were out at meetings all day late in April, with Dr. Aziz. We got a ride to the Kuwait Ministry of Animal Health. While we were there, we saw Dr. Fatima, the veterinarian who has a few pet cats of her own, and I took a photo of her. Dr. Aziz kept asking for photos. When we got back to our flat and had a chance to talk, he told me that ALL of the bosses at the Ministry of Animal Health are women. Not only that, they also all go home by 1:30 or 2 p.m. to cook and clean for their families. I said that their husbands must be spoiled and unwilling to deviate from sharply defined gender roles if they have to cut their workdays 3 hours shorter than men do. Dr. Aziz seemed startled.

Something else occurred to me after that conversation: if the wife gets home in the early afternoon, before the children arrive home from school but after the husband returns for lunch, the couple will have some time alone together. This enforced availability of wives keeps a husband's options open: he could come home from work, take a long lunch and have sex...or not. The wife never knew whether or not she could have some time to herself.

The reason why wives have shorter work-days turned out to be the usual one: their work-days are actually longer, with no real time off.

A Wife Sees the Agd on the Wall...

Hamid Al-Qasim told us all about his divorce as we drove along, after eating at a fancy Chinese restaurant with a Roman name in Salmiya (but not while we were there). He was very unhappy about it. He and his wife were separated; they had 3 little girls, ages 5, 2, and 1. According to Hamid, the problem was that he didn't spend enough time with the family, because he was always out in the evenings attending diwaniyas, so his wife became unhappy and asked for a divorce.

He told us all about it. We didn't ask him to – he just started pouring out all his troubles to us in the car on the way home. He protested so much about her reasons for wanting a divorce that I began to wonder about this woman's point of view. Eventually, I figured out what was going on: she had reproduced 3 times but had no sons, and saw the handwriting – no, the Arabic script of a co-wife's agd (wedding contract) – on the wall. She didn't want a co-wife. I didn't blame her.

The Al-Qasim family is one of the oldest and most influential in Kuwait. On the way back to our apartment, we passed a police checkpoint. Hamid pulled up to the cop and told him his name (first and last). The cop didn't even ask for anyone else's identification, because he recognized the name. We drove on, and Hamid told us that he was one of the last adult males in his family; most of the others had died, either of illnesses or other causes. [In the 1970s, he mentioned, 2 of his uncles were driving through Iraq. They were shot to death just for the money in their wallets, further depleting the Al-Qasim family of adult males.]

This diminishing supply of adult males is what drove him to attend so many diwaniyas. Only men can go to these gatherings, and Hamid was the only available adult male in his family. (He didn't mention whether or not he had any nephews, and we didn't ask.) The purpose of this was to maintain and increase his family's sphere of influence in Kuwait, mostly by attending at least 2 or 3 diwaniyas each evening. That was why he did not spend more time with his family. This made Hamid himself plus his family known to many people, so that if any member of his family needed something or had a problem, he could get his friends to help. That wouldn't work if no one knew him, so he maintained a regular presence at diwaniyas.

He told us that 60 years ago in Kuwait, if a couple was divorcing, it would usually be done without the courts, so as to not require the children to appear in court and feel the effects of the split so much. The couple would amicably work out an arrangement whereby the mother would take the children most of the time, and the father could see them for a couple of days per week. That way, the family's problems would be kept private. Women's families would say, okay, you don't want our daughter/sister, we will take her back and share time with the kids. Not now – so he was forced to go through the courts, and he hated the whole thing. He really wanted to confide all this in someone; he seemed to just need to talk.

As we rode down the main streets, I noticed some large signs with 2 photos on each one – one Kuwaiti man, one Kuwaiti woman. They were in Arabic, so I asked Hamid what they said. The reply: marriage counseling pleas/ads from the government, trying to reduce the divorce court's docket of cases.

We DID know someone with another wife...

I tried not to think about this much, but Saleh has had additional wives. Often when another culture is discussed, there are calls to be tolerant of it – but tolerance is an insult.

It turned out that Saleh had brought a mistress (that was what David said Saleh had told him) to our place before I arrived. That made no sense after I had learned about the lack of dating in Islamic culture – so she would have to have been a second wife.

How did this information come up?

Well…I have a strong sense of smell. Especially when my nose is up against the thing that smells, or just a foot away from the same smell in a different place after that.

I slept all day to get over jet lag when I first arrived in Kuwait.

The apartment was furnished.

The sheets smelled awful, and with a smell I had never smelled before. An odor.

Neither David nor I smelled like that. Ever. And I know what my husband smells like, both clean and in need of a shower.

So I asked him about it.

It was Saleh and his mistress – Saleh had asked David if they could use his place while he was out during the day. David said yes.

When I sat near Saleh in the car, and in offices, this added up – he smelled the same:

So...we did know someone who had multiple wives in the present. We weren't just hearing about the marital status of a dead person, as with Assim's father. This was real, in the present, and a subject that was being avoided by its perpetrator.

So one day, while out with Saleh, I not only queried him about the Islamic heaven fantasy, I also asked him point-blank "How many wives do you have, Saleh?"

Nervous laughter...followed by blatant lies: "I have one who visited me while I was sleeping on a mattress in your living room in the United States, another who visits me at work, another who comes to me..." he went on for a bit with his litany of fiction, then stopped.

By then I was sitting with a disgusted expression on my face, unconvinced, glaring out the car window at traffic. It didn't matter; I knew the truth. Saleh was a bigamist who justified his disloyalty to Raidah with religion.

A Loaded Question

When I visited with Raidah at her house shortly after arriving in Kuwait, the atmosphere there had a rather heavy feel to it. An oppressive sadness hung over the place, for 2 obvious reasons: her 2 oldest children are dead.

That wasn't all. As we sat down to dinner, Raidah put me off a very short while into the meal. She turned to me and asked very pointedly, "So, what do you think of Islam?" I felt ambushed. I don't care which religion it is that someone is absorbed with; I don't like to feel cornered by opposing preferences. With no time to consider it, I told her that I thought Islam to be a perfectly good religion, and very interesting, and then countered with "Why do you ask?"

She didn't have much of an answer to that, and wouldn't just admit to curiosity. Okay; I had been polite and held back. But when Raidah asked me this same question again a little while later, I decided that the satisfaction of saying "Too many wives," was worth it. It was; she said, "That is a problem."

It really seemed a bit early to ask me to discuss the topic at length, because I had just arrived in the Islamic world. How could I possibly be ready to talk intelligently about it without staying in this environment for a while and observing people?

Raidah is very Islamic herself; she wears a hijab and abbeya, holds religious gatherings in her living room, and despite the fact that her religion puts herself and other women at a distinct disadvantage, she is loyal to it. She wouldn't be winning me over to it; I saw enough while I was in Kuwait to know that, plus I had studied enough on my own before going there.

Chapter 14
Crime, Victims, and the Kuwaiti Media

As this is a book that is told from a woman's point of view, by a woman, this chapter will deal with crimes that concern women: rape; punishment for sex out of a male-sanctioned situation; and attitudes about both the crimes and the punishments. We have the same crimes all over the planet, but not the same attitudes toward and responses to them.

Reading the local newspapers, called *The Arab Times* and *The Kuwait Times*, was one source of news about crime. Talking to people was another. Reading books – well, one book with a mysterious and disturbing photo on its cover – was still another. What follows are the results of delving into these sources.

An Islamic Endocrinologist Shares His Views

My husband knew a Syrian doctor – an endocrinologist – who lived in Kuwait. He had an office in Salmiya, and an apartment there as well. On 3 or 4 occasions, he and his wife invited us over for dinner. It was fun; the food was interesting and delicious and led me to try some recipes that I had never heard of. His family was nice, too. And I saw an apartment inhabited by a non-Kuwaiti family. At first, David and the endocrinologist, whose name was Dr. Alim, discussed science until it got so technical that I stopped trying to follow it.

What I really hoped to find out, as I spent time with this doctor and his family, was cultural data: what did they think and do in their daily lives, how, when and why? What about women's issues – voting (Syrian woman can vote, I found out), hijabs, education, careers, demeanor, interaction with a husband, etc. On this particular day, I sat in the front seat of Dr. Alim's jeep and he headed out into traffic towards his home for an Eid dinner party. It was January; a grey, overcast, drizzly day.

And so my education in the Arab and Muslim mentality continued as we drove along: the topic of rapists and attitudes towards both criminal and victim were discussed.

What was interesting was Dr. Alim feeding me a line of nonsense – culturally programmed nonsense – that Muslims are raised to believe that rape is always the woman's and never the rapist's fault. Why? She must have looked too attractive for the man to resist his impulse to attack her. She should have worn a hijab, or no makeup, or...the list of lame excuses goes on and on. Fascinating and alarming. Westerners expect men to control their impulses or pay the price.

The way Dr. Alim talked about it led to a bout of me scolding him. All that got me was a line about how he knows the scientific workings of males, and how these urges are fueled by body chemistry, because he knows endocrinology. I didn't buy this excuse.

We got started on this because I refuse to live in Iran. David mentioned that we almost ended up on a business trip there until – happy inconvenience – it turned out that bringing our cat to both Iran and Kuwait in rapid succession would cause all sorts of bureaucratic snafus. As it was, we still thought that we would be visiting Iran, so I had bought some hijab scarves. Dr. Alim's wife and daughter both wear them. I absolutely did not want to wear one – not even if it meant an adventure in yet another country.

The upshot was that we knew that I was not only learning a lot, but also finding more and more reasons to intensely dislike this culture, fascinating though I found it. I knew from past reading about this upside down attitude about rape in Arab and Islamic thinking, but here it was again, open for discussion and analysis. This was priceless in its way, but I was happy to think about other things for a while at the party, such as sympathizing with Mahibah, the family's one daughter, about her older brother, who was studying pharmacy in Jordan and missing the family at Eid while he cooked macaroni.

Blaming – and Disposing of – the Victim

In late March, a news item that I had been following in the *Arab Times*, concerning a lunatic who went on Hajj, then came home, shoved his daughter up against a wall, turned her face towards Mecca, and slit her throat contained an update. He had been duly and promptly hauled off to jail, and had been there ever since. The criminal was arrested in late January, and then this follow-up story appeared. At first, the monster's name was unknown, and the reporters got the girl's age wrong – she was 11, not 14 years old. More facts appeared in this week's story: the perpetrator divorced his wife 50 days before he killed his daughter. Now his wife was suing for alimony and custody of their other 3 children. The murderer was behind bars, so I didn't see how she was going to get anything out of him – not custody of the kids, not money – nothing.

Now we knew who he was and his daughter's name. He was A.K. Al-Enezi, and he was a Kuwaiti citizen. His daughter's name was Asmaa. The other 3 children's names were listed in the paper as well, but I won't include them here. He claimed it was an "honor killing" – this usually means that some male relative has molested a girl, and whether she gets pregnant or not, the usual response is for the girl to suffer for it by being murdered by either her father or an older brother. Any male relative can do the deed, as long as the rape/incest victim doesn't live. The problem with letting her live is that she is no longer a virgin, so they would view her as damaged goods – not as a person. There was another case like this in Palestine recently, in which a Muslim father raped his daughter, and after the resulting pregnancy was aborted, her brother killed her. It amounts to blaming the victim.

One last interesting detail about this story...the murderer, Al-Enezi, was an employee of the Islamic Studies Department at the Awqaf Ministry. The word Awqaf means Islamic Affairs. How nice – criminals and lunatics are provided with a ready-made explanation for their inexcusable behavior – "Allah made [them] do it." In the West, it is "the devil made me do it." Here, God takes the blame. (It gave me that upside down feeling again – complete with déjà vue.) Either way, a crime has been committed by a lunatic. At least they weren't letting the perpetrator out.

Justice here can also be very permanent – I would check, but I suspected that death was the punishment. But that was okay, the criminals seemed to believe, as long as – in their view – the family honor had been cleansed. Fatin told me a while ago that rapists get a heavy punishment. Al-Enezi likely committed that crime, too. Which makes it sound as though he attacked his oldest daughter after his wife left, taking his access to religiously sanctioned sex with her. It was completely his fault – he divorced her and wouldn't let her take her children – total selfishness, as crimes tend to be. Good riddance – but there will probably be other crimes like it in the future, complete with the "Allah made me do it" line.

Dishonor Crimes

Honor crimes – the murder of a female relative who has had sex outside of marriage, whether by consent or force – happen with enough frequency in the Islamic world to merit some mention here. They are mentioned from time to time in some form or other in newspapers here, and one has even become a book, called *Burned Alive: A Victim of the Law of Men*. Souad, a Palestinian woman who nearly died as a result of her brother-in-law pouring gasoline over her head, has had her story written down by a French woman, one Marie-Thérèse Cuny. It has been published in a small paperback book, showing a woman's face on the cover – with a white mask over it. There are cut-outs for her eyes and mouth. Black cloth surrounds her head and neck in the portrait.

Souad was lucky – her face wasn't destroyed. Her scars – 24 operations later – are on her upper back, shoulders, chest and neck. She has married a nice Italian man, had 2 daughters with him, and even had her son (by the cowardly boyfriend who dumped her) move in with them all. She cannot write, but she learned to read with great difficulty as an adult. She can never go anywhere near her homeland again, because if her family finds out that she is living – or worse yet, if the villagers do – they will try again to kill her. Families such as hers consider its honor to be compromised when a daughter's virginity is lost. They don't care how it happened, even if it was by rape or incest. In Souad's case, she was seduced by a cute guy who made false promises, but the response of her family wouldn't have been any different.

Estimates put the yearly number of these crimes at 6,000, and some Middle Eastern countries actually have laws on their books that allow for very lenient punishments for the murderers, who are treated as heroes at home. The present and past kings of Jordan, Hassan and Hussain, have called these crimes "crimes of dishonor," and want them stopped, but convincing uneducated people who blindly pass on old customs is like asking them not to go to the bathroom. Most of the people who follow such customs are Muslim, but uneducated even in the details of their own religion. The Quran, it turns out, bans execution by fire – so Souad's family actually went against their own customs without being aware of it.

A woman named Jacqueline rescued Souad from a hospital in Palestine, with the aid of a young male Palestinian doctor and some Israeli officials, who knew that she was helping children. Souad was 15 years old when all of this happened. The Israelis helped because Jacqueline helped both Palestinian and Israeli children; the doctor helped because he knew that his people were committing crimes. Jacqueline also found Souad's son – a 2-month-old baby – and took him to Switzerland with them, where he was later adopted and raised by the same family that helped Souad adjust to life in Europe. He and Souad reconnected when he grew up. He was furious at his biological father when he heard the story of how he had used and then ignored his mother.

Jacqueline is now involved with SURGIR, a Swiss foundation that helps women wherever they are in the world who have been subjected to traditions such as dishonor crimes. The contact information is:

Banque Cantonale Vaudoise

1001 Lausanne
SWITZERLAND
Account #: U 5060.57.74
Website: www.surgir.ch
E-Mail: office@surgir.ch

I found this book in the Marina Crescent Mall on Easter Sunday evening while David was enjoying a water-pipe. It was a can't-put-it-downer. Soon David was hooked – he read the whole thing, too. While I was still reading it, I showed it to Rola Al-Dashti, Kuwait's superstar woman suffragist. She immediately mentioned that Jordan was one of the countries that actually had laws condoning these crimes. Women's rights attorneys in that country keep working to get rid of these laws, but as of now they are still there. The president of the Iraqi Kurdish National Assembly has condemned honor killings. I wondered about Kuwait – I couldn't read the laws for myself, but the Al-Enezi family murder came back to mind.

Reading such things reminds me that on the whole, American women have good lives. I also prefer the method of the Western world for avenging the family's honor after a rape: either kill or prosecute the rapist; not the victim. In the Middle East, for some mysterious reason, the opposite is done. This presents 2 problems: 1. It unjustly terminates the rape victim's life; 2. It leaves the monster still out in the world somewhere, able to commit the crime again and ruin someone else's life. I realize that I am speaking not of law but of ancient, primal instincts, but these different responses are the outcomes that go with the primal urges associated with each culture.

Rapists, Victims, and Reporting

The Arab Times ran several stories about rape cases, including one about catching the Farwaniya Hospital rapist in Bahrain, another about a maid from Indonesia who was brutally beaten at a home in Saudi Arabia (It's good that it actually made the newspaper – with a photograph of the bruised woman in her hospital bed. Clearly, working in Saudi Arabia is not advisable. But many women from Southeast Asia can't afford not to take such jobs.).

The hospital rapist said that he liked having sex with pregnant women – that figured...he was obviously criminally insane. Imagine going to a hospital to give birth, or because of complications associated with pregnancy, and not being able to stay in a bed unmolested. (On second thought, don't...) The Bahraini police handed him over to the

Kuwaiti police. He would have to stand in a police line-up and wait while the patient whom he raped and the woman doctor whom he attempted to rape identified him.

The maid who was brutally beaten in Saudi Arabia had asked for her pay, a meager $160 per month. A closed society provides many opportunities for such abuses, and Saudi Arabia is just such a society. To its credit, the country does investigate many cases of abuse of domestic help. But there is no excuse for locking a woman in a bathroom all night every night with infected cuts and bruises. She was at risk for having some fingers and toes amputated thanks to having had untreated injuries for days on end. The article didn't mention any punishment for her wealthy employer.

We stopped at a bakala – convenience store – close to our building before coming home. I got a paper – the *Friday Times* edition of the *Kuwait Times* – and took it home. In it was a photo of the accused Farwaniya rapist on the second page. He is hanging his head rather than looking into the camera, but it showed part of his face. He had short hair and a short beard. He had been identified by both the pregnant woman that he raped and the woman doctor. He also admitted to raping other pregnant women at that hospital, most of whom didn't report the crimes out of fear of enduring the shame they would likely face in their culture and families. At least he had been caught; I hoped he never regained his freedom.

A few days later, the paper ran a new article about an unrelated rape case, a gang-rape of a Philippina woman. She had been walking at night, when the weather is cool enough to go outside and do heavy work such as carrying many bags of groceries. That was why she was out alone – her employers wanted her to go out alone to buy their groceries. They wouldn't drive her. The four rapists grabbed her from behind and kidnapped her in a van. They raped her and beat her in that van, then let her out.

They were all arrested, and she thanked the police for arresting them. It sounded okay thus far, until I looked to the left of the text – her photo was there! At least her name wasn't – the stupid journalists left her *some* privacy, but not enough. Kuwait needs a law like the ones in the United States that forbid publication in a newspaper or broadcasts on television of rape victim's pictures, photos or names. It is possible that she consented to the photo, but I find it highly questionable.

The story was enough information. A few days later another story appeared, with a group photo of the 4 teenaged monsters. 4 big boys in dishdashahs, all bareheaded, stood in a row looking into the camera. I doubted that much would happen to them, not in court, not in a jail, not even when their futures were contemplated. How would Kuwaiti women be able to avoid marrying one of them?

Servant women need legal rights aimed at protecting their security. It's the least that Kuwaitis can do if they expect these women to leave their own families and countries to wait on them.

And Kuwaitis need to change their attitudes about rape victims. They need to decide that rape is never the victim's fault, always the rapist's fault, and punish only the rapist. Counseling, sympathy and friendship should be extended to the rape victim.

I realize that I am looking for progress in a culture and country that is mentally in medieval times while enjoying modern conveniences and technology, but I won't let that hold me back.

Thinking about Kuwaiti Rape Victims of the Invasion

All this made me wonder whether many – or even any – of the many women, Kuwaitis, their guests and servants, who had suffered rape by the Iraqi invaders had been taken back by their families and husbands, or simply been cast out.

What about the wives – had their husbands accepted them again, or cast them out?

What about the daughters – had their fathers and brothers loved them and considered them eligible for marriage in the future, or damaged goods?

Any woman who has suffered a rape will feel psychological trauma. Would Kuwaiti husbands, fathers, brothers, and other relatives make life better or worse for them later? Would they even have a future life?

These were the things that no one was going to tell me – leaving no answers to questions that haunt me still.

All I could do was hope that those women got what they deserved: good lives after it all.

Chapter 15
Invasion Stories

On August 2, 1990, Saddam Hussein, the President of Iraq, ordered his troops to invade Kuwait. He wanted Kuwait's oil, and he wanted Kuwait's territory, which would have extended the coastline of Iraq considerably if he could have annexed Kuwait to Iraq.

The President of the United States, George H.W. Bush, responded by sending American troops to Kuwait. The troops landed in Saudi Arabia, got organized and, along with British, European, and Japanese troops, routed the Iraqi invaders out of Kuwait. Bush Sr.'s reasons for doing this were outwardly humanitarian, but there is another side to his action: Kuwait is a gas station nation to the U.S., and we needed continued access to oil.

On February 26, 1991, Kuwait was liberated by U.S. and other foreign troops.

Some historical facts about Abdaly Road: It leads away from Kuwait City and goes north into Iraq. At the end of the Iraqi Invasion, the U.S. military told the Iraqis to get out of Kuwait by a particular time, or else. The Iraqis stayed until the absolute last minute, looting Kuwait City of property, including vehicles and citizens. Then the Iraqis complied and their entire garrison evacuated the city, moving north on Abdaly Road toward the border town of Safwan.

Approximately 30 kilometers out of Kuwait City, they were attacked by (mostly) U.S. and British aircraft. Using a combination of cluster munitions, napalm, air-to-ground rockets and mini-gun strafing, the U.S. and British military killed virtually everyone in the convoy – including the many kidnapped Kuwaiti civilians. This left a 10-kilometer stretch of the highway littered with loot, vehicles and corpses.

The outcome was that Kuwait was rid of the invaders, and the Kuwaiti people could calmly return to their own country, clean things up, rebuild, and resume living there. For this reason, Kuwaitis love Americans. This is a Muslim nation that openly likes Americans – infidel Westerners, with a culture that is dramatically opposite to theirs. This is not to say that people from other Islamic nations don't also like us, but we felt very welcome and safe in Kuwait.

What Resistance from Kuwaiti Militia?

Shooting back at invaders seems like the most natural and patriotic response. It also seems like the honorable one, and possibly the response with the best chance of survival. But this was precisely what many Kuwaiti soldiers failed to do.

I just can't get over my amazement that few Kuwaiti forces actually shot back in 1990 as the Iraqis invaded their country. If foreign invaders came into my country, Americans would, as in the past, fight back by any means available without waiting to be told or to be granted permission to do so. No one in a position of authority would find fault with any of us for doing so. In fact, American laws allow us to defend our own homes and persons with lethal force in cases of invasion, be it by criminals or foreign soldiers. We are NOT expected to just roll over and die. If we lived and died like that, the final chapter of our history would have been written by someone other than an American.

David managed to shed some light on this for me. He said that the Al-Sabah family created this pathetic situation all on its own by ordering that the Kuwaiti militia be trained never to shoot back at anyone without an express order to do so. Why would they do such a thing, I wondered aloud? Because, David explained, the royal family was afraid that the military might turn on them. This keeps the threat of such a possibility at a minimum. How nice, I said, but it also made Kuwait a sitting duck when the country was invaded.

Only one unit fought back, so there was only one battle between the Kuwaitis and the Iraqis in 1990. And – you guessed it – that unit had express orders from its general to fight back. The unit lost, but at least it didn't just stand around and quietly let the invaders walk in and terrorize the citizens. Granted, that is exactly what happened anyway, but the point is that some effort was made to stop this.

Don't shoot back without orders, even if you're being shot at – seriously?! American military units, by comparison, are trained to fight back by any means necessary right up until the end, David told us. What our governments want is another issue, but they come and go, so they won't tell us not to defend ourselves. Defending others, though – our government had our soldiers do that to protect a country that has long served as a gas station to others, including ours.

Regardless of that cold and selfish reality, I'm glad the Kuwaitis have their home back. It's theirs, not someone else's.

Aiesha and Assim's Escape

Assim told us what happened with his family during the Iraqi invasion. He and Aiesha had just returned from their graduate studies in the U.S. They already had 2 kids: a 6-year-old girl named Zahra, 5-year-old Hassan, and Aiesha was pregnant with their next boy. 2 weeks after they came home, the Iraqis took over Kuwait.

Everything got very quiet, and ominously so. They only went out for groceries.

It took a couple of attempts to successfully leave Kuwait. They left by driving off of the usual roads, straight across the desert and into Saudi Arabia...passing Iraqis as they did so. Most people who did this lost their papers, making it hard to prove their identities as Kuwaitis later on, but they were lucky and managed to keep them all.

It sounded, from their brief description, as if they were incredibly lucky to get out without being murdered, and also as though they had the innate sense to leave soon enough – before things got any worse. From Saudi Arabia, it was on to the U.S. to wait out the war. Some of their children were born in the U.S., so being there was no problem.

Environmental Catastrophe

One afternoon, I finished reading a very important book: *The Iraqi Invasion of Kuwait, An Environmental Catastrophe*. It was written by a Kuwaiti biochemist, one Dr. Jassim Mohammed Al-Hassan, Ph.D., who worked at Kuwait University as a researcher. He was a leader in the Kuwaiti effort to study and clean up the environment after the Iraqis left. His book is extremely helpful in understanding the Kuwaiti ecosystem both before and after the disaster. Unfortunately, the book suffers from 2 serious deficiencies, one of which is not his fault: 1. the Iraqis stole all lab equipment from Kuwait during the invasion, which seriously hampering his ability to properly document and analyze the destruction; 2. the book is very poorly edited, making reading and understanding its contents needlessly laborious and time-consuming.

That being said, it should be mentioned that the book makes some valuable observations. I can add to some of these observations in light of the reading I had to do in order to assist our friend Assim in preparing his lecture for the academicians who will meet to discuss public administration studies in Florida. First, the reading for Assim's paper told me that Kuwait University has tried, both in the 1980s and 1990s, to create a Master's in Public Administration program. Thus far, all that both visitors from Harvard and MIT, and other groups (including Kuwaiti professors) have managed to produce is a series of papers which document their ideas. They know what needs to be done, but lack dedication and follow-through, so the effort remains unfinished.

Further reading about Kuwait society – plus conversations with Kuwaitis who have worked in this society in their chosen professions for a number of years – led to the conclusion that Kuwait suffers from an overload of a combination of wasta (influence) and nepotism. This combination cripples its administrators' ability to effectively manage Kuwait's resources. Public administrators need to consider work ethics and the merit of job applicants before granting employment, which is currently done merely on the basis of political and family connections. Kuwaiti administrators often don't know how to manage resources, let alone care to expend the necessary effort to do so properly. Too many Kuwaitis – as I have mentioned before – simply expect to be given prestigious, high-paying jobs that require a minimum of effort. They would rather let the system carry them from the cradle to the grave with free health care, education (and let someone else write their term papers), social security, and easy jobs.

This deficiency showed itself in the Kuwaiti effort to clean up the nation's environment after Saddam's troops vacated the country. If – and this is a huge "if" – Kuwaiti public administrators had been better prepared to manage what resources remained to them after the invasion and destruction, the Kuwaiti environment might have fared better much sooner. The chief resource that remained to Kuwaitis after the disaster was human. People were still here. This is their country, and those whose home country needs remediation tend to be those who care most about remediating it. Had Kuwait University had an M.P.A. program in place in the 1980s, some graduates of it might have been well-equipped to handle this situation and to properly assist and organize the environmental scientists who freely gave of their time and skills to repair Kuwait. But they were not.

Reading Dr. Al-Hassan's book pointed out specific instances in which Kuwait as a society could have profited by having a fully functioning, properly planned system of public administration to fall back on after the Iraqis left. When people know what to do and how to do it, even when those people lack material resources they can organize quickly, efficiently and effectively. Dr. Al-Hassan talks about a lack of organization among Kuwaiti environmental administrators, which meant that the freely given efforts of the Kuwait Environmental Action Team (KEAT) were not fully utilized by all who needed them (page 155).

There is no excuse for this; there are only explanations. Foreign environmental scientists also came here, but none of them communicated at all with their Kuwaiti counterparts, who were all working on the same problem (page 156). That Kuwait was not paying the way of these foreign teams is no excuse. If these groups had assembled their findings neatly into one user-friendly report in all languages, the environmental scientists would have had the most effective remediation tool possible in terms of world and Kuwaiti efforts to protect everyone from the poisons dumped into the desert, the Gulf, the marshes, and the air.

Air Raid

Our Egyptian friend Shakir had a new girlfriend. He had been dating her for 3 months when he told me about her. They were just 4 years apart in age. They met briefly a few years ago when she was just starting high school and his sister was a senior in high school, and they remembered each other when they met again. Now they were dating. She lived in the hotel where she worked as the general manager's assistant, in staff housing. Her name was Manar, and she was Egyptian. Shakir took her to breakfast at Kuwait Towers. It was nice to hear about...until he told us about her family. Someone was lost during the invasion.

Manar has a father and a brother, but no mother. Her mother worked as a nurse at a hospital in Fahaheel, but she died in an air raid during the invasion. Manar was there with her when they heard planes overhead – an air raid. They both crouched against the wall, hiding their faces, with no other place to run to on short notice. The windows suddenly shattered, and a piece of glass came at her mother, decapitating her. Manar saw it happen.

That was the most horrifying war story I heard; no rape stories were shared. (I have to assume that Jean Sasson pried all of those out of women shortly after the war. That is the kind of story that women tell each other only on condition of anonymity, with no witnesses.)

The Sheikh Who Stayed

Sheikh Azby Fahd Ahmed Al-Sabah ran the Kuwaiti resistance during the Iraqi invasion and occupation. Saleh was one of his deputies. Sheikh Azby was the one Al-Sabah sheikh who didn't turn tail and flee the country during the invasion. The rest got the first flights out of Kuwait before the airport was taken over by the invaders, leaving the citizens and foreign servants to suffer the consequences of the occupation. This sheikh stayed here until the Iraqis were gone, collecting information, supplies and weapons.

I should add something to these comments: there is a benefit to having the rulers of a nation flee in times of war. The benefit is denying the invaders the satisfaction of capturing the leaders of the vanquished nation, thus preserving a sense of hope for continuity when war is over for that country's citizens.

David and I saw one of his younger brothers arrive at a mall in Kuwait City one afternoon. We were out with Assim, and he recognized him, quietly telling us that he was what is known as a "bullshit sheikh." What did this mean? It means someone who is one of so many sheikhs that it is possible to enjoy the royal family's wealth, but not the responsibilities of leadership. So he just lives the good life, with no duties, followed by bodyguards. Sure enough, he wasn't alone. Security officers in dishdashahs got out of the SUV and covertly cased the area.

Of course, David wanted to meet his illustrious older brother, so I took a photo of the three men together – David, Assim, and the Sheikh Bullshit, whatever his name might be. I handed the young sheikh David's business card, he shook our hands (including mine), and an invitation was issued to a diwaniya given by Sheikh Azby. Nothing further came of this meeting – somehow Sheikh Azby wasn't available at the appointed time, but at least I learned about him. I would not have met him, anyway, because women don't attend diwaniyas.

Saleh's Patriotic Treachery

David told me about what Saleh did to fight the Iraqis during the Iraqi invasion and occupation of Kuwait. Saleh stayed – unlike many of those in power then and now – facing danger and covertly fighting the invaders. He was a professor of immunology at Kuwait University. The Iraqis assumed – erroneously – that they could use him because of his ethnic and religious sectarian background.

Saleh is a Shia Muslim in a mostly Sunni Muslim nation (the Al-Sabah royal family are Sunnis). Saleh is also an Arab, like the Iraqis, but Kuwaitis are Arabs too – the invaders weren't thinking this through – they were just being predictably greedy. As a result, they assumed that he would work with them rather than against them. [Apparently, the invaders forgot that in the early 1980s, Iraqis had kidnapped, tortured and murdered one of his brothers.] So, they installed Saleh as dean of Kuwait University's Medical School.

Sheikh Azby Fahd Ahmed Al-Sabah organized Kuwait's resistance, and Saleh became one of his chief deputies, working by day for the Iraqis and by night against them, passing information and supplies to Kuwaitis. And why not – they had kidnapped his brother, taken over his homeland, and had no right to expect him to do otherwise. In the end, as the Americans attacked and the war was ending, the Iraqis figured out what he was doing. When Saleh realized that they were on to him, he knew he had to get away immediately.

Instead of simply running away, Saleh secretly gathered case after case of Coca-Cola that was destined for Iraqi troops and officers. This is the part of the story that he told me himself. He took it to a basement at the university, and teamed up with some people who had machines that could open and close the tops of the soda cans without leaving a trace of tampering. They opened the round tops – not the tabs that consumers pull to open them. Saleh added cyanide to the soda, the tops were resealed, and then he sent the cans on to their destinations. Lots of Iraqi invaders died slowly and painfully, thanks to Saleh. Saleh did this at night, working as the deputy of the one Al-Sabah sheikh who stayed in Kuwait to fight. Only then did he run for his life – well, drive for it.

That was why Saleh fled late in the war, driving through Iraq and into Iran with his whole family, less than 2 hours ahead of the Iraqis after they found him out. Saleh escaped by packing his whole family into the car – his wife and 5 sons – and going on a daring drive north, out of Kuwait, right through Iraqi territory, and into Iran, to his wife's relatives in the southern part of that country. Good for him – he made it, and came home when the trouble was all over. Once inside Iran, they took a plane out of the country and on to the U.S., where they waited out the war. Some of their sons were born in the United States, so doing this was no problem.

Mansoor's Nightmare and Escape

One evening, Mansoor visited and told us what happened with his family during the 1990-1991 Gulf War and Iraqi occupation of Kuwait. One month before the Iraqis arrived, Mansoor's mother, Busr, had gone to Egypt to visit her relatives, leaving her children in Kuwait. She goes every year, but that year she found herself separated from her children for far longer than she had intended. The Iraqis invaded on August 2, 1990. Mansoor's mom had already been widowed twice, so she was a single mother with 4 daughters from the 1st marriage and Mansoor from the 2nd one. The family was living in the Sha'ab district, in an apartment.

Mansoor's oldest sister, Farah, was the only one who was married – to a Saudi guy. But she was back at home visiting her younger siblings when the Iraqis invaded, and her husband was in Saudi Arabia.

Telephone calls were not possible. He did not know what was happening until the war was over and she had returned to Kuwait; then they got back in touch. As an aside, I asked Mansoor what had happened with them...why the divorce? He said that the Saudi had seemed very nice when he was asking to marry Farah, but afterward he showed that he was not so nice, and Farah was very unhappy with the Saudi requirement of covering up her face. I caught a glimpse of Farah once – she wore Western clothing with a hijab, not the full Saudi getup of a black abbeya, hijab and nekhab.

So there they all were – all 5 of Busr's children – stuck in Kuwait without their mother. Legally, all 5 were Kuwaiti citizens, because their fathers were Kuwaitis. But by then, both fathers had died, and the 5 children were living with just their mother. Their mother is a citizen of Egypt, who is legally permitted to reside in Kuwait to be with her children. She was horrified when she realized that she would be separated from them for an indeterminate amount of time during the invasion. She went to the Egyptian and Kuwaiti embassies many times to ask for help and arrange for their escape from Kuwait. Meanwhile, the 5 of them were holed up in the apartment for 7 or 8 months with no telephone or television, afraid to go out.

In those days, Kuwait gave free groceries to its citizens, even providing home delivery service to those who desired it. This came in handy for Mansoor and his sisters, who were afraid to go out and thus trapped at home. Only Farah might have been able to leave the house unchaperoned; but as a lone woman she was not about to do so if she could avoid it – the risk of meeting a rapist just wasn't worth it.

Thus began months of long periods of boredom punctuated by short bursts of intense anxiety whenever the doorbell rang. It was the grocery guy, either coming for a shopping list or bringing the goods. The kids had no news at all about anything until close to the end of their stay in the apartment. Luckily, the gas and electricity worked, so Farah and the older girls could cook for the family. They did not need to go outside.

After months of begging for help and planning, Busr succeeded in arranging for her children's escape to Egypt. A stranger came to their apartment from the Egyptian embassy in Kuwait. He had a plan worked out with their mother: he would take the children's Kuwaiti passports to the Egyptian embassy, where officials would create Egyptian passports for them using copies of their photographs from the Kuwaiti passports. Fake names would be put into these passports, and the Kuwaiti ones would then be concealed in their luggage, sewn into blankets, to be taken out in Egypt. The Iraqis were allowing all non-Kuwaitis to leave Kuwait.

A short flight later, the family was reunited in Egypt, where they waited out the remaining months of the war plus one more, returning to Kuwait after perhaps 3 months. During their stay in Egypt, the Kuwaiti embassy was somehow able to access money, which it liberally dispensed to any of its citizens who were stranded there.

Mansoor told us that each Kuwaiti citizen was given 500 KD per month, as did was his mother because she has Kuwaiti children. So each month while they were away, the family collected a total of 3,000 KD! This went for food and other living expenses. When they returned home, the cash flow ended but the grocery service resumed. [Today, the Kuwaiti government no longer pays for its citizens' groceries.]

Mall Therapy – a Reaction to the Invasion

Mansoor told us that before the 1990 Iraqi Invasion of Kuwait, Kuwaitis used to regularly drive up Abdaly Road and into Iraq to go shopping. This was for recreational shopping, not groceries. Just outside of Kuwait is a township called Safwan, where Kuwaitis and others could go to whatever malls are there.

Not any more: the construction of the Sharq mall, completed just 4 years after the invasion ended, was a reaction to the Invasion. Now Kuwaitis can go shopping within the safety of their own borders, enjoying the convenience of a short drive and the safety of home; Souq Sharq is located within the limits of Kuwait City. It is the perfect retreat and hangout for the Kuwaiti citizen who wants to spend some quality time safely frittering away hours at a mall.

Kuwait has other shopping malls, many of which are also quite luxurious, and also built in reaction to the invasion.

Chapter 16
The Retched Blessings of ZamZam Having a Pet Cat in Kuwait

Bringing our cat to Kuwait was a lot of work but well worth it. We got to keep her with us, and say that she was returning to her homeland for a visit. She had a very good time, and didn't mind traveling thanks to a lifetime of doing so with David. Scheherazade was a small shorthaired black-and-orange-and-white calico cat. She was born on Failaka Island, Kuwait, in the winter of 1990 (most likely December, judging from her size when David first met her), and adopted by David the following spring, after seeing her playing with a cluster munition. The warning doubtless saved several lives; they were walking among thousands of these bomblets.

He was still in the U.S. Army, however, so he couldn't take her home with him when the unit demobilized back to the States. So he left her with a Kuwait navy captain, where she spent the summer of 1991 on one of Kuwait's 3 navy ships. I am deliberately not telling which one it was, because if I did, David tells me that Awqaf, the Ministry of Islamic Affairs, would seriously inconvenience everyone associated with that ship by dispatching an imam to do a ritual on it; Muslims vary in their attitudes toward animals. What they really don't like is dogs, I have been told, but cats sometimes seem unclean to them. Others adopt them as pets.

This Kuwaiti navy captain was the one who suggested Scheherazade's name, for the Arabian philosopher woman in the Arabian Nights saga of 1,000 living-saving tales. Our cat had a tail and a tale, hence her name. David asked this navy captain to take care of her over the summer, when he left for the States, and so he did, keeping her on the ship. She killed all of their mice, and the crew knew her story, so they thought that their ship was blessed by this lucky cat. Our cat had a streak of white that went up between her brows and ears, and some Muslims believe that this is also evidence that a cat has been blessed by Allah. I don't know if they thought so, but they took good care of her.

David returned to the United States, was honorably discharged from the Army, and thought that he would never see that cat again. Then he accepted a job that would bring him back to Kuwait as a civilian scientific researcher, and one of the first things he did in Kuwait was retrieve his cat.

By this time, she was back on land, but on the mainland, as Failaka Island was now uninhabited by humans. She was living with an Indian guy, a foreign worker, in an apartment that was occupied by 8 men. David found her leaping out of the top shelf of a closet, delighted to see him again. He took her to his apartment at Kuwait University, in Shuwaikh.

She lived there with him for 3 years, while he did research with Saleh in the Department of Immunology at Kuwait Medical School. He met Fatin there, and she also participated in the experiments. Both Fatin and Saleh were professors there (they didn't get along, but the work continued). Scheherazade knew nothing about all this, of course, nor did she care. She was living in the lap of luxury in an 8-room apartment, a far cry from starving on the desert island where she was born. Her entertainment was David, with the only excitement being the time that she chewed through the phone cord in a futile attempt to stop the obnoxious contraption from distracting her human from doing her bidding and petting her. She hated that phone. (The attempt was a failure – she got zapped, and men came in the next day to replace the cord.)

After 3 years, David was ready to go home again, but this time with his cat.

The research at Kuwait University had ended. David had always wanted to earn a Ph.D. – ever since he was a little kid. Both of his parents had earned theirs, and he wanted one in immunology. He already had a Bachelor's degree with honors – a double major in biology and chemistry – and the next logical step was a Ph.D.

He was still friendly with a veterinarian at the U.S. Army base in northern Kuwait, so he brought Scheherazade to see him and get whatever vaccinations and papers were necessary for travel: a rabies shot, a certificate attesting to it, and a kitty passport with a mug-shot of the cat's head and a paw print.

Then he was off to the airport for an Alitalia flight to New York City via Rome. With no cat carrier, the airline people gave him a canvas bag for her. Big mistake: during takeoff, with the plane at a 45-degree angle, David heard a ripping sound, and then she was gone, racing up the aisle through the curtains into the first class seating area.

Suddenly there was an odd, loud screech. It sounded like Scheherazade and some other creature. It was. The next thing he knew, David watched as Scheherazade emerged from the curtains, screeching and yowling, pursued by an Arabian hunting falcon with its hood hanging off to one side, wings flapping, as it screeched angrily: "Awwk! Awwk!" It had quite a wingspan – perhaps 3 and a half feet.

Half the people in the plane were freaked out by this sight, while the other half were falling out of their seats, doubled over with laughter. The Italian flight crew just added to the comedy, trying to grab both animals, crashing into each other, yelling incoherently in Italian. To David, who spoke no Italian, it sounded like: "Pizzeria! Mama Mia!" and other such nonsense.

At last both animals were captured. The falcon was returned to its owner with profuse apologies. Scheherazade was returned to David with less cordiality: "Here is-a you cat. We do not like you. We do not like-a you cat. Please do not fly Alitalia again." They had some nerve, I thought, giving him an inadequate container and then blaming him when she broke out of it.

The crowning blow to the ride was when the Arab prince with the falcon poked his head out to see who Scheherazade's human was. He had restored order to his pet, having re-fastened the blinding hood and re-strapped the falcon to his shoulder. He saw David, pointed at him, and cursed out his ancestors in Arabic, calling them goats, sheep and camels. David was fluent in Arabic, so he understood every word.

Scheherazade Cat, cooing and purring. She smiled at lot, too.

Scheherazade had a good time in the States with David, and was with him for most of his studies. She had a few brief stays at a cat sanctuary in northwestern Connecticut when he wasn't allowed to have a pet where he lived, but was otherwise with him. When I moved in, after we had both finished graduate school, she accepted me happily enough. I love cats, and had changed her food, given her a new bed and some toys, new dishes, new litter box, new everything, and, to her chagrin, new nail clippers.

Life was good; she rode in the car with us, and not just for trips to the vet. She enjoyed car rides, including a long one to Washington, D.C. where David did some grant-writing.

Then we found out that we were going to Kuwait, and we were determined to keep her with us. It meant lagging behind David for a month and a half so that the cat's shot would be in order, but that was fine with me: it meant that I wouldn't go to Iran and have to cover myself in cloth, and I could stay with my parents and the cat I shared with them until it was time to go.

Our War Heroine Goes Back to Kuwait

When I started researching what would be involved in international travel with a cat, I did not know that it would be over a month before I could go to Kuwait to join David. U.S. law required that she have a rabies vaccination before we left the country. That wasn't all – the shot had to be a month old, and she needed a United States Department of Agriculture Veterinary Health Certificate. This certificate had to be issued within a couple of weeks after the rabies shot, and used within 10 days of receipt.

As if that weren't complicated enough, I would have to carry a file with me including: 1. the story of the cat's life, 2. the original rabies vaccination certificate signed by the veterinarian, 3. the U.S.D.A. Veterinary certificate, 4. a paper stating that she can handle temperature fluctuations during air travel, 5. a Home Again Microchip record (she had a microchip installed under the scruff of her neck with a reference number for her address and I.D.), 6. a faxed copy of an animal import permit from the Kuwait Ministry of Animal Health. To come to Kuwait, she needed the rabies shot and a feline distemper shot. This cat will not need any more medical care for a while, and she is in perfect health. She was 14 years old at the time.

David and Saleh faxed me the necessary form, all filled out, and I taped the cat's name and information all over her new carrier. With this and a few travel supplies – small litter box, bottled water, little metal dishes, and some dry food in a zip-lock bag, we were good to go. 48 hours of travel later, we were in Kuwait with David.

A few days after that, we were in the apartment that we would live in for the duration of our stay in Kuwait. The cat liked it very much. She had a lovely view of airport road, 2 beds and lots of toys, and her litter box and food were in the kitchen – spaced well apart. We never let her go out, of course.

Delivery Guys and Government Vets

November 24th was a big day for our cat – she got little rest or relaxation, which is always a huge imposition on a pet cat (what a life!). That was the day that our furniture arrived, brought from Al-Ghanim. After that, it was back in the cat carrier to meet a veterinarian at Kuwait's Ministry of Animal Health. The real purpose of going there was to enable David to meet the virologist there, have a tour of the facilities, and network with the scientists there. A lot of his work deals with experiments on lab animals – rodents, for the most part – and he needed to find as many laboratory scientists who were interested in immunology as possible.

When the furniture arrived that morning, it was in boxes, with much assembly required. Fortunately, it was delivered with a small army of Indian and Egyptian men – all of whom spoke Arabic but none of whom spoke English – to assemble it. This took 3 hours, and the men brought 2 elaborate tool boxes full of gadgets and power drills to help them do the work. I locked Scheherazade in her kennel for the duration.

She wondered what was happening, and would periodically start meowing. The men looked up, startled by the sound, so I held the cage up and they all peered at her through the kennel door. Sometimes the men meowed back at her while they worked. A couple of times when they did this, I brought her kennel around the flat to let her see what was going on. That quieted her down. As the saying goes, cats are curious. I also showed them the news article from the small paper in rural Connecticut, with a large color photo of her and David on the front.

David arrived when the furniture was almost assembled, and when it was, we hurried out – dressed up and with our cat – to get into Saleh's car. He took us to the Kuwait Ministry of Animal Health, located in a marketing district called Souq Al-Juma (which means Friday Market). We parked and went into a sand-colored, one-story building decorated with photos of dogs, cats, birds and other species. Some were about dealing with rabid animals; others merely identified wild animals and birds that lived in the deserts of Kuwait.

David had been led to expect that we would meet a member of the Al-Sabah family – Kuwait's royal family (it was typical of Saleh to tell us some grand but untrue tale). Instead, we met a representative of the Al-Sabah family member who oversees the Ministry of Animal Health, a veterinarian. She was a lovely lady with a black scarf decoratively draped around her head, glasses, attractively applied (not heavy) makeup, and the owner of a pet cat herself. We enjoyed meeting her. David told her the entire story about how he met and adopted our cat.

Also present was a veterinarian named Dr. Mohammed Aziz, an Egyptian national who had prepared Scheherazade's import certificate for Kuwait. Dr. Aziz was also a virologist who had developed a new application for using the extracts of some kind of mushroom in suppression of the hepatitis-C virus (a precursor to cancer). He needed permission from the K.N.P.C. (Kuwait National Petroleum Company), the parent organization of K.O.C., to develop this. This was really why we went to the meeting – to see Dr. Aziz. He and David made plans for more meetings. We did not know it then, but Dr. Aziz would be very helpful to us and our cat later on.

Saleh took us all home after that. We then let our cat out of her box and moved all of our things into the new furniture. And then...we went to sleep at 2:30 p.m.! It felt great after sleeping on the floor for 3 consecutive nights.

Umm Scheherazade

David got into the habit of referring to me in company as Umm Scheherazade – Mother of Scheherazade – because of the Kuwaiti custom of calling mothers by their children's names with the word for mother in front. Often, but not always, the same goes for fathers. So David could be called Abu Scheherazade – it sounds silly with a cat, but we don't care. It's fun.

Our cat had settled into life in the Abraq Khaitan apartment easily, and was enjoying her beds, food, view from the living room window – we had piled 2 cardboard boxes up with her fleece bed on it – and watching television from between David's feet every night. She also liked to hide in his wardrobe, despite our repeated attempts to discourage her from doing so.

Scheherazade enjoying the apartment: sunshine at the window; David's feet; her favorite forbidden closet.

We had brought a large stash of cat food from the States for her, which David had put both high up on top of the upper cabinets and inside the lower ones where I could reach it. Our cat had always thrown up a lot, so we hadn't wanted to just buy whatever was sold in Kuwait – we wanted Science Diet sensitive stomach formula dry food, and another kind of canned food.

We had been giving her bottled water since we arrived in Kuwait, because the tap water was desalinated sea water which flowed brown when we first opened the taps – questionable, to say the least. So we all drank bottled water. Also, Kuwait's water may have lead in it.

I also had fun learning the Arabic word for cat: gatwa. I was compiling a glossary of Arabic words, collecting a long list of frequently-used ones. No one seemed to be playing any jokes on me with this project, at least. Probably this was because women in this serious society didn't approve of teaching newcomers bad words. [I was glad; David had some unpleasant excitement over that during the Gulf War.]

Life went on for her with no difficulties for months, and she was quite happy.

So were we – if our cat was happy, then we were happy.

Merry Christmas to Our Cat

Our cat couldn't believe her luck as she approached the dish: she stared some more, then dug in happily.

We bought a cardamom-coated roast chicken for Scheherazade Cat's Christmas dinner. We unpacked it, put it in a new rose dish, put it on the floor where her small metal canned food dish usually went, and then David held her there, staring in utter disbelief at it while I photographed her. It was hilarious. After that, we cut up some of the white chicken meat – her favorite – and put that into her dish, and put the rest of it away for our dinner the next night. I took some more pictures of her eating it – she was very happy. Merry Christmas to our cat!

Kuwaiti Cats are a Breed of Their Own

There is something about Scheherazade that made me notice the Kuwaiti cats in our area. They lived all around, most of them on the street, with no homes, poor cats – some of them limped on 3 paws until foreign objects worked their way out. People were terrible litterbugs, and stray cats suffered for it. It made us glad that our Kuwaiti cat had a nice, clean home with beds, a litter box, toys, and plenty of special food and clean water.

For years, I had listened to Scheherazade's "Mrrrrooww!" and realized that it was quite distinctive in the States. Our Kuwaiti cat did stand out among American cats when she talked.

When we looked at her, she seemed similar to the American shorthair cats, but her voice and speech were significantly different from theirs. [My mother had told me that she has not seen a cat with markings like Scheherazade's before, or colors quite like hers either, but she blended in well enough with other cats in America. It was her voice that didn't.]

Now that we were in Kuwait and seeing other Kuwaiti cats when we went out walking, I realized that our cat belonged to a particular breed: Kuwaiti shorthair calico. This was just interesting – nothing that would get her registered in any cat fancier association or cat encyclopedia, but it was definitely a distinct group.

I had seen many other calico cats in Kuwait since arriving, and they all had her exact color shades, and similar patterns. Scheherazade's markings were, however, the prettiest of any that I had yet seen, just for the record. (Of course, I'm totally biased.) As for the sounds she makes, all I can say is, so did they.

The males tended to be white-and-gray (not gray-and-white, because they were more white than gray). A stray cat around our building was one of these; Assim had seen him several times sitting on the stairs just outside our apartment door, apparently hoping to meet our cat. I saw him too when Assim pointed him out to me. We heard him mrrroowwing outside often, not always outside our door. I finally figured out where the sound is coming from: the roof.

Hajji Saleh Brings Us the Blessings of ZamZam

Saleh went on Hajj in January. He goes every year, because he likes to take a vacation alone, because he feels the need to atone for another year's worth of sins, because he likes being called Hajji Saleh, and because he likes to bring back little individual-sized bottles of water from the holy spring at ZamZam. He brought one for us. We all tried it later, including Mansoor. It tasted heavy, as though it were full of minerals, and even seemed a bit gritty. It went down okay, but we were amused when Mansoor said, "I don't like it," and made a face.

Predictably, David announced that he had shared the holy water of ZamZam with our cat. He thought that it might do the cat some good to have holy water – bless the cat – even though none of us had liked the stuff. She drank it, having nothing else, and a couple of days later, puked clear fluid on the quilt. I sponged it up – no lasting harm done. That afternoon, I noticed more dried clear stuff on the floor behind our open bedroom door, and mopped that up. I thought I heard some retching in the night recently – it had to be our poor cat, puking up the ZamZam water. Of course, I put her right back on bottled water.

Feline Dental Problems

It's always nice when life with your cat is boring. That's means that she's okay.

Early in March, I noticed that she wasn't okay. She had had some rotten teeth extracted a couple of years earlier, and everything had been fine until now. Suddenly I noticed that she was avoiding her dry food, her mouth smelled bad, and she kept licking her gums. Poor cat!

It was frustrating, because I had done everything I could before leaving Connecticut to make sure that she wouldn't need anything, but it hadn't worked. It appeared that an upper molar, midway along her right side, had come out, leaving a large, red, painful hole. I didn't understand this, nor did I want the poor cat to wind up toothless.

She had good food, both dry and canned. I brushed her teeth with a special cat toothbrush and toothpaste. But now she had a problem again. I spotted it because she hid under the bed. David called Fatin, who knew where the veterinary clinic in Kuwait was.

Fatin had been told about this, and said that Zaki was out of town, or he would have driven me and the cat to the vet. Fatin told us both that the veterinary clinic she used was in Shuwaikh, and that her brother could drive us – and she would come with us – in the evening. That was a relief. I didn't want our cat to die of an infection.

Scheherazade Cat got upset again when she and I got up, because David had taken the cat carrier down from the top of the wardrobe, and when I put it on the sofa, in plain sight, the cat settled down onto the coffee table, crouching there facing it, and contemplating it. She knew she had a problem. While I got our food, she sat on top of the television, watching me. She never sat on either the television or the coffee table, so she was obviously upset.

I cuddled her and put her down, and she went to curl up in her ring pillow bed, where she fell asleep. She saw me change into my house clothes when I finished talking to Fatin – which meant that we weren't going out anywhere just yet.

I realize that all of this may seem like a long and very boring sob story, but it is a case in point for anyone considering how it would be to travel with a pet. If you leave the pet home, you won't be there if it gets sick. If you take the pet with you, then you have to navigate the difficulties of taking it to a foreign veterinarian in a foreign environment.

In the afternoon, Assim rang the bell – a screechy thing that I wasn't used to hearing – offering to take our cat to the vet. He was very sweet, saying that David had called him, desperate for help, saying that the cat is our child, prompting Assim to say that those words "broke his heart," a favorite catch-phrase of his. The reason why his sympathy was stirred is that he is very attached to his own 6 kids; he loves kids. He saw the parallel, and unlike some other people we met in Kuwait, did not believe that we should love only what he loves and consider whatever he considers irrelevant to be so. We certainly appreciated it.

I called up Fatin and she told me again about the details of going to the vet. She was pleased that Assim would take us there. The place she used was in Shuwaikh; she gave directions and a phone number, and said that the doctor she trusts is a Philippino veterinarian named Dr. Andro. She didn't know his last name. She also gave me his cell phone number, but when I tried it, someone else answered and said it was the wrong number. Oh, well. We would just go there and see him.

The Al-Dohama'a Private Veterinary Hospital in Bayan

We went to the Al-Dohama'a Private Veterinary Hospital in Bayan, and we were very impressed with it and with Dr. Andro Satumbaga, D.V.M. It was fascinating – we met several hunting falcons. I had heard all about them from David, but had never met or seen any. They were quite safe, having been tamed by trainers before being sold.

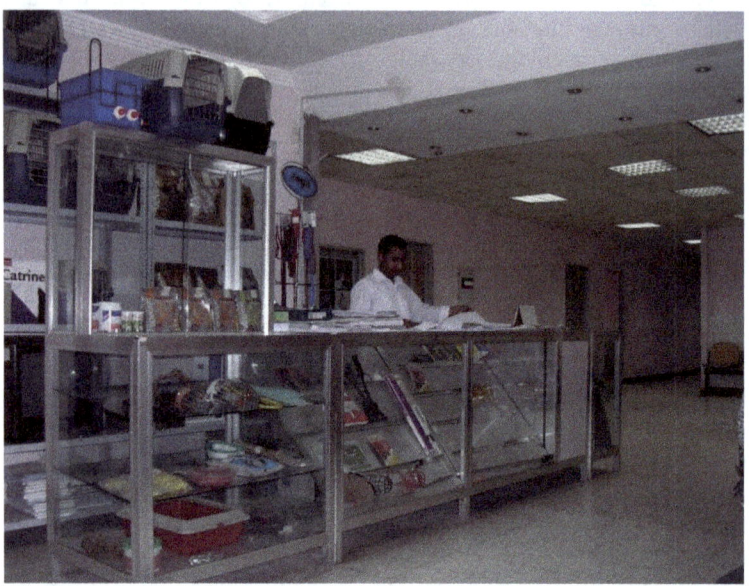

The Al-Dohama'a Veterinary Clinic in Shuwaikh: the check-out counter and store.

The place was near Shuwaikh, off a main road and down a dirt driveway past a sheep market. It was an ugly little square-shaped building with signs all around identifying it. A courtyard set into the side of the place led to the door. I saw a couple of Kuwaitis carrying their pet falcons, both with and without hoods. Inside, it was clean and comfortable enough. To the right was a desk with a receptionist, surrounded by glass display cases of cat, dog, and bird-care supplies. If you wanted one of these items, you paid the receptionist and another worker brought one from the supply room. I bought a pair of cat nail clippers for Fatin for 3 KD.

The Kuwaitis with pet falcons – I think I must have met 4 different falcon owners – were very nice. They held their pets out on gloved hands for me to see, and took off their hoods. The birds were beautiful, majestic creatures with a mixture of brown and cream colored feathers, in an even, patterned mix of color all over, and their eyes were large and round and interested in the surroundings. The legs were tied loosely together so as to keep them from flying away, but not to make them uncomfortable. A rope connected each falcon to a heavy glove, which the owner wore with good reason: the talons were long, pointed things that could do a lot of damage whether the bird meant it or not.

Kuwaiti guys with pet falcons.

We met one owner in the hall beyond the waiting room, the one whose falcon had been injured by another falcon, and chatted with him for a while. David told everyone he spoke to about our famous war heroine of a cat, and this got people into a friendly, chatty mood. This particular falcon owner was a twentysomething Kuwaiti named Nasser who ended up inviting us to go shooting in the desert, a popular pastime in Kuwait. His falcon was a little different from the others in that most of its feathers were cream-colored. The falcon's name was Sayah, and we both felt very sorry for him, because he was hanging his hooded head as he waited on a red cabinet, sitting on his glove. Another falcon had bitten his right shoulder 7 days earlier, and after that, he got bitten again in the same spot.

Nasser kept Sayah in an aviary with several other birds. Perhaps he should keep him apart from them until the falcon recovered completely, I thought. As we chatted with him in the hall, Nasser offered to let one of us hold him. David immediately said, "Yes, let's have a picture of Stephanie with Sayah." What?! I wasn't sure about this thanks to the one that had menaced Scheherazade on that Alitalia flight. But Nasser insisted, and coaxed Sayah off of his glove, which was for the left hand – all of the falcon owners used their left hands to hold their pets – and started pulling my hand into it. I stopped resisting; this could be fun.

Here I am, with Sayah the falcon perched on my gloved hand.

This is a close-up of Sayah the falcon, perched on Nasser's hand.

The falcon was no problem at all. Nasser persuaded him, still wearing his hood, to get onto my hand, and then he removed the hood. There he was, calmly regarding me from his right eye. He was beautiful – ruffled on one shoulder – but quiet and calm. I spoke to him in low tones, telling him that he was a good boy, and a beautiful bird, and that I hoped he would be okay soon. After I put him down, I discovered that the falcon didn't mind having his wings stroked and being given more sympathy, so I enjoyed him some more. We saw them again after our cat had been seen, and Nasser said that the prognosis was good – Sayah would recover.

When our turn to have Scheherazade examined came, we found Dr. Andro ushering us into the exam room near the main door. It proved to be a large, white-tiled room with a desk and computer in one corner, a small metal exam table across from it, and a sink in the far corner. A veterinary assistant came in with us, and we opened the cat carrier. Predictably, she did not want to get out of the box, and I had to pull her by the shoulders with David pulling on the back of the box. Once she was out, I shut the door. The doctor looked at the mess in her mouth carefully, and said that yes, she had just lost another tooth, and yes, the area was infected and inflamed.

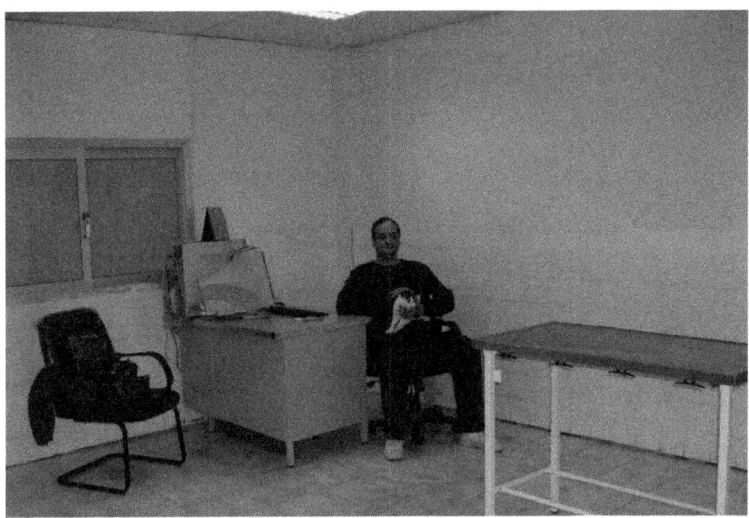

David waited by the desk with our cat until he arrived. It was a plain, bare room in an old building with windows and a sink – the bare basics.

Dr. Andro then left us, saying that he wanted to give her some injections, as pills would be unreliable in this case – her mouth hurt too much to force her to swallow them, and they might get lost. He came back with 3 different syringes: an antibiotic, a vitamin B complex, and an anti-inflammatory. He gave our cat the shots, then instructed David in the rest, saying that he was giving us 4 more days' worth. David would inject her while I held her. Dr. Andro asked to see her again in 5 days. Hopefully that will solve the problem. If not, he would have to anesthetize her and do more work on the affected area.

For all of this, we paid 3 KD. That's right – you read this correctly – 3 KD. Not 30, not 13, not 33, but 3, and much cheaper than in the States, which would have been $10.30. Dr. Andro said not to worry, that this was a common problem for older cats, and that we would be able to keep her for several more years. He loved the story about how David found her on Failaka Island, and how she had warned his group of soldiers about the cluster munitions. The vet said that he has cared for other such "lucky pets" and found out their stories after wondering to the owners why they wanted a particular, seemingly scruffy and unremarkable animal so much. David was always trying to protect our cat by telling any veterinarian this story. It did seem to make Dr. Andro pay more attention to what he was doing.

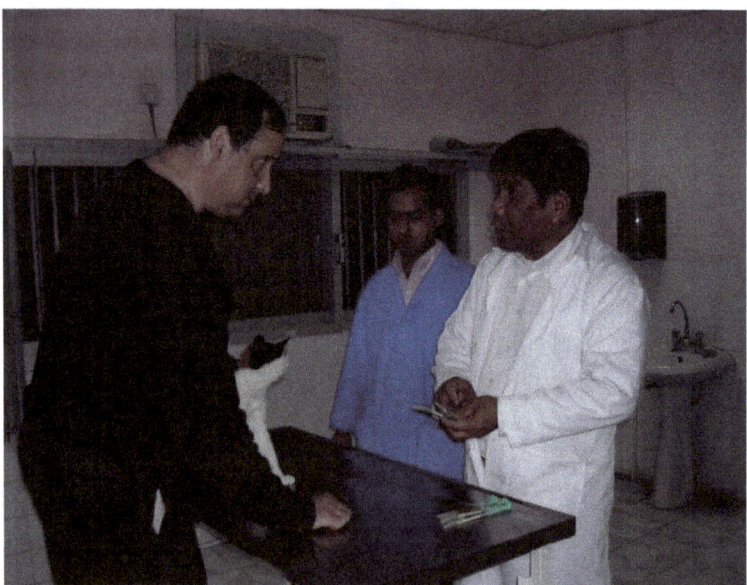

In the exam room with Dr. Andro and his veterinary technician.

Dr. Andro also mentioned that before the Iraqi invasion, veterinary hospitals had been run by the government. After the reconstruction of Kuwait, however, the vet clinics all went private, and there were now 15 or 16 of them. It was better this way, he said, because the competition improved the quality of the animal health care offered. I hoped so – our cat was important to us.

We met some really cute kittens of varying ages, and one huge, fluffy orange cat. There was a miniature collie, a Siberian husky, a red-blue-and-yellow Macaw, a cockatiel with a yellow plume, a gray parrot, and a little green parakeet. The bulletin board was covered with lost pet notices and ads for kittens and puppies.

At last, we headed out and Assim appeared, ready to take us all home. He was glad that the cat was going to be okay. So were Mansoor and Abdul Mohti when we arrived at our building. We had seen them on the way out, and I had told them what was wrong. They both said "Poor Scheherazade – meskeen Scheherazade!" both before and after the outing. Hours later, she was sleeping deeply on the corner of our bed, breathing peacefully.

5 days later, we went back there. We got a good report on our cat. Assim very nicely drove us there and back again, and also to the grocery store. He waited in his SUV with our cat in her carrier while we shopped at the Khaitan supermarket. The weather was still fairly cool every day – getting warm, but easily within comfort levels. After dark it was breezy and pleasant; I went about in sandals with no socks, wearing long cotton pants and a tee shirt. In other words, perfect weather for leaving the cat in the car for a few minutes. It would be lethal in hotter weather, I was sure.

As for Scheherazade Cat…the infection had healed, the swelling in her mouth had gone way down, and Dr. Andro was very pleased with us and with her. Her mouth bled when he opened it to peer inside, but he said not to worry. He gave her a shot to stop the bleeding, another one to boost her appetite (vitamin K), and then more pills. One pill was to stimulate her appetite – morning – and another was for pain – evening. She didn't need anything else yet. All this for 2 KD ($8)! After 10 days, we were to bring her back.

A few days later, I made David look at Scheherazade's tooth again. It looked rather gross, and still smelled bad. We had expected it to be much better by this time, and he got worried. The Al-Dohama'a Veterinary Hospital wasn't open – it was Friday, so that came as no surprise. David called the veterinarian that we met with at the Kuwait Ministry of Animal Health, the nice Kuwaiti lady who had cats of her own. She immediately recommended someone who was an expert on cat health. We would hear from this person soon; meanwhile, we intended to see Dr. Andro at Al-Dohama'a the next evening as planned; an x-ray would cost 5 KD – not bad at all.

The next night we were told that the cat would live, because she did not have what David had been rapidly convincing himself that she was infected with: calcivirus, a rare but usually fatal virus endemic to the Gulf region. David panics when he thinks something might be true, while I panic when I know that something really is true. So I was calm and he was not.

Dr. Andro thought that Scheherazade might have a tooth fragment left up under the gum, and he said that the area was still infected. He gave David more syringes and me more pills. To x-ray the cat, she would have to be anesthetized, because no cat would hold still while someone poked at its mouth – especially if the cat's mouth hurt.

Anesthesia was not possible because Dr. Andro lacked the right equipment. He added that most vets used injections, which could kill a 14-year-old cat. Dr. Andro had ordered the right equipment, but it wasn't there yet. Any day now it would come, but meanwhile…some company sent him the kind of anesthesia gas that kills rather than keeps an animal safely asleep. It's absurd; he is in the business of healing animals, not finishing them off!

The good news was that the cat was eating a lot, running into the kitchen to demand that we put more food in her dish at least twice a day, and then gobbling it up. She did this when we got her home. We called it "cracking the whip" – but she wasn't a tyrant; she just really wanted the food. We were to go home in 6 weeks, if we could just preserve the cat that long.

Kuwait's International Veterinary Hospital in Ahmadi

At the end of March, Dr. Andro sent us elsewhere with our cat. He just didn't have the right equipment, and she couldn't wait 6 more weeks, so he told us where we could get what she needed. He told us what the problem was: Kuwaitis tended to be rather prejudiced against people from Southeast Asia and less wealthy nations, and to ignore foreign experts from such places. He lacked the clout to get whatever he needed quickly, and he did not own the clinic – only Kuwaitis could own businesses and property. With no one listening to him, he was stuck.

So he referred us to a different veterinary hospital, in Ahmadi City.

Scheherazade ended up staying all day at this place. Her mouth had not healed, because she wouldn't eat food with a crushed antibiotic pill in it – it tasted bad, and of course the logic of the situation cannot be discussed with a cat.

When we got there, we were very impressed. On the road to Wafra was a beautiful, new, flawlessly maintained, properly-equipped hospital. The grounds were green – covered with dark green grass that was kept well-watered. The smell of the grass made me long for spring in Connecticut. Americans and other foreigners were bringing pets (cats and dogs, mostly) for treatment, and an army of Labrador Retriever tracking dogs were being led up the driveway.

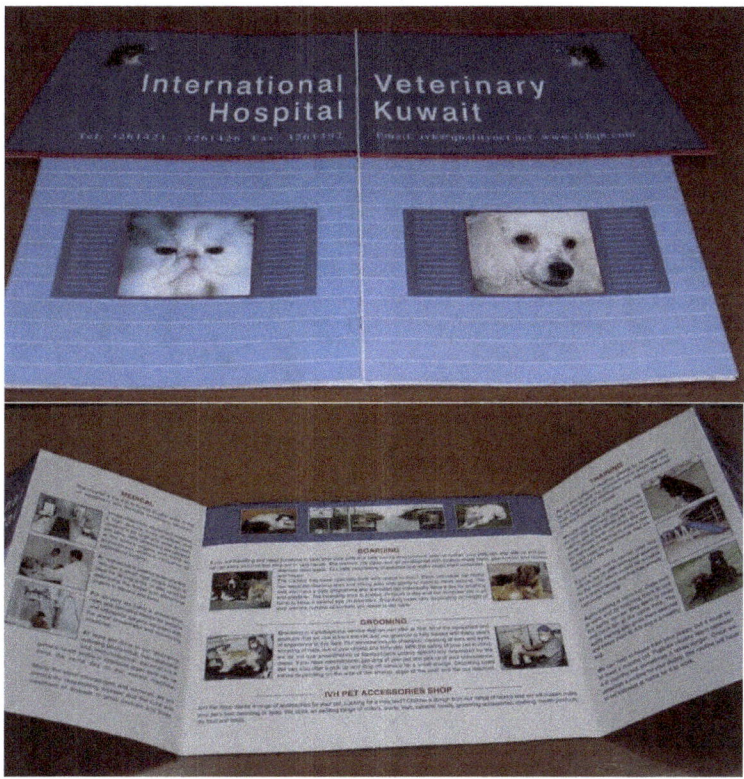

The place was staffed by a British woman administrator and 2 Italian veterinarians, plus many Philippino workers to help keep it spotlessly clean. A Kuwaiti who was fanatical about cleanliness owned the place. They also had some fancy brochures.

For readers who bring pets to Kuwait, I am including the contact information:

International Veterinary Hospital
P.O. Box 9275
Ahmadi 61003
KUWAIT
Telephone: 965 326-1421/1426/1382

Fax: 965 326-1392
E-Mail: ivh@qualitynet.net

To get there from the north, we took the Fahaheel Expressway south to Exit 306 Wafra, then turned right and went through 3 traffic signals. The hospital was directly across the street from the Equestrian Club, on the right. Partha, Hamid Al-Qasim's driver, brought us there.

The doctor who examined Scheherazade was a friendly northern Italian woman who listened to the entire story of the cat's life, that she was a war heroine and so on, and decided that she wanted to take no chances. The cat needed surgery to get a tooth fragment or whatever infected tissue out, but she wanted at least one if not 2 other doctors to participate. It would be done that afternoon. We felt much better after meeting Dr. Zavatti and looking around. They promised us that our cat would be okay when we came back, so we went home to wait.

This was the main reception building of the International Veterinary Hospital, and its parking area.

The cat boarding wing of the International Veterinary Hospital was a really beautiful luxury hotel for cats.

We met another couple with a pregnant pet cat in the waiting area, and spoke to them about the place. The husband was American; the wife was Romanian. She had boarded cats at this place before, and she insisted that I follow her into the back of the place to see everything. I did, photographing everything. There was a kennel for cats, with lovely cat-condos for each pet. There was another one for dogs. Both areas were decorated with stuffed animals and pet sculptures, and carpeting for the cats inside the condos. Everything was cleaned daily.

There was a pet grooming area, with a large tub for big dogs, and all kinds of grooming equipment lined up on some shelves, neatly organized. A German Shepherd was up on the table, waiting for its grooming to resume. This area was on the right, in the back of the hospital.

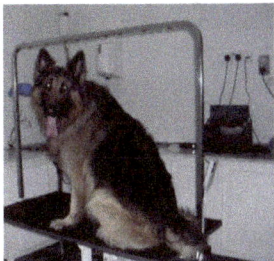  

The dog grooming salon: trimming table, radio, lotions, tools, a bathtub – you name it, they had it.

A hallway led to the right of this office, straight to the back of the building and out. The first door on the right in this hallway led to a nice bathroom, followed by isolation rooms for animals that were recovering from surgery – dogs, mostly, or other larger animals. On the left are the operating room, x-ray room, laboratory, and cat cages for those who needed treatment. Going outside into the backyard, I noticed a yard for horses and 2 smaller areas enclosed by chain-link fences – one for dogs and one for birds.

 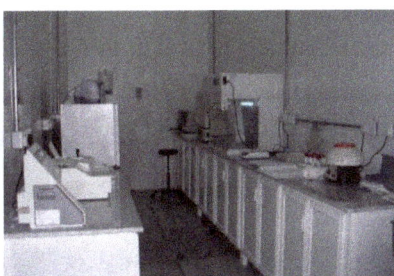

The bathroom and laboratory: the laboratory was very impressive; David checked it out and was thrilled. Any test that our cat might possibly need before and after surgery could be dealt with at this place.

Coming around to the left area, I found myself back near the examining rooms and the administrator's office, a lovely wood-paneled carpeted room full of colorful drawings of exotic birds and waterfowl. With the tour completed, I went back to the waiting area, stopping to talk to the lady from London, England. She told me all about the place, and chatted with me for a few minutes. The tooth extraction was 30 KD ($103), but we didn't care – our cat was worth it.

We returned to the International Veterinary Hospital at 4 p.m. to retrieve our cat. 65 KD and 3 hours later, we left with Scheherazade. There was no tooth fragment in her jawbone, but there was a lot of infected gum tissue, which Drs. Stefania Zavatti and Walter Tarello cut out. Then they stitched her gums shut, and brought her out of the anesthesia-induced sleep. They took x-rays first, and showed them to us when we arrived.

This was where the exam rooms were, around to the left of the reception desk; above, the waiting room.

We had to wait a while after arriving before the doctors could see us. I immediately went backstage and found Scheherazade in the same top left metal cage, sitting in the crouch position with her tongue protruding, a runny nose, a dirty face, and drool coming out of her mouth. Another pet's cage in the room needing cleaning, and it stank.

Our cat in her cage in a cage waiting, and the reception desk, with the nice worker who cleaned her area.

While David scrutinized the x-rays, I found one of the nice veterinary technicians – all of them were young Philippino people, mostly men – and ask him to clean it up. He spoke very little English, so I led him to the stench and pointed. He got the idea right away and cleaned it up, which quieted the white dog and made all of the cats and kittens around the dog much happier. Then the tech wanted to know which cat was mine and what had happened to her. I pointed her out, and gestured at one of my own upper right molar teeth. This explanation seemed to satisfy his curiosity. He must like animals – I realized that he needed this job, but he seemed to enjoy the animals, too.

When the doctors were ready to talk to us, we were led – with Partha – to a separate building to the left of the main entrance, which was devoted to the care of falcons. Huge, framed color photographs of falcons adorned the walls of the reception room, and Dr. Tarello was waiting for us in the exam room, which contained an x-ray viewing board, a couple of taxidermed falcons, and some paintings identifying the various species of falcons. David spent a long time going over the cat's x-rays with both Dr. Zavatti and Dr. Tarello in there.

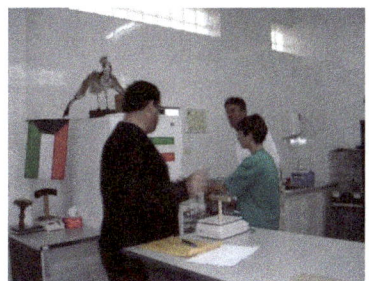 

David spent a long time discussing our cat's health problem with the Italian veterinarians in the Falcon House.

The upshot of it all was that our cat had a chronic condition that would probably make this happen again. David wanted to try out some of his immunotherapy on her to prevent it and make her live longer – poor pin cushion, we said to each other later on. The cat would have to swallow round antibiotic pills for 20 days, and David insisted that the vets also sell us 4 doses of pain-killing injections for her. We were to water down her canned food and feed it to her through a syringe…she was going to hate that.

As we waited for Dr. Zavatti to prepare these items for us, we met the brother of the owner of the hospital, a Kuwaiti man in a white dishdashah and guthra. Of course he asked us whether we have any children, and David said that the cat is our child, complete with his routine of reintroducing us as Umm Scheherazade and Abu Scheherazade. The man looked rather nonplussed at this, but he soon adjusted. Wealthy Kuwaitis have traveled and discovered that other cultures do not tunnel-focus on marriage and then children as Arabs and Muslims do. His name was Saud Yacoub Al-Anzi, and his brother's name is Duaij. We exchanged business cards, and told him how impressed we were with the place.

David chatting with the brother of the clinic's owner; a certificate of appreciation from U.S. Army officers.

There were even some framed certificates on the waiting room wall in the main building from some U.S. soldiers, thanking Mr. Al-Anzi for caring for their military dogs and for hosting a party for the soldiers. The waiting room was stocked with magazines in both English and Arabic. The doors of the International Veterinary Hospital's brick buildings were all stainless steel with vertical grooves, and very tall ones at that. The overall impression conveyed by the style of the buildings is one of relentless cleanliness and antiseptic fastidiousness.

Exercise areas around the hospital for dogs, falcons and horses. The place was both a hotel and a hospital.

The next day our cat seemed much better, and we followed all of the new instructions.

After Ahmadi, Nothing Else Measured Up...

A few days later, David wanted me to bring the cat to the Kuwait Department of Animal Health and sit with him while Dr. Mohammed Aziz gave a 2-hour lecture, so I did. He left me the good phone to call Dr. Aziz with so that he could tell the cab driver how to get there. We were lucky enough to get a ride home from the Director, as no cabs went anywhere near it. It was surrounded by a metal fence, giving the impression of being closed when people first arrived, looking quiet and deserted. We hadn't been there since November.

Dr. Aziz gave a nearly 2-hour-long lecture on animal vaccinations. Our cat went to sleep for most of it. When at last it was over – and I could tell that Dr. Aziz really knew his subject well – people got up, took some food and chatted. I was asked to tell the heroic tale of our cat warning David and his other soldiers about the bombs on Failaka Island, and the vets were interested in our famous cat.

David and I met 2 Egyptian veterinarians introduced to us by Dr. Aziz, who were both full of advice and plans for analyzing our cat's health, starting the next morning, early. The more I heard, the less I liked their plans: they wanted me to stop the antibiotic pills so that they could sample her tissue and fluids. Stopping the antibiotics was what had made her so sick in the first place, I informed them, saying that I did not want to do any of what they proposed. I managed to explain the entire 6-week saga of Scheherazade's dental illness, and they suddenly didn't like their own plans. David agreed with me; instead, he waited until the antibiotic treatment was completed, then had me bring her back for tissue samples. He would analyze the data with his colleagues in New York City, he decided.

The next day, I edited Dr. Mohammed Aziz's PowerPoint presentation...77 slides, including the ones that thanked Allah for being merciful and benevolent. It looked a lot nicer, both aesthetically and grammatically, with proper spelling, punctuation, spacing and other effects. The whole thing was in English, though he had delivered it all in Arabic. I suspected that he was perfectly capable of lecturing in English too. However, David said that it was much too long; I thought so too, but that wasn't up to me. Scientists reuse their presentations, so this would make a nice thank-you gift for helping us with our cat.

What Dr. Aziz had done for us was get an animal import permit for our cat, which served as her entry visa. That no official checked it was beside the point. He would also be getting the samples of her tissue ready for David to deal with in the States.

One Lavender-Soaked, Embarrassed Cat

One evening, just as I was about to take a bath, our cat entertained us with an accident.

I had just filled the tub with warm water, scented with lavender bath gel. But I didn't get into it right away, because as usual, I still had a few more things on my mind to write. David was watching television, and sitting directly across from the bathroom.

While I was in the bedroom typing away on the laptop, I suddenly heard a splash. David called out: "I *don't* believe it! The cat jumped into the tub!" Scheherazade Cat had gone into the bathroom, smelling the air, and leaped into the tub without looking. She yowled and leaped out, raced into the hall, skidded across the floor into the living room, and then ran into the dining room, where she jumped up onto some of David's files.

Of course, I came out and found the cat. She was sitting on a file folder, on a chair in the dining room. David was sure that she meant to say "Don't look at me!" But we paid no attention – she was soaking David's important papers. She tried to hide under a table, but we cornered her and David toweled her off while I mopped up all the water. She run under our bed to hide, mortified. She had assumed that the tub was empty. Crazy cat – we got a kick out it.

Pharmacy Errand – Interrupted by a Muezzin

Late in April, with just a week left in Kuwait, our cat needed some more medicine. We had met a nice Kuwaiti veterinarian at the Ministry of Animal Health who wanted to study in the United States, and so we called him. He came to get us and take us with our cat to see Dr. Andro again at Al-Dohama'a Veterinary Hospital. (We couldn't go all the way back to Ahmadi.) Dr. Andro said to definitely put the cat back on the medicine that the Ahmadi vets put her on, so the Kuwaiti vet took us to the pharmacies around the Souq Al-Juma to look for a new bottle of it. He tried 5 pharmacies before he found it, for 2 KD – half of what we had paid in Ahmadi.

He called his brother for directions, interrupting prayers in the process. At last, we got to the Souq Al-Juma. The place was just a lot of cheap shops on a huge block in Shuwaikh; many small front shops lined the outside of large buildings, with long, merchandise-lined hallways that led into a huge concrete room with a high ceiling beyond the smaller shops that was filled with all sorts of junk. Our host said that the merchandise was mostly Persian stuff. The only thing I would ever want to buy there would be the Persian rugs, with a guide to help me, but the moray eels in a fish-pet shop were interesting.

Suddenly a muezzin started the next call to prayer, and the veterinarian left us to roam the souq for an hour while he prayed. I hoped that the pharmacy would still be open when he came back; it was after dark. I found myself nostalgic for the Protestant work ethic culture of the United States, in which work is seen as a way to get closer to God rather than prayer leading to Allah. Things don't stop for prayer times in the States.

An Exit Visa for the Cat – What a Hassle!

On April 30th, not having known I would need such a thing, I got the cat's exit visa from the Kuwait Ministry of Animal Health. I had taken her back there for the tissue samples to be extracted, as planned, and would never have found out about this requirement if not for the nice Indian veterinarian who did the work. He was the only one of the group who seemed to know what he was doing, and who showed some sign of a work ethic.

He was great – very serious, kind to the cat, and absolutely disgusted with the laziness that he saw all around him. This, while being very careful to not only work hard but to be seen to be working hard...always important in Kuwait for anyone who was not Kuwaiti, or from a wealthy Gulf nation, or American, British, or European...or a follower of one of the 3 monotheistic religions of the world. It was patently unfair, and he was acclimated to it.

David went out to do some final work on the asthma study with Saleh while I was left with specific instructions about Scheherazade Cat. I was to take her to the Animal Health Department in Shuwaikh, where Dr. Aziz would do a bacteria culture test to see if the infection in her mouth was resistant to her antibiotic medicine. With the impression that this was all that the cat needed, I got a cab and took her there. Lucky me – the cab driver missed the exit, got lost and had to stop and ask some friends at a car wash how to get there. I called Dr. Aziz 3 times for directions, and finally I was walking into the gate of the Animal Health Department.

I didn't know it, but I was about to get help and a lesson in cultural differences from a new source, without realizing what I needed until I was getting it from a Good Samaritan. The Good Samaritan turned out to be a Hindu veterinarian from Madras, India. Dr. Aziz introduced me to him. I went into the main building, which was designed like a small square around a central courtyard. Its outdoor courtyard was shaded by an overhang, leaving almost no view of the sky, because another building sits inside that courtyard, containing more offices and some rest rooms, filling the entire space.

Many Indian men worked at this office and lab building as servants, getting tea and coffee for people, and cleaning. One of them called out to me and led me to the office of this Indian veterinarian. I went in, sat down, felt confused, and asked about Dr. Aziz. The man said he would help me in a moment and continued to look at something at his desk, which made me even more confused. He spent such a long time rummaging in the desk without looking up that I called Dr. Aziz on my mobile phone one more time. Perhaps he was wondering why I hadn't appeared; no one had told me that Dr. Aziz wouldn't be the one doing the test. With that, Dr. Aziz came in and ushered me into his office, which was across the driveway in another building, and explained that the Hindu doctor would be doing the test.

Now I understood; Dr. Aziz was more of a laboratory analyst that a patient care-giver. He understood the theory of helping animals, but his strength was as a virologist. Dr. Aziz insisted on having one of the servants bring me a Nescafe (with milk). I gave him the newly edited curriculum vitae that I had promised him.

At this point, the Indian doctor came in and sat down, looking serious and businesslike, and began to ask me about the cat. (I still did not know his name.) He started by quizzing me but guessed wrong, so I discouraged this method and [briefly] told him the story of her life followed by full details of her dental illness. Now he felt ready to proceed. He would do the bacteria culture, then flush her mouth out with a 2% hydrogen peroxide solution. No sooner had he announced his plan than the Egyptian doctor with the huge, prayer-induced callus on his forehead appeared.

This was Dr. Sharaf (whose name means honor/chastity). Like Dr. Aziz, he gushed politeness and asked many irrelevant but good-natured questions. Dr. Aziz was very religious too, but his personal habits left him looking like a well-groomed, handsome pharaoh, with no callus on his face. The Indian doctor did not smile at all, so it took some time to warm up to him on my part, as I did not understand right away that the reason for his constant frown was this time-wasting, irrelevant, overly drawn-out politeness and banter of the Egyptian doctors.

The oddest moment was when the Indian doctor had to instruct Dr. Sharaf in making a 2% hydrogen peroxide mixture! This, to even a non-scientist such as myself, seemed odd. Wasn't this the most basic of chemistry skills, learned in college, early in a veterinarian's training? Off went Dr. Sharaf to mix it up, and I asked the 2 remaining scientists what was with him. Dr. Aziz looked embarrassed and disappeared for a few minutes. Dr. Sharaf had forgotten how to do his job somehow, it seemed, in all of the friendly, time-wasting chatter.

The Indian doctor looked annoyed, and muttered something about Egyptians wasting other people's time with talking, talking, talking and irrelevant questions. I noticed that the Indian vet wore a gold ring, and suspected that he was probably a Hindu, not a Muslim – a difference which would further set him apart from them, both socially and professionally in this bigoted culture that would dub him "qaffer". I was right; a little while later we had an opportunity to talk at length, after the cat had been treated and supplied with many tiny syringes and a batch of the solution that Dr. Sharaf managed to prepare properly.

During the treatment, I had to hold Scheherazade still as she shrieked, terrified and confused. One of the Indian servants was called forward to help hold her still. He looked terrified, too, so I felt bad. As soon as it was over and I had packed the cat back in her cage, I turned to the man and picked up his hand, shook it, and looked him straight in the eye. "Thank you for helping with my cat; I could see that she scared you. She was scared, too." The man looked astonished. He was probably used to be treated like he just didn't matter. I couldn't let him walk away without doing just the opposite.

After that, I went back to see Dr. Aziz and take care of whatever details David had asked me to discuss. When I was ready to leave, I announced my intention of going on foot to Al-Ghanim (across the busy road) to buy an ink cartridge for the printer. He looked at me strangely and ran off to ask a colleague to give me a ride there and home. It turned out that he got the Indian doctor to do it. This was when I learned his name – Dr. Ramayanth – and all about him. He had lived in Kuwait for 10 years; his siblings were all physicians living in different cities in England. His wife was a physician who dealt with HIV-positive orphans in India and traveled all over the world to conferences in Europe, Washington, D.C., and Brazil, etc.

As we rode along, we talked about life in Kuwait. He asked me if I liked it there, and I admitted that I didn't like the culture – only my individual friends. That really opened things up. He didn't like it either. Kuwaitis didn't work hard; they just drank tea and goofed off while foreigners did the real work. I added that they treat non-monotheists as non-humans, and told him that I had learned the word "qaffer" to name people who are not Muslims, Christians or Jews. It's like you are not in the club if you are not one of these, I said, so my husband had told me not to tell the more fundamentalist Muslims that I am a Wiccan – just say Episcopalian. Dr. Ramayanth completely agreed with me there, because he was a Hindu, which fell under the category of qaffer to Muslims, and he was often treated as a non-human who didn't matter.

This really struck a chord with him; when I added that it is insulting to be told that I ought to drop my own religion and switch to Islam, he agreed and said that he had also been treated to this same suggestion. Why should we do so, we said? We are not weak of character and personality, so that when we travel and meet different cultures and ways we will suddenly abandon our own.

It was also rather amusing to hear him tell me that he thought that hijabs and especially nekhabs are ugly. Why, Dr. Ramayanth said, when God has given a woman a pretty head of hair and a beautiful face, should she cover it all up, as though she is ashamed of it? A female colleague of his had gotten married and come back covered like this, so he had asked who she was. She identified herself, and told him that it was her new husband's wish that she wear this costume. He was appalled, but hid his opinion from her. Not from me, however – he said that husbands should not be jealous if others see her face, worried that everyone will be carried away with lust. These are sick people to be so obsessed with sex and to actually believe that a mere handshake or the sight of a pretty face will turn men on to the extent that they can't focus on behaving politely and rationally. He was preaching to the choir's soloist, I thought, noting that someone from an ancient culture was commenting on another ancient culture.

This being agreed upon, I hurried through my business in Al-Ghanim, which was so close to the Animal Health Department that we could see it from there before leaving in Dr. Ramayanth's silver jeep. I thanked him and said it was very nice of him to drive me not only home but to stop for this errand. I also suspected that as a qaffer he was getting stuck with a "servant" kind of favor-request, so I made an extra effort to be pleasant and thankful.

As it was, I felt sorry for the real servants in his workplace. Dr. Ramayanth had told me, as we prepared to leave his office, that they were paid 17 KD per month, and that their pay had been withheld for 3 months due to government carelessness. How, he had wondered, could they live? These men seemed to be afraid of their own shadows, and afraid to complain.

Dr. Ramayanth realized that his Egyptian colleagues knew their professions, but he also thought that they wasted an enormous amount of time talking about unnecessary things. He wanted to work efficiently, and I suspected that this was just the way he preferred to operate. He liked to get things done. He also disapproved of treating particular groups of people with respect because those groups have helped Kuwaitis in the past (Gulf War I) while treating others without as though they didn't matter, and he told me so.

As we approached Abraq Khaitan, he asked me when I was going to the States. When I said Tuesday, he got upset. Why hadn't I said so at the office? All this talking, and the Egyptian doctors got their work done, but I didn't get mine done! Dr. Ramayanth insisted that I rush up to the apartment, leave the cat, collect her paperwork, and run back down and go back with him to the office, and hope that everyone would still be there long enough to prepare her export permit, so that she could go home. So…there was a requirement that I get a paper allowing me to take her back out of Kuwait! More rules to worry about…

Dr. Ramayanth scolded repeatedly until I had to say that I had never been told about this requirement until he did. He understood and stopped fussing. We drove back and saw an Ethiopian man who said he would make a form, and copied down a description of the cat after viewing her rabies and distemper papers. Next, Dr. Ramayanth drove me, worrying about the time every few seconds, across the highway – which was on a bridge and had to be crossed with a long traffic light stop – to the Kuwait Ministry of Animal Health.

The Animal Health Department is only a sub-branch of this larger government branch. He drove down a long, speed-bump riddled driveway, past palm trees and well-kept desert grounds, turning left to head for a building all the way down at the end. We could see the highway just beyond the back fence. All of the signs except those informing us that this was the Kuwait Ministry of Animal Health were in Arabic; I would never have found anything without help.

He hurried me out of the jeep and inside, where we found a heavyset young man in Western dress drinking tea and smoking a cigarette in front of a word processor. This man was supposed to type a description of the cat into a form on the screen, and to fill in Dr. Ramayanth's name, print it, and let him sign it. It sounded simple enough, but he was so lumbering and slow about it typing by the hunt-and-peck method with one finger, making lots of errors, that I just reached across and finished it for him.

He printed the document, Dr. Ramayanth signed the bottom, and then he rushed me out again after I paid half a KD. Dr. Ramayanth snatched up the document and raced out, leading me back to the jeep. He drove to the opposite end of the grounds and we jumped out again, this time to a beautifully decorated office populated by Kuwaiti officials in dishdashahs. The sign outside informed us, by the way, that we were at the Kuwait Ministry of Animal [W]ealth [sic].

Dr. Ramayanth slowed down a little here, because to get this part of the job done he had to be a bit obsequious, but he never let his guard or his dignity drop for a moment, and the Kuwaiti veterinarians in there, despite being relaxed and busy chatting and drinking tea, respected him as a professional colleague. I was pleased to see this; they offered both of us tea, but didn't insist when they realized that we were in a huge rush.

Kuwaitis shut their offices down completely at 1:30 p.m., and they realized that we were racing to beat this deadline. As the official behind the desk stamped it sent it off for another signature, a very relaxed Kuwaiti veterinarian who obviously liked to do some work in the field (but not with a heavy workload) came in to change his shoes and drink tea, telling Dr. Ramayanth about a camel that he had worked on. Dr. Ramayanth listened politely; he had just told me earlier about taking care of Indian elephants for a zoo. He could treat a wide variety of species.

The form was returned to us, and Dr. Ramayanth rushed me back to his silver jeep. As we headed off down the speed-bump driveway, he chatted a bit, since the time in the vehicle was inevitable. He also agreed that the worst part of this mad dash was now over. Now he mentioned that last year, he used to take the ferry out to Failaka Island a lot to care for camels there, to the tune of 10 KD each time, and that Sheikh Hamad had never seen to reimbursing him. He had asked for the money – probably 100 KD – but the Sheikh hadn't made much of an effort to get it for him. Shame on him, I said, and that is very un-Islamic of him and others like him. And they go around saying that they are such good Muslims, too.

We got back to the Animal Health Department and found the Ethiopian man. He seemed to resent the fact that Dr. Ramayanth had heroically taken care of this important form for my cat – like it was a competition to be the one who helped the American woman. Dr. Ramayanth was getting the glory and thank-yous from me, but they were well-deserved. 2 KD later I was free to go. Dr. Ramayanth relaxed now; we had beaten the deadline, so my cat could go home with me. I thanked him profusely, and said that I would write all about him, and tell my husband all about what he had done for us and for our cat. He seemed really pleased.

Then he told me to wait with him until exactly 1:30 p.m. in his office, at which time he would bring me back to my apartment. He had to be seen there until that time. We chatted a bit, and then Drs. Aziz and Sharaf appeared, full of apologies and excuses for not having taken care of this form. It is only fair to add that Dr. Aziz had no car, so he could not have done any this, and Dr. Sharaf gave me the creeps, so I would not have ridden off with him. Dr. Aziz felt bad though – he could have summoned someone to help me if he had realized that I needed this exit visa. David was planning to work with him on a nutraceuticals lecture series, so I just reassured him that all was well, and they left. I explained this to Dr. Ramayanth after they had gone, and he understood that I had to seem friendly.

When I told David about all of this, he was sorry he could not have met Dr. Ramayanth.

He was a dedicated lover of animals, and I would never forget him.

Chapter 17
Holiday Weekend at the Wafra Oasis

Kuwait has 2 non-Islamic holidays each year, one right after the other. Notice that I said non-Islamic, not un-Islamic. What I mean is, these holidays are secular – not related to religion – but it is perfectly in line with religious beliefs to celebrate them. These holidays are all about giving thanks for being independent politically, and safe to live their lives as Kuwaitis. February 25th is Kuwaiti Independence Day, commemorating the day in 1961 when Kuwait was given its independence by the British, who then pulled out of the country and went home. February 26th is Liberation Day, celebrating the day in 1991 when the last of the Iraqi invaders left Kuwait, thanks to the liberators from 34 other nations.

To celebrate both Liberation Day and Independence Day, Kuwaitis carry Kuwaiti flags, put them on their cars, wear them as hats and scarves, and let their kids spray canned white foam at passing cars (we didn't like this – it made driving dangerous!). Teenagers and young men also drive drag-racing cars around like maniacs (we didn't like that, either). Other than that, nothing alarming happened, and we were endlessly fascinated and entertained.

Our friend Hamid Al-Qasim had invited us to his house at the Wafra Farms Oasis on both of those days, with one overnight stay. Scheherazade Cat was also invited, but we left her home with lots of dry food and water after some careful deliberations. We would have a much better time knowing that she was safely locked inside our apartment than if she were to stay someplace that left us worrying about a servant opening the door. She would have dashed out.

So, we spent two days and one night at the Wafra Farms Oasis (not to be confused with Wafra the town, which is northwest of the oasis) as guests of Hamid. I couldn't tell anyone the addresses. No such thing was disclosed at the time – and if one looks at the area on Google Earth maps, every road in the area is unhelpfully labeled "Paved Road." In any case, we had a fantastic and fascinating time. There were many interesting people to see, some of whom were the elite big-shots of Kuwait, plus lots of beautiful plants and animals, and some interesting places. I even got to attend a real diwaniya; unheard of for a woman.

The Drive South

Hamid's Sri Lankan driver, Partha, picked us up on Thursday morning. We gave him a cup of coffee, and he insisted on washing out the cup himself when he was finished. Hamid was very tough on him because his previous driver quit, so Partha was perpetually nervous. He had worked for Hamid for only one month, and was still learning where every place he must drive to was located. He was a nice person and very willing to do his best – so we hoped Hamid would come to appreciate him.

We packed, as Hamid had instructed, our own pillows and a blanket, plus an overnight bag. David insisted on bringing the computer, but I was the only one who used it, downloading photographs from my camera. We left our cat home with extra food, fresh water, and our bed unmade so that she could enjoy burrowing under the quilt.

We stopped to pick up someone we did not know across Airport Road in Farwaniya. He was an old man in a dishdashah and guthra. He came alone, saying that his wife wasn't feeling well, and he brought 3 tiny porcelain cups with no handles into the car, a carafe of hot spiced Arabic coffee (that stuff tastes terrible!) and fresh dates.

We didn't see him bring an overnight bag, but off we went. I was in the front seat, and he passed me one of the tiny porcelain cups with that weird hot drink in it. I sipped at it to be polite, then gave up and poured the rest out the window. The man just smiled happily and said, "Halas?" and took his cup back. Halas means finished, so I assumed that I had drunk enough to be polite.

We were taken to look at a little house in the desert with no one in it. The servants had been ordered to clean it, which they had done by hosing it down – the halls and floors in every room. It was dark, dank, and the beds were tossed apart. We were immediately glad not to have brought our cat; she definitely would have bolted and caused a lot of anxiety for us, and the servants definitely would have not understood that we didn't want her to get out. We didn't want to stay there. David said not to worry, that we wouldn't have to. Okay – I hoped he was right.

We drove for over an hour to get to Hamid's house in Wafra Farms. We went past the Burqan oil fields, past camels, goats, sheep, and herders. We saw an occasional dead goat or sheep on the side of the road, and David said that often one will wander away from the herd and die of thirst and hunger, lost and unable to rejoin the others. What an awful way to die – though I suppose that the only pleasant way to die is in one's sleep, feeling at ease with one's past and comfortable with the thought of death. In any case, the ride was pleasant enough otherwise.

In Hamid's Diwan

The first thing we did was sit for a while in Hamid's diwan, which was inside his house. Hamid was sitting in there, against the cushions that are placed along the walls, smoking and listening to his guests, who were chatting and drinking tea. Hamid was wearing his usual navy pin-striped dishdashah and a white khaffiah, but no guthra and ekal. This was his outfit for relaxing and hanging out with the guys. We were given fresh dates, water, tea, and a hot drink made from boiling a kind of dried lemon.

Hamid's house at the Wafra Farms Oasis; a guest, Hamid, and David in the diwan. David seems to be getting the hang of relaxing. ☺

David had to make a concerted effort to relax – painful to a workaholic who is anxious to earn a living, but necessary. No one else wanted to work – this was a weekend, and a holiday weekend at that – he could not take their much anticipated fun time away from them by trying to talk business. I told him, and Hamid told him, that he had to just visit people at the weekend house without mentioning business. To have any dealings with rich and comfortable people, you must not appear to be too eager to work, even if you are. Relax, and they will like you and deal with you – tense up, and you will get nowhere. David protested that he knew that, but couldn't relax.

Polyandry at an Ostrich Farm

After about an hour or so of sitting there, Hamid got up and announced that he would take us to see ostriches. I was excited about this – we still had the signed ostrich egg that he had sent us, for lack of a way to cook it. We got back into the car with Partha and followed Hamid in his white pickup truck to the ostrich farm.

The place was spread out over several acres, with adult ostriches pacing around in large pens, and a house for hatchlings. We began the tour in a tiny building that contained a freezer full of ostrich meat, some ostrich plume feather dusters, and ostrich eggs that had been emptied of their contents. We bought 4 of them for 1 KD apiece, and made it home with 3 intact. We would give them to our relatives.

Before we saw the farm's residents, we got a preview of their fate: feather dusters, hollow eggs, and steaks.

The adult ostriches were funny to watch. The females are gray, and it is their feathers that are used to make feather dusters. The males are black with white feathers just on the tips of their wings, and have a hilarious habit of puffing out their long necks. To flirt with a female, they would squat down near her and spread out their wings and swing their long necks back and forth. This seems quite pointless, because the female was not impressed, and because she was not at all hard up for sex – sooner or later, a strong male will simply sit on her and mate with her, and if she didn't mind, she wouldn't toss him off. Meanwhile, she would run off if the group of males pestered her too much.

A male ostrich (black) flirting with a female (gray); ostrich hatchlings eating indoors under lamps.

We went on to see the ostrich hatchlings next, which were housed in a long, darkened building lit with heating lamps. There were 4 or 5 pens in a row with several hatchlings in each one. The babies' legs were tied together, perhaps to keep them from leaping over the low walls and out into the viewing area. We petted one and found that its feathers were very rough. David was particularly fascinated with some antibiotics that were being given to the hatchlings. This medicine would prevent some infections, but not all, and not infections with something called the Newcastle Virus, which the ostrich farmer had been particularly counting on the drug to prevent. Hamid passed this information on, but who knew what will come of it.

A Bee Farm

Next, Hamid instructed Partha to take us to a bee farm. He gave directions, and it was clear that he would not be going with us – he had more guests to entertain back at his house. Off we went, and Partha found the place. We had to walk towards the back to find anyone, so we looked at beehives as we went.

We found a house with some hijab-clad women on the patio. Instantly, the beekeeper appeared, ushering us into the building to the right, where honey was processed and jarred. He didn't want us going into his house, and when I tried to shake his hand, he offered me his sleeve-covered wrist. I declined in disgust, disguising my reaction from him.

 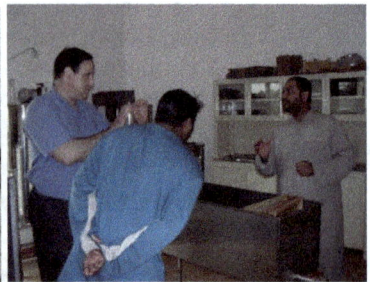

The building where the beeswax was processed; the beekeeper explaining the honey production process.

Honey canisters and finished products with a chart; a vat of honey being prepared.

Beehives: all were outdoors, some in boxes, and some in more familiar-looking slides, one for each hive.

The bee and honey tour was fun; the beekeeper showed us huge vats of honey, a centrifuge for removing the caps from the individual, hexagonal cells, and photo-explanations of different honey-producing stages and processes. We ended up walking back to the gate, where we saw pet dogs running around, rabbits in a hutch with cabbages all around, and a stand and delivery truck. We were given 4 jars of honey as a gift, and then we left.

Looking back at the front of the farm – the hives were behind us; a worker who packed some honey for us.

An Animal Farm

Next, Partha drove us to a palace, through its front gate, around it, out its back gate, and into the farms beyond it. We saw white camels grazing in a field, sheep and donkeys penned together, and greenhouses with tomato vines. The palace was the most interesting, mostly because of its massive gates. We drove right up to the gates. Partha honked the horn until an Indian man pulled one of the huge doors open. The doors were beautiful, traditional Kuwaiti-style ones, with huge nails in rows across them, ending in clusters of 3 nails on either side.

A pair of cheek-to-cheek white camels.

The Al-Dahi palace, built in the traditional Kuwaiti style.

Lunch with Kuwaiti Men

After this, we returned to Hamid's house for lunch. I was the only woman present, but all of the men were pleasant to me, and the nearer ones helped me scoop food onto my plate. The servants and cooks were all Indian men. They had set up lunch on a long, low, white table, with no chairs. We were meant to sit around it on the floor. David and I sat next to each other, and it seemed that this was expected, because this is a culture that normally separates men and women.

Our male hosts seemed to feel perfectly comfortable with my presence there as long as I sat with David. So did I for that matter, though I realized that they were all wealthy Kuwaitis who had traveled in the West and found nothing strange or offensive about me. This is why most Kuwaitis are not bothered by American women as we are – visible with makeup and pretty clothes. They spent the lunch hour talking in Arabic, leaving me to people-watch. Many of them could speak English fluently, but they were enjoying each other's company and leaving me to my own devices most of the time. Two boys, perhaps aged 10 or 11, also ate with us.

The lunch was very interesting to look at: 3 large, round plates had been placed at intervals on the table containing parts of a sheep. The plate in the center contained the sheep's head. As an honor to us, a pair of visiting Americans, we were seated in front of the sheep's head. We were not required to eat it, only to sit in front of it. The plates on either side had that wonderful Arab rice, cooked with saffron and golden raisins plus a little onion and garlic and other spices. On top of that were cooked sheep parts. One plate had its ribs, and the other had its heart and a huge leg and joint. I had some joint meat and rice.

Hamid's dining room: that door led out to the back yard and diwaniya tent; the neatly laid out meal.

David, always the intrepid diner, ate an eye, part of the sheep's tongue and brain, and some of the head meat. He will eat anything! I didn't watch; I just gave him more rice. There were also dishes of lamb and tomato gravy full of vegetables, and a bowl of barley with tomato and other unnamed items inside by each plate. This last was a bit gluey, and almost no one ate it. Everyone had a small plate of salad, and there was water and laban to drink. Most people ate with their fingers, but David and I used the flatware.

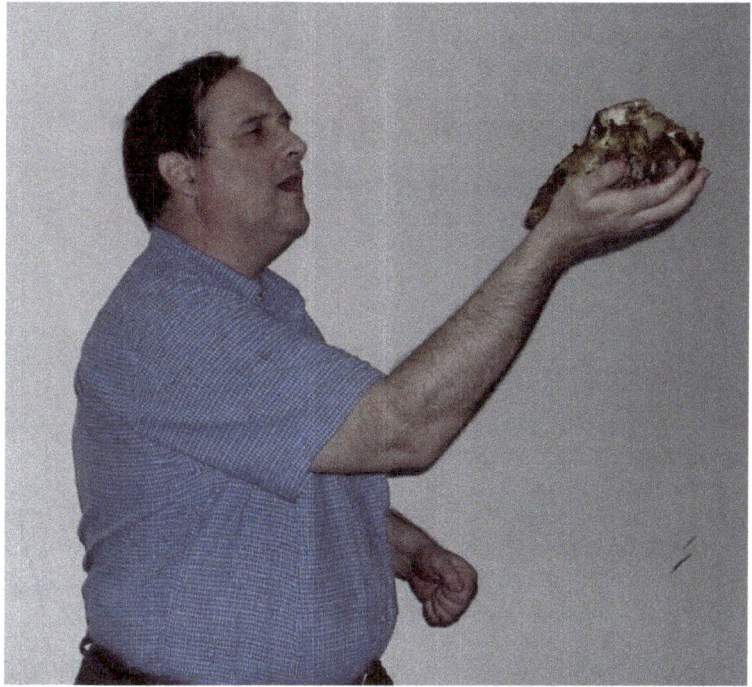

David hammed it up with the sheep's head after the room had cleared: "Alas, poor Yorick!" he said.

After we ate, we were told to eat as much fruit as we liked from the huge pedestal of fruit on display behind us. It was loaded with products from the farms: the best fresh, red, juicy strawberries, bananas, oranges, grapes, etc. A visiting Arab journalist in Western clothing insisted that David, I, and another guest crowd around it and pose eating strawberries so he could take our picture. He intended to publish it the following week. After he left, we stood around eating more strawberries – they were that good.

To the right is the bowl of that wonderful, perfect fruit – especially the red, ripe, juicy, sweet strawberries.

Abu Omran

Next, Hamid told us to go across the street to visit Abu Omran, an old man who had eaten lunch with us. Abu (which means "father of") Omran spoke almost no English, and when he spoke Arabic, it was rather quietly, so David was hard pressed to understand. I managed to sort out a little by guessing. Abu Omran was very old, and his hands had constant tremors. He told us he would soon have open heart surgery in Toulouse, France. His family was away, traveling, and so he was temporarily alone – he thought traveling would be too much bother, he added. All this we found out over Nescafé coffee and mineral water in his house after the grand tour.

The grand tour was great fun. It started with long greenhouses for strawberries and tomatoes. The strawberries were a Spanish variety, grown in neat rows sticking out of thick white plastic. The tomatoes were on long vines suspended on strings from the ceilings of the greenhouses. A foreign employee was working there, and Abu Omran ordered him to package some fresh fruit and vegetables for us. We had no idea that he intended to give us so much stuff until we saw the collection on his porch after the tour. All we knew about was the huge styrofoam tray of strawberries, because he gave it to us outside the strawberry house.

Abu Omran's strawberry greenhouse – they were a Spanish variety; David with a whole carton of them – for us!

Abu Omran had some nice dogs on his farm, one bigger than the others, perhaps the mother of the puppies. They all followed us through patches of herbs and vegetables. All of his patches were made up of several rows of varying items. The first one we saw had fennel, then flat-leaf Italian parsley, then kohl rabi, then eggplant. One corn stalk stood at the beginning of each row. We continued on to see Japanese parsnips, and cabbage and potatoes, then across to see date palms that would bear fruit in 3 more years, plus baby carrots, lettuce, and curly-leaf parsley. Abu Omran was one of McDonald's suppliers (lettuce and tomatoes mostly).

Abu Omran's dogs (shoe thief in front); tomatoes destined for McDonald's; Abu Omran with a Japanese parsnip.

When we had seen all of his crops, we went to his house, which was the first one on the right as we entered the farm. We sat in his living room and he told us about his upcoming heart surgery. There was an old photo of him as a young man next to his uncle on the window sill. Then he took us to the house next door – the women's house – and made coffee for us.

David had dutifully left his sneakers outside – a standard procedure when entering an Arab home – and one was missing when we went out. Of course the mother dog had to have taken it; she was the most mischievous one. Abu Omran knew exactly what she had done with it, and headed wordlessly across the yard to a spot next to the gate. The dog was long gone, but the shoe was there, along with many, many others – only one each from pairs she had robbed! I was glad that I had left my sandals just inside the door…thanks to a vague hunch about that dog.

I took this photograph of Abu Omran calmly walking back to David with the sneaker. He looks so serious in it, with his dark green dishdashah, huge glasses, and red-checked guthra. He seemed not to mind that we thought it was all really hilarious…and there was just a hint of a smile on his face.

To the right, inside the gate to the property, Abu Omran stood in front of his house.

Desert Truffle Mushroom Hunt

Our next outing was to some land where cars were forbidden, because Kuwait's desert truffle mushrooms – called fagaes – grow there, and cars are death to these delicacies. I was reminded of French truffle mushrooms, which are also delicacies, and said so. The Kuwaitis knew all about them, and we briefly discussed how the French train pigs to find the black and white truffles in the forest, letting the leashed animals lead the way.

This was different; someone had been there ahead of us and left styrofoam markers indicating where the biggest mushrooms were. Groups of people crowded around these spots. The Kuwaitis had all come to the hunt with their Indian servants (men), who videotaped the whole event, and some of their children and grandchildren (both boys and girls – the girls were young enough not to be wearing hijabs).

People arriving at the truffle grounds, with little girls and boys.

Kuwaiti men finding the first raised crack that indicated a desert truffle was growing there.

We had a lovely time watching as Kuwaiti men and their servants used sticks to carefully unearth the fagaes without breaking them. They are huge white things, full of sand, and must be carefully washed and cooked into omelets before 2 days pass. There were also some smaller, brown ones that looked like little odd-shaped buttons – bad ones that had started to go moldy. David was given a small piece of one of the big white ones. The way to look for the mushrooms is to find a raised, cracked spot in the dirt. The land was covered here and there with desert brush, a scratchy kind of low bush, plus other plants growing in among the brush with yellow and lilac-colored flowers. A wall surrounded this land.

An Indian servant doing the digging; a big-shot with truffles; Indian servants flanking party guests with the truffles.

Around the corner were two huge, red, woven carpets, where the servants were setting up tea, baklava and a container of delicious sweets including halwa with chocolate on it, and nut paste on top of the chocolate, finished off with green, ground pistachio nuts. The Kuwaitis all grouped around the carpets, each holding some of the huge white truffle, and posed in a row for the 2 newspaper photographers who had come along.

Setting up a photo-op of V.I.P.s on Bedouin carpets with desert truffle mushrooms – fagaes.

It was then that we realized that the purpose of this outing was to serve as a photo-op for showing off Kuwaiti big-shots. Later, I found out who these guys were: the Kuwait Police Major General; the son of the Speaker of the Kuwait National Assembly, the director of the social club for the Ministry of the Interior, and some wealthy landowners, including Fahad Al-Dahi, whose land we were truffle-hunting on. Hamid Al-Qasim posed with them; he was important too, as THE go-between guy of Kuwait, who was responsible for arranging entertainment and security for major social events.

We met a nice Syrian family at this truffle hunt. The father was a journalist, and he was finishing his Ph.D. in Kuwait while supporting the family with his camera. His wife, a pretty lady named Farhanah, smiled and spoke to me a little. She and I did not know enough of each other's languages to talk much. She had long brown-blonde hair, nice makeup, and wore an interesting parka-and-pants outfit. Her children were a 12-year-old girl with a Kuwaiti flag for a scarf on her head, with her long brown hair hanging down her back, and a younger boy. They were quietly having fun running through the groups of Kuwaiti guys as they all crowded around each mushroom site. The journalist wanted to start a university when he returned to Syria.

David chatting with the Syrian couple.

The group of Kuwaiti V.I.P.s posing for a newspaper photo with truffles.

When the photographers left, David asked the police major general – a guy with a brown beard and a grin who wore a Nike hat and a Tommy Hilfiger sweat-suit – about the mushrooms. What the difference between the white one and the little brown one?

The major general pointed at the white one and called it Zubaidy (that is a kind of fin-fish), and then at the little brown one and called it halas (finished or no good). I thought he was teasing, but he was serious.

David held out examples of Zubaidy and halas fagaes/truffles.

We went back to Hamid's house after this and found the men all watching the new truffle hunt video. The first part looked unfamiliar, and they all laughed and said that Fahad, the one with small eyes and a round face, had gone there the day before to confirm the existence of truffles before letting Hamid call the media and his colleagues. He didn't want to be embarrassed by a lack of mushrooms. Then the scene abruptly changed to all of us at the hunt.

A Diwaniya and a Bisht

In the evening, I got a surprising cultural treat: a chance to attend a diwaniya – something that really surprised me, because women never get invited to these events. It was held in the brown and white Bedouin tent at the back of Hamid's yard, and the inside was filled with AlSadu House weavings.

Most of these were beautiful red, white, and black pillows. There were carpets all over the floor, and one side was open. This was the best possible diwan to visit – thanks to its traditional Kuwaiti décor, which was all hand-made by the women of the famous craft museum.

The diwaniya tent shown from the outside in daylight. I realized sometime after our visit that it and its contents were hand-crafted by the women of Al Sadu House in Kuwait City.

A fire was set up in the ground outside, and a large round dish over another, portable fire was off to the far side. The servants used this dish to cook large, sticky crackers, some with beaten eggs inside. We also ate hot chick peas, small fruits called knar with large pits that looked like golden apples and tasted slightly sour, and there was hot milk (halib in Arabic) with sugar, cardamom, and ginger in it. That was absolutely delicious.

Inside, authentic AlSadu House-woven rugs and cushions.

We did not know what the situation was that made my presence there permissible, so we asked Hamid about it. David told him that I was having a great time, and he wondered whether I would be allowed back. That was when Hamid told him that of course I would be welcome again, that this was his diwaniya, so what he says goes, and if the others didn't like it, they couldn't say anything. But they didn't seem to mind me at all; I kept sitting next to my husband, and I was a foreigner anyway. They were quite friendly to me all weekend. This was their weekend fun time, and they spent it chatting merrily in Arabic together most of the time, and sometimes they would speak English for me so that I knew what was happening.

The servants set up an outdoor camp-kitchen to cook for us. They had a table of materials and an open fire.

Here were the treats that we all enjoyed: sticky crackers with egg; knar fruits; cardamom milk; chick peas.

Hamid lent me a brown bisht with brown embroidery on its edges during the diwaniya, because I was cold and Partha had driven to Fahaheel with most of our things still in the car. David took a couple of photos of me wearing it in the diwaniya tent. I had a lovely time, taking photos of the guys at the party, eating and drinking what they had, and looking at the weavings. Hamid confirmed my thoughts about them being from AlSadu House. I wanted to go there.

Me in Hamid's diwan, attending the diwaniya. Hamid is at right; David had gotten up to take the photo.

Several of the V.I.P.s that we had seen at the truffle hunt attended the diwaniya, and this was when the son of Jassem Al-Khorafi, the

Speaker of Kuwait's National Assembly, was pointed out to me. He might have been twentysomething, or in his thirties. All of the guys let me take their photos as they sat around chatting; I preferred candid shots when I could get them. The son of the politician only stayed for a little while; he seemed to be making the diwaniya rounds. I'll bet he didn't usually have the chance to relax and just enjoy a visit – he was too busy networking and helping his father keep track of other people.

The guests at the diwaniya: unknown smiling man; Fahad; Al-Khorafi's son; Abu Omran; more guests chatting.

During the diwaniya, a pair of complete strangers suddenly arrived, and I saw an old Arab custom of hospitality at work. I first learned of it as a kid watching the movie called *The Black Stallion* (of all sources). If a traveler is lost and needs temporary shelter, no matter who he or she is, that individual is given safety, shelter, and food, and is treated as a guest – even if the guest and host are enemies. The 2 guys who arrived were nervous about an extra police checkpoint on the road, and had driven near it 6 times before heading past Hamid's place. They saw his name on the archway and thought that this would be a good place to calm down.

The police were looking for reckless drivers celebrating the holiday weekend, Hamid told them, not traveling salesmen, which is what they turned out to be. The guy in the business suit with the long beard was the more nervous of the two, and he asked what David had in his plastic box, just as a way of making conversation. David had saved the halas and Zubaidy mushrooms. A servant carried it over to him, and he tossed the halas mushroom into his mouth and ate it, to the amazement of everyone around him. David was upset – he had wanted to show them to Mansoor. The police general couldn't get over it, and kept talking about it after the strangers left – "He ate the halas mushroom!" he kept saying. Oh, well…

They began to relax, and we enjoyed seeing the electrolysis gadget that the guy in the suit had. These visitors were trying to market a water filtration system. They had brought some brochures with them. The brochures were in Arabic and English – 2 separate ones – and contained photos of American families washing with water processed by the filters, and drinking it. The one in English was a mess: bad punctuation, poor sentence structure, incorrect words, etc. I gave him my business card and offered to fix it. Hamid immediately said he would arrange it all, just let him do the talking (bit a paying contract from this never happened).

The water filtration gadget: Phase One, Two and Three. Kuwait's water is undrinkable, so it might sell.

After the diwaniya ended, with our computer and everything else back from its ride to Fahaheel, we were given a choice of sleeping in Hamid's house rather than the deserted and remote villa that he had shown us earlier in the day. We chose to stay in the house with him and the others. He informed us that breakfast would be laid out at 5:30 or 6:30 a.m., at the table where we had eaten lunch, next to the entertainment system. Our presence was not expected at that hour; he merely required his servants to present breakfast early, just in case someone wanted to eat early. Hamid planned to sit in his indoor diwaniya room all night, watching the TV in there, because he is an insomniac.

The bedroom we stayed in was just inside this ornate doorway, to the right. It had no lights, and no windows.

We were put in a bedroom next to the bathroom. The bathroom had a bidet, a toilet with no seat, a shower with no curtain, and a sink. Just outside it were 2 more sinks, directly across from our bedroom. It turned out that this was the most private bedroom – the others had glass walls showing inside from the halls! Those rooms had several mattresses on the floor, and the other visiting guys slept in there. They had left their wives at home, so they became roommates.

Meeting a Saudi Wahabi and Tasting Camel's Milk

The next morning I worried about flooding the bathroom, then decided to stop mulling it over and just take a shower and wash my hair. After that I got dressed, did my makeup, and came out with brushed wet hair to eat breakfast. Breakfast was hard boiled eggs, sweet muffins, one flatbread, a little piece of cheese, water, and more of that delicious hot milk. A buffet was arranged down the middle of the table, and people had been sitting down at the table all morning to eat. I did this at approximately 9:30, and a servant showed me the hot milk. Hot tea, milk and Arab coffee (thin and spiced) were on a heated tray at the far end of the table.

The next thing I intended to do was dry my hair, because the weather was going to be overcast and probably rainy, not warm and sunny like the day before. The outlets in Kuwait are all meant for plugs with 2 huge prongs and one bigger square one. The hair dryer has 2 smaller prongs only – not the standard. U.S. outlets can accommodate anything, without further ado, but not Kuwaiti ones. As I looked around, carrying the hair dryer and brush in a plastic bag, something funny happened.

The cheerful, friendly Kuwaiti who was always smiling – Nami was his name (the clubhouse director for the Ministry of the Interior) – rushed up to me and grabbed my wrist, and said he wanted me to meet Fahad Al-Dahi's older brother, who had just arrived from Saudi Arabia, bringing camel's milk with him. Sure enough, here was a guy with a red guthra, brown dishdashah, white beard, and small eyes just like Fahad's. What was missing was a smile. David had told me that Saudi Arabs look just like Kuwaitis but are less friendly, and this one was true to type. All the while, Nami – devilishly and deliberately oblivious to the unpleasant expression on the elder Al-Dahi's face – was grinning and introducing me to him. He knew exactly what he was doing, and he was having some fun.

There I was, a woman with long wet hair, unacceptably uncovered by Saudi standards. Well, I knew what was expected of me, and I did it: grinning broadly and feeling mischievous, I put out my hand and said cheerfully, "Salaam Alaikum!" The guy shook my hand with obvious reluctance, giving it one pump, a socially correct handshake certainly, and then dropped it, never quite meeting my eye, and only grunting vaguely at me. If someone was going to be impolite, I thought, let it be someone other than me! The man obviously felt forced to be polite to me because he couldn't avoid it, and I thought it was hilarious.

Of course I understood that this guy was a Wahabi Muslim. Wahabism is a sect of Sunni Islam which considers the slightest deviation from the original teachings of the Prophet Mohammad to be "kafir" – an example of ungrateful and therefore amoral behavior. The idea is based on some 18th-century scholar's view that innovation in Islam is a bad thing and should be rigidly suppressed. But, this Al-Dahi brother had chosen to cross the border from his insulated society, so I wasn't going to worry about his religious obsessions.

At this point, Nami tried to get me to join him and Fahad's unfriendly brother for a taste of camel's milk. But the joke had gone quite far enough and my hair was wet and cold, so I begged off, showing him the plug for the hair dryer, saying that I didn't know how to plug it in. He said okay, and called the ubiquitous Indian servant to help me. The servant led me back to the bedroom, knelt next to the long extension cord with four standard outlets, and did something that I would not have dared to try: he stuck a piece of clear plastic in the larger part of one outlet, moving something inside the mechanism slightly. He then seized the plug of my hair dryer and put it in. I thanked him, dried my hair, and came out to try the camel's milk.

Finding David out there, I sat down next to him at the table – across from Fahad's brother – and drank a teacup full of camel's milk. Fahad's brother and I ignored each other; the Kuwaitis were perfectly friendly toward me. They did not think I was offensive, and would glance at me and include me in the visit. They never stared; they had traveled extensively, and so had been socialized both in Western and Arab culture. The milk, lower in fat than cow's milk, disagreed with me. It felt, for about 3 hours, as though I had swallowed something metallic. David was surprised, but I am still glad I tried it. The point of travel is to have food adventures and meet new people, after all.

This is Aunt Fill-in-Her-Name – She'll Take Care of You

After I tried the camel's milk, there were a few minutes with nothing to do, so I sat on the sofa facing the television to load photos onto the laptop. The Indian man who had plugged in my hair dryer walked by, saw his photo being labeled, and smiled happily; I grinned back. Everyone was going into my files – not just the elite and guests who were there to have a good time. These were the people who made it all possible while being hurried, bossed, and hardly thanked while living away from their own families for years on end, sending their pay home.

Hamid sat down across from me and told me that his daughters were coming to see him. "That's nice – you'll get to visit with them," I replied. He told me, looking very unhappy, that he didn't like to see them because it reminded him of his divorce. I didn't know what to say to that. My attitude was that he would just have to maintain a relationship with them because they were his, and that was only fair to them. (I was still trying to understand his divorce – and was getting closer to the realization that his wife refused to passively accept him taking a second wife – a co-wife to her – and reproducing again to get sons.)

Hamid's daughters and nanny arrived after this. He had 3 little girls, but the one-year-old wasn't feeling well and had stayed home, so we only met Dalal, aged 5, and Yasmin, aged 2. Their nanny was a middle-aged Indian woman with a braid. She was very patient with them, and they were reasonably well-behaved girls, though the younger one cried annoyingly a few times. I don't like babies and young children, and neither does David, but he can deal with them better than I can. The reason for this is that less attention to children is expected of men – in ANY culture – than is expected of women. I won't coo and fuss over children, even if it's expected.

Hamid said to Dalal, "This is Aunt Stephanie – she will take care of you." With that, I turned and stared a long unhappy glare at David. Then I turned to the little kids and said, "I'm not your aunt, and I won't take care of you – but it's nice to meet you. Now smile, I'm going to take your pictures to give to your father later." They did, and I shot a few good ones.

Any other response spoken by me would most likely have led to being required to stay close to the little kids all day and fuss over them – an unacceptable outcome. I had been having a great time, and I would not have it ruined. I knew about this Middle Eastern custom, but I would not go along with it. I had made up my mind about this a few months earlier, when I read an article about it.

David told Hamid a few minutes later, aside, that I don't like to be expected to fuss over children. The pressure stopped. This is a culture that loves children and expects every woman to want nothing more than to have babies, and neither David nor I wish to have any. The world is overpopulated as it is anyway! David is the best husband in the world; he sat in the back with the nanny and the kids while we toured more farms, removing me from more annoying expectations. No one expected him to fuss over the kids! This pressure would come up every now and then, and I would refuse to cave in to it every time.

Recently, David told me that something funny had happened before and after that. Before the children arrived, when I was not in the living room, Hamid was pacing up and down, rubbing his hands together, saying, "My children are coming – Stephanie will love this!" David looked at him as if he were speaking gibberish. Hamid would just have to learn from experience, David decided.

After I had met the kids and left the room: the Kuwaiti men had come in and sat down on the sofas to watch television. Hamid must have told them what had happened, because they all inadvertently mimicked the Munchkins of *The Wizard of Oz*, repeating in tones of wonder, "Stephanie doesn't like little kids?" "Stephanie doesn't like little kids..." I like older people – they have great knowledge, life experience, and stories. People should only have kids if they really want them – otherwise, it's not fair to the kids.

300,000 Dinar Worth of White Camels

Our next trip was to Fahad's palace farms again to see the 3 white camels again. They cost 100,000 KD apiece, so we were looking at over a million dollars' worth of camel. Camels can be white, black, red, or brown...different people choose different colored camels. Price is determined by the quality and health of the animals. One slobbered all over Hamid's leather jacket as he posed with me and the little girls – David got a photo of that. Partha rushed over and mopped at the slobber with Kleenex. Then we got back into the car and followed Hamid in his white pickup truck to the next event. He never rode with his daughters – he just drove separately ahead of us all. David piled into the back seat with the nanny and the girls.

Here we all are, posing with the out-priced camels, and the one on the left is slobbering all over Hamid. The one on the right promptly took over that job for the next photo.

The Friday Farmers' Market

The next stop was the Friday Market – a farmers' market in the town of the Wafra Oasis. As we drove into the parking lot, we noticed teenagers and younger kids with cans of white foam, which they were spraying at passing vehicles – celebrating Independence and Liberation Days in a most annoying fashion. It made seeing to drive safely a chore, and more than once Partha had to wipe down his windows before we returned to Hamid's house.

The market was great – we saw lots of birds and fowl for sale, every kind of fruit and vegetable plus some eggs on display, even a rose bush in the back of a truck, and some sheep and goats. All of these birds and animals were alive and in cages and pens, and two brown horses were tied off to one side. The birds and fowl for sale were great fun to see: guinea hens, pigeons, geese, chickens, chicks, ducks – any species one might wish for, it seemed.

Horses and chickens under the market roof.

Radishes, beets, carrots…a gourmet chef's paradise.

Eggplants, tomatoes, strawberries, tomatoes, eggs…

…even a rosebush was brought in for sale.

The market was under a huge open roof, and it was full of vendors, mostly Indian employees of rich landowners, and all male. A few women walked around in abbeyas, some with nekhabs, and some without. I was the only bareheaded one, and the only American.

The main selling floor of the Friday Market; caged guinea hens; very tightly caged roosters for sale.

Lots of Kuwaitis were wandering around. We found Nami, happy and smiling as usual. I took a nice photo of him with Hamid, Dalal and Yasmin. I liked those girls well enough – I just didn't want to assume a care-giving relationship with them, even for a short visit.

Fair prices for fowl! Just kidding – I don't know how much they wanted for geese, pigeons and ducklings.

Hamid seemed to be paying lots of attention to them at the market, picking them up and talking to them. Good – he wasn't ignoring them. It wasn't like he could send them back, as though someone got his order wrong in a restaurant. Girls are smart and interesting, but they weren't what he wanted.

A Kid's Zoo

After this, we went to a kids' animal park, where people were riding horses, looking at goats, and a giant domed cage held lots of chickens. Hamid talked to Dalal, asking her to tell us about the time he arranged for the park to be open just for his kids for a whole day, and the huge domed cage had contained monkeys. One had escaped after scaring Dalal, who told her nanny to put her on her shoulders and run – cool thinking under pressure at age 3.

After recalling that, Hamid bought some of that canned foam for his daughters, and promised to withhold it until they got home. At least Hamid was paying attention to his children personally, I thought. But I thought wrong.

Reckless Entertainment

Onward we drove with Partha, to see another farm – without Hamid but with vague directions. We never got there. Poor Partha got lost and nervous, apologized that he had only had this job for a month, and we realized that he was still learning where everything was in Kuwait without a map. What a difficult task. We told him it didn't matter, just relax and slow down, and don't worry – we wouldn't tell Hamid that he couldn't find the place.

It was raining, and a crazy teenage driver in an orange car scared us all, so we went home and swore to Hamid that that was why we didn't see the farm. We even took down the license plate number: 15373. The idiot kid was showing off by spinning the back wheels of the car on the wet pavement, and we thought he would kill someone. Partha was very upset, and had trouble skidding around in the mud. The nanny stayed calm, though, so the kids did, too. Predictably, the cops were nowhere in sight. We told Partha to pull over and relax for a minute, which helped.

Lunch at a Harim

The next item on the agenda was lunch, a much talked about event that was to include fish. I was excited, because we don't get to eat much fish. As it turned out, I was expected to leave and go eat with Fahad's wife, Talibah. I must have looked alarmed at the thought of leaving David and going elsewhere, because Fahad said to me, "Please visit my wife," so I said I would go. (David later told me that the fish was dried out and terrible.) Before going there, I was told that they were honored that Americans were there, and that Fahad's wife would love to meet me. He was perfectly at ease with me hanging out with the guys, accepting that this is normal for an American woman, but there was no way that he could bring her among them.

I did not want to go, but felt forced to, and it was not until I returned and David explained what was going on that it began to make sense and seem less awful for me but much more awful for Talibah. Until that happened, all I knew was that I was being dragged to a harim – a house for only women and children – where I could count on being harangued yet again about having babies and quizzed about my life. Sure enough, this is exactly what happened. However, the harassment came not from Talibah but from her teenage daughters and nieces.

There were some boys there too, but they were quiet. I recognized the 2 boys from the lunch the day before, and said "hi" to them, and then the girls crowded all around me, asking lots of personal questions. I immediately found myself surrounded, ambushed, and in airhead land. I have met lots of teenagers, some very interesting and intelligent people, but not these kids. They loved McDonald's, *American Idol*, *Titanic*, and babies.

They had absorbed the worse aspects of American culture. It was hell. I didn't even have a chance to meet Talibah at first – I had no clear idea where she was, or which of the women in the next room she might be. The moment I walked in the door, the kids surrounded me and herded me into the next room, where they ordered me to sit.

The house had 2 huge living rooms side by side, with beautiful, matching décor: huge Persian carpets, pretty curtains, and pretty sofas. This was the women's living room and visiting area. The first living room was where the women and toddlers and nanny sat; it was a Bedouin-style room, with cushions around the perimeter of the room forming sofas. The second living room was exactly the same but with Western-style sofas running continuously around half of the room. This was where the teenagers hurried me to. A bathroom was visible through a door between these two rooms.

Once I was seated, 2 Indian maids abruptly appeared with a tray containing 2 dishes of mixed nuts, a plate of cookies, a plate of 2 slices of delicious saffron cake, a plate of chapatti bread, and a cup of tea with milk in it. One maid brought this while another dragged over a small table for it. These maids looked like sisters; they were smiling, they were dark with long, frizzy braids, and had on long housedresses. Perhaps they were happy because they really were sisters and had found a job together. Off to the side was a depressing sight, though: another maid with a beautiful face, a white hijab, a long pants outfit, and a very sad expression. I gave her a weak smile, but it is very hard to look cheerfully at someone who is so obviously unhappy with her life. I felt terrible for her – who would want to be a maid, I thought?!

Americans just don't have them unless they are super-rich and live in mansions – not a common thing.

About the teenagers: Talibah had 3 children, an 11-year-old boy and 2 older girls. One girl was pretty and somewhat thoughtful – I thought she might turn out well when she was older and went to school. Her name was Najwa, and she had a long dark braid. She was probably fifteen years old. She sat to my right. Her cousin Munirah sat with us and went on and on and on about *American Idol* and how its contestants cheat a lot – as if the show mattered. This girl was somewhat pretty, but she wasn't very interesting. She told me that she tells everyone to call her Monica rather than make them learn her name properly.

Other, slightly younger girls sat nearby, listening, but saying nothing. They let the older girls run the conversation. The first thing I heard was in incredulous tones: "No sugar in your tea?!" as I stopped the maids from adding it. One of the sisters had seized the tongs and grabbed a cube of sugar as soon as she set the tray in front of me. (The question actually sounded less insane coming from children than it did when Egyptian guys in restaurants asked it.)

And then there was the other sister: she might have been fourteen; I wasn't sure. She was overweight, and had a long dark ponytail. (She was the one who had asked about the sugar. I pointed out all the sweets on the tray: "Here is the sugar – I don't need any more.) When her mother came in to talk to me, I found out why she was so heavy: she loved McDonald's, and ate no fruit – just sweets and other junk.

These kids made pests of themselves and then went outside to spray that horrible white foam at anyone and everyone in the vicinity. Would I like to join them? Absolutely not, I answered. I stayed and faced the tray of goodies, thinking sadly that I could probably just forget about a real lunch while the guys all ate fish. I enjoyed the chapattis, one slice of the cake, and drank my tea, grateful that it had milk. I also managed to head off one of the cheerful Indian maids, who tried again to add huge cubes of sugar to it.

At last, Talibah came in to talk with me, her loud and persistent children, nieces and nephews gone for the time being. This lady was very interesting. I was glad to have met her...and sad. Between her English and my Arabic, we had a labored but fun conversation. Her children spoke English almost as well as Americans, but she didn't.

She told me that she knew lots of geography, and had a master's degree in history. She had traveled extensively around Europe, and she particularly enjoyed the green vistas of Austria, especially the towns and villages near Salzburg. She knew that Salzburg was Mozart's home town. She used to teach history at a girls' high school, until she became the headmistress. When she had her children, she retired. It was her husband's wish that she become a housewife, and not go out any more.

Her own mother had had 10 children, 5 daughters and 5 sons, all of whom attended graduate school. Her sister was an oncologist. Talibah did not want 10 kids – she was tired after having 3. I didn't blame her. Talibah had a gold front tooth, and she asked how old I was: 35, I answered. How old was she, I asked? "I am old," she said. "No you aren't," I said. Yes, I am 40 years old. (At this point I was shocked – she looked like she was 60 years old! But my acting skills passed muster – I concealed my reaction.)

"That is young in America," I said. Talibah's children had said that 40 and 50 are old ages when they were haranguing me…I had replied that I did not think so, and that this was not a very good thing to say to someone whose husband would soon be 50 – plus he looked much younger than that. Had I married a Kuwaiti guy, the kids asked? No, an American – I showed the photo in my wallet. Who did I work for? No one – I am an independent writer and editor.

When were done chatting, she called for lunch to be brought to me. It was a tasty meal of chicken on saffron rice with fried onion bits and golden raisins. It felt odd to eat this after having had cake and cookies, but there was nothing to be done about that. I glanced up from it and found the beautiful maid staring at me. She looked very unhappy. I tried to smile at her in a friendly manner, but she continued to look terribly sad.

I wondered about her life. She probably had to stay in Kuwait for at least 2 years (or 3, depending upon her contract), away from her family while she sent her pay home to them. She probably wondered why I looked upset; I was feeling stressed from noise and too much social interaction at once. That was nothing she ought to worry about, however, I thought to myself.

After I ate, I got up and used the bathroom, which was nicely tiled and clean – though the floor was all wet and soaked my socks. Then I went to find Talibah again. She was sitting in the other living room, on the floor with a neighbor from across the street. This woman was pregnant and covered with a black abbeya and hijab. She was nice, but didn't seem terribly bright; she had covered the top joints of every finger with black magic marker because it amused her older children. Poor Talibah – this was what she could look forward to for conversation. It was a shame – she was so smart and intelligent.

It was a sad outing. When Partha reappeared, I almost leapt from the room.

Back at Hamid's house, I found David and whispered to him, almost in tears, that I had had a miserable time. (I did not realize that the stress of the day was giving me an Aspie meltdown – that was a concept that we would learn about a few years later.)

David wanted to hear all about it, so he led me right to the bedroom. Then he told me that Hamid had told him that Talibah is desperately unhappy, because she never goes anywhere and is trapped in this hellish, air-headed environment all the time, and she grasps at any chance to meet interesting people and talk to them. I could see that – that rather dull woman was likely her only company. It just made it all the more upsetting; I feel strong empathy for nice, intelligent people who are unhappy.

I felt sorry for Talibah and that sad maid. This is what happens when an intelligent woman lives in a closed society. She knew interesting things, thought interesting thoughts, and was trapped inside her mind and her boring, closed environment. She couldn't return to work; she had to go from one of her husband's many houses to another, following her husband's schedule while never being included in the fun and interesting events of it. Islamic societies are closed – there are many, many limits on tourism, and women do not go out into the open much, even where their governments do not demand hijabs or nekhabs.

Once again, I was SO glad to be an American, and to be included in as many of the interesting parts of life as possible, either thanks to my husband sharing them with me, such as the weekend in Wafra Oasis, or to my own connections. I know that as a secular American woman, I have many more opportunities for an interesting and happy life than this wealthy, comfortable Kuwaiti woman did. I did not have wealth or financial security, but I have a great husband who is my best friend. He would never try to make my world narrower, or try to control me. Visiting this harim made me appreciative of my life, culture and husband.

Abu Khalid's Fish Farm

Before we went home, Hamid wanted us to visit one more farm – Abu Khalid's farm. We saw strawberries, eggplant, cucumbers, fish, olive trees, and horses. Abu Khalid and his son showed us the Nile River fish that they were raising in huge concrete pools, and took one out to show us. They threw it back after we had seen it. Abu Khalid spoke no English, but was determined to drive us to every interesting thing on his farm. He was a very serious but nice person, and a good host.

The fish farm had long pools that stretched across most of the property.

Abu Khalid stood at one end of the tanks.

We drank tea in their weekend house, and met the daughter and son-in-law. The daughter was happy – no hijab, and rather beautiful. She was wearing jeans and had her dark hair down long, loose and attractively styled. The son-in-law was very nice – a journalist and former Kuwaiti Army chemical weapons officer. David enjoyed talking with him.

Here is Abu Khalid with his son Khalid, showing David some pickling cucumbers, which were grown on strings.

Abu Khalid's name was also Khalid, by the way. Here was his son-in-law, the Kuwaiti Army chemical weapons officer, with David, the U.S. Army chemical weapons officer. It was cool, to say the very least. ☺

After this, we thanked Abu Khalid and his family, and went back to Hamid's house with Partha and the nanny and the little girls to get ready to leave.

The Drive North

It was after dark, and as we gathered our things, the power went out in half of the house – predictably, the half where our stuff was – so David didn't realize that he was forgetting to pack his blue shirt and black pants. Off we went in the rain, and we all told Partha to drive slowly, not to hurry. There was no reason to hurry, we said, and the nanny translated for us – we didn't want to die in a car crash.

Someone else did, though: halfway back, we were in a long traffic jam. We got close to the source after a while and saw cars merging right, and police lights. Then we saw a blue work truck – a huge one – that had crashed through the cement barrier, jackknifed around in the opposite direction, and then lethally and messily ejected the poor driver through the windshield. David saw blood on the pavement; the body was gone, and a crew was trying to figure out how to remove the truck. Some poor foreign worker was dead. He wouldn't be sending money home to his family any more, and they would never see him again.

The kids and nanny got dropped off at home in Shamiya, just south of Kuwait City, and then Partha took us home. We made him come in for a cup of tea – after almost 2 hours of stressful driving in a rainstorm, we didn't want him to go right back out without a rest. It is safer to pause in the middle of a big job like that. He had his tea and then took off. Hamid probably wanted him to come right back, but we knew he wouldn't die if his servant took proper care of himself. After Partha left, I relaxed, cleaning the laundry, painting my toenails, and eating more of Abu Omran's wonderful strawberries.

We had a great weekend, and Hamid welcomed us to visit again.

Truffle-Hunting in the News

About a week after the fun at Wafra Oasis, we stopped at a convenience store at 3:30 a.m., found the newspaper that Assim had seen with the photo of the mushroom hunt. David grabbed one and bought it for me. Sure enough, there was a photo on its front page of the was in Arabic, so I couldn't read the picture's short caption, and truffle hunters, including Fahad Al-Dahi, the Kuwait Police Major General (I still didn't know his name), and Nami Al-Hamdullilah. The whole paper I didn't know who the other 3 guys in the picture were, but I didn't care. I had my cool souvenir! The title of the newspaper was *Al-Qabas*. There was nothing in English, so I just saved it, and didn't worry about reading it.

Chapter 18
The Museums and Crafts of Kuwait

I had warned my workaholic husband that I would not accompany him to Kuwait only to sit quietly in the apartment or in some office waiting area all the time while he worked nonstop, day in and day out, and then went off to an endless series of meetings without me. The travel guide to the Middle East had a section on Kuwait, with a list of the nation's museums. Armed with this smattering of data, I curious to study the place, I also wanted a collection of books to take home at the end of the trip. I was also determined to have a wonderful time in Kuwait, and to create something of my own: a written and visual memory of it all.

Shortly after arriving, I found a book which served as a taste of wonderful cultural experiences to come: it was about a British expatriate who had lived in Kuwait with her husband, a member of the British Foreign Service. It was his wish that she remain in their house after his death. She really liked Kuwait.

When she spent summers in England, she would say to people, "Can you believe that they actually don't serve dates with the coffee?!" Her own culture had become foreign to her. Queen Elizabeth II knighted her – Dame Violet Dickson. She was often called Umm Saud, after the Arab custom of calling mothers by their oldest son. Her house is still standing in Kuwait City, on Arabian Gulf Street near Seif Palace, and when I told David about it and showed him the book, it was settled: we intended to tour it.

AlSadu House and Kuwait National Museum

On March 10th, we went to 2 museums in one afternoon. The 2 places, Kuwait National Museum and AlSadu House, are next-door neighbors, enclosed within the same walls and facing Kuwait Bay on Arabian Gulf Street in Kuwait City. [We had attempted to visit previously and found the place locked with no explanation, despite a sign that listed the hours…which included the time at which we had arrived. I had been very upset, imagining that we would waste our time trying to visit, and waste cab fare, never being able to rely upon any information about a Kuwaiti site. David said that I had sized up the situation correctly.]

But the second time was the charm in every sense of the phrase. We went out to Souq Sharq, and then on to the museums...and everything was open! We saw everything in great detail, taking our time. That is what we both consider enjoying a place when traveling. As I said to David on the way out of the museums, I can tell that I married judiciously, because we both believe that it doesn't compute to come to a faraway place – even if it is to work – and not visit its museums and cultural centers. David said "likewise" with a big smile on his face.

Arriving and Entering

When it was time to leave for the museums, we went outside to hire a cab. It seemed that because we were at a ritzy place, the taxi drivers at Souq Sharq were trying to fleece us of as much cash as possible, demanding 1.5 KD to take us just a short distance away, just down the street! David held out until he found one for 1 KD, but he thought .5 KD would have been more reasonable, considering how close our destination was to the mall. Off we went though, for 1 KD, and were soon walking into the guardhouse of the Kuwait National Museum.

The guardhouse was a little odd; the metal detector was turned off, and the guards did not search my handbag. All they wanted us to do was leave our bags of groceries next to the desk, where one guard was sitting reading. We did, and they were still there when we were ready to leave. We walked through the metal detector, and they didn't even turn it on or turn on the X-ray machine. They really must not be worried about the artifacts on display, I thought. Or perhaps they assumed that Americans would never hurt them after getting rid of the Iraqis.

We came out the other side of the guardhouse and found ourselves heading down a long paved driveway with palm trees and flowers in the parking lot, facing the museum buildings. The buildings are 3 identical modern structures with empty water fountains. The grounds are pleasant, with more small gardens lining the edges of the walkways.

To the right is AlSadu House, an old Sharq area, gypsum and coral building with huge, carved wooden doors that have curved, pointed arches made of glass and wood above them. AlSadu House itself was a mess; it was under restoration and therefore closed to the public.

The door to AlSadu house. The gypsum and coral house, a historic building on Arabian Gulf Street, was undergoing extensive restoration. It is over 100 years old, so it wasn't surprising that it needed work.

Not a problem, though: Bayt Al-Badr House, built between 1838 and 1848, was right next door – touching AlSadu House, in fact. This house is an example of traditional Kuwaiti architecture, complete with huge, heavy doors with rows of metal nail-bolts that end on either side in clusters of three. It was convenient that the weaving society could keep its displays there until their building was fully restored.

The first place we walked to, however, was the Heritage Museum of the Kuwait National Museum. We approached and realized that it was only in the building on the left; the other two were still empty shells, gutted by the Iraqi invaders 14 years earlier. Only one of the 3 had been restored and reoccupied. The artifacts used to fill all 3 buildings, but the Iraqis destroyed or stole them all. The stolen things were eventually returned, but many of them were damaged.

This was the sight that greeted us upon entering the museum gates: 3 buildings and a courtyard. Only the building to the left contained any exhibits; when we looked into the other 2, they were dark and full of concrete rubble, still not restored from the Iraqi invasion. AlSadu House was on the right, before the fountain, which was empty.

As we came closer to the Heritage Museum, we noticed that several wooden benches were set up along either side in front of the door. A worker was putting out AlSadu cushions and lining the seats of the benches with AlSadu rugs. They were all very colorful and beautiful. A guard was seated on the bench closest to the door, and I started excitedly photographing all of the AlSadu things.

At left is the guard who greeted us; he waited for museum visitors on these benches.

Another museum employee put out cushions and cloths woven at AlSadu house, which was located across the courtyard.

The guard stayed seated, but immediately began pointing at my camera and at a huge sign in English next the door – it forbade photography inside the museum. He did not speak English, but it wasn't difficult to figure out what he was trying to tell us. I let him see that I understood, and then pointed in the direction of AlSadu house – was it open now? Yes, he nodded.

AlSadu House – The Cooperative Women's Weaving Society

David was a bit reluctant to go back, but I insisted – AlSadu House was what I had been begging to see for weeks, and I wasn't sure that it would stay open if we waited. That persuaded him, and we went across and into the courtyard of Bayt Al-Badr House. A center display of Bedouin-style teapots decorated the courtyard, and off to the side was (under an overhang to protect it from the elements) a huge, elaborate baby's cradle made entirely of Bedouin weavings.

The courtyard of Bayt Al-Badr House, temporary hostess to AlSadu House.

A cradle woven by its craftswomen.

Off to the left as we came in, we noticed 2 women with ponytails taking pictures of a small room, and we followed them. I went in, taking photos. It was a room full of things for sale. There were small mats, table runners, rugs, bags, and other things. Prices ranged from 6 to 40 KD.

I had intended to buy one souvenir for myself plus one each for my aunt (an artist), and David's 2 sisters. I chose 4 bags, and found a book on the weavings when we went to the next room to pay. A Kuwaiti man in casual Western clothing was on duty there. Not a single Bedouin woman was in sight; they all leave at 1:30 p.m. They only weave in the mornings.

Looking back at the entrance to the courtyard (the door on the left). Above it is the Kuwait Communications Liberation Tower, built after the war, and not open to the public.

The next room was another shopping area, with larger, more expensive items – mostly rugs. I did not see any pillows; perhaps Hamid had specially commissioned his. According to the book I bought, Bedouin people couldn't travel with pillows, so they were a relatively new product, begun since giving up their nomadic lifestyle for a settled one in modern Kuwait.

The door to the left of the palm tree led to the room with the merchandise, and the door at the extreme right led to the bookshop.

The room with the wall hangings and rugs that were for sale.

We walked down the courtyard and found 2 more rooms of interest; one room had several looms laid out in one long row, with a couple of baskets of yarn of varying colors across from them. There was also a long stick with some yarn wound around one end of it – a spindle. At the end of the room was a huge brown-and-white wool thing, a tent like Hamid Al-Qasim's diwaniya tent – a monument to the old nomadic Bedouin lifestyle. There were some colorful seat cushions on several of the looms, and a display of wool types: mohair, cashmere, alpaca, etc.

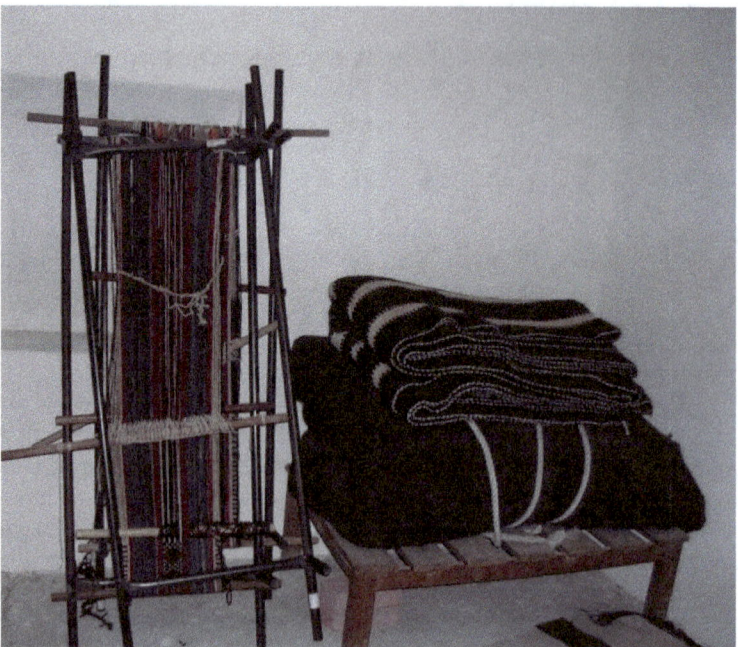

This was where the Kuwaiti Women's Cooperative Weaving Society met to produce its famous textiles.

Moving on down the courtyard, we went to the room, where completed items are arranged as if in a living room. Outside were 2 more examples of looms, one a traditional style, which Bedouin women used to disassemble, pack up, and reassemble in the sand, flat, when they got to their next camp site, and a new, experimental, upright style loom. We also saw some wool out there, and a sheep-skin.

2 forms of Bedouin looms: traditional, and the new experimental upright one.

Inside was a room decorated entirely with AlSadu weavings: pillows, rugs, runners, looms, and 2 tapestries (one at either end) propped up on easels. The room was a lovely profusion of reds, whites, and blacks, with a few other colors here and there in the weavings.

Every design was represented here: the most complex one, Al Shajarah, was prevalent throughout the display, as were a couple of others, most notably the 'Uwairjan and the Midhkhar. No one was around, or I might have watched the video. The machine was turned off, so David and I contented ourselves with photographing it all and looking at the room very carefully.

At left is an example of the Al-Shajarah weave pattern – black-and-white parts – stripes in the red of a wall hanging. Across to the right, a pair of long couches were laid out with more of these beautiful things, including pillows that depicted Air Force planes and traditional-style Kuwaiti earrings, which are long, flat, wide things. Paintings of old Kuwaiti buildings – perhaps scenes of AlSadu House itself – were arranged in the nooks above the couches.

AlSadu House is an independent cooperative weaving society which aims at preserving Bedouin skills and heritage by making sure that the craft is remembered by both Kuwaitis and foreigners. Most of the weavers are aging women who need to find younger women with an interest in learning this millennia-old skill. There are some younger women, but not many.

The door into the display room with the video setup; a pillow; another pillow next to an upright loom.

The view to the right after entering the display room: the woman in the picture next to the wall hanging is the award-winning weaver, Abab Farhan Al-Azmy, a.k.a. Umm Nasser. She lost her son (Nasser) during the Gulf War, and weaves war planes into her Al-Shajarah patterns.

The most famous of the weavers is Umm Nasser – her real name is Abab Farhan Al-Azmy. She won the 1996 prize for Women's Creativity in Rural Life at the Women's World Summit Foundation in Geneva, Switzerland. We enjoyed seeing that a woman from a closed society had won fame and recognition for her achievements.

The Kuwait National Museum

After this, we returned to the Kuwait National Museum to see the Heritage display and, upstairs, the ancient Greek and Bronze Age and Stone Age artifacts from Failaka Island and the other small islands offshore from mainland Kuwait. We first walked through a long series of mannequin displays of scenes from old Kuwait – Kuwait as it used to be before oil wealth changed it. This was followed by exhibits housed behind glass of jewelry, writing implements, pearl grading and measuring instruments, old documents of Sheikh Mubarak the Great, and then some old, framed photographs of people in early 20th-century Kuwait.

The guard kept reappearing every now and then to make sure that we weren't taking any photographs. David insisted that I do so and kept a vigilant lookout while I did it, enabling me to photograph a small version of a Kuwaiti door with the nail-bolts and a door-knocker, plus several beautifully executed scenes of pre-oil Kuwaiti life: a coffee house, a diwan, a bridal chamber and a madrassah school, complete with life-size dolls in traditional costumes.

Another woman who was taking pictures wasn't so lucky; I saw the guard coming and hid my camera, trying to warn her about him. But he had seen the flash, and he spent several minutes scolding her. My husband is such a rule-breaker so, to please him, I took a few photos. ☺

This scene shows a Kuwaiti coffee house being patronized by ship-owners who would wait inside until sailors came to find them and apply for jobs on their ships, for merchant voyages to Madagascar and India.

A Kuwaiti bridal chamber: it has a beautiful bed, and the bride is wearing a traditional Kuwaiti gown in green and gold. Her husband is wearing a cream-colored bisht with gold embroidery and tassel-ties.

When we were finished looking at everything, we went around to the side of the museum that is closest to Arabian Gulf Street (hidden from the street by a high wall) and saw a huge boom on display, with a large brown-and-white Bedouin tent. Unfortunately, it was after dark at this point, so the photos I took aren't worth showing. After that, we took a cab home. The driver was an Indian man who did an excellent job; after running up against a traffic jam, he wove the vehicle through every back road in Abraq Khaitan to get us quickly to our building. I was impressed and told him so – I added that that is exactly how I drive in America, using back roads to avoid heavy traffic.

This is a reproduction of a traditional Kuwaiti door (to nowhere!); note the clusters of bolts on one side. The scene next to it depicts a group of men hanging out and relaxing at a local diwan, playing a game of damma, which is like checkers. The pieces are round, domed wooden things that are moved on a symmetrical grid.

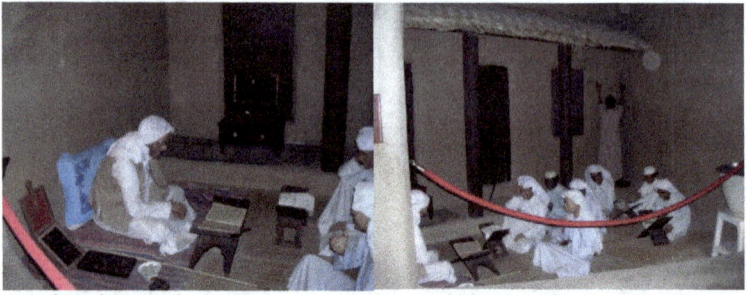

A madrassah scene: the teacher leans over a Quran, which must never touch the floor, so it rests on this stand. The method of learning is by rote, and the unfortunate boy in the corner with his arms over his head made a mistake in his recitation of the holy book. Who knew how long teachers would drag that punishment out…

I loved seeing that there are craftspeople and artisans of Kuwait who still practice their old arts rather than letting them die because modern conveniences have relieved them of the necessity of practicing them. Bedouin weavers who win international prizes, such as Umm Nasser did in 1996, are wonderful examples of Kuwaiti culture.

Unfortunately, the reading materials that I found on this expedition told me that other crafts are endangered.

Bisht weavers and embroiderers are no longer working in Kuwait now that wool can be bought from importers. A bisht is that beautiful outer garment that Kuwaiti men wear over their dishdashahs in the winter or at ceremonial occasions. Our friend Assim Al-Tikriti wore a nice black one with standard gold embroidery on the edges for his wedding (I remember seeing it in his and Aiesha's wedding pictures). They also come in grey, brown, beige and cream (I wore a brown one at the Wafra Oasis). So where are bishts made now? The answer is Saudi Arabia, for one place, but not Kuwait.

Boom and dhow builders are no longer constructing ships, because there is no longer any demand for them – except perhaps from museums. Even the old Kuwaiti style of architecture is no longer practiced, thanks to the ready availability of concrete. The remaining historic buildings in the old style – with the wood for their doors imported from India – are the ones that have undergone historic preservation efforts.

Dickson House

Just 2 weeks later, we enjoyed an absolutely fantastic museum visit at Dickson House. At approximately 2:30 p.m., Assim picked us up. Before leaving, he very sweetly and patiently photographed us. We were both dressed up; I wore my hair down with a blue flowered dress. People were starting to ask us for photographs of us, so I wanted to get a nice shot ready to print.

After this, Assim drove us to Dickson House, passing Al-Ostad Street – a salute to Aiesha's boom-building ancestors – a street with a sign marking it, which used to connect to Arabian Gulf Street. He pulled in next to the house, giving us a view of Dickson House to our right, and a lot with an ancient, crumbling Kuwaiti house on our left, set back from Arabian Gulf Street.

We could see that it was a traditional Kuwaiti home, with a diwan courtyard in the middle. Assim told us that that piece of property was worth at least 1 million KD. We knew why without being told: location, location, and location. We all laughed and he drove off.

The million-dinar piece of property with the ruins of an old Kuwaiti mansion next to the Dickson House museum.

Dickson House was beautifully kept, whitewashed with all of it balconies painted a lovely shade of bright blue, with flags out front, a huge traditional Kuwaiti door made of wood with clusters of bolts at the outside ends of its rows of bolts, and brass name plates identifying it as Dickson House in English and Arabic. Another brass plate listed the museum's opening hours in English and Arabic. The numbers were readable to us, but the weekdays were all in Arabic. We looked around outside, took each other's photos in front of the house, and entered, looking up at the palm-leaf ceiling as we went.

Dickson House, facing Arabian Gulf Street, showing its wooden front door and posting of museum hours.

The front hall contained many items attesting to the history of Kuwait: AlSadu weavings; a huge model of a boom with a Kuwaiti flag on it; a large brass plaque listing the museum's founders; a large guestbook with muted photos on each page of the front of Dickson House; framed old photos of the house and Kuwait City in black-and-white; and a huge Arabic and English copy of an agreement between the Turks, the British, and Kuwaiti Sheikh Mubarak I the Great aimed at keeping Kuwait independent by allowing the foreigners to think that the Turks owned the place and the Brits would not have to worry about losing control of Kuwaiti territory to other Europeans. A hall leading perpendicularly off of this one contains photo portraits of all of the British Foreign Political Agents to Kuwait, up until 1961, when Kuwait was officially declared independent.

The front hallway is a testimonial to Kuwait's history and culture, with a model of a boom and portraits of sheikhs and British Foreign Political Agents, including Harold Dickson.

A copy of the 1899 Treaty between Kuwait and Britain, signed by Sheikh Mubarak the Great and British officials, promising that Kuwait would only deal with the British – no other foreign powers. At right is the front hall, with the guest book on the left, and Faiz Moh'd Khan's room at the end. He was Dame Violet's house companion in her old age, and now he gives tours at the museum twice each week.

This mud-brick house was built in 1899, and in 1904 it became the base of the British Foreign Political Agent. Harold Dickson was the British Political Agent from 1929 to 1936. The Dicksons liked this house so much that they returned to it after briefly living in a newer building, and never moved out of it until Dame Violet had a stroke in April of 1990. The house is whitewashed every year, as it was when they lived in it, and although the back courtyard has been paved with brick, it was a packed dirt and sand yard when the Dickson family lived there.

Dame Violet, also known as Umm Saud, when she was young.

Harold Dickson, the British Foreign Political Agent.

The Iraqis had looted this house just as they had looted many other places, and Iraqi soldiers had occupied it. When the Kuwaitis returned, Sheikh Saad Al-Sabah, the Crown Prince, who had known Dame Violet personally, was determined to restore the house and turn it into a museum. To accomplish this, he contacted Faiz Moh'd Khan, Dame Violet's Pakistani servant. We were lucky enough to meet him yesterday. Faiz Khan had lived with Dame Violet because she needed someone to stay with her in her later years, with her husband dead and her children living in other countries. He had a job with Kuwait Airways at the airport, and he sent money home to his relatives while living in a room at the left end of the front hall of Dickson House.

The Iraqis had stolen most of Faiz's things, except for some important papers that he had just taken home on a recent visit, but it is still his room. Sheikh Saad set him up as a tour guide at Dickson House. His old room is his office, beautifully refurbished with black leather sofas, a phone, a fax machine, and a copier. We hit the jackpot by visiting on this particular day – he only works there twice a week. Faiz had a lovely time showing us everything; we could see that he was in his element, recounting his past experiences as Dame Violet's companion. He said that she treated him like a grandson. His father had been the Dicksons' butler for 26 years, and it was when he died that Dame Violet invited Faiz to come to Kuwait. She sponsored him (no one can legally work in Kuwait without a sponsor), and he came to live in her house.

David found Faiz in the dining room, and I answered David's calls to find them both seated at the table, which had an AlSadu runner down its center...and 2 signs warning visitors not to touch anything. As a former historic interpreter (at the Mark Twain and Harriet Beecher Stowe Houses in Hartford, Connecticut), I was appalled...until I found out that Faiz was a former resident there. This was his house. He had lived here, eaten dinner with Dame Violet at this table, and so on, so if he wanted to touch these things, it would be entertaining to watch any curator try to stop him. Faiz insisted on taking a photo of me and David seated there.

Our pair of museum heresy photos: the shocking sight that greeted me when I walked in, of David sitting among the "Don't Touch" signs and chatting with the man who turned out to be so authorized to sit there that it wasn't debatable...

…and the photo that Faiz took of us duplicating the travesty. I still refused to actually touch anything…

    Faiz was delighted to point out each and every artifact and feature of the house to us and to tell us all about them all. There were century-old, Kuwaiti-made chests in some of the upstairs rooms, plus some furniture that had belonged to the Dicksons; this was where the Dicksons spent most of their time. Not many of the original furnishings remained; the Iraqis had either ruined or stolen many irreplaceable items that represented the family's history and travels to India and Persia. Somehow, Violet's medals from Britain's Queen Elizabeth II had survived and were on display in glass cases, and her bed was in her bedroom.

    But mostly we had to rely on the photographs which hung in frames in every room, including a color photo of Dame Violet and Colonel Harold Dickson in 1958, the year before Harold died. This was hanging in their living room. Throughout the house, there were many photos of Saud and Zahra, the couple's children, and of their children, supplied by Saud and Zahra during the restoration after the invasion. The grandchildren used to visit Dame Violet at this house, as did her children.

The living room, upstairs: as it looks today, and as it looked when Harold and Violet lived there.

The Iraqis stole most of the original artifacts, and Saud and Zahra, the Dickson children, helped with the restoration by sending lots of photographs of the home and their parents, showing how things had looked in the past, when it was all perfect.

Outside, Faiz showed us the back courtyard, mentioning that Dame Violet had fresh eggs from her chickens, and that she liked to go out there with the pet cats and poultry, feeding the hens and other birds on the packed sand. There is an Iranian tanoor bread oven towards the back of the yard, near the stables. A dead tree stands off to the left; it remains because when Dame Violet lived there, it was a huge, living tree that provided shade over the entire back yard. Every year, Faiz said, Kuwait Oil Company provided her with a new Mercedes car, for which she kept a chauffeur. He took us out in front of the servants' wing, behind the front wall, to show us the little yard there.

Dame Violet with her K.O.C. Mercedes, out on a picnic in the desert.

We saw a photo of Dame Violet crouching in her back yard with a couple of turkeys and guinea hens, and some chickens. Faiz told us that she kept 12 pet cats. He also mentioned that the long ramp in the back yard was built in 1954 for Harold, when he had the lower part of his right leg amputated. He lived for 4 ½ more years after that, and Violet took great care of him.

There was another photo of her riding her white horse, which she rode as long as it lived up the street to Seif Palace to visit the Sheikh (they would chat on the street – he sat in his car). We saw photos of Dame Violet with her grandchildren – Saud had 2 sons and 1 daughter, and Zahra had one daughter and one son – photos of Violet at parties, photos of Violet and Harold in the house, and a last one of Violet taken at age 90.

Dame Violet on her horse out front.

The backyard of Dickson House; the tree where she fed her chickens was on the left. The round white shape is a tanoor bread oven, and to its left is the garage door.

This other view of the courtyard was taken from the upper level veranda, which stretches around the entire upper story.

This is Harold's ramp at the back of the house, built because his leg swelled up painfully; the back of the house.

The house, I later realized, was built in a European style out of local Kuwaiti materials. It is made of clay and brick, and whitewashed yearly, but it has no diwan or harim, no separate courtyards for men and women, and it integrates the sexes of the household just as in other Western homes. It is a Western home located in the Middle East.

Dame Violet could come home to the culture she was raised in while living among Arabs and their culture. The house has 2 wings: the main part of the house is for the family, and is 4 times the size of the servants' wing, which is off to the left of the main house and set back from it. The main house has a small porch running along the back, and a balcony-veranda running all around the upper level.

Upstairs: Dame Violet's bed; a wardrobe in another bedroom.

This old, Kuwaiti-made, wooden and metalwork chest was in one of the bedrooms.

It was on this veranda, on the front side of the house, that Dame Violet liked to sit in a rattan chair looking out over Dhow Harbor at Kuwait Bay directly ahead and the Gulf to her right, in the East. I walked all around it, finding a narrow, blue-painted bridge leading off to the servants' wing, and 2 long white-cushioned benches on the wide front of the veranda.

No rattan chair was to be found. Most likely, the Iraqis destroyed it. A set of blue-painted stairs with one railing led to the roof. I'm acrophobic, but I climbed partway up and took some photos of the sunset from there. The roof and the veranda both afford views of the dhows in the harbor and the new Fish Souq, showing the service area with delivery trucks pulled up to the building.

At the top is the spot where Dame Violet's rattan chair used to be, and where she would sit looking at the view in the evenings. She was a fixture in the city historic neighborhood, and so people were used to seeing her there. The middle image shows the view that she enjoyed so much. The bottom views show Dhow Harbor and the Fish Souq.

Downstairs, Faiz had some more things to show us. He took us down the back hallway to the right side of the building and into a modern lecture room with lights, wood-and-steel chairs, and video display equipment. He told us that this room had been the kitchen, and had been outfitted with Italian-made electrical cooking fixtures, but that the Iraqis had gutted it. From there, he led us to his office, which used to be his bedroom, and on to 3 other rooms with framed black-and-white photographs on the walls.

The back hallway leading to the kitchen; here is the former kitchen, now a lecture room. Restoration of the kitchen was deemed a hopeless proposition after what the Iraqi invaders did to it.

When we came to the photograph of Harold Dickson standing under a sidr tree with a Kuwaiti man, Faiz had a very special story to tell us. This tree, which stands in the Burqan desert, appeared in a dream that Harold Dickson had…5 times.

It had to be significant, Harold thought, because the dream kept recurring, and because it featured a spring of water, so he got some Kuwaiti friends to help him find it. Claudia Farkas Al-Rashoud's book tells it differently, though, saying that Harold dreamed that he and Violet unearthed an ancient woman's grave, and that this woman came back to life, and that they protected her from crazy old Kuwaiti men who tried to kill her.

Harold had the dream interpreted, and it led not to water but to oil – the first successful location of an oil well in Kuwait! So Harold really helped to make Kuwait Oil Company a successful enterprise. This entitled him and Violet to many retirement benefits.

David and Faiz with the photo of Harold's sidr tree in the Burqan oil fields.

David signing the guest book.

We thanked Faiz for the wonderful tour and each wrote notes to him in the guest book. We signed them, having called him a piece of living history and a wonderful tour guide, feeling thoroughly delighted to have met him. He then walked us down the street to a bus stop, where we paid 150 fils each for the Bus Ride from Hell – it included motion sickness and over an hour wasted not getting to our destination – then bailing out and switching to a cab. We were trying to go to an office in Salmiya to pick up our passports, and David apologized for my motion sickness and our wasted time as the cab took us quickly to our destination. We were not far from it, at least not by car.

It could have been worse; David kept soothing my motion sickness as we rode the bus just by apologizing, agreeing, and being sympathetic. The bus was full of foreign workers who looked at us like we had just beamed down from an alien spaceship – what were a couple of Americans doing using it anyway? The seats were nicely upholstered in cloth, just like a Greyhound or Peter Pan bus, but the ride just got us lost. David agreed to take cabs from then on, because despite the higher fares, we could at least get wherever we were going.

Before leaving, we took photographs of each other outside. Next to us was the gate that the car went in and out of when Dame Violet lived in the house.

A little while later that evening, David told me that when he was in Kuwait after the war as a soldier, he had gone into Dickson House. He saw the damage that the Iraqis had inflicted on it, and it was obvious that the place had once been a gorgeous home and someplace significant. He just didn't know what it was – the damage had been that severe that he could not guess by looking around. No helpful clues remained. The sheikhs of Kuwait had obviously made a point of restoring Dickson House to as close to its pre-invasion condition as possible. Dame Violet and Harold Dickson had been that special to them and to their nation's history.

The Tareq Rajab Museum of Antiquities

One afternoon in April, David and I planned to visit the Tareq Rajab Museum in Jabriya, which contains examples of Islamic art in the basement of a villa. It is open from 4 to 7 p.m. on Fridays. Tareq Rajab was Kuwait's first Minister of Antiquities, and he set up a beautiful museum on Failaka Island containing many of the fascinating artifacts that were excavated there.

He and his wife, Jehan Sayid Rajab, have each written many books full of beautiful color photos on various Middle Eastern arts, crafts, and history. They met in London at a university, and fell in love there. The couple and their 3 children used to spend a lot of time with Dame Violet Dickson, touring and enjoying the beaches of Kuwait and Failaka Island together.

Early in our stay in Kuwait, I found a book on Failaka Island that included photographs of the couple and their children. Interestingly, Tareq is shown wearing traditional Kuwaiti clothing, while Jehan was dressed in conservative Western clothing with no hijab. The photographs are approximately 40 years old; they show the couple enjoying Failaka Island with Dame Violet Dickson, who loved to go there. Unfortunately, the Iraqi invaders completely trashed Tareq and Jehan's work on Failaka Island in 1990-1991.

We called the Tareq Rajab Museum. It was closed, and an Arabic-speaking person informed David that it would be open the next afternoon from 4 to 7 p.m., so my workaholic husband agreed to go with me. So we went to Jabriya the following afternoon.

It was great! We saw: clothing from all over the Arab, Islamic, Moghul, and North African world; jewelry from the same areas; swords; embroidery; calligraphy; ancient Quranic texts in beautifully decorated books; carved wood; inlaid mother-of-pearl in furniture; ceramics; marble; coins; a couple of Stars of David adorning two different clay bowls; paintings; Hands of Fatma; a talisman undershirt covered with Quranic writings; Indian children's robes; and an enormous array of musical instruments, including all sorts of lutes and drums.

The clothing on display was all beautifully embroidered, and I came away from the place with not just the museum's general publication, but also a book by Jehan about women's costumes in the

Arab world. Jehan S. Rajab is from Scotland, I found out as I read her book, which explained at last why she had her husband last name. She has obviously enjoyed an interesting and privileged life as Tareq Rajab's wife.

This view, taken from across the street, shows the house in which the Rajab family lives, with the museum in the basement.

The museum has a small bookshop. The rest of it is a series of well-lit rooms full of glass cases, with explanations in English and Arabic. The calligraphy room has a poem in the back, translated from Arabic to English, describing the process of cutting and fashioning a writing tool. I thought to myself, wow, I had it easy when I learned calligraphy – all I had to do was buy a really good pen and take care of it. The poem tells the calligrapher to pray for a steady hand before beginning…good advice.

Everything was beautifully and carefully preserved and presented in glass cases in the basement of the Rajab family villa. At least, we thought that it was their house before going there, and again when a rather large and perfume-scented male cat, white with a couple of asymmetrical black markings on its head, appeared outside while we waited for a cab.

We were enjoying the lovely breezy evening on a bench in front of the building after the museum closed when the cat appeared, sauntering up from the garden area. It came around the back of the bench, and it calmly let me pick it up and settle it into my lap, whereupon David and I petted it and smelled the perfume. When we put it down, it pulled itself up over the high wall behind us and into the villa's enclosed front gardens. That was what convinced us that we had petted the Rajab family cat.

The entrance to the Tareq Rajab Museum.

Later, I found out that the school that Nuwwar attended – a private school, because non-Kuwaiti citizens must pay for private ones – is the same one that Jehan founded. It is around the corner and down the street from her home and museum, and she was on its board of trustees. Her son ran the school.

I didn't find any information about how that school and its staff and students fared during the Iraqi invasion, but I did read that Jehan was very worried about her collection in the museum. She stayed in Kuwait and packed up every last artifact in boxes and stacked them carefully, remembering where each thing was. She made the basement look as boring and unremarkable as possible: like an ordinary basement that was merely extra space to the family.

It worked, thanks to her cleverness and pure luck. The Iraqis never noticed that it was a museum; the sign was removed also, and put back when they were gone, as was the entire collection of wonderful artifacts.

Jehan had saved her life's work.

Chapter 19
Kuwait's Woman Suffrage Movement

Of course an American woman could not go to a Muslim nation without wondering about the legal rights of its female citizens – especially not one who had majored in Women's History and minored in Women's Studies in college. Could Kuwaiti women vote? Wait...did the men vote? It seemed that Saudi Arabians did not vote, so what about Kuwaitis? Well, the answers to the questions in Kuwait turned out to be that men could vote in national and local elections and women could not. Pay dirt! An issue worth focusing on...

But did Kuwaiti women care about having the right to vote? There must be some who cared and wouldn't be quiet, docile, religious personalities who wouldn't dream of making a fuss about this. After all, as the Harvard professor Laurel Thatcher Ulrich said, "Well-behaved women rarely make history."

Winning the right to vote usually means encountering resistance from men who don't want to share ANY political clout, which means a fight with – at the very least – words, and possibly the laws that are already in place being used against the women.

At first, the only method of satisfying my curiosity appeared to be watching the newspapers, what with the sporadic access I had to the Internet. Accordingly, I watched the stories of national political Kuwaiti news until the issue cropped up.

It seemed highly unlikely that it wouldn't; the majority of nations on our planet have voting rights for educated and politically involved women. Many Kuwaiti women have college educations; some even have graduate degrees. They all seem to be literate, from what I was able to observe: their children attend school, usually coeducational if private or not if public. Most Kuwaitis are able to say at least a few words in English. This is a first-world, developed country, albeit with an entirely foreign servant class.

In short, it stood to reason that Kuwaiti women must have a few suffragists in the mix.

The population is 2.2 million, with perhaps 800,000 to 900,000 of those being Kuwaiti citizens. The rest are the foreign servants plus foreign professionals, from nations such as the United States, Britain, France, Germany, Italy, Japan, Pakistan, India, Egypt, Kenya, Thailand, the Philippines, and Indonesia. Quite a list, and I have not attempted to include each and every nation that actually has a citizen living and working in Kuwait – the point is merely to show what regions of the globe foreigners come from.

Of the portion of the population that consists of Kuwaiti citizens, only a small number are adult males. The rest are women and children. With the women voting, that would likely double the number of voters.

In mid-January, after checking my Lonely Planet guide to the Middle East, and after asking around about freedom of speech, I had a sense of what Kuwaiti woman suffragists might be up against. The point of checking for freedom of speech – or the lack thereof – was to see what the stakes of making a fuss about women's rights might be. It was no surprise to learn that there is no such thing as free speech in Kuwait. Instead, there is the very real threat of execution if it is discovered that anyone has spoken against the government.

The specifics on voting rights were that voting is allowed for men only, and they may vote for 2 members of the National Assembly every 4 years, plus local municipal representatives. The people – only men – vote only for politicians and never on any political questions. Political cartoons here depict candidate kissing the hands of voters before elections, and the reverse going on after elections. So the politicians do NOT look after Kuwaiti people's interests once in office – only their own.

I wanted Kuwaiti women to have the vote – and I felt quite sure that there were Kuwaiti women who felt the same way.

There is a story called *Night of Terror* about American woman suffragists. They had endured being force-fed in jails for "disturbing the peace" and President Woodrow Wilson tried to have a psychiatrist declare Alice Paul, the leader of the woman suffragist movement, insane. The psychiatrist refused, saying publicly – in open court – that courage in women is often mistaken for insanity. We got the vote 3 years later.

It is always good to have a say in the running of one's country, however small that say may seem. To leave all decision-making up to men is folly. Men will think of themselves and their needs and wishes first and foremost, and they will forever claim that now is not the time to make a fuss about women's issues. The rub is that now will never, in their view, be the time to do that. Women need to understand that since that is the reality facing them, men's view of the matter is utterly irrelevant.

Did enough Kuwaiti women realize this to make a difference?

Following the Local Woman Suffrage News

Finally, in February, I saw a newspaper article about woman suffrage. The Emir (ruling Sheikh) whose name was Jaber, was making what was not his first attempt to get Kuwaiti women the right to vote. Who knew whether or not it would work, but Aiesha wanted to vote, and she said "insh'allah" they will get it. Good for her, wanting it – and having it, *The Arab Times* had helpfully stated, is not un-Islamic. In fact, the article I read went on to say voting rights for women is in line with Sharia law – that is Islamic law. There is no excuse for the current situation; it is just pure selfishness and foolishness on the part of the all male politicians who don't want to share voting rights with Kuwaiti women.

However, Emir Jaber could not unilaterally decide to grant women the right to vote. Despite the fact that a royal family was in control of a significant portion of Kuwait's assets, the government was not an outright dictatorship; it was a constitutional monarchy of sorts. The National Assembly, made of entirely of men complete with a Speaker, could vote on the issue and prevent women from ever having a say as to who represented them politically. The Prime Minister was always a member of the Al-Sabah royal family, but he would appoint a Cabinet member to assist him with running the various governmental ministries – and thus far, they had always been men. I realized that I might be in Kuwait at the right time to witness some herstoric changes, and I was cautiously optimistic.

It wasn't long before I began to see herstory unfolding in the newspaper.

On March 1st, 2005, *The Kuwait Times* reported that Kuwaiti politicians who favor women's suffrage have contradicted those who don't, calling them Islamic extremists and saying that they are distorting Sharia law for their own personal agendas rather than reading it as it really is. They backed up their statements with Sharia scholars analyses of the Islamic law. A quote by a liberal Member of Parliament, Mohammad Al-Sager, reported him as saying "some people here are abusing Islam by highlighting isolated interpretations that do not give women their political rights," adding that "the pretext that women's political rights are in contradiction with Islamic Sharia has been denied by Muslim scholars." A simple majority is what is required under the Kuwaiti Constitution for the bill to pass.

Maybe it would happen soon. Maybe. I told David what I was watching for, and he helpfully made sure to get a newspaper for me every time he went to the bakala.

Just 2 days later, another article about this exciting issue appeared. It talked about what Kuwaiti women plan to do once they won the right to vote and to run in local and national elections. If I could meet Kuwaiti woman suffragists, I would give them an article that I had brought from Connecticut, which listed quotes from American men and women who said why they valued their right to vote and other freedoms. Meanwhile, I read on:

The Al-Sabah family leaders, both Sheikhs and Sheikhas (princes and princesses), were pushing for woman suffrage. Sheikh Mohammed, the Foreign Minister, looking around at other Gulf countries, said that it was a shame that Kuwaiti women could not vote while women in most of these other countries could, and added that Kuwaiti women are capable, enthusiastic and patriotic, bolstering his argument in favor of Kuwaiti women's suffrage. Sheikha Nisif wanted Kuwaiti women to have the same rights as men do when they marry foreigners, citing gross iniquities in the Personal Status Law. I would have to find out more about that law.

Kuwaiti women college professors and political leaders said that with a political voice, women would be able to improve the attitudes of Kuwaiti youths, who were becoming more and more apathetic and feeling more and more entitled to whatever comforts are handed to them, rather than contributing actively to their society. It is these women who seemed likely to do the most good with that article I brought from Connecticut.

The Kuwaiti political group which backed women's suffrage was called the Islamist Ummah Party, and it was first Sunni Muslim group in the country to do so. Voting is one of the things that makes life worth living. It reminds everyone who can vote that we do not have to passively accept whatever fate hands us if we don't like it.

The news article continued, giving the male chauvinist Islamic politicians some attention. They had organized themselves under the name Islamic Salaf Alliance. A photo was published showing 4 of them at a political rally. They thought it would be shameful to give Kuwaiti women the vote, and believed that liberals were actually distancing Muslims from their religion by doing this.

They sounded like the usual childishly insane types who have cropped up in history every time a nation has faced its own woman suffrage fight. I thought about my Egyptian friend: Fatin voted, and her rather doctrinaire husband didn't want her to refrain from doing so. Fatin obviously didn't think she shouldn't vote either, and she is definitely a devout Muslim, in touch with her religion. Well, Gloria Steinem did say that "logic is in the eye of the logician." The Islamic Salafs were applying their own logic, however faulty, to the situation.

Always remember who says what and what their point of view and agenda is.

So woman suffrage was of interest to Kuwait's politicians, and without naming my sources, I found out that the Islamic Salaf Alliance was considered to be a minority of individuals who are a disgrace to

Islam by the majority in Kuwait. These extremists drank alcohol, married additional concurrent wives, and committed adultery right and left, said one Kuwaiti source. The idea that granting women the vote would be shameful and distance Kuwaiti women from Islam was ridiculous – these guys were the epitome of the pot calling the kettle black. Again, Aiesha and Fatin were both good Muslims, and both wanted the vote, so this was just absurd. The Salaf guys were not backing up their statements with logic or Sharia scholarship; they were simply pushing their own wishes.

In *The Arab Times*, an article on women's suffrage talked about one MP called Dr. Waleed Al-Tabtabaei. I wondered what he was a doctor of – if it was Sharia Law, I would be amazed. The Kuwait Women's Cultural Society planned to sue him for saying that "supporters of the draft law on women's political rights are encouraging homosexuals and illegitimate children." The Society charged that his statement was a "misuse [of] the Parliamentary immunity to insult others," and I was glad to hear that they slammed him for his outrageously stupid and obnoxious remarks. It is amazing that such people still exist in this world. This guy sounded like someone from 19th-century American politics or even science. When I was studying women's history in college, I came across many similar remarks made by men in the past. They imagined all sorts of absurd things about women who wanted social and political equality, none of which any sensible, thinking or reasonable person would take seriously.

David had reminded me that this was a medieval society with modern conveniences.

I thought about the benefits of having the right to vote. When women are represented at all levels of a government, women's interests are represented, and laws that protect us and make our lives worth living are enacted. Kuwaiti women didn't have any such benefit. Some were lawyers, but they were not represented in their government, and they could not vote, neither as Members of Parliament in the National Assembly nor as citizens electing those Members.

The next newspaper articles told me such helpful facts as: to get Kuwaiti women the right to vote, the first article of the country's constitution would have to be amended, because it restricted the vote to Kuwaiti males aged 21 or older. Kuwaiti women lawyers had been repeatedly quoted as saying that Islamic law does not restrict the vote to men.

The behavior of male Kuwaiti politicians certainly begged the question: what is a Kuwaiti woman supposed to do in order to take care of her family's external affairs – marry the first man who comes knocking at her door and then trust him to look after her interests? That may work for some, but no blanket rule works for all. Some men might be good, but others might abuse that trust. The only viable solution, the only guarantee of a woman's security would be to enable her to legally look after her own interests.

Meanwhile, those male Members said that women's suffrage was not a priority. Of course it wasn't – for them! They only cared about their own priorities. It was tantamount to proclaiming to the world that they were selfish and didn't think that women counted. It was a slap in the face to women all over Kuwait. I wondered how these guys could face their own wives, daughters, mothers and sisters when they went home. I had been thinking about this not long before I read it, and now they had gone and said what I had expected of them. They were following the usual pattern of a fight for woman suffrage.

There was a pattern of patriarchal sociopathology at work here. Unless and until Kuwaiti women started demanding their rights and making life inconvenient and unpleasant for Kuwaiti men, I didn't see them getting their just right to vote. That is how American and British and other women got the right to vote. Being obedient and quiet achieved nothing. [Not that I intended to advocate window-smashing, but some sort of indecorous behavior seemed in order.]

The next *Arab Times* article on woman suffrage had an obnoxious a title: "Government Plotting to Muster Support of MPs on Women Suffrage Law." Granted, the newspaper was published in English by journalists whose native language was NOT English, but the phrasing of this title read like an accusation – perhaps by design.

Of course the government was actively seeking support for whatever it has on its agenda – that is what governments do. The Emir, the Prime Minister and the Crown Prince were not "plotting" to do what they are doing – they were simply doing it. The *Times* headline gave the impression that anti-woman suffragists had written the article...until I read it. It came across as reasonably objective, simply reporting what was going on. Reading it gave the impression of business as usual, by moving the bill along in the Kuwaiti Parliament. It even had some good news: 10 Islamic fundamentalist MPs had withdrawn their request to refer the bill to the Constitutional Court, and now consented to debating it in the National Assembly.

The March 14th article on the women's suffrage bill quoted an MP, one Hassan Jowhar, as saying that currently, only 15 percent of Kuwaitis could vote – so adding women to that percentage would therefore assist in reversing this contradiction of democracy. Even more helpful, another MP, one Ali Al-Rasheed, said that although the

1st Article of the Kuwaiti Constitution restricted the vote to Kuwaiti males, another provision – found in Article 29 – stated that "people [are] equal, regardless of sex, origin, language, or religion." This was clearly a contradiction in the Kuwaiti Constitution, and one that reinforced the practical contradiction found in the country's efforts to provide democracy. It ought to help with the woman suffrage effort. Amending the Constitution would almost look like editing out a typo.

The next commentary on the issue informed the readers of the existence of an obnoxious former MP called Mubarak Sunaideh who ran something called the Islamic Constitutional Movement (ICM). This character spent a significant amount of his time trying to block woman suffrage. His remarks were to the effect that because most European countries didn't grant women the right to vote until over 100 years after becoming democratic, Kuwait had another 60 years or so left before it ought to be required to do so.

Hmm...how nice to know that Kuwait had a comedian commentating on this hot political issue, I thought. Watch out Letterman and Leno – you've got competition! (American comedians have been known to notice and comment on such things...)

Women in the countries he referred to got the vote because they demanded it, loudly and often militantly. They weren't subservient about it, they weren't quiet, and they weren't usually the leaders of their households – neither was that last item deemed relevant to the issue, not by the women nor by those who ceased withholding their right to vote. Sunaideh was just coming up with any and every silly and childish reason he could to prevent Kuwaiti women from voting.

He added that there were many other laws which discriminated against women, so why should they have the right to vote? Why indeed...so that they can vote to redress these imbalances. His commentary degenerated into whining as he claimed that granting Kuwaiti women the vote would result in a demographic imbalance in voting constituencies from area to area...as if that were a valid argument. He thought he had some valid arguments, but they only seemed to reinforce arguments in favor of woman suffrage – again, following the herstorical pattern of fights around the planet for this right.

The next article did not disappoint: Member of Parliament Jassem Al-Khorafi, the Speaker of the National Assembly, refuted charges that the government was trying to force the legislative assembly to pass the women's suffrage bill. He added that he and many others were committed on their own to passing it. What was interesting here was the wording; "government" seemed to mean the Emir, the Prime Minister, and the Crown Prince – all members of Kuwait's royal family, the Al-Sabah family. To an American outsider observing this language, the word government is usually meant to encompass both the executive and the legislative branches of lawmakers and administrators in a nation. Here, it only to indicated the executive branch.

There seemed to be a great deal of optimism about the passage of the women's suffrage bill, despite the existence of so many efforts to stop it. Another article mentioned that this has been an issue since the 1970s, and still women in Kuwait didn't vote. I tried to imagine myself as a Kuwaiti woman who wanted to be able to exercise this right *in my own lifetime*.

Woman suffragists in other countries have been very angry not to have won their voting rights in time to vote in their own lifetimes, and felt very anxious as time passed and still they could not vote, wondering whether or not they would be able to do so before they died. Elizabeth Cady Stanton said that this bothered her, and she and Susan B. Anthony both died before ever seeing the result of their efforts – when or how it came about. They got no sense of closure.

Voting is a privilege – a right – and when one possesses it, a duty. Men should not keep it to themselves. It is humiliating to have to beg a legislative assembly for the right have a political voice. I couldn't blame the women suffragists for booing members of Parliament as they watched the debates about their issue, which they did in mid-March. In fact, this raised my respect for them, because it showed Kuwaiti women suffragists demanding rather than begging for their rights.

March 19th brought 2 more *Arab Times* articles. The first one reported on an article – not cited – by a columnist called Ahmad Al-Fahd, who was against granting women's suffrage. He thought that Kuwaiti women should care about one political issue and one only: naturalizing their foreign husbands.

How, I wondered sarcastically, were Kuwaiti women supposed to fix their inability to grant citizenship to their husband through marriage to them if they couldn't vote?! The article moved on to discuss something else: the idea that granting Kuwaiti women the right to vote in municipal but not national elections would be a way of distracting Kuwaiti feminists from their goal of gaining the right to vote in all elections. The writer did not endorse this as a strategy. He quoted the warnings of someone named Nasser Al-Abdalli that it was the Kuwaiti Constitution that needed changing. Until an Amendment was passed, the fight would not be over.

What was interesting about these articles was the tone, both as written and titled. A typical article – regardless of the topic – would have a dramatic title, with perhaps a brief paragraph or two that referred to its subject, and then the rest of the story would move on to some other subject that might or might not relate to the title. By the time I finished it, I often found myself wondering how I ended up reading about the other topic. Sometimes the entire mention of a dramatic issue or charge would be contained in the title, with no further discussion of the charge in the text of the article.

Another article on the same page surprised me by dealing with both of the items mentioned in its title, but did not explain much about what either one had to do with the other. One issue was women's suffrage; the other was a gas deal with Qatar. Apparently, MP Mohammed Al-Saqer visited Qatar to talk about a gas deal, and some other people went with him to talk about "enhancing the democratic process in the [Gulf] region," so as to enable citizens of the Gulf States to elect a Gulf parliament. When they all returned to Kuwait, it was Al-Saqer who commented on both issues.

David said that we ought to get in touch with Kuwaiti feminists; I agreed.

To prepare – and to identify these women – I made a list of the ones who were mentioned in *The Arab Times* and *The Kuwait Times*. The names of the Kuwaiti feminists, the organizations that they belonged to, and their professions, all went onto my list. Kuwait had no white pages directory for looking up individuals, but there was a book of yellow pages. Perhaps by looking up the organizations I would be able to track them down. Also, some of them were Kuwait University professors – so we thought that maybe Assim can help me find them.

Meeting a Piece of Living Kuwaiti Herstory

On March 20th, David had some exciting news: Assim Al-Tikriti had gotten the phone number of a Kuwaiti feminist by the name of Dr. Rola A. Al-Dashti, Ph.D. She worked as the Chairperson of Kuwait Economics Committee, and her photograph had appeared in the day's *Arab Times* with some other Kuwaiti women, showing them trying to convince Kuwaiti men to sign a petition in favor of women's suffrage. I hoped they would get lots of signatures.

Page 6 of the newspaper showed me something that I had long hoped to see: a woman behaving badly. Finally! It briefly mentioned that a male lawyer who was not a public official was suing a Kuwaiti woman suffragist – a complete stranger to him – whom he saw stomping on her own Kuwait nationality certificate while the National Assembly discussed women's suffrage. This pompous attorney's name was Mohammed Al-Jumai, and he had the gall to call her behavior a "betrayal of gratitude."

Just what, I wondered, did he expect her to be grateful for?! Is it for having no say as to who will represent her interests? That is nothing to be grateful for. American and British suffragists smashed windows; all this woman did was stomp on her own legal document – it caused no harm to any other person. He says he will defend the dignity of Kuwait – what dignity can it claim to have while treating half of its citizens with so little respect as to deny them a political voice?! I saw no dignity in him; only pomposity and a sense of entitlement.

The actions of the Kuwaiti feminist reminded me of those of the militant women suffragists of the United States and Britain. It was only when such tactics were used by these past feminists that American and British women achieved a political voice. No men listened until their voices became shrill and demanding; politeness got women nowhere, but loud militancy did. The proof is in the 19th Amendment to the U.S. Constitution – American women can vote.

The most exciting event mentioned was a fatwa – a religious edict – issued by Awqaf (the Ministry of Islamic Affairs). It was written by the Minister himself, Abdullah Al-Matouq, and it said that the decision on whether or not to grant Kuwaiti women the right to vote should be left up to the Emir of Kuwait, Sheikh Jaber Al-Sabah. The precedent for doing so can be found in the Quran, he said in what appeared to be a well-researched, balanced analysis of the Quran.

The report went on to say that MPs who favor women's suffrage – now 35 of them – will be very happy about this, because they were very upset about being called un-Islamic by fundamentalists when they announced that they favored amending Article One of the 1962 Kuwaiti Constitution. If the Emir were to unilaterally grant women the right to vote, these guys would have an easy political out – they could agree with the act while expending no effort, and offending none of their constituents, and thus have it both ways.

An opinion article by Ahmed Al-Jarallah gave a well-argued and carefully thought out analysis of the current international political situation as it affected and related to both Kuwait as a democracy and Kuwaiti women's political rights. He compared other democracies with Kuwait's, saying that it didn't measure up, and added that men and women ought to be equal partners in this society. He hoped that the Emir would be able to grant Kuwaiti women the right to vote soon. The way these articles were written was creating an atmosphere in which the Emir would look very odd indeed if he didn't grant women the right to vote in his next decree. That would be wonderful to see.

The next day, a thrilling phone call came: it was Rola Al-Dashti. She wanted to meet us! We made a tentative plan to meet her on Wednesday afternoon, March 23rd. She would call us again to confirm it, when she was more certain of the rest of her schedule. Apparently, she taught economics at Kuwait University; this was how Assim was able to put us in touch. She seemed pleased, and I looked forward to meeting her. I wondered how much she knew of the history of women's suffrage fights in other countries. I wished I had some books with photographs about this to give her; I have read many on the subject.

Before I met her, I made sure to review the news articles that mentioned her. I promptly came across a newspaper photo of her from the day before. In it, she was pitching her petition in favor of women's suffrage, attempting to garner signatures. She wore no hijab, her hair was in a ponytail, and she was wearing jeans and a tee shirt that read: "WOMEN ARE KUWAIT TOO!" She was leading other younger Kuwaiti women in this activity, and they weren't wearing hijabs either. [I should mention again that Kuwait had no requirement that women veil; it's optional.]

The way they were dressed did not surprise me, but it was be a good thing for all Kuwaitis to see Kuwaiti women in all forms of dress demanding the right to vote, and few photographs of Kuwaiti feminists had appeared in the newspapers. If Muslim women could be seen demanding the right to vote and have a political voice while wearing abbeyas, hijabs, nekhabs, blue jeans and tee shirts with hair visible, or any combination of these, that would be helpful to their cause. It would show that there is such a thing as a woman who is both a feminist and a devout Muslim.

There was also some good news in the day's *Arab Times* article about women's suffrage and other political rights for women: a former Kuwait MP by the name of Dr. Yaqoub Hayati was quoted as saying that denying women as a group the right to be observers in the Kuwait National Assembly was a violation of Kuwait's Constitution. He even said specifically that this was a violation of Article 30 of the Parliamentary bylaws, which prohibited this, and added that many MPs had been taking for granted the mistaken idea that they were above and immune from criticism, which they were not. They could be questioned, and they have to face criticism.

It was delightful to read this: a man telling off male chauvinists. Meanwhile, Speaker Jassem Al-Khorafi kept getting lots of good press coverage for favoring women's rights. Perhaps the majority of Kuwaiti MPs could see the handwriting on the walls of their assembly hall, and realized that they will have to share the political life of Kuwait.

The next day it was made official: tomorrow afternoon at 3:30 p.m., we were to meet the illustrious Dr. Rola Al-Dashti in Kuwait City, at an upscale mall called the Courtyard Marriott Complex. This woman suffragist was a living piece of history – herstory – and it would be fascinating to meet her for this reason. I was thrilled just to have a chance to talk to her.

With that, I looked at the day's *Arab Times* and found a photograph of foreign expatriate women who had just assisted the Kuwaiti women suffrage work by attending, as a group, a session of the Kuwait National Assembly. The group consisted of American, European and other foreign women, and they went to hear the discussions about granting Kuwaiti women the right to vote in all elections in their own country.

A useful piece of information on the Kuwaiti political process was outlined in the accompanying article: to pass a law in the Kuwait National Assembly, a majority of one-half is required. There are 50 Members of Parliament in the National Assembly, plus 15 Cabinet Members, totaling 65 politicians who are allowed to vote on a given issue. This meant that for the bill to pass, 33 of them would have to vote in favor of it. At last tally, the woman suffragists had verified that 30 or 31 were on their side, and they wanted 2 more to be certain of passing the law. I hoped they would get more than that to ensure a clear, comfortable margin of victory.

Rola Al-Dashti was also working on another issue: transparency in government. Apparently, Kuwaiti institutions needed to put more effort into conducting business in an open, on-the-record fashion so as to prevent corruption and under-the-table dealings. She hoped that aligning her group, the Kuwait Economics Society, also called the Kuwait Economists Committee, with a German-based group called Transparency International, would help.

The following afternoon, at approximately 2:30 p.m., Assim Al-Tikriti arrived. Before leaving, he very sweetly took this photograph of me and David. We were both dressed up, and David even kept his eyes open! He often squints at cameras.

After this, he drove us to the Courtyard Marriott Complex in Kuwait City to meet Rola Al-Dashti. He had to go home to pray and eat lunch, so we went inside alone, and found ourselves in a beautiful, upscale mall full of high-end stores such as Burberry. Not very many people were in there, because it was time for afternoon prayers, and shops closed down in the afternoons until around 4 o'clock. But 2 fancy cafés were open, and we sat down at first one and then the other. (We moved because David called Rola and she said she would meet us at the other café. The first one was a modern-styled place called Café Supreme. The second one was called Richoux, and it served mostly elaborate, showcase desserts and fancy coffees, teas, and Belgian hot chocolate, which is what I had. I took several photos while we waited, until a guard told me to stop. Later, I found out that this is due to copyright concerns; store owners worry that the styles of their stores and signs may be pirated.)

David and Stephanie, ready to meet a piece of living Kuwaiti herstory.

Meeting Rola was quite a thrill. At first, the conversation was slow, because I was being careful not to stare at her as if she were a famous statue rather than a living person, and because meeting new and fascinating people is still really just meeting people who are strangers. I didn't want to seem off-putting, but I was very excited to exchange contact information, take her photograph, and give her the newspaper full of voters' quotes from Connecticut. That felt like a lot to say and ask for, especially with David sitting next to me, determined to ramble on for the first 5 to 10 minutes or so (as we had agreed in advance). He stopped after that, though, and let me take over. Women's history is, after all, my area of interest.

We each ordered a hot drink, and then talked for about an hour. Rola immediately took out 2 of her business cards, and I saw that the correct name of her group was the Kuwait Economic Society (*The Arab Times* kept changing it rather than checking before printing it). Her mobile phone rang almost immediately after we got settled, so I took the cards and gave her ours. That took care of the contact information. When she hung up, we each told her a little bit about ourselves, including my background in women's history, and then she sat for a photograph, which came out very well. After that, we heard about her past, growing up, education, etc.

Rola A. Al-Dashti, Ph.D. – Kuwaiti Woman Suffragist.

We had an absolutely fantastic afternoon and evening. The sunlight was beautiful throughout the afternoon and evening, and we were thrilled and fascinated by it all. Rola was a lovely person, and she invited me to come to her office in Kuwait City and help her to prepare articles in English for foreign readers, so that they would know all about the Kuwaiti women's suffrage efforts.

Rola grew up with a Lebanese mother and a Kuwaiti father. She lived in Lebanon for her teenage years, and began attending college at the American University in Lebanon when civil and political unrest forced the family to leave and come to Kuwait. With a Kuwaiti father, she found herself entitled, with her good academic record, to benefits from the country's system of free education for all at all levels. She was offered a chance to study in America or Britain, and she chose to go to America. Where, the officials asked her?

All she knew then was Texas and California, so she said California. San Francisco or Los Angeles, they asked? What was the difference, she wondered, not knowing much about America or California. She told us that she has found a similar lack of knowledge about Arab countries in Americans, most notably hearing that their entire impressions of Arab women consisted of the lives of Bedouin women as gleaned from their daughters' school reports. By the time she was ready for graduate school, she knew enough to choose to study for her Ph.D. in economics at Johns Hopkins University in Maryland.

It was my background in women's history even more than my education as a lawyer that most interested Rola. She had been hoping to meet an American woman who could describe the history of the American fight for women's suffrage, and she got her wish when she met me. I told her about the Seneca Falls Women's Right Convention of July 18-19, 1848, about the 19th Amendment to the United States Constitution, passed in 1919 and effective as of 1920 – just in time for a Presidential election year – and mentioned Elizabeth Cady Stanton, Susan B. Anthony, Marilyn Joslyn Gage, Ida Wells-Barnett, and Alice Paul. I also wrote these things down for her, and added Gloria Steinem's name to the list, because she is alive and working now.

Rola was looking forward to having me e-mail her the story about Alice Paul and the psychiatrist who refused to certify her as insane, saying that "courage in women is often mistaken for insanity." I told her several herstorical anecdotes, and answered her questions about woman suffragists' tactics in both the U.S. and Britain. I added a caveat to this; I was not encouraging her to break windows or destroy property. What I was encouraging her to do was to fight the "invisibility factor" of life for women in Arab and Islamic society, and indicating that being polite and taking a back seat gets women nowhere fast in efforts to achieve equal political rights. She agreed with me about both things.

Of course men don't see women's political equality as a priority, she agreed. But in answer to our questions about the Emir of Kuwait and his attempts to pass decrees or amendments or whatever would work for women's suffrage in this country, she told us that Emir Jaber Al-Sabah sincerely wanted Kuwaiti women to have voting rights, and at the national level. That was great to hear; to further assure us that this is true, Rola added that she had met with the Emir and spoken to him about it, so she wasn't merely spouting wishful thinking.

Dr. Rola also informed us that Emir Jaber issued something called a raqba in 1999, attempting to grant women the right to vote. We knew that he had issued a decree of some sort, thanks to Kuwait's national website, but that was about it, other than that the National Assembly voted it down in 2000. Now she explained how a raqba works: it is actually both a wish and a decree. It is usually most effective when the wisher-decreer has not asked for much in the past, which Emir Jaber had not.

Unfortunately, it was issued when the National Assembly was in recess, and is came along with 60 or so other wishes – pitched as "emergency" items – which ALL got voted down and rejected when the

National Assembly returned to work the next year. This time, Emir Jaber was trying to do this during a regular Parliamentary session. It was as I had guessed: he couldn't make unilateral decisions about constitutional issues.

The conversation moved on to some other things, including her invitation to me to come to her office some mornings and assist in the writing and distribution – in foreign publications – of articles about Kuwaiti women's suffrage efforts. She wanted this publicized to foreign women so that they could blitz Kuwaiti politicians with e-mailed letters demanding voting rights for Kuwaiti women – perhaps on International Women's Day, or at a time when the law was about to be voted upon. I would have to get to her office on Saturday. She pointed it out to us; we exited the door next to the Richoux café and looked across the street and to the left. The KES Office was on the 2nd floor of a building with a large blue sign, across the street from the Courtyard Marriott Complex.

David now imagined that ALL of my time would be taken up assisting with Dr. Rola's efforts for Kuwaiti women's suffrage rights. David imagines many things before he knows for certain how other people's schedules work, so I intended to just go to Rola's office on Saturday and see what it was like. Who knew what would happen next; right then, it all seemed rather vague, but I was sure it would make sense once I sat down at a computer in her office.

Working with Rola

It turned out to be Monday before I could go to see Rola Al-Dashti. Going there meant taking a taxi alone, something that worried me because I hadn't done it yet. How would I find a driver who understood what I was saying? Well, I couldn't do anything about it until then, so I read the newspaper again.

The day's *Arab Times* article on women's political rights contains an amusing story. Apparently, 2 different diwaniyas were held on 2 separate occasions. The first one was held by an opponent of women's voting and other rights, an imam by the name of Nasser Shamsuldeen. The second diwaniya was held by a supporter of women's rights, an MP called Ali Al-Rashed. During this second diwaniya, the Secretary-General of Awqaf Public Foundation, whose name was Dr. Mohammed AbdulGafer Al-Shareef, gave a speech detailing Sharia Law's support of women's political rights. Shamsuldeen and approximately 20 other Islamists kept trying to interrupt him, so the host threw them out.

MP Al-Rashed's action seemed reasonable – he was holding a social gathering, and these guests kept trying to disrupt it. The funny part was that another MP, one Mohammed Al-Mutair, made a big fuss about it, criticizing Al-Rashed for not allowing Shamsuldeen to express his views *during* the speech. Of course he didn't – expressing one's views during someone else's lecture or speech is called interrupting and is rude. Opposing views are for the discussion period. Al-Mutair made a fool out of himself by objecting to this. His behavior just marked him as an opponent of women's political rights, which was the real issue.

Another *Arab Times* article on Kuwaiti women's suffrage rights briefly mentioned that Kuwait's Deputy Prime Minister, Sheikh Jaber Al-Mubarak Al-Hamad Al-Sabah (he happened to have the same first name as the Emir, plus the same last name, just to keep things confusing), who is also the Defense Minister, spoke about the issue in the United Arab Emirates. He said that Islamic religious leaders no longer unanimously speak against this issue. The Emir wanted women in Kuwait to be able to vote, so it should be made possible. He said he hoped that the National Assembly would make it so soon. After that, he went on to talk about other issues of Gulf countries. Political meetings are held on a regular basis in the United Arab Emirates, in Dubai, for the Gulf Cooperation Council (GCC).

A few days later, I found myself visiting Rola's office every day – for at least a few days. Her office was in an old building in the Sharq district of Kuwait City, and was really 2 offices, one across from the other. She also had an office at Kuwait University, where she taught economics, plus another office elsewhere for the Kuwait Economic Society. She shared this one with her mother, and they ran an interior decorating business out of it. It turned out that they had decorated the interior of the Courtyard Marriot Complex. The secretary was a friendly Indian girl from Goa who spoke little Arabic but fluent English.

Our plan was to e-mail letters to individuals in the media, academia, politics, non-governmental organizations (NGOs), and whatever professional groups that we could find e-mail addresses for. In short order, thanks to my writing skills and donated time, we each had a letter to send over the Internet. I wrote mine using my own logic and arguments plus that 1917 story called *Night of Terror*. I also wrote Rola's letter with her sitting next to me telling me what sorts of things she wanted to say. Once we had several sentences on the screen, she had me change the order of them, and then it was done. We planned to attach these letters to short notes addressed to Kuwaiti Members of Parliament.

We set up our e-mail accounts with many addresses in them. Our plan was to acquire the e-mail addresses of all 50 of the Kuwaiti MPs as well. Then we intended to send out the letters in such a way that recipients could sign their names to one for the MPs and then e-mail it to them. This meant that the MPs would receive many copies of our letter asking them to vote to pass the bill into law that would grant Kuwaiti women the right to vote at all levels. Rola had stacks and stacks of business cards from people all over the world, and I spent a significant amount of those few days entering them into a new e-mail account.

The difficulty seemed to be in getting the e-mail addresses for all of the MPs. Rola thought that we would just e-mail the Prime Minister, Sheikh Sabah, and MP Jassem Al-Khorafi, the Speaker of the Kuwaiti National Assembly, but I said that we might as well not bother if we just rely on 2 men to inform all the others of our arguments. Why would they bother?!

They could vote – they didn't feel the outrage of being unable to vote – and in any case they were not likely to read the whole letter to the other politicians. It made some excellent and convincing points, but each of the MPs would need to receive a copy of it for it to make a significant impact. If you want change, I tried to impress upon her, you must be prepared to bother everyone – not just a few people. You must make a thorough though polite nuisance of yourself.

With 65 MPs to either vote or abstain – 15 Cabinet Members and 50 Members of Parliament (this includes the Speaker) – we hoped to make a difference. One Cabinet Member would abstain, Rola told me, while the other 14 intended to vote in favor of passing the bill. So she wanted to focus our efforts on the MPs.

Fine, but we needed ALL of their e-mail accounts. She told me that she had an Arabic-speaking secretary at the Kuwait Economic Society office who would call and get each and every one. I had to convince her of the necessity of doing this...the day after I helped her write the letters, she only had the Prime Minister's and Speaker's addresses, and was going to leave it at that. No, I told her – that wouldn't work.

I began to wonder just how much help I could be if I had to depend on the inaction of others. Regardless, I decided that I would stick around long enough to make sure that I had done all that I could.

After all this, the Islamic weekend started, so work stopped. The vote was planned for sometime in mid-April, so we had time to get those e-mail addresses and send our letters out.

Getting to Rola's office was interesting. I took cabs from Airport Road 55, which I could find out in front of our apartment building in Abraq Khaitan. It usually cost me KD 2 to get to Kuwait City and KD 1.5 to get back home. I suspected that I was being charged by the destination – the distance is the same. Cabs in Kuwait don't have meters; you negotiate the fare with the driver before taking off, usually while standing outside the cab just before saying okay and getting in. David, who was concerned about my safety, advised me about safe cab-hiring the first day: only take a cab that is marked as a cab – don't get into any unmarked vehicles. He added that I should only do that when I am with him.

The cab drivers all assumed that they should turn on some sort of American music when they picked up an American, and it was useless to try to tell them otherwise. This meant listening to rap music and rock music all the way. I told them to please take me to the Courtyard Marriott Hotel in Kuwait City on Hillali Street. This is not as simple as it sounds, because there is a J.W. Marriott Hotel (older) on the other side of the city. The Courtyard Marriott Hotel is only 8 months old. It was easier to tell cab drivers to go there, and then say that I wanted to go to a place right across the street.

The second day that I went there, the driver took a slightly different route – farther east – and I saw why as we headed north: four lanes of vehicles were stopped, creating a highway parking lot. Ahead of them, a score of police cars appeared with their lights flashing (sirens off) as they escorted the President of the United Arab Emirates to the airport. The cab driver, who was from India, had listened to the radio in advance, so he knew not to go that way. I congratulated him on his cleverness and thanked him.

Since I couldn't go to Rola's office over the weekend, it was back to following the news.

The *Arab Times* has had several more articles about women's suffrage, including one which referred back to that new fatwa that analyzed Sharia law and concluded, after careful scholarly research, that Islam does not preclude political participation by women. This was on March 20th. On the 29th, I read a spate of mournful, lamenting wailing by a Muslim cleric called Nazem Al-Mesbah, who complained bitterly about this fatwa, wishing that the 1985 one that had banned women from voting could have remained in place forever.

Here is an example: "Those who want equal rights for men and women are infidels." Several other whiny comments by this guy were quoted, further demonstrating his prejudices and propensity for making absurd pronouncements. At least he had provided some entertainment, I laughed to myself.

I spent April 1st contemplating the constitutional rights of women in Kuwait, the U.S., and other nations. This was thanks to, as usual, reading the day's newspapers. For some reason, the paper was free – the *Friday Times* of the *Kuwait Times*.

Page 3 had a story by a *Philadelphia Inquirer* reporter about the political setbacks that may likely take place – and have taken place in the past – for Arab women in many countries. It included a passing mention of Kuwaiti women suffragists. Then it talked about the veiling law that women in Iran are subjected to. "When male politicians quarrel, women become the sacrificial lambs," it said. That remark reminded me that I always look at the women in any situation – it helps with the assessment process.

I recalled Ali Al-Baghli's latest editorial, in which he commented about ultra-religious Muslims who can't bear to see other people happy. Free women are happy, and traditionalists wanted to put a stop to that, as if there were something terrible about it. Their attitude made me glad to be free, and made me all the more determined to support Kuwaiti women suffragists, who happiness, liberty and quite possibly their lives could be at risk without it. Whenever a group's freedoms are chipped at, soon that group's safety is threatened as well.

The April 3rd edition of *The Arab Times* had a piece of useful information for Kuwaiti women suffragists: Kuwait is a member state in the Inter-Parliamentary Union (IPU). The IPU favors women's political participation in any country, and has a committee on women's affairs. Even better: the IPU has a reputation for decreasing the allotment of votes to any member nation that does not allow women to participate in its parliamentary processes.

That was delightful news. Currently, fatwas from Kuwait's Awqaf Ministry of Islamic Affairs said that Sharia law allowed for women to vote but not to be Members of Parliament. There are women in this society who are good Muslims and who might wish to both vote and sit in Parliament. This could help them if Kuwait's government decided that it was not willing to be left out of international decisions, or to accept lesser roles or voices in those decisions.

On this particular day, I did not go to Rola's office. Taxi rides cost KD 3.5 round-trip, and I knew that she had just returned from traveling somewhere late the night before. I had already loaded many e-mail addresses into the new account, but unless and until she acquired the e-mail addresses of the 50 Kuwaiti Members of Parliament, this would be useless. Rola would now to direct her Arabic-speaking secretary to begin this task. Actually hunting down all of these addresses would take some time, so there was no need to rush down there yet. I tried to call Rola, but her phone was switched off – Kuwaiti people switch their phones off a lot.

I couldn't afford to go into Kuwait City every day without knowing that something useful would be accomplished. David agreed.

Meanwhile, I had a book by Tracy Chevalier that I intended to give to Rola, called *Falling Angels*. I wanted to give it to her because it was about British suffragette history, and it was not yet available in Kuwait. I wrote Rola a message inside its cover:

> To Rola Al-Dashti, Ph.D. –
>
> Here is a piece of British women's history, about the suffragettes. I am glad to be able to give it to a piece of living Kuwaiti history.
>
> – Stephanie C. Fox, J.D.

The previous evening, at 8 o'clock, Assim brought me and David over to his and Aiesha's house for a visit. David caught up with some research and writing on their computer while I chatted with Aiesha. Aiesha looked at my letters for the Kuwaiti suffragettes, and thought they would do some good. She and Assim both agreed that I could not be expected to take a taxi to Rola's office every day just to type in e-mail account names any more – I have already done that 3 times, to the tune of KD 11.5 – that was $36.

I had called Rola to explain this and add that I was eager to return when she had the MPs e-mail addresses. She thanked me profusely for my help, and shared her progress with me. She spent Saturday and Sunday traveling and had collected promises of e-mail support from more allies of Kuwaiti suffragettes. She also intended to prepare a version of her letter in Arabic for some of her allies. She would definitely call me when her secretary at the Kuwait Economic Society office had collected the addresses, and would check her progress on this task each evening. All I could do was keep up to date on that, so I concerned myself with reading again.

On April 5[th,] *The Arab Times* had yet more to report about woman suffrage in Kuwait. Kuwait's Minister of Health had faced a major grilling by the MPs the day before, and offered his resignation when it was over. They hadn't accepted it yet, but it didn't look good for him.

His name was Dr. Mohammed Al-Jarallah, and he was one of the 15 men in the Cabinet – Ministers of the various Ministries of this nation. I wondered about the 14 votes from the Cabinet that Rola said were promised for the Kuwaiti suffragettes' bill. They needed all the votes that they could get; suppose this guy was one of the 14 promised yes-voters? Even if he planned on abstaining, a replacement might ruin things by voting no. I would call her about this and ask.

Meanwhile in Brussels, European Union External Relations Commissioner Benita Ferrero-Waldner met with Gulf Cooperation Council foreign ministers and commented about Kuwaiti women voting. She said she would like to see Kuwaiti women gain their political rights, but couldn't force the issue. However, she could endorse it by actively supporting Kuwait, Kuwaiti women, and the Kuwaiti government if they passed the suffrage bill and granted Kuwaiti women the right to vote. She made a point of saying that women make up 50 percent of the society, so of course women ought to be able to vote.

The next day's *Arab Times* duly announced that the Health Minister, Dr. Mohammed Al-Jarallah, had officially resigned, and that the Prime Minister, Sheikh Sabah, had responded by dissolving Parliament. There would be no vote on women's voting rights.

Sure enough, the next issue of the paper dealt with this, complete with a prediction that one of the many outcomes of this will be that the government will be able to "ensure full political rights to women" in Kuwait. Hopefully, this would mean voting at all levels. I had Rola's phone numbers – mobile phone, Kuwait Economic Society office phone, and 2 numbers for her office in Kuwait City. I wanted to know whether and how our strategies would change. But it was tough to discuss that with someone who didn't answer her phone.

The Personal Status Law of Kuwait

The following Thursday's *Kuwait Times* ran an article describing a nagging legal problem for Kuwaiti women, one that a political voice would give them some hope of redressing: it was an interview with a Kuwaiti woman who had married an expatriate, and it detailed the legal and financial ramifications of such a marriage.

This particular woman, named Salama Al-Noman, found that while she herself did not lose her Kuwaiti citizenship, extending the same to her new husband and any children by him was not possible. Only a male Kuwaiti could offer that to his spouse and children. This meant that the benefits of free health care, education and social security were lost to them. Kuwait's patriarchal rules assume that husbands will provide all this. Also gone was the right to own a home in Kuwait. The exact reverse is true when a Kuwaiti man marries a non-Kuwaiti woman. Full benefits are extended to both the new wife and any children that they have.

The Kuwaiti woman in this article decided to return to Kuwait because it is her home, and she loved her home. She lived in a rented apartment, and used her job benefits to provide health benefits to her children. But what would they have when they grew up? I hope that by passing this story on, I am stirring up outrage that will change this.

The Debates and Tactics Rage On

The April 9th issue of *The Arab Times* painted a bleak picture of the outlook for the future of Kuwaiti women's suffrage. (Either that or the paper was giving the opposition equal time in press coverage.) An anti-women's rights MP by the name of Dr. Muslem was quoted extensively in an article with a title that claimed that the woman suffrage bill had been "forced" on Kuwait. Muslem went on to make the tiresome remark that the issue was not a priority, so again I must point out that remarks such as this are a standard tactic of men who don't want women to win legal rights.

Muslem was quoted as supporting the ideas that women ought to stay at home and have no careers, that women should be housewives and raise children, doing nothing else except for remaining invisible and out of men's way. If men like him got their way, half of the population – with many bright and talented individuals – would have no opportunity to share the benefits of their abilities with others or to express themselves. Put up and shut up, he seemed to be saying, accept the role that he believes Islam forces upon women, and obediently put on the shackles, handcuffs, leg-irons, and gags that enslave you to live a fundamentalist life.

Fortunately, the article gave its final third over to the supporters of women's political rights. Dr. Ayyed Al-Mannaa, a columnist and advisor to the Kuwait Journalists Association, said that "these people" – including Dr. Muslem – are not more knowledgeable about Sharia law than the issuers of the 2005 fatwa which favors women's political rights. He went on to name particular Muslim clerics who were careful scholars of Sharia law, including the authors of the fatwas. He called women's rights opponents "retarded and ignorant" and accused them of allowing themselves to issue their own fatwas against women's rights. His comments, though eminently satisfying to read, were not part of the first impression conveyed by the article, with its glaringly large title. They were, however, the last word in it.

Back to the Office

After carefully reading that, I called Rola on her mobile phone – no answer. Her secretary answered at the family office, however, and assured me that Rola was in the country...she was just busy and out of the office. I asked her to please have Rola call me, and to say that I was concerned about our efforts, the potential dissolution of Parliament and what that might mean for our efforts and their outcome, etc. David once again reminded me of how difficult people are to communicate with in Kuwait...they just don't answer their cell phones if they don't feel like it, and that is often.

Not Rola, though – she called me back a bit later, with good news and bad news. Bad news first: the Kuwaiti MPs didn't have government e-mails. They would in the future, but the system wasn't organized yet – just ordered. Good news: we could still e-mail Speaker Jassem Al-Khorafi and Prime Minister Sheikh Sabah, and lots more people in surrounding Arab and Islamic countries that Rola had met or spoken to who wanted to be included in our mass e-mailing. Okay – I would return to her office tomorrow afternoon, and bring with me the latest news articles from *The Arab Times* – she hadn't seen them.

We would probably modify our letters using quotes from opponents in the National Assembly. Perhaps we could send copies of our letter – the one meant for all of the Kuwaiti Members of Parliament – on paper to them all. Also, the Cabinet Minister who planned to abstain from voting on the women's suffrage bill turned out to be the Minister of Justice. He didn't want the bill to pass, but it wasn't politically expedient for him to vote against it. Interesting.

So on April 10th, I went back to Rola's office and we revamped our letters to the Kuwaiti lawmakers, addressing them only to Prime Minister Sheikh Sabah Al-Sabah and to Speaker of the Kuwaiti Parliament Jassem Al-Khorafi. After that, I e-mailed mine out to all of the people whose business cards Rola and I had – media, academicians, businesspeople, non-governmental organizations, politicians, friends, etc. Included in the letter from me was the attached letter to the Sheikh and the Speaker, with their e-mail addresses.

When that was finished, Rola told me that she now had to send hers out, along with another letter in Arabic, which she had written out by hand but not yet typed. She had written it on the plane home from Jordan over the weekend, while she was full of ideas from meeting more people. After Rola told me about that, I told her that I would like to continue working with her as a liaison to American media and other professionals when I go home. She was interested. If there was any chance of returning to Kuwait, great, and if not, there was always e-mail.

With Rola satisfied with the day's efforts, I proceeded to photocopy for her the articles that I had been reading and saving. Anita the secretary helped me. Rola told me that if Kuwaiti women got the right to vote, she won't stop there – Kuwaiti women had other problems. The personal status law and its effect on Kuwaiti women who marry foreigners (and their children) needed changing. Rola said that she would welcome help from me, and we discussed the citizenship conditions of women in other nations as a basis for comparison.

With that, I said goodbye, and Rola took note of when I was to return to the United States, because she wanted to see me again and plan our next moves before I went home (it was less than a month away).

News Again...

April 11th was a quiet day; I stayed home and looked at 2 day's worth of newspapers. Dr. Al-Jarallah's resignation had been accepted – so now it was official: he had quit his job. Interesting how someone quits a job in government...in any country. They say that they quit, and then they have to wait for their resignation to be formally accepted. What a lot of fuss. Meanwhile, everyone swore up and down that the Kuwaiti Parliament wouldn't be dissolved, and that business as usual would continue in the land of the lawmakers. Bills will continue to be debated and either passed or rejected.

Oddly, it was the News in Brief report that made the most interesting story. The Rector of the American University of Kuwait, Dr. Shafeeq Al-Ghabra, was talking hypothetically about what would happen in Kuwait if women here were actually granted full political rights. He wondered – would the genders be mixed in the Parliament, as in most countries where men and women have equal political rights?

This got me thinking along similar lines. How would the National Assembly function in this sexually segregated culture? What was next – separate debating rooms for male and female politicians? How would that work, anyway? I could see how stock brokers could function in a gender-segregated environment – the Kuwait Stock Exchange had separate trading floors. Watching the buying and selling of stocks on a computer board above rows of seats can be done without talking to anyone, but debating issues in a political assembly must be done together.

Would Kuwaitis actually have a room of debating men and a room of debating women, tally up 2 rooms worth of results from voting on the issues, and then add them all up? Wouldn't the politicians then want to debate together, which would be impossible without coming face to face? What would they do...have a chat room on an Intranet? Would 2 separate debates' worth of text be published after the fact for the press? How balanced would the political and media attention to each group of politicians be? Also, what if only 3 women got elected to the National Assembly? Will they really go to all that trouble for such a small number of politicians? If they didn't, how would those women politicians be heard, or be effective?

This last question made me wonder how the Quran would be involved: it demands that for every witness, a male witness is worth 2 female witnesses, whereas one female witness isn't enough to take seriously. Would anyone suggest that women are liars, and must independently corroborate everything that other women say, but that men never lie? How would all this work in politics, a profession notorious for liars? It seems like too much quibbling over who gets how much attention and in what way. Giving everyone equal time in the same space seems better. I felt like a Vulcan visiting Earth and expecting logic, which I just wouldn't find.

The Arab Times ran a story that listed several articles of the Kuwaiti Constitution which helped woman suffragists, especially number 75; it says that the Constitution can only be amended "to provide more freedom and equality." Also helpful was a comment by a former MP and current Secretary-General of the Democratic Forum, Abdullah Al-Naibari, who pointed out that "Kuwait has signed an international agreement to end discrimination against women and pass laws which provide for justice and equality between men and women." I wouldn't hold my breath or get overly excited, but it seemed promising, I thought.

Kuwaiti Women Get the Vote....Sort Of

Extra, extra, read all about it! On April 20th in *The Arab Times*, it was close, but it wasn't the desired end. The Kuwaiti Parliament had passed into law a bill that gave women the right to vote...in municipal elections. With 48 out of 65 officials voting, it passed by a vote of 28-20. Of course the Justice Minster abstained, as promised. He didn't even show up during the voting. There were speculations about his absence, but they were brushed aside by Sheikh Sabah, saying that it didn't mean anything.

So now women could vote, but not in all elections at all levels. This is what is called hali-wali – a disparaging term for things that are below acceptable standards – a piddling little thing, an incremental granting of voting and political rights – an insult to our intelligence and our status as human beings. The article, which quoted Rola Al-Dashti and Sheikh Sabah, contained the usual rude remarks by male chauvinist, selfish politicians – including MP Al-Muslim – who claim that women's voting rights were not a priority, that all women should do is stay home and raise children, that soldiers and 18-year-old males deserved the right to vote more than women did, and on and on. It reminded me of Molly Pitcher being denied a veteran's pension after taking over her fallen husband's cannon in the American Revolutionary War.

Rola hoped that women would run in municipal elections. (Well, why not – get noticed and on the political record.) Another Kuwaiti women's rights activist, Naima Al-Shayeji, lamented, "Why do women have to get their rights in doses?" This response is a poignant reminder and warning that was voiced by others as well, suggesting that male politicians are likely to expect Kuwaiti women to quietly accept this as a pacifying measure rather than continue to push for full political rights. That will not happen, but women suffragists were worrying that progress in Kuwait on this issue might grind to a full halt.

Another article quoted a Muslim woman by the name of Kamilia Hilmi Mohammed denouncing Western feminists for "ruining Muslim countries." Here was another patriarchal woman undermining and betraying her own gender. She did this at a meeting of the International Islamic Committee for Women and Children, which is affiliated with the International Islamic Council for Propagation and Relief, in Shuwaikh. In her speech, she charged Western feminists with many ridiculous actions and motives, twisting their words and portraying them as deliberately anti-Islamic. Her overall charge was that they get anti-Islamic but pro-women proposals adopted at international women forums. As for her particular charges, she accused Western feminists of rejecting heterosexual marriage outright, plus motherhood and childbirth. She ought to talk to me.

As a married feminist – in a heterosexual relationship! – I find her charges laughable. Sadly, she has plenty of [deliberately] mistaken company. Many Islamic fundamentalists in the world, both male and female, do not want Muslim women to have any choice but to get married to whomever their fathers decide to marry their daughters to.

After that, they insist that women should do nothing but raise children or, if not only that, that it should be women's top priority, with all other life ambitions taking a back seat to child rearing. Not every woman wants the same thing, however, and forcing it upon them is not the best thing for women or for children. Children should be wanted or not had in the first place.

Fortunately, the article went on to quote an opposing view, one put forth by Kuwait University political science professor Dr. Massouma Al-Mubarak, who said that women must have full political rights. She added that women make up three quarters of the world's population (I would love to check that statistic. It sounds a bit high.), and that "despite religious teachings guaranteeing their rights" many women around the world are suffering from various forms of discrimination. This suffering can range from a lack of voting rights to murder dressed up as "honor" killings, and having the right to vote would be a step in the right direction towards changing laws that protect men and others who perpetrate it.

The weekend's *Arab Times* was full of news about the incremental victory won by Kuwaiti women suffragists. There were 2 articles – one jubilant story called "Joy That Now It's Finally "Us"," and another from the United Nations, praising Kuwaiti lawmakers and congratulating Kuwaiti women, while urging Kuwaiti woman suffragists to keep pushing for full political rights. The U.N.'s meaning is carefully spelled out: voting rights at all levels and the right to hold political office in the National Assembly and on the Cabinet. Quotes came from representatives of France, Italy, Russia, India ("better late than never"!), and Jordan. Rola Al-Dashti was again quoted in the jubilant article, filling 2 paragraphs in which she urged Kuwaiti women to make the most of this victory by voting in the October municipal elections.

As for other quotes in the jubilant Kuwaiti article, there were many, including, interestingly, those of a male political writer named Shamlan Al-Essa. There have been repeated comments by lawmakers to the effect that 18-year-old males and males in the Kuwaiti military service ought to get precedence in voting rights, and Al-Essa disagreed with them. He went on to express disapproval for other iniquities faced by Kuwaiti women: even at age 21, a Kuwaiti woman may not choose her own husband; she must marry whomever a male relative deems acceptable. She also cannot pass on citizenship to her children or extend it to a foreign husband. It was delightful to find a Kuwaiti man saying that this just wasn't right. He accused Salaf party members and Bedouins, who have many relatives in the military, of opposing women's rights.

Apparently, a large number of Kuwaiti males were willing to share voting rights with women, and saw nothing un-Islamic about doing so – at any political level. The problem lay in the selection of the members of Parliament, made by Kuwaiti [male] voters. How did the National Assembly get so many fundamentalists into its numbers?! I suspected apathetic voter turnout – it happens in so many countries, including, unfortunately, my own. People think that their vote won't make a difference, so they don't even try to affect the outcome of elections by showing up at the polls. The results speak for themselves.

This issue of the paper included a useful inventory of Gulf States which include voting rights for women – at all political levels (which my Lonely Planet book lacked): Oman, Qatar, United Arab Emirates, Bahrain and Syria. Kuwaiti women were not happy about lagging behind, as evidenced by 3 paragraphs' worth of quotations by Fareah Al-Saqqaf, a Kuwaiti women's rights activist. They are finally catching up – sort of.

One More Visit with Rola

A few days later, David came with me to meet Rola, and it was just as well that he did, because he saw how things really were with her, with her office, her schedule, and how difficult it was to communicate with her or to maintain a stream of conversation with her. She didn't make it difficult willfully; she was just very, very busy. We met her mother and one of her brothers while we were there – nice people – but they never saw her and had to leave before Rola even arrived. The meeting with Rola, when it finally took place, was peppered with interruptions. Her secretary, her 2 telephones, her painters...all of them constantly interrupted her throughout the meeting. It felt like a miracle that we actually understood her and she understood us.

The purpose of meeting with her was tie up all loose ends of my time in Kuwait and assess how much help I had been and could be to her in the future. I was not delighted with the outcome of my efforts: my letter, signed by me, had not been read with interest by the feminists of the Gulf States. The problem was that, despite the fact that it had explained who I was and with whom I was working (namely Rola), they had never heard of me and so did not want to deal with me. It was the classic problem of wasta. With no counterpart to the men's diwaniyas and no way to jet around the Middle East at will, I could not know them.

Despite this setback, Rola told me that she wanted to stay in touch and continue our association. I was surprised, and doubted that we would achieve much more if she couldn't be relied upon to answer her e-mails regularly. Well, at least David saw this for himself, and would now understand the problem, which was a classic one of non-communication.

The meeting also cleared up a few key misconceptions: Rola is not affiliated with Kuwait University; her connections in the Kuwait Economic Society were limited to economic work and woman suffrage fact-finding; the women's group she met with was just an unofficial group of 6 or 8 women who ate Thursday morning brunches together; most of her work was done out of the Alor Group/Faro International business, which she ran with her mother.

The only letterhead that she could use for her woman suffrage work was the business letterhead. David had ideas about Rola getting me funding for travel and other business expenses related to doing this writing and publishing work, ideas which I knew were unrealistic, so I had brought him along to hear this for himself. Sure enough, Rola could not accomplish such things. She operated at her own expense.

We were supposed to meet with her at 10 a.m. this morning, but as our cab approached Kuwait City, we spoke to her on the phone and found her in a big hurry. She could only spend 10 minutes with me; she suddenly had a really important meeting, etc. No good, we said, we had more to talk about – could we meet later in the day? Okay, at half past noon. Fine. We didn't want to waste the cab fare to the center of the city now that we were halfway there.

We went to Rola's office and found Anita the secretary, who was friendly and welcoming to us as usual. She let us use the phone to confirm our airplane tickets – and even helped us by getting the right people on the phone. It turned out that they were all set with pre-arranged electronic reservations…except for David's Kuwait Airways flight out. That one would have been cancelled without a phone call.

While we waited, we met Rola's mother. She was interesting to see: she looked like a slightly older version of Rola with glasses: a nice lady with her hair fully visible and tied into a tight bun with a scrunchie (ribbon-covered elastic). She wore a casual pink outfit – pants with a long-sleeved cotton shirt and sneakers – no abbeya.

Rola's brother was there, too, waiting to see her. His name was Payman, he worked in Virginia, and lived across from a shopping mall that we knew well in McLean, Virginia. Small world – he knew Washington, D.C., and his company made frequent trips to Beacon Falls, Connecticut. He was just visiting in Kuwait, and had lived in the U.S. for 28 years. He added that this was the third anniversary of their father's death, meaning that the family members would visit his grave and meet each other at some point during the day. It all sounded so normal and unremarkable. After listening, I politely asked how many brothers and sisters there were.

The answer was anything but unremarkable: 23 total. I found myself asking how many wives he had when he was alive: the answer was 4. He didn't have them consecutively, either – he had them concurrently. Payman said that he grew up calling the other 3 of them "mom" and that Rola's mother is not his mother, but he wanted to visit her while he was in Kuwait. Rola's mom appeared to be happy, but then she was fully visible and independently working with a business, and widowed. She did not have to deal with her Al-Dashti polygamist any longer. As for Rola, I had asked her whether she was married or not, and she had said "single and happy."

There was absolutely no time to talk to Rola about any of this. We met with her, discussed our intentions, made an agreement, took some photographs of her with me and with her secretary (who was soon to be married – the couple were Indian Christians from Goa), and we said our good-byes. All this we did with numerous, constant interruptions of all kinds.

Anita, Rola Al-Dashti Ph.D., and Stephanie C. Fox, J.D.

Payman told us that Rola was the only Kuwaiti he knew who worked from 8 a.m. to 11 p.m. every day, and we believed him. Rola was heard to say to one person, over the phone, "Wake him up!" when she found that someone was following a normal Kuwaiti schedule of taking a mid-afternoon nap when she needed an answer from him. She was a very energetic, hard worker in a slow-moving society. Rola promised not to leave us waiting for too long for replies from her once we get home, but response times could vary from 48 hours to 2 weeks, depending upon how heavy her workload and schedule are at any given time.

We thanked her very much and went away feeling somewhat hopeful. I would work on the manuscript for my book about our time in Kuwait when we returned home, and see what else developed, without depending on Rola or anyone else.

On April 29th, *The Kuwait Times* ran a story about an MP who didn't really want Kuwaiti women to have any voting rights at all, one Waleed Al-Tabtabaei. He was attempting to delay enjoyment of their new right to vote in municipal elections by demanding a women's voter list before Parliament went into recess. Of course this raised the question: was there already a list of registered male voters? Well, there ought to be; all voters should register themselves, male and female, so that no one can vote more than once. Supposedly none of this nonsense would delay women from voting.

I spent May 1st, just 3 days before my departure, reading the news yet again. The lure of information about woman suffrage had proved irresistible day after day; I had only read herstorical accounts of such fights in my own culture and country.

There were 3 stories about giving Kuwaiti women the right to vote in municipal elections. One story mentioned that the National Assembly approved this right on April 19th as a "rehearsal" for granting full voting rights to soldiers and 18-year-olds, and that a total of 228,000 Kuwait women were eligible to vote in municipal elections as of the last available statistic, dated December 31, 2004. It went on to talk about other countries' records on women's rights, suggesting that Kuwait was not the only nation which set a shameful example in this regard. Suggestions about adopting a quota system for female politicians in Kuwait's National Assembly, similar to Iraq's new system, were rejected.

Another story was full of congratulations from other countries to Kuwait for passing the law the allows women to vote in municipal elections, saying that these countries are certain that Kuwait will continue to grant women more rights until they have full political rights. This was just a veiled and politely phrased message in diplomatic terms that amounted to telling Kuwaiti politicians to grant women full political rights and get on with it or be considered to be treating women disgracefully. The day's paper had the Prime Minister of Kuwait, Sabah Al-Sabah, saying something very similar.

Home Again – and Kuwaiti Women Win at Last

I was glad to be home when the time came. David arrived a day after I did, and he brought me 2 more issues of *The Arab Times*. One talked about Kuwaiti women's chances of voting in the fall in the municipal elections. It didn't seem likely at the time.

The Kuwaiti Parliament had ruined it for them, postponing the vote until after the date necessary for it to be logistically and legally possible for Kuwaiti women to enjoy voting that year, but still making it possible to pass the law in time for the 2009 elections.

The objection was that including them would change the voting demographics in each municipal area, thus making the outcome far less predictable. (Sooner or later, they would have to face that situation!) Men who were betting on winning this year's elections were not at all convinced that they would win with women as a part of the equation, so they put it off. Rola Al-Dashti was quoted as hopeful for the 2009 elections…hopeful that women would vote in them.

On May 18th of 2005, 2 weeks after I got home, I read the great news. 2 days earlier, on May 16th, 2005, Kuwaiti women had won the right to vote at all political levels! In a vote of 35 to 23 with one abstention, the law has been passed, and Rola Al-Dashti was quoted as jubilantly intending to run for office in the 2007 elections. A careful reading of articles in both *The Arab Times* article (on-line) and an editorial in *The Hartford Courant*, Connecticut's state newspaper, suggested that there would be plenty more news for a while on Kuwaiti women's rights.

One thing in particular immediately jumped out at me: the threat that female politicians might be required to wear abbeyas and/or hijabs. Rola doesn't wear them – she dresses as a Westerner. If she accepted a restriction such as this in exchange for the vote, she would have lost one huge freedom in exchange for another one. I wondered what would happen next.

As it turned out, she ran for political office and lost the following year, but she was one of 11 women who ran. We tried to keep in touch but, true to cultural type, she did not return any of my e-mails. I realized that it was no reflection on me.

Nearly a month later, I was still thinking about Kuwaiti women's suffrage.

One question –that Zahra had asked – stayed with me after all this: how would the lives of Kuwaiti women be changed by having the right to vote? (She didn't see how it would change her life – yet. Wait until she has a husband and wants to do specific things, I thought.) I have always known, since I was aware that the right existed in my country, that I would have it when I became of age to exercise it. I don't know what it's like not to have it. She knew, but had not been taught that it is important, nor had she thought about it much on her own. This is how it has been for women of every country where there have ever been woman suffragists: some appreciated and fought for this right, while others occupied themselves with other things.

Many of those women did not support the fight for the right to vote.

Many of those same women went ahead and enjoyed the spoils of the efforts and sufferings of the women who had fought for them.

Many women in many nations who have had this right for decades or longer take this right – this feeling of autonomy and self-determination – for granted, sometimes voting without a thought for how and why they are able to do so, and many others do not bother to exercise their right to vote at all. They are too busy, or think that their vote won't make a difference.

None of them would want to live in the situation of the past, however.

I know that the U.S. government sent its military to oust the Iraqi invaders from what it essentially viewed as its little gas station in the distant desert, but when I saw what happened not long after I came home, I was pleased that this had been done for yet another reason.

It was just 3 weeks after I returned to the United States that Kuwaiti women won the right to vote at all political levels.

Aisha's mother-in-law went right out and voted the first chance she got.

Four years after that, Rola Al-Dashti was elected to a seat in Kuwait's Majlis (Parliament), also known as the National Assembly, on May 16th, 2009. She was one of 4 women who won seats.

Chapter 20
Home – Culture Shock All Over Again

On May 4th, 2005, Saleh drove me and our cat – with David – to Kuwait International Airport. We were going back to the United States via Air France, just as we had come to Kuwait. David would follow via American Airlines in 2 more days.

Packing to go had stressed me out a bit, but David dealt with that by telling me that he and Saleh would deal with the furniture – just get all the small stuff put away for him and he would handle the rest. So I did: the quilt set got bagged up (alas, I couldn't wash it out, and it was terribly dusty), and I packed all of the dishes in newspaper. That was it; David said he would have Saleh sell our furniture, and keep the smaller stuff in case he needed it on some future visit to Kuwait. (I think our stuff – all of it – is still in some back corner of Saleh's house, though.)

I brought back all of the books that I had collected during the trip, even though I had to pay extra. It was worth it, and I still have them, plus the Fulla doll, the AlSadu House bag, and the handmade nail from the Al-Boom restaurant.

David assured me that everything would be fine, and it was – in 2 more days he was safely back in the United States with me.

But first I had to fly home with Scheherazade Cat, repeating our steps the previous fall in reverse. This time, the airport officials did want to see her paperwork, asking for the exit visa. David told me that they were hoping to extract a huge bribe from us, but they had no leverage when they saw that we could produce that document.

We had to wait for an hour or so before it was time for me to walk through the last gate to the terminal seating, so David and I sat with Saleh downstairs in the fast food area. I noticed a group of American soldiers in the McDonald's seating, and smiled and waved to a woman soldier. She gave me a big smile and a wave back. They were either going to or returning from the U.S. Army base near the Iraqi border, in northern Kuwait, David told me.

The Kuwaiti security people did not pat me down; they were all men.

This did not escape my notice, considering the events of 9/11 and all the effort put into security that I observed in France – a woman at the Charles de Gaulle International Airport did in fact pat me down – and upon arriving at Newark Airport. I was simply ushered into the plane.

Once I had kissed David good-bye and lost sight of him as I walked toward the gate, I found that I was really excited about both the trip – I was going to pass through Paris, after all – and getting back to my home culture.

Flying on a French plane would mean wine with dinner, something that I had foregone for months without complaint, and perhaps some haram food, which was how I had jokingly come to think of bacon, and most likely some baked goods that tasted right. I would likely have to wait for the transatlantic flight for that, but so what – it was in my near future.

The trip home was fun. The cat was fine, too. She seemed to really know the routine, and she accepted every opportunity for food, water and toileting that I offered. She slept a lot and was no trouble. I was seated next to a cat lover, a woman who was my age or perhaps a little younger, on the Paris to Newark flight, so getting along was no problem at all. Speaking French was a plus, too: I ordered some food in French, helped an airsick woman who moaned and wretched, and found my way around Charles de Gaulle Airport.

That airport is interesting: it is divided into 6 segments, with its terminal buildings labeled A through F; one boards a bus to change terminals. The French people in the airport were very nice – I saw none of the snootiness toward foreigners that one often finds in Paris (well, this was an airport – they would never get people through the place if they acted like that).

Something really funny happened there: I met a guy from Houston, Texas when I deplaned. He had just left Kuwait, too. We stopped at a little booth to ask young airport security man where to go next. The Texan just walked up to the booth and asked his question without preamble, and the French man wouldn't answer right away; he kept saying, "Good morning," in English, and the Texan just kept asking his question, until I told him, "Say "Good morning" to him, and then he'll tell you how to get where you're going." "Oh, is that how it works?" he said to me. He took my advice, and then the French man helped him. Funny – but imagine the French man's point of view…he probably was trying to avoid hating his job.

Terminal C was great fun. I found Fauchon chocolates for sale, and Côte D'Or chocolates, and Valrhona chocolates. After buying some of these, I browsed the stores for other items, ending up with some reading materials in both French and English. There were famous and high-priced stores to look in, such as Galleries Lafayette and Hermes, with scarves for €80+, ties for €120+, etc. I ate some strawberries and a chocolate croissant with a cappuccino in a modern cafeteria. A nice French lady was getting a meal there with her husband. She offered to help me work the coffee machine, but I hadn't decided what I wanted just then. I smiled and thanked her anyway. I was having a wonderful time.

Some man from a southern African nation saw my cat when I sat down to wait for boarding time and asked me all about her – they liked cats. I told them all about her, because they wanted me to, and then I got nervous about meeting the plane and got up to wait as close to the gate as possible. The plane wasn't ready on time, and it turned out to be a huge airbus on the far side of the airport. The passengers were all ferried over to it on a ground bus.

I was so happy to be away from the restrictive Islamic world that I had some white wine with my delectable gourmet dinner on that second plane ride. It was included in the cost of the ticket, so why not? Dinner was a fish called straith with a lemon butter sauce, rice pilaf and carrot purée. There was a wedge of Brie cheese, bread and butter, strawberry yoghurt (the good kind with fruit on the bottom), mineral water, an appetizer of chicken satay on Middle Eastern carrot and rice salad, and plum pie. I thoroughly enjoyed it, and the wine, which came in a small bottle, gave me a slight buzz. The wine was my celebration of what felt like an escape from the Islamic world with its many restrictions on enjoyment. The food on the Kuwait to Paris flight was okay, but nowhere near as spectacular as the food I ate over the Atlantic Ocean.

Arriving in Newark was the point at which I learned how differently trips to the Islamic world are viewed from trips to, say, Europe or Japan. Everyone had to go through a booth with a cop, regardless of where we had been; there was a huge, long row of such booths – half for U.S. citizens and half for visitors to our country. What was different for those of us who had visited Islamic countries was what came next. Instead of being finished there, an immigration official took us to a back room full of seats with round seals on the wall that said "United States Department of Homeland Security" – thank you, John Ashcroft.

The cops loomed above everyone from a raised platform where they looked down on us as they asked us which countries we had been to and why and what we had done there. They typed the information into their computers and then let us leave. I was the second person to be called, and a young male cop wanted to know, as he leafed through the pages of my passport, what I did in Kuwait and Iran. Kuwait: I helped my husband research a book on Arabian foods, and wrote a journal about my experiences there, taking digital photos and visiting every museum that I could see. Iran: we didn't go because we couldn't afford it, and I was so glad, because of that insulting head scarf law for women. He seemed quite satisfied, especially with my attitude about

Islam. Cops in the area surrounding New York tend to be skeptical of it, thanks to 9/11.

As for my attitude about Islam, I don't think I will ever be a fan of it, but I also don't see any reason to hate and fear every Muslim on the planet. I made several new friends in the Islamic world. None are extremists or potential murderers; they are just people with careers and families whose religion has always been Islam. I don't like the way Muslim women are often treated by Muslim men, but as long as they are living by their own choices (hijabs, etc.), I am content to mind my own business to a large extent. If they are unhappy, however – this being considered on a case-by-case basis – my attitude changes. I will not operate on the idea that their culture is different so therefore noninterference is okay, even when they ask for help. Ask for help and I will try to give it – even if someone calls me insensitive to Islam.

When the cops were through with me in that room, I wheeled the cat out and got my luggage. I had to pay $3.00 for a cart to move it around on, and a nice airport worker helped me and another woman (I had the cat to wheel, and she had a little girl to wheel, so we needed some help) to put our bags onto these carts and then push them over to the next officer. The next officer was a chatty, friendly sort who asked what I had been doing in Kuwait and did I have any food with me? I didn't mention the 4 packages of Turkish coffee. He seemed easily satisfied and told me not to worry about fees for the goods I had bought – I had spent way below the $800 exemption, so I was free to go. But first, I had to clear the cat for passage into the U.S.

Another cop appeared to look at the cat's paperwork. Leaving Kuwait, I had been required to show her export "visa" paper, but entering the U.S. this guy wanted one thing only: the original, signed rabies vaccination paper. I had to pull out the whole stack of papers and turn them over one by one to get to what he wanted. He commented on them as I started off, saying that no, he didn't want that one or that one, until I said I had to find the page he wanted. He quieted down and let me get it, then wanted to know whether I had any open cans of cat food on me. I gave him the one that I had opened in the Paris airport. Scheherazade had eaten 2 meals out of that one. The cop was a bit zealous, and began carrying on about how it might have picked up some germ on the way; it had to be thrown out, and on and on. I said he didn't need to convince me of anything; if the rule was to get rid of it then by all means take it – I wouldn't argue. He stopped fussing and walked off with it, looking happy.

With that, I walked out and saw my father staring earnestly into the distance, just beyond the glass doors. Then I saw my mother, too. They were glad to see me, and after a brief stop in the rest room – where I reveled in the abundance of toilet paper and the absence of water hoses – we went to the car, loaded everything in, and drove off. 3 hours later, we pulled into a Ruby Tuesday's restaurant, where I made a point of ordering cheese fries with bacon – I wanted some "haram" food. We drove home after that, and I slept for about 24 hours, with one afternoon call from my Aunt Joan to welcome me home.

Friday afternoon, I went to see my grandmother, who lives 5 minutes (by car) away from my parents. My mother brought me to her house, where I told her all about the trip, and showed her a few exhibits: the Fulla doll, the Shajarah bag woven at AlSadu house, and the 3 hijabs I had bought. I also showed Nana and my uncle how to wear them, both Fatin's way and Aiesha's way – Egyptian and Kuwaiti. I gave them the chocolate bar from Paris, and they were delighted.

Cookie, the black-and-white male cat who lives with my parents, was camped out in my room constantly. Teddy Bear, the Sheltie dog that I had given to my grandmother happily went out for a walk with me. I took him through my grandmother's neighborhood to Gledhill Nursery, where I feasted my eyes and nose on everything that I had been telling my Kuwaiti friends that I looked forward to experiencing again: lilacs, wisteria, irises, lavender, peonies, roses, and sweet, freshly cut grass. A woman was mowing her lawn near the nursery, and I smelled the wonderful, sweet grass.

David brought me two more issues of *The Arab Times*; one talked about Kuwaiti women's suffrage. The other had Ali Ahmad Al-Baghli's usual weekend editorial. It said that a religious government was not the best thing for any nation. This was mostly a rehashing of the previous week's editorial, but it would make a great exhibit at the Mother's Day party when I could point out that Kuwait was not a land infested with religious extremists. Instead, it is a land populated by people whose religion happens to be Islam. Kuwaiti people think about other things besides their religion, just as other people do.

Last but not least, it had another jinn article by Claudia Farkas Al-Rashoud. This one showed a beautiful color photo of a black cat. Apparently, jinn sometimes appeared as black cats, but they could do so as helpers. So much for the superstition that black cats bring bad luck – this jinn was good luck! ☺

I now had nothing more to worry about than to watching myself for any signs of culture shock as I settled back into life at home.

Glossary of Arabic Words

English to Arabic (Kuwaiti Dialect)

cat	=	gatwa
fox	=	thaalab
thank you	=	šukran
hello or peace	=	salaam
welcome (you're welcome)	=	'afwan
finished	=	khalas
In the name of God, the Merciful, the Benevolent.	=	Bi's-mi'llah, al rahman, al rahim.
no	=	lāi
yes	=	aioua
God willing	=	insh'allah
maybe tomorrow	=	insh'allah bokram'allesh

This is frequently tacked onto "insh'allah."
It means that one can just forget about it…whatever "it" is.

Devil	=	Shaitan
good-bye/with peace	=	ma es salaam
influence	=	wasta
Hey! How's it going?	=	Salaam alaikum!
milk	=	halib
tea	=	chai

poor	=	meskeen
sleep	=	nayim
dad	=	baba
father	=	abu
mother	=	umm
lettuce	=	khas
strawberry	=	farawla
mango	=	manga
garlic cream-sauce	=	thoom
mushroom	=	fagae
sheep	=	harouf
sucer	=	sugar
mall or market	=	souq
morally bad	=	haram
bad	=	kharban
zein	=	good
women's visiting room	=	harim
men's visiting room	=	diwaniya
lawyer	=	muhammi
marriage	=	zawaj
wife	=	zouwja
husband	=	zouwj

no good	=	hali-wali
astonishing	=	ajib
strange	=	gharib
building superintendent	=	bouab
women's head scarf	=	hijab
non-human, as in a non-Muslim/Jew/Christian	=	qaffer
rest room or bathroom	=	hamam
genie(s)	=	jinn(i)
without	=	Bedoun

Describes people with no citizenship papers. They are literally without a home country.

Arab ruler	=	Emir or Amir
Islamic religious edict	=	fatwa
Amiri wish-decree	=	raqba
business plan/proposal	=	iqtirah
"The machine is off."	=	"El jihaz mohillaq."

Recording heard whenever someone calls a Kuwaiti's cell phone. This is because the owner usually has it switched off.

one	=	wahad
Mafay mishkla!	=	No problem!
Southern rural Egyptian	=	Saeedi
small pitted fruit of sidr trees	=	knar

jinn exorcism ceremony	=	zar
left (direction)	=	shemel
right (direction)	=	yeimine
straight ahead	=	sidha
bribe money	=	baksheesh
thin wool over-robe for men edged with gold embroidery	=	bisht
women's over-robe that completely covers clothes	=	abbeya
men's robe	=	dishdashah
men's head cloth	=	guthra
fastener for men's head cloth	=	ekal
men's cap (under cloth)	=	khaffiah
women's head scarf	=	hijab
women's face veil	=	nekhab
grocery store	=	jamiyah

Bibliography

1. Sheikha Altaf Salem Al-Ali Al-Sabah, *Kuwait Traditions: Creative Expressions of a Culture*, Printed in Kuwait, 2001.

2. Claudia Farkas Al-Rashoud, *Dame Violet Dickson: "Umm Saud's" Fascinating Life in Kuwait from 1929-1990*, Al-Alfain Printing Press, Kuwait, 1997.

3. Jehan Sayid Rajab, *Failaka Island: The Ikaros of the Arabian Gulf*, Tareq Rajab Museum, Publisher, 1999.

4. Arab World Map Library, *Kuwait – Scale 1:500,000 with city maps of Central Kuwait and Kuwait Urban Areas*, Published by GEOprojects (U.K.) Ltd., www.geoprojects.net, 2002.

5. National Geographic Society, Washington, D.C, *National Geographic: The World*, www.nationalgeographic.com/maps, Printed August 2004.

6. Ali Kazuyoski Nomachi, Photographer, and Seyyed Hossein Nasr, Essayist, *Mecca The Blessed, Medina The Radiant: The Holiest Cities of Islam*, Motivate Publishing, 2004.

7. Jassim Mohammed Al-Hassan, Ph.D., *The Iraqi Invasion of Kuwait, An Environmental Catastrophe*, Printed by Fahad Al-Marzouk, Kuwait, 1992.

8. Andrew Humphreys, John R. Bradley, Paul Greenway, Anthony Ham, Paul Harding, Siona Jenkins, Virginia Maxwell, Richard Plunkett, Grace Pundyk, Deanna Swaney, Jenny Walker, and Pat Yale, *Middle East*, 4th Edition, LONELY PLANET PUBLICATIONS, 2003.

9. William Facey and Gillian Grant, *Kuwait by the First Photographers*, I. B. Tauris & Co., Ltd., Publishers, 1998.

10. Claudia Farkas Al-Rashoud, *Kuwait's Age of Sail: Pearl Divers, Sea Captains, & Ship Builders Past & Present*, Husain Mohammed Rafie Marafie, Publisher, 1993.

11. Staff Writer, "Voting: It's Hard Work – Why Vote? 2004" *The Hartford Courant*, Tuesday, November 2, 2004, Section D, pages 1 and 4.

12. Larry Geber, "Learn Arabic by Practical Method," *The Arab Times*, No. 12054, Sunday, December 12, 2004, page 19.

13. Dr. Sami Al-Rabaa, "Kuwaiti Academics," *The Arab Times*, No. 12088, Thursday-Friday, January 20-21, 2005, pages 1 and 6.

14. Mansour Al-Sultan, ""Hajji" Returns, Kills 14-Year-Old Daughter," *The Arab Times*, No. 12093, Wednesday, January 26, 2005, pages 1 and 6.

15. Staff Writer, "Kuwait to Push Political Rights for Women," *The Arab Times*, No. 12115, Monday, February 21, 2005, pages 1 and 8.

16. Raed Yousef, ""Give Priority to Women's Issue, Instead of Referring it to Court,"" *The Arab Times*, No. 12115, Monday, February 21, 2005, page 2.

17. Khalid Al-Hajri, ""Ummah" Backs Women's Rights...ICM Yet to Decide," *The Arab Times*, No. 12116, Tuesday, February 22, 2005, pages 1 and 8.

18. B. Izzak, "Cabinet to Discuss Preparations for Vote on Women's Suffrage, *The Kuwait Times*, No. 12848, Monday, February 28, 2005, pages 1 and 4.

19. Kuwait, "Kuwaiti V.I.P.s Hold Desert Truffle Mushroom Hunt," *Al-Qabas*, Tuesday, 1 March 2005 – 34th Year – No. 11395 – KUWAIT, page 48.

20. H. Hashim Ahmed, "Kuwaiti Women Set Legislative Agenda," *The Arab Times*, No. 12124, Thursday-Friday, March 3-4, 2005, pages 1 and 8.

21. Raed Yousef, "MPs, Al-Matouq on Collision Course Over Rights for Women – Women's Society to Sue Tabtabaei for "Derogatory" Remarks," *The Arab Times*, No. 12125, Saturday, March 5, 2005, page 3.

22. Ben Arfaj Al-Mutairi, "Liberals Lobby for Women Ahead of Monday Debate: Government Cool to Teen Vote, Poll Rights to "Boots"," *The Arab Times*, No. 12126, Sunday, March 6, 2005, pages 1 and 8.

23. B. Izzak, "Women's Rights Battle Rages – Islamist Leader Threatens Counter-March to Women's Rally," *The Kuwait Times*, No. 12854, Monday, March 7, 2005, pages 1 and 4.

24. Anne-Rhona Crichton, *Al Sadu: The Techniques of Bedouin Weaving*, AL SADU, Kuwait, 2nd Edition, 1998.

25. National Council for Culture & Art and Letters, *Kuwait National Museum – Popular Traditional Museum*, Al-Bader Trading Co., W.L.L, 2003.

26. Claudia Farkas Al-Rashoud, "Jinn: Cast from the Flame of a Smokeless Fire...in the Service of God and His Creation, Part One of Eleven," *The Arab Times*, No. 12130, Thursday-Friday, March 10-11, 2005, page 24.

27. Najeh Bilal and Shawqi Mahmoud, "Women's Political Role Vital for Development of Society: Rujaib," *The Arab Times*, No. 12131, Saturday, March 12, 2005, page 6.

28. Salem Al-Wawan, Raed Yousef, Mohammed Al-Khalidi, and Khalid Al-Hajiri, "Crisis Brews Over Suffrage – Islamists Gear Up to Kill Bill," *The Arab Times*, No. 12131, Saturday, March 12, 2005, page 6.

29. Agencies, ""Gov't Plotting to Muster Support of MPs on Women Suffrage Law" – No Date Specified for Discussions: Al-Faji," *The Arab Times*, No. 12132, Sunday, March 13, 2005, page 6.

30. KUNA, "PM Reiterates Support for Political Rights for Women," *The Arab Times*, No. 12133, Monday, March 14, 2005, page 4.

31. Raed Yousef, "Loyal to Ruling Family...Shia Mosques "Apart" – All Mosques Under Awqaf Supervision, Says Minister," *The Arab Times*, No. 12135, Wednesday, March 16, 2005, pages 1 and 8.

32. Abdullah Al-Hajiri, "ICM Members Hit Out at Gov't Law on Giving Women Political Rights," *The Arab Times*, No. 12135, Wednesday, March 16, 2005, page 6.

33. KUNA, "Women Should Work in Tandem for Political Rights: Al-Khorafi – Speaker Urges Respect for Opinions, Decisions," *The Arab Times*, No. 12136, Thursday-Friday, March 17-18, 2005, page 2.

34. KUNA, "Parliament Will Approve Women's Rights: MP Saleh Ashour," *The Arab Times*, No. 12136, Thursday-Friday, March 17-18, 2005, page 2.

35. Claudia Farkas Al-Rashoud, "Jinn: Ajib & Gharib, Part Two of Eleven," *The Arab Times*, No. 12136, Thursday-Friday, March 17-18, 2005, page 20.

36. Photo by Sheikh Abdul Shakur. "A Bangladeshi man was killed on the King Fahd Expressway Wednesday night after he was hit by a car driven by a citizen as he was crossing the road. The impact was so severe that the Bangladeshi's leg was separated from the body at the hip. The victim is said to have died on the way to the hospital. Above: The leg of the victim lies near a police car." *The Arab Times*, No. 12136, Thursday-Friday, March 17-18, 2005, page 6.

37. Najeh Bilal, "Move Condemned: "Suffrage Only in Foreign Pressure,"" *The Arab Times*, No. 12137, Saturday, March 19, 2005, page 3.

38. KUNA, "Gov't Determined to Grant Political Rights to Women: Kuwait Hopes Qatar Gas Deal Clears Hitch," *The Arab Times*, No. 12137, Saturday, March 19, 2005, page 3.

39. Moamen Al-Masri, "Woman Faces Suit for Insulting Nation," *The Arab Times*, No. 12138, Sunday, March 20, 2005, page 6.

40. Khalid Al-Hajri, "Matouq Fatwa Will Help Win Support for Suffrage," *The Arab Times*, No. 12138, Sunday, March 20, 2005, page 6.

41. AFP Photo, "Rola Dashti (wearing a tee shirt with the slogan: WOMEN ARE KUWAIT TOO!), head of the Kuwaiti Economic Committee (KEC), accompanied by young Kuwaiti women, tries to convince Kuwaiti men to sign a petition during a campaign in support of women's political rights March 19, Kuwait City. Kuwait's Ministry of Islamic Affairs on Saturday entrusted the Amir to rule on a controversy over whether to give women political rights, in a new fatwa, or religious edict." *The Arab Times*, No. 12138, Sunday, March 20, 2005, page 6.

42. Agencies, "Fatwa Outlines Suffrage Options: Ruling Belongs to Amir," *The Arab Times*, No. 12138, Sunday, March 20, 2005, pages 1 and 8.

43. Ahmed Al-Jarallah, Opinion, "Women Rights an Amiri Wish," *The Arab Times*, No. 12138, Sunday, March 20, 2005, pages 1 and 8.

44. Associated Press, "Woman Leads Muslim Prayer Service," *The Arab Times*, No. 12138, Sunday, March 20, 2005, page 16.

45. Agencies, ""Denying Women Suffrage Violates the Constitution" – Khorafi Mantle of Democracy: Dumaitheer," *The Arab Times*, No. 12139, Monday, March 21, 2005, page 6.

46. Agencies, "Political Disputes, MPs Unease Must Not Hamper Women's Rights – Kuwaiti Women Launch Door-to-Door Petition Bid for Suffrage," Photo: "A large number of expat women visited the National Assembly on March 21 and attended the Assembly session. The ladies group pose[d] for a photograph in one of the halls." *The Arab Times*, No. 12140, Tuesday, March 22, 2005, page 6.

47. Abdullah Qunais, "Khaitan Raid Nets Asians for Gambling, Prostitution – Police Arrest Two Opium Traders," *The Arab Times*, No. 12140, Tuesday, March 22, 2005, page 5.

48. KUNA, "Deal Linked to Fight Graft: Report to Be Worked Out," *The Arab Times*, No. 12140, Tuesday, March 22, 2005, page 5.

49. Moamen Al-Masri, "Enezi's Detention Extended – "Daughter Murdered for Honour"," *The Arab Times*, No. 12140, Tuesday, March 22, 2005, page 5.

50. Claudia Farkas Al-Rashoud, "Jinn: Partners in the Peaks and Valleys of Creation, Part Three of Eleven," *The Arab Times*, No. 12142, Thursday-Friday, March 24-25, 2005, page 23.

51. Khalid Al-Hajiri and Mahmoud Shawqi, "MPs Spar on Women's Rights," *The Arab Times*, No. 12143, Saturday, March 26, 2005, page 3.

52. KUNA (Dubai), "Let Women Have Political Rights: Senior Gov't Official – We Are Alive to Regional Developments: Deputy PM," *The Arab Times*, No. 12144, Sunday, March 27, 2005, page 4.

53. Riyadh, NEWSWATCH, *The Arab Times*, No. 12144, Sunday, March 27, 2005, pages 1 and 8.

54. Salem Al-Wawan, Raed Yousef, and Mohammed Al-Khalidi, "Women to Contest Municipal Poll as First Step to Full Rights: Sharar – Gov't May Delay Vote on Suffrage," *The Arab Times*, No. 12145, Monday, March 28, 2005, page 6.

55. Abdullah Al-Hajiri, "Muslim Cleric Criticizes 3 Fatwas Issued on Women Political Rights: "Quit Blind Following of Western Values" – Al-Mesbah," *The Arab Times*, No. 12146, Tuesday, March 29, 2005, page 6.

56. Kuwait City (AP), "MP Denies Comments on Suffrage – Hurt Women Plan to Sue Tabtabaei," *The Arab Times*, No. 12146, Tuesday, March 29, 2005, page 6.

57. Kuwait City, "Women Won't Gain Respect of Society," *The Arab Times*, No. 12147, Wednesday, March 30, 2005, page 2.

58. Ali Ahmad Al-Baghli, "Kiss for Mom, Joy at Easter," *The Arab Times*, No. 12148, Thursday-Friday, March 31-April 1, 2005, page 1.

59. Riyadh (RTRS), "Bruised, Bandaged, Maid Tells of Abuse – Case Probed: Saudis," *The Arab Times*, No. 12148, Thursday-Friday, March 31-April 1, 2005, page 7

60. Claudia Farkas Al-Rashoud, "Jinn: Migration of Souls Across the Millennia, Part Four of Eleven," *The Arab Times*, No. 12148, Thursday-Friday, March 31-April 1, 2005, page 23.

61. Souad, in collaboration with Marie-Thérèse Cuny, *Burned Alive: A Victim of the Law of Men*, Warner Books, July 2004.

62. Trudy Rubin, *The Philadelphia Enquirer*, "Democracy May Set Back Arab Women," in *The Kuwait Times – Friday Times*, No. 12876, April 1, 2005, page 3.

63. KUWAIT, "Farwaniya Alleged Rapist Identified by Victims," *The Kuwait Times – Friday Times*, No. 12876, April 1, 2005, page 2.

64. Manila (KUNA), "IPU Offers to Back Law on Women's Rights," *The Arab Times*, No. 12150, Sunday, April 3, 2005, page 3.

65. Tracy Chevalier, *Falling Angels*, Penguin Group Publishing, October 2002.

66. Lidia Qattan, "Pioneers of Kuwait: Jahra Incident Shakes Whole Country – Everyone Joins Hands to Fight Off Invaders," *The Arab Times*, No. 12151, Monday, April 4, 2005, page 20.

67. H. Hashim Ahmed, "Jarallah Offers Resignation After No-Confidence Call – Future in Doubt After Marathon Grilling," *The Arab Times*, No. 12152, Tuesday, April 5, 2005, pages 1 and 30.

68. Brussels (KUNA), "Waldner Backs Rights for Kuwaiti Women – FTA Deal Very Soon: EU Official," *The Arab Times*, No. 12152, Tuesday, April 5, 2005, page 3.

69. Dubai (AFP), "4 Alleged Gays Face Lashes, Jail," *The Arab Times*, No. 12152, Tuesday, April 5, 2005, page 7.

70. Zahed Matar, "Day by Day – Campers Leave Trash After Dismantling Winter Tent Grounds," *The Arab Times*, No. 12152, Tuesday, April 5, 2005, pages 1 and 30.

71. Kuwait Today, "Prayer Timings," *The Arab Times*, No. 12152, Tuesday, April 5, 2005, page 2.

72. News In Brief, "Imam Punches Citizen in Face," *The Arab Times*, No. 12152, Tuesday, April 5, 2005, page 5.

73. Kuwait (Agencies), "Jarallah Resigns: Leaving "Proud"," *The Arab Times*, No. 12153, Wednesday, April 6, 2005, pages 1 and 8.

74. Ahmed Al-Jarallah, "Sheikh Sabah "Set to Dissolve Assembly" – Analysts Point to Need for New Political Class: Move "Crucial for Stability"," *The Arab Times*, No. 12153, Wednesday, April 6, 2005, pages 1 and 8.

75. Claudia Farkas Al-Rashoud, "Jinn: Frankincense & Fire Shield the Soul, Part Five of Eleven," *The Arab Times*, No. 12154, Thursday-Friday, April 7-8, 2005, page 23.

76. Legal Clinic, "Visa Change," *The Arab Times*, No. 12154, Thursday-Friday, April 7-8, 2005, page 21.

77. Ahmed Al-Jarallah, "A Grilling Too Far…Uncomfortable – Crisis as Parliament Dangles Near Dissolution: Assault on Unity," *The Arab Times*, No. 12154, Thursday-Friday, April 7-8, 2005, pages 1 and 8.

78. Velina Nacheva, "Kuwaiti Women Suffer From Marrying Expats: My Home is Not My Fortress," *The Kuwait Times*, No. 12882, Thursday, April 7, 2005, page 5.

79. Abdullah Al-Hajiri and Najeh Bilal, "Law to Grant Women Political Rights Forced on Kuwait -- MP – Gov't Realizes Issue Has Failed: Dr. Muslem," *The Arab Times*, No. 12155, Saturday, April 9, 2005, page 6.

80. Tareq S. Rajab and Jehan S. Rajab, *Tareq Rajab Museum*, Published in Kuwait by the Tareq Rajab Museum, 1994, Reprinted in 1997.

81. Jehan S. Rajab, *Costumes From the Arab World (Saudi Arabia, Syria, Jordan, Palestine, Lebanon, Kuwait, Iraq, Arabian Gulf, Oman and the Yemen) in The Tareq Rajab Museum*, Published in Kuwait by the Tareq Rajab Museum, 2002.

82. Ben Arfaj Al-Mutairi, "Khorafi Sees No Intent to Dissolve Assembly – Special Session to Discuss Audit Review of Sharar Grilling," *The Arab Times*, No. 12156, Sunday, April 10, 2005, pages 1 and 8.

83. Kuwait City, (KUNA) and Agencies, "Amir Accepts Resignation of Health Minister – Sheikh Ahmed Holds Portfolio; "Dissolution Not Considered – We Deeply Advocate Democracy"," *The Arab Times*, No. 12157, Monday, April 11, 2005, pages 1 and 8.

84. News in Brief, "Women Rights Backed," *The Arab Times*, No. 12157, Monday, April 11, 2005, page 3.

85. Kuwait City, ""Women Qualified to Join Politics" – Kuwait Signs Int'l Accord to End Female Discrimination," *The Arab Times*, No. 12160, Thursday-Friday, April 14-15, 2005, page 6.

86. Claudia Farkas Al-Rashoud, "Jinn: Iron Out the Wrinkles, Part Six of Eleven," *The Arab Times*, No. 12160, Thursday-Friday, April 14-15, 2005, page 26.

87. Claudia Farkas Al-Rashoud, "Ecology - Once and Again: Once There Were Green Fields," *The Arab Times*, No. 12160, Thursday-Friday, April 14-15, 2005, pages 24-25.

88. Kuwait (KUNA), "Free to Choose...Just One – Secret Citizens Cautioned," *The Arab Times*, No. 12162, Sunday, April 17, 2005, page 1.

89. Kuwait City (AP), "Baghdadi Writes Come-Back Column After Enezi Provocation: Pens at Fifty Paces...Columnists Duel – Professor Revisits Teachings of Islam," *The Arab Times*, No. 12162, Sunday, April 17, 2005, pages 1 and 8.

90. Geneva (AP), "Europeans Fail to Protect Muslim Women," *The Arab Times*, No. 12164, Tuesday, April 19, 2005, page 9.

91. Melanie Britto, Arab Times Staff and Agencies, "First Nod for Women to Vote Municipals: Sheikh Sabah Lauds Win...Sees Step to Legislative Polls – Activists Optimistic," *The Arab Times*, No. 12165, Wednesday, April 20, 2005, pages 1 and 33.

92. H. Hashim Ahmed, "Gender Equality Sows Discord – Western Feminists "Ruining" Muslim Societies: Expert," *The Arab Times*, No. 12165, Wednesday, April 20, 2005, page 8.

93. Claudia Farkas Al-Rashoud, "Jinn: Secret Sharer, Part Seven of Eleven," *The Arab Times*, No. 12166, Thursday-Friday, April 21-22, 2005, page 21.

94. Valiya S. Sajjad, "Joy That Now It's Finally "Us" – Over the Moon on Municipals," *The Arab Times*, No. 12166, Thursday-Friday, April 21-22, 2005, pages 1 and 8.

95. United Nations (KUNA), "Parliament Move on Women Right to Vote Wins Worldwide Acclaim – Continue Struggle Until Full Political Rights: U.N.," *The Arab Times*, No. 12166, Thursday-Friday, April 21-22, 2005, page 6.

96. World News Roundup, Photo with Caption: "U.S. President George W. Bush walks hand-in-hand through Texas bluebonnet wildflowers with Saudi Arabia's Crown Prince Abdullah on his ranch in Crawford, Texas, April 25." *The Arab Times*, No. 12171, Wednesday, April 27, 2005, page 12.

97. Claudia Farkas Al-Rashoud, "Jinn: Tongues Feed Flame of a Smokeless Fire Born in the Mists of Time, Part Eight of Eleven," *The Arab Times*, No. 12172, Thursday-Friday, April 28-29, 2005, page 22.

98. Ali Ahmad Al-Baghli, "The Religious State," *The Arab Times*, No. 12172, Thursday-Friday, April 28-29, 2005, pages 1 and 8.

99. Baghdad (Agencies), "Iraq Crafts Rainbow" Cabinet – Insurgents Assassinate Female MP," *The Arab Times*, No. 12172, Thursday-Friday, April 28-29, 2005, pages 1 and 8.

100. Ben Arfaj Al-Mutairi, "MP Sees Trap in Gov't Strategy to Allow Women to Vote in Local Polls – Info Minister Seeks Time on Panel Inquiries," *The Arab Times*, No. 12172, Thursday-Friday, April 28-29, 2005, page 2.

101. Kuwait City, "Rapists Beat Filipina Before Raping Her," *The Arab Times*, No. 12172, Thursday-Friday, April 28-29, 2005, page 4.

102. Toronto (AP), "And Then There's the Hair – Rebel Takes on Radical Islam," and "Reform Without Fear – Project Ijtihad" (2 Related Articles), *The Arab Times*, No. 12172, Thursday-Friday, April 28-29, 2005, page 16.

103. Photo (AP), "Jewish settlers and opponents of Israeli Prime Minister Ariel Sharon's plan to pull out of the Gaza Strip and four West Bank settlements stand atop a mosque's minaret in the northern West Bank settlement of Sa Nur, April 28. About 10,000 Israelis streamed into the nearby settlement of Homesh, one of the West Bank settlements slated for evacuation to protest against the evacuation plan." *The Arab Times*, No. 12173, Saturday, April 30, 2005, page 1.

104. Ahmad Al-Shimmari, "Hotline to Hear Expat Complaints…434-4954 – Pay or "Pay"," *The Arab Times*, No. 12173, Saturday, April 30, 2005, pages 1 and 8.

105. Al Shal Report, ""Better Efforts Needed by Gov't for Positive Results on Women's Rights" – "KFH Report on Real Estate Sector Commendable"," *The Arab Times*, No. 12173, Saturday, April 30, 2005, page 2.

106. London (KUNA), "Kuwait Strives to Improve Life of Its People: Al-Hajji – Gov't Takes Strides Towards Women's Rights," *The Arab Times*, No. 12173, Saturday, April 30, 2005, page 4.

107. News in Brief (AFP), "Briton Detained in Dubai," *The Arab Times*, No. 12173, Saturday, April 30, 2005, page 9.

108. Kuwait (KUNA), "Suffrage: Make it Happen: PM," *The Arab Times*, No. 12174, Sunday, May 1, 2005, pages 1 and 8.

109. Melanie Britto, "MPs Fail to Pass Suffrage for Municipals – Women in Limbo – Try Again Today," *The Arab Times*, No. 12176, Tuesday, May 3, 2005, pages 1 and 8.

110. Ahmad Al-Jarallah, "Enforce the Will of the People," *The Arab Times*, No. 12176, Tuesday, May 3, 2005, pages 1 and 8.

111. Abdullah Al-Hajri, "MPs to Work for Citizens' Rights, Not Afraid of Constant "Threats" – Discussion on Important Issues Being Deflected: MP Akash," *The Arab Times*, No. 12176, Tuesday, May 3, 2005, page 6.

112. Melanie Britto, "Suffrage Fails for June 2 Municipals – PM Calls Delay...Poll Swapped in Bid for Rights Passage – Dashti Hopeful for 2009," *The Arab Times*, No. 12177, Wednesday, May 4, 2005, pages 1 and 32.

113. Ali Ahmad Al-Baghli, "Other Voices: Disadvantages of a Religious State," *The Arab Times*, No. 12178, Thursday-Friday, May 5-6, 2005, pages 1 and 8.

114. Kuwait (Agencies), "21 Register for All-Male Municipals – Kuwaitis Lament Pace of Change," *The Arab Times*, No. 12178, Thursday-Friday, May 5-6, 2005, pages 1 and 8.

115. Claudia Farkas Al-Rashoud, "Jinn: Alive in Legend & Look Behind You, Part Nine of Eleven," *The Arab Times*, No. 12178, Thursday-Friday, May 5-6, 2005, page 22.

116. Kuwait, "Legislative Blitz Amends Election Law; Women Win Political Rights," *The Arab Times*, Web Edition No. 12189, Wednesday, May 18, 2005, page 1.

117. Editorial, "A Half-Step Forward in Kuwait," *The Hartford Courant*, Eastern Edition, Volume CLXIX, Number 139, Thursday, May 19, 2005, page A14.

Stephanie C. Fox, J.D. is a historian, writer, and editor. She is a graduate of William Smith College and the University of Connecticut School of Law.

Ms. Fox has written several books on a variety of topics, including the effects of human overpopulation on the environment, Asperger's, and travel to Kuwait and Hawai'i.

She runs an editing and publishing service called *QueenBeeEdit*, found at www.queenbeeedit.com, which caters to politicians, scientists, and others. Her imprint is *QueenBeeBooks*.

Her areas of interest include – but are not limited to – history, biographies, women's studies, science fiction, human overpopulation, ecosystems collapse, law, international relations, Asperger's, and cats.

www.ingramcontent.com/pod-product-compliance
Lightning Source LLC
Chambersburg PA
CBHW071134300426
44113CB00009B/965